NDEA Summer Institute in History

Administering
educational
media

Administering educational media

James W. Brown

Graduate Dean
San Jose State College

Kenneth D. Norberg

Professor of Education and
Director of Audiovisual Services
Sacramento State College

McGraw-Hill Book Company

New York   St. Louis   San Francisco
Toronto   London   Sydney

Administering Educational Media

Preface

This book is concerned with media in education—the problems involved in organizing and administering their use.

In it we deal with all the common educational media, including print, although major emphasis is given to so-called "new" media—television, films, various forms of graphics, programmed instruction, recordings, and the like. This emphasis reflects a rapid growth in the use of such technological means of instruction and the multiplicity of problems arising out of their applications in education. Some reasons for dealing with the total spectrum of educational media as a complex are introduced in the opening chapter and expanded in the last.

In the past, the traditional administrative arrangement for managing books and other printed materials has been known as the "library," and it has been a more or less autonomous feature of the educational establishment, with its own areas of concern, its own science, its own training programs. In many respects, the library continues in this way today; it operates according to firmly established organizational plans and procedures, and its concerns with new media are quite commonly absorbed within the existing "print" context of its administrative framework.

Although ancient in lineage, librarianship is nevertheless a changing field in which there are now many signs of vigorous growth. In recent years, for example, many librarians have begun to show increasing interest in a more inclusive approach to educational media. Some actively promote the concept of an entirely new kind of library—one that would house a full offering of instructional materials and devices, including those ordinarily called "audio-visual." Concurrently, many so-called "audio-visual specialists" have seen perhaps more clearly than the librarians themselves the need for a fully integrated organization of instructional materials services and learning resources.

In practice, there are many different types of administrative organization for the management and use of educational media, although the traditional separation of services for printed materials and most other media is still the most common arrangement. Combined instructional-materials centers have been established in some school systems, particularly at county and district levels, and growth has been more rapid in some states (notably Florida, Pennsylvania, and Washington) than others. A recent upsurge of activities in television, programmed instruction, and language-laboratory facilities has focused greater attention on the administrative problems involved in these somewhat diverse instruc-

v

tional resources. Television is often a complex and expensive operation, and it tends to become a separate enterprise with its own administrative structure—especially if open-circuit broadcasting is involved. Programmed instruction has ambiguous administrative implications because it involves both printed materials and often the newer technology as well. Language-laboratory facilities represent a distinct departmental instructional interest on the one hand and a new technological resource with broader implications on the other. Modern teaching calls for integrated and highly organized use of instructional resources, but the present situation is characterized (and complicated) by the persistence of traditional patterns of instructional organization and practice and the encroachment of new ideas and new technology. For this reason, our uses of educational media are still uncertain and experimental, and administrative provisions for their management are tenuous, varied, and changing, to say the least.

Making systematic use of the various educational media seems to entail some examination of the *total* range of technological resources and exploration of the need for coordination. In this book we do not affirm that all instructional media must be brought together in one closely knit administrative unit. Whether this would be desirable in any particular case may depend not only upon such general considerations as coordination and economy, but also upon the circumstances of the local situation —the size of the institution or system, the existing physical facilities, the personalities involved, and that always delicate balance of the traditional past and the emerging shape of the future. But we do assume that *at some level* of administrative planning and organization, all facets of the instructional-communications technology must be viewed as parts of a comprehensive whole.

Educational administration involves many concerns of widely varying importance. As school systems and institutions of higher learning multiply and grow in size and complexity, so do administrative problems. Schools are sometimes criticized for putting too large a portion of the educational dollar into administration and administrative services and not enough into teaching. Does it follow that the wisest course is to limit any increase in educational media services and continue to provide only media that can be offered through the traditional administrative framework? Or would it be wiser to expand educational media services, enrich materials and equipment collections, and add to teaching and administrative staffs persons professionally or technically prepared to provide needed assistance to students and classroom teachers?

It may also be asked: Why not leave educational technology to the technicians? Why must professionally trained persons be used for this work? One answer to these questions has been framed quite pointedly by Charles F. Hoban, Jr., professor of communications at the University of Pennsylvania: [1]

---

[1] Charles F. Hoban, Jr., "The New Media and the School," *Audiovisual Communication Review,* vol. 10, p. 354, November–December, 1962.

The problem of new media in education, as with almost all of the problems of new technologies, are not those of mechanics or the machinery involved. The engineers and the technicians do a reasonably good job with the mechanics and the machinery of technology. The real difficulty is much more complex. It arises from the reorganization of procedures, the introduction and wider use of management on a higher level of skill, the changing role of the men and women in the process or system, and the evaluation of goals made possible by the productivity of technology.

Thus it seems that our main problem will not be solved merely by adding more administrative personnel, nor will it be eliminated simply by buying more films, more books, or more projectors. The problem is much broader than that. We need an insightful recognition of the proper roles of instructional media in the total process of education and willingness of all concerned to reorganize media services as required by changes in curriculum goals and patterns, the nature and size of our student groups, and the teachers' classroom needs. Fundamentally, a more inclusive form of management of instructional resources than we have known in the past is involved.

This book is intended for use primarily as a college text by persons who will assume positions of leadership in the field of educational media: the media generalists, audio-visual specialists, librarians, television specialists, graphics production specialists, and others. It should provide orientation to the many special aspects of these positions and emphasize their relationship.

To provide this orientation, we begin with an examination of the background of the field—the relationship of educational media to the purposes and conduct of education today and the nature and requirements of current professional opportunities in educational media. We continue with analyses of the fundamental elements of educational media programs—physical facilities; procedures and standards for administering materials, equipment, and production services; budgeting; improving utilization; and administering textbooks, television and radio, and self-instructional programs. We then consider these same elements in the context of actual programs in the single school, county and district systems, universities and colleges, and state departments of education. Finally we examine the function of research and the possible future implications of a "systems" approach to planning instructional programs.

The authors wish to express their appreciation to the following individuals whose contributions of materials, ideas, or advice aided greatly in the preparation of the manuscript for this book: Lee Campion, C. Ray Carpenter, Thomas D. Clemens, Lee Cochran, Sol Cornberg, J. Wesley Crum, Edgar Dale, Amo DeBernardis, Robert DeKieffer, Margaret Divizia, William H. Durr, Ralph Ellsworth, Donald P. Ely, Carlton W. F. Erickson, Gene Faris, James D. Finn, John Flory, Morton Gassman, Robert Gerletti, Leslie P. Greenhill, Robert Hall, Fred F. Harcleroad, Horace Hartsell, Elton Hocking, Thomas W. Hope, Shirley

Hopkinson, Ronald L. Hunt, Anna P. Hyer, James W. Jacobs, Leslie Janke, Jerrold E. Kemp, L. C. Larson, Richard B. Lewis, Ralph Leyden, Robert McAdam, Lewis Mayhew, Earl Mennett, John Moldstad, Barry Morris, Francis Noel, J. E. Oglesby, Murray G. Phillips, Ward Phillips, Philip Tyrrell, the late Paul C. Reed, Henry C. Ruark, Jr., David G. Ryans, Paul Saettler, Edward Schofield, Robert Shanks, Len Singer, Harry Skelly, Verne Stockman, Richard Szumski, Jack Tanzman, James W. Thornton, Jr., Ernest Tiemann, J. Lloyd Trump, Lyndon Vivrette, Hobart D. Wagener, Roger Walters, Selden Watkins, Don White, Paul W. F. Witt, Charles Wright, Raymond Wyman, and MaryLouise Zingheim. Special thanks should also be given Ruth Aubrey for her valuable assistance in typing the manuscript.

James W. Brown
Kenneth D. Norberg

Contents

Administering educational media

chapter 1

Education and educational Media

Educational institutions reflect the purposes and problems of the society in which they are nurtured. They must also rely upon the human talents and technical capabilities of the culture in which they must discharge their functions. As the tasks of any modern profession increase in size and complexity, two immediate effects can be noted: a growing demand for more highly trained professional workers; and a tendency to marshal technological resources to assist or amplify the efforts of professional workers and reduce the drain of mechanical and repetitive chores. This is the case with modern education. Both quantitatively and qualitatively, we have here a truly formidable task. Never before has any society been faced with the problem of providing so much learning to so many and with so much at stake. Never before has any society had a greater potential to train the necessary teaching force and provide teachers with such powerful tools to do their work. This is one of the great challenges of our time.

In this book, we are not concerned with the first half of the problem, the training of teachers, but with the means of teaching that must be placed in their hands. These are the media of instruction—especially the modern technological resources of communication and learning. It will be noted that the subject is media in general, although focal attention is directed to the so-called "new media" of instruction. The phrase "new media" became current in the 1950s with the rather spectacular development of educational television and the growth of interest in programmed instruction and teaching machines that began in the middle of that decade. Since the term was also applied to the more conventional audio-visual devices, it was used as a convenient label for a wide range of instruments of modern technology that were applied to instructional procedures. The weakness of the concept was and is this: It splits the technology of communication down the middle—with print and lithography on one side and the audio-visual and electronic media on the other. A growing interest in the more inclusive concept of a total complex of "educational media" or "instructional media" is reflected in this book. The idea of an inclusive approach to educational media also can be traced back to various types of instructional-materials centers that combine printed and audio-visual materials and related services in one organization. The concept has been brought into new

1

The impact of technology upon the conduct of education is emphasized through "multi-media" presentations at the University of Wisconsin. (*University of Wisconsin*)

focus recently by the growing tendency to look upon the problems of storing, handling, and circulating instructional materials as a complex of related processes that lend themselves to new and ever-changing technological means of implementation.

This chapter reviews some of the explosive changes and pressures that have created the present crisis in American education. It outlines briefly the confrontation of education and modern technology and some of the doubts and fears of those who question the expanding use of new media in solving instructional problems. Finally, we observe how these rapid changes and emerging trends challenge administrative leadership in the modern school.

THE SCHOOL IN A CHANGING SOCIETY

Our schools and colleges have felt the shock of a series of explosive changes that have created a crisis in contemporary education. The surging national population is flooding the public school classrooms with steeply increasing enrollments. The number of students grew from 25 million in 1950 to 36 million by 1960. A projection given by the U.S. Office of Education for 1970 is 50 million! In the colleges and universities, enrollments are increasing even more rapidly; they feel a triple impact—population growth, the rapid expansion of knowledge, and constantly increasing demands for technical and high-level training that characterize our highly developed society in this age of vigorous scientific and technological development. The recent college enrollment of about 3.5 million is expected to double by 1970. Although we have had a system of universal education for many years, the startling fact is that our school population is increasing more rapidly than the population as a whole.

The information explosion has already been mentioned as a factor in the growth of college and university enrollments. Equally important for education at all levels are the ferment and new patterns of organi-

An experimental classroom, designed by Rensselaer Polytechnic Institute's School of Architecture, incorporates systems for front and rear screen projection, together with television projection and monitor viewing. The projection systems are operated by the lecturer from a specially constructed podium. Through the medium of television microscopy, a class in Embryology views a cross section of a chick embryo while, for comparison, two different images of the gross embryo (2- by 2-inch slides projected from the rear) are held on adjacent screens. (*Rensselaer Polytechnic Institute*)

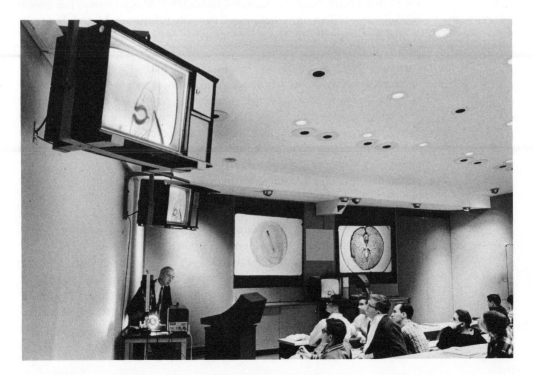

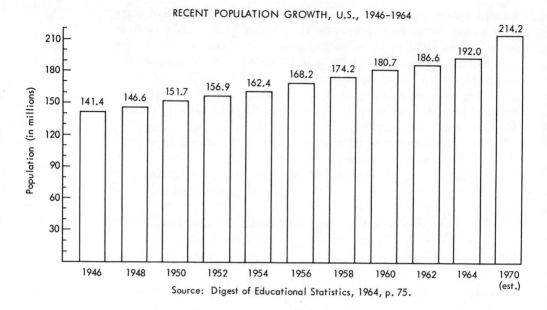

RECENT POPULATION GROWTH, U.S., 1946-1964

Source: Digest of Educational Statistics, 1964, p. 75.

zation of knowledge in various fields. There is more to teach; there is also the age-old questions of what to teach and how to teach it. One of the most notable developments of recent years has been the increasing number of subject-matter specialists and scholars who have collaborated with educators in revising curricula to bring their content into line with current scientific trends and developments. Examples of such efforts have been the School Mathematics Study Group, the Physical Science Study Committee, the Chemical Education Materials Study.

Parenthetically, it should be noted here that the new media have played a crucial and rather conspicuous part in implementing recent curricular changes in physics, mathematics, and other fields. The first "Continental Classroom" broadcasts in 1958 used a national television network to bring thousands of high school physics teachers abreast of new subject matter and changing emphases brought about by nuclear developments. Television and motion pictures have been used widely to disseminate new content and methods in mathematics, chemistry, and biology. A Western college offered an extension course in the "new" mathematics in 1963, and more than 1,300 teachers signed up for the course. This was an astonishing and unprecedented enrollment for an extension course given by this college; but how else could such a large number of teachers in that community quickly bring themselves up to date on important recent developments in their field?

Added to the sheer quantitative growth of enrollments and the tremendous task of teaching an expanding and changing curriculum are mounting pressures to improve the quality of education in various ways. The problem is aggravated by a severe shortage of well-trained teachers. The recently tabulated teaching force of 1.3 million is considered about 10 per cent under the number needed in the public and private schools.

Anyone associated with a college or university knows how difficult it has become in recent years to obtain properly trained instructors—especially in those fields in which industry offers competition. Ironically, the steadily increasing demand for scientific and technical training drains the teaching force that is qualified to supply that training. Trow summarizes the plight of the schools as follows: [1]

> More students are crowding into the schools than ever before, each one of whom deserves individual attention, but they find themselves in larger and larger classes or even on part time. Special certificates are being issued to untrained teachers because there are not enough who have the proper preparation, and both the children and the public at large are the losers. . . .
>
> These downward constrictive pressures are met by upward pressures for the development and improvement of the school program. And the schools are caught between. Many wish to retain students in school longer, to provide new buildings, a more enriched curriculum, better teaching, a larger proportion of graduates who are trained in the disciplines, less disturbed mentally, less inclined to delinquency, and more competent professionally. The pressure for excellence demands that the schools satisfy the intellectual and cultural needs not only in mathematics, the sciences, and the humanities, but in producing good citizens.
>
> It is a kind of squeeze play the public is using on the schools, as a consequence of which they can do one of two things. They can either continue in their traditional ways to struggle along, or they can streamline their operations, and taking advantage of the present interest and concern, introduce the necessary innovations.

What innovations are needed to cope with the imposing tasks that now confront the schools? At the outset of this chapter, it was proposed that the present crisis in education requires more and better-trained teachers, as well as a modern technology of instruction to lend optimum force to their efforts. We will now consider technology and the new media as developing forces in modern education.

EDUCATION AND TECHNOLOGY

Still another cultural explosion that has engendered pronounced changes in education is the remarkable expansion of technology—especially in the field of communication—since the turn of the century. It has made possible the earlier audio-visual methods and materials and, more recently, the growing use of other new media in the schools. The organized use of these new resources in education has followed the rising arc of technological development, although trailing at some distance behind its growth in other fields.

[1] William Clark Trow, *Teacher and Technology: New Designs for Learning,* Appleton-Century-Crofts, New York, 1963, pp. 170–171.

5

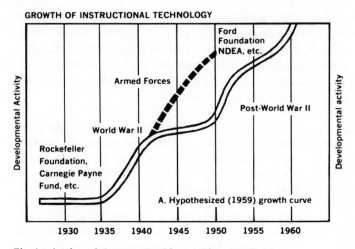

Finn's plotting of the growth of instructional technology.

Prior to World War I, a few large city school systems had established educational museums, and there was some interest in the use of lantern slides. Chicago established its Bureau of Visual Education in 1917, and this was followed by other visual education departments in the early 1920s.[2] These early prototypes of audio-visual or educational media programs were organized to circulate slides, motion pictures, and some other materials—but on a very limited scale. This development gradually continued and expanded during the late 1920s and the 1930s, but it was not until after World War II that the schools and colleges began to make systematic and wide-scale use of motion pictures, radio, magnetic recordings, filmstrips, and other audio-visual media.

National surveys conducted by the National Education Association (NEA) in 1946 and 1954 revealed that the number of sound–motion-picture projectors in the schools had increased 140 per cent compared with pupil enrollment. During the same period, the relative number of motion-picture titles owned by the schools had more than tripled. A national survey conducted by the U.S. Office of Education in 1958 revealed that over 500,000 prints of educational motion pictures were housed in 1,009 16mm film libraries operated by educational institutions or agencies.[3] In the same year, it was estimated that almost 8,000 motion-picture titles were available for primary or exclusive use in education.[4] This growth has continued, and today the motion

[2] Paul Saettler, "The Origin and Development of Audio-Visual Communication in the United States," unpublished doctoral dissertation, University of Southern California, Los Angeles, Calif.

[3] Seerley Reid, Anita Carpenter, and Annie Rose Daugherty, *A Directory of 3,660 16-mm. Film Libraries,* U.S. Department of Health, Education, and Welfare, 1958.

[4] John Flory and Thomas W. Hope: "Scope and Nature of Nontheatrical Films in the United States," *Journal of the Society of Motion Picture and Television Engineers,* June, 1959.

picture is an established medium in education, although its effective use as an integral part of instruction is perhaps still infrequently realized.

The growth of educational broadcasting can be traced back to 1920, when the first university-owned radio station was licensed in Madison, Wisconsin. However, the major development in this field has occurred since 1952—and this has been, of course, mainly in the field of television. By 1964, there were more than 80 educational television stations on the air, and well over 400 closed-circuit television stations were in operation in universities, colleges, and school systems.[5] Another spectacular and even more precipitate development has been the increasing interest in programmed instructional materials and various kinds of teaching machines—up to and including the use of electronic computers. By 1964, a U.S. Office of Education catalog listed 352 instructional programs, many of them complete courses of study, that were available from various commercial sources. Hundreds of schools and colleges throughout the United States were using programmed materials and/or autoinstructional devices, although much of this was still on an exploratory or experimental basis.[6] Still another highly significant development—one accompanied by marked changes in teaching foreign languages—was the widespread introduction of electronic sound reproduction and recording installations, known as "language laboratories." From a few scattered installations prior to 1958, the number of language laboratories mounted rapidly to approximately six thousand in 1962, and the growth has continued vigorously since that time.[7]

It is apparent that education has made substantial gains in the application of modern technology, but some feel that progress has been slow in comparison with fields such as medicine and industry, for example. In a comparison of technological expenditures in industry and education, Columbia University economist Harold Clark examined the changes that have taken place since the turn of the century. In 1890, both industry and education distributed capital outlay for new plant in a ratio of three-quarters for the shell of the building and one-quarter for the tools to be used by the occupants. Recently, the ratio for industry had been reversed—one-quarter for the building, three-quarters for the tools—but the ratio for educational structures continued about the same.[8]

American educators, often very progressive in their views in many

---

[5] A detailed discussion of the development of educational television and radio will be found in Chap. 10.

[6] See Lincoln F. Hanson (ed.), *Programs, '63: A Guide to Programed Instructional Materials Available to Educators by September, 1963,* The Center for Programed Institution, Inc., U.S. Government Printing Office, 1963.

[7] A detailed discussion of language laboratories, as well as other autoinstructional facilities, will be found in Chap. 11.

[8] Harold F. Clark, *Cost and Quality in Public Education,* Syracuse University Press, Syracuse, N.Y., 1963, pp. 8–9.

areas, sometimes have been very conservative—even rigid—in thinking about their own practices.[9]

> . . . American school methods and facilities have evolved from what society deemed best at a given moment. They have been molded by other cultures, by custom, by regulation, and even by law. Today, acceptable ideas of school scheduling, size of classes, teacher load and responsibilities, instructional materials, and architecture have become hardened. These practices have not been changed basically for generations, and their inflexibility makes it difficult to alter them now.

It is difficult to predict the future shape of education in a changing society, but two brief observations may be helpful in summarizing the present state of affairs:

❯ We have already witnessed the beginning of a technological revolution in education.
❯ Despite significant developments and important changes thus far, it appears that education is trailing far behind other sectors of the society in its use of modern technology.

Many factors affect the rate of innovation in education. Some relate to the community setting. It has been noted, for instance, that community size and level of financial support have positive effects upon the incidence of change in school systems.[10] Still, a good deal of responsibility for the instigation and acceptance of innovation rests upon those who teach or hold positions of leadership within the educational enterprise itself. Why are many educators and teachers slow and/or reluctant to face up to or adopt new practices involving technological applications in education? There is no simple answer to this question, but it may be useful to consider some of the questions, doubts, and fears that arise with the use of the new media. Some of them are of concern not only to professional educators but to the community as a whole.

SOME QUESTIONS AND DOUBTS CONCERNING THE NEW MEDIA

In the 1950s, some of the strongest criticisms of audio-visual devices and materials in education came from literary sources or educators who felt that the new media are somehow competitive with printed materials. The following rhetorical question posed by Joseph Wood Krutch is a

[9] J. Lloyd Trump and Dorsey Baynham, *Focus on Change: Guide to Better Schools,* Rand McNally, Chicago, 1961, p. 4.
[10] Matthew B. Miles, "Educational Innovation: Some Generalizations," paper read at the Symposium on Identifying Techniques and Principles for Gaining Acceptance of Research Results of Use of New Media in Education, University of Nebraska, 1963, p. 11. (Mimeographed)

classic example of literary scorn and distrust of nonverbal methods of communication: [11]

> Are what our school principals call "audio-visual aids" usually anything more than concessions to the pupil's unwillingess to make that effort of attention necessary to read a text or listen to a teacher's exposition?

The comment of historian Arthur Bestor in his book *Educational Wastelands* is another good example of the view that the new media provide weak and debilitating forms of learning experiences, lead to dilution of subject matter, and tend to interfere with the development of reading skills. Conceding the possible value of visual aids for the very young, he feels that: [12]

> The human mind advances from pictures to words and abstract symbols. Once it has made the advance, many kinds of visual aids become time-wasting, roundabout, burdensome methods of conveying information that can be got more quickly, accurately, and systematically by means of the printed word.

Although increasing sophistication and wider acceptance of instructional technology today tends to date such attacks, the underlying attitude still runs deep and wide in a civilization that has so long regarded the book as the storehouse of culture. In an age of electronics, nuclear energy, and space travel, it is still difficult to realize that verbal and other information can be stored and transmitted in many ways. Even more important, it is not always apparent that print and the new media are not alternatives, not competitive, and the use of one does not necessarily diminish or preclude use of the other.

Actually, audio-visual or "concrete" materials are interchangeable with verbal symbols only for very limited functions of communication. While much is still unknown about the nature of nonverbal or analogical signs and symbols, it is apparent that nonprint materials often do not afford communication adequate to deal with generalizations or abstractions. The essential role of lingual communication in human learning cannot be questioned. On the other hand, verbal symbols have their own characteristic limitations when used alone. For instance, they do not suffice when there is an inadequate background of concrete reference. The relationship between print and the media that traffic in nonverbal signs and symbols is not competitive but complementary.

The charge that audio-visual methods and materials degrade subject matter and interfere with the development of reading skills seems also to assume that literacy is merely the mastery of verbal symbols and that, once this mastery is attained, intellectual growtth can be sustained

[11] Joseph Wood Krutch, *Human Nature and the Human Condition,* Random House, New York, 1959, p. 134.
[12] Arthur E. Bestor, *Educational Wastelands,* The University of Illinois Press, Urbana, Ill., 1953, p. 51.

perpetually on a diet of printed materials. Language is, of course, the great essential tool of human thought and communication. Without a full command of reading and other lingual skills, no one can function effectively as a learner or citizen in modern society. However, matchless tool though it is, language is a *means* of getting at life's meanings, not the substance of meaning itself. Literacy is not absolute. It is a constantly changing capacity that must grow or wane with the individual and his total grasp of life's concerns and activities. Literacy cannot feed upon itself.[13]

> A human child denied all contact with other lingual humans would of course not learn to talk, or to read, and would hence remain something less than civilized, if indeed not less than human in behavior. But a human child denied all sensory-motor contact with his environment would be doomed to an existence even lower than subhuman, and if by some freak of circumstance this same child could be exposed only to auditory and visual stimulation by verbal symbols, no amount of such stimulation would lead the child to talk, to read, or to think. Indeed, he would have nothing to talk, to think, or to read about.

Modern instructional practices in education do not entail a conflict between new media and printed materials; the requirement is to fit the various media together in an ordered pattern that will make optimum use of their complementary functions.

It would be a serious mistake to assume that all resistance to the new media comes from the literary tradition and the conservative or antiprogressive elements in education. Undoubtedly, there is also a great deal of concern among teachers in general—especially, among those whose views and practices are best described by the now more or less archaic term "progressive." Many teachers feel threatened because they believe that recent technological developments tend to put greater distance between the teacher and the student. Shimabukuro points out that the earlier audio-visual media, including films, filmstrips, slides, recordings, display and three-dimensional materials, were not so threatening because they did not disturb the central role of the teacher in the instructional drama. With the new instructional media, which are designed to teach the core of various courses, it is quite different. "At best, the use of these media robs him [the teacher] of the star role and reduces him to the ignominy of an aide; at worst, it raises the worrisome specter of technological unemployment in education." [14]

Taba has expressed the feeling that "the media are trying to figure out a curriculum by themselves and for themselves in place of acting as media." Her statement that "within any technology lies a compulsion for 'packaging,' for mechanizing, and rationalizing," points

[13] Kenneth Norberg, "AV and Books," *The Instructor,* vol. 71, p. 48, June, 1962.
[14] Shinkichi Shimabukuro, "Programed Instruction: Threat or Challenge?" *Audiovisual Instruction,* vol. 9, p. 277, May, 1964.

to the source of a serious danger. She suggests that the success of the media in communicating knowledge has been overemphasized and that this may have obscured the need to explore their potential for implementing other important educational objectives, such as the development of values and attitudes and thinking.[15] Taba's thoughtful article helps to make explicit a probably widespread concern that some of the newer media may emphasize limited approaches to learning (at the expense of others), or that instructional goals and procedures may be tailored to an overriding technology that is dominated by its own compulsions rather than educational considerations. Her point is not that education should reject technology or the new media, but that we can exploit their full potential only if we recognize their dangers and the limitations of their improper use. This important concept will be amplified in the following discussion of the fear of technology in its wider aspects.

THE FEARFUL PATH TO TECHNOLOGICAL CHANGE

The long-delayed advance of technology in education has entered a stage of acceleration. Increasing use of newer media in the classroom calls for many changes: new designs for school buildings, changes in the organization and scheduling of classes, sometimes rather drastic changes in instructional procedures that seem to strike at the very heart of the teacher-pupil relationship.

Just how will these changes affect education? Will they tend to "dehumanize" the instructional process? Will instructional devices displace or degrade the teacher? Will the new technology destroy the privacy of the classroom—rob the instructor of his autonomy? Will it place too much emphasis upon economy and efficiency, too little upon quality? Will the growing use of a complicated technology, including the mass media, tend to overcentralize curriculum control, thus weakening the American tradition of local autonomy in education?

That many teachers and school administrators are troubled by such questions is hardly surprising. After all, the questions are real, and the answers are not yet in. Moreover, the uneasy forebodings aroused by modern technology are not limited to education. They represent one of the most pervasive emotional syndromes of our time. Bettelheim has made the penetrating observation that when modern man is haunted, he is not haunted by other men, but by machines. Ironically, man learns to dread his own technological creations while at the same time relying upon them for his protection or even his very salvation. Bettelheim proposes that the answer to technology's threat is not denying it or running away from it or refusing its benefits,

[15] Hilda Taba, "Evaluation Techniques? First Some Fundamental Questions," *Audiovisual Instruction,* vol. 9, pp. 271–272, May, 1964.

but facing its dangers and using it "without letting it deprive us of our humanity." [16]

It is becoming apparent that contemporary society affords no refuge from an advancing technology and the stresses and strains that result from its impact upon institutions and habitual patterns of conduct. Dealing with the total problem, Lewis Mumford has emphatically stated that we must "humanize" the machine. What would this entail in education? An answer is suggested in the 1963 publication *New Media in Higher Education.*[17]

> The first requirement is to recognize that the machine exists—that technology is now a fact in education. The other is to make sure that the positive force of technology is openly and responsibly directed by democratic instructional policies that are timely, clear, and explicit and not by obscure pressures and counter-pressures reflecting confusion, fear, or the desperation that comes when overdue decisions are forced by the sheer weight of circumstance. If these requirements are met, there is no need to fear that the machine will displace, degrade, or regiment human teachers—or that it will dehumanize education. On the contrary, a humanized technology can free the teacher from the servitude of mechanical and repetitive chores and amplify the force of his creative and distinctively human efforts.

The problem is to face up to change without forgetting what we wish to keep unchanged. It is frightening to have to look to technology for solutions to problems that technology helped to create; and there is always the lurking suspicion that new means will destroy cherished values, even when the faltering of old means has already placed the survival of these values in jeopardy. In a provocative "position" paper that appeared in 1963, Morris and others suggested that a culture such as ours has no other course than to look to its characteristic (technological) resources for solutions to its problems. They propose that the foundations of a technology of instruction have already been developed by pioneers working in education and the training programs of the military services and industry. They assert that the time has come to apply all that is known about communication and learning in developing a modern science of instruction; doing this requires "a massive infusion of technological capital and personnel into the system as well as a massive program of research and development." This would require a technological leap forward—in education. The decision of any school system to attempt this leap must be made in relation to certain assumptions. These are quoted as follows: [18]

[16] Bruno Bettelheim, *The Informed Heart,* Free Press, New York, 1961, p. 56.

[17] Kenneth D. Norberg, "A Rationale for the Use of New Media in Higher Education," in James W. Brown and James W. Thornton (eds.), *New Media in Higher Education,* Association for Higher Education and Division of Audio-Visual Instruction, 1963, p. 15.

[18] Barry Morris (ed.), "The Function of Media in the Public Schools," *Audiovisual Instruction,* vol. 8, p. 11, January, 1963.

Present instructional programs are inadequate to meet certain obvious needs of students who will grow up and work in the world of the 1960's and 1970's.

A new technology for instruction has been developed and proved through basic research and practice. This development has now reached a level that will permit rapid expansion of application and of further innovation.

The new educational technology is capable of meeting and solving certain of the schools' major problems in instruction, organization, and administration.

Application of the new technology will result in major changes affecting the administration, organization, and physical facilities of the public schools.

Methods of instruction will be modified to a major degree, particularly in the presentation of information.

Teachers and learners will have new roles and changed activities as a result of this technological change.

A new kind of professional will be required to provide leadership in design, implementation, and evaluation of programs of education which make the fullest use of new media. The functions performed by this leader and the resources he brings will be among the essential determinants of success or failure in tomorrow's schools.

If the crisis in modern education requires a technological leap forward, we must examine this imperative as a challenge to administrative leadership, which poses the essential problem of this book. In the following section, the main dimensions of this problem are summarized from the preceding discussions contained in this chapter.

SUMMARY: THE CHALLENGE TO ADMINISTRATIVE LEADERSHIP

A surging population has inundated the schools and the colleges, creating a shortage of qualified teachers in a society that demands fully educated citizens and highly trained manpower as never before. The advance of modern scientific inquiry has brought about an explosion of human knowledge that adds much to the already staggering task of education. But the same explosion has resulted in a modern technology that can help the schools accomplish their critical and difficult work.

Education has been very slow to make use of technological advances that have already produced revolutionary changes in industry, medicine, and other fields. The development of an audio-visual movement in education quickened after World War II. A definite acceleration of technological change came about with the advent of television and the increasing attention given to other electronic devices in

1950s and early 1960s. It was during this period that the concept of a truly modern complex of educational media, based upon a twentieth-century technology, took form.

Contemporary man has ambiguous feelings concerning technology; these feelings are evident in education, where the powerful modern instruments of communication are regarded as at once promising and threatening. As long as technology is used in the continuing quest for better solutions to human problems, it will be feared and resisted for the dislocations it brings and the dangers it creates. Whether it will help to solve critical problems in education or only create additional ones will depend upon planning and organization. This is the challenge to those who must administer the educational media in the schools.

In the opening paragraphs of this chapter, we outlined our position that all facets of the instructional-communications technology must be viewed as parts of a single comprehensive pattern—at some level of administrative planning and organization. We assume that instructional functions can be facilitated and strengthened by combining human judgment and skill with modern technical instrumentation. But the modern instruments of communication and teaching are not like a kit of carpenter's tools that can be carried around and operated by individual teachers. Television systems, language laboratories, and computers are only three rather conspicuous examples of a growing trend toward the use of more powerful, more complicated, and more costly devices in education. Obviously, the central coordination and management of such apparatuses adds new dimensions to the problems of educational administration.

On the other hand, we must realize that the fundamental problem in the administration of educational media is not the care and operation of elaborate technical systems, but the reorganization and re-orientation of instructional procedures and human tasks that are involved. The aim is to help people assert more powerful, more creative, and more humane roles in teaching—through technology. To mistake the mechanics of instruction for the substance would be a serious mistake, but one that can and sometimes does occur.

The problem is not to mechanize education, but to *humanize* it by amplifying the effectiveness of human beings and releasing them from machine-like chores. When Mumford talks about "humanizing the machine," he is really talking about humanizing people. This can be done by bringing the use of machines under the dominance of purposes that are informed and truly humane.

FOR FURTHER INFORMATION

Brown, James W., Richard B. Lewis, and Fred F. Harcleroad: *A-V Instruction: Materials and Methods,* 2d ed., McGraw-Hill, New York, 1964.

Dale, Edgar: "The Teacher and Technology," *The News Letter,* vol. 29, pp. 1–4, October, 1963.

Ely, Donald E.: "The Changing Role of the Audiovisual Process in Education: A Definition and a Glossary of Related Terms," Monograph 1, Technological Development Project, NEA. *AV Communication Review,* vol. 11, January–February, 1963. (Entire issue)

Finn, James D.: "Technology and the Instructional Process," *AV Communication Review,* vol. 8, pp. 5–26, Winter, 1960.

Miller, Neal, and others: *Graphic Communication and the Crisis in Education,* Department of Audio-Visual Instruction, NEA, *AV Communication Review,* vol. 5, no. 3, 1957.

Office of the Superintendent of Public Instruction: *Instructional Materials,* Illinois Curriculum Program, Administration and Supervision Series, Bulletin A-3, Springfield, Ill., 1963.

Ruark, Henry C., Jr.: "Technology and Education," *Phi Delta Kappan,* pp. 387–392, June, 1961.

Schramm, Wilbur (ed.): *New Teaching Aids for the American Classroom,* The Institute for Communication Research, Stanford University, Stanford, Calif., 1960.

Taba, Hilda: "Evaluation Techniques? First Some Fundamental Questions," *Audiovisual Instruction,* vol. 9, pp. 271–272, May, 1964.

Trow, William Clark: *Teacher and Technology: New Designs for Learning,* Appleton-Century-Crofts, New York, 1963.

Trump, J. Lloyd, and Dorsey Baynham: *Focus on Change: Guide to Better Schools,* Rand McNally, Chicago, 1961.

Schuller, Charles F. (ed.): *The School Administrator and His Audio-Visual Program,* Department of Audio-Visual Instruction, NEA, 1954.

chapter 2

Requirements and opportunities for educational media personnel

The new and growing interest in improving education through application of educational technology, as discussed briefly in Chapter 1, leads directly to the need to recruit and educate professional educational media personnel to carry out such programs. In calling for "a technological leap forward in education," the (DAVI) task force in 1962 recognized that: [1]

> A new kind of professional will be required to provide leadership in design, implementation, and evaluation of programs in education which make the fullest use of new media. The functions performed by this leader and the resources he brings will be among the essential determinants of success or failure in tomorrow's schools.

This chapter treats in broad outline some of the many professional opportunities in schools, colleges, universities, branches of state and Federal government, business and industry, and social welfare agencies that use the products of this technology of education to improve communication and learning. As the following discussion indicates, each organization provides opportunities for professional educational media personnel to perform as generalists or specialists. The distinguishing characteristics of these two roles will be examined first.[2]

THE EDUCATIONAL MEDIA GENERALIST

The educational media generalist differs from the specialist primarily in the breadth of his preparation and his responsibilities. While generalists may function temporarily as specialists (during their training period or while awaiting assignment), specialists seldom function as generalists.

[1] Barry Morris (ed.), "The Function of Media in the Public Schools," *Audiovisual Instruction,* vol. 8, p. 11, January, 1963.
[2] Much of the following material is adapted from a paper prepared earlier for the Study for the Technical Education of Materials Specialists (STEMS), an NDEA-supported project undertaken at California State College (Hayward), Robert Hall and Fred Harcleroad, project directors.

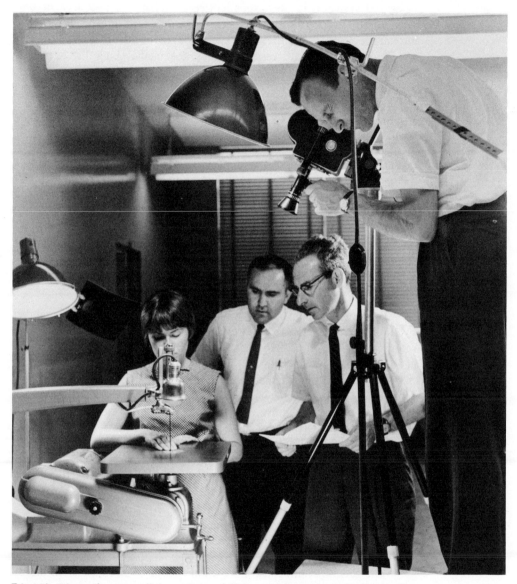

Educational media generalists and specialists contribute importantly to the achievement of modern educational goals. A photographic technician at San Jose State College follows action filmed for local use in demonstrating shop safety procedures. The college instructor and the Audio-Visual Center materials preparation specialist direct the action. (*San Jose State College*)

The generalist serves as the director, coordinator, or manager of an educational media agency and works closely with or under the supervision of an administrator who is responsible for a larger program. He may be a director of educational media services and responsible to a principal or an assistant or associate superintendent (in a school

17

or school system), to an academic vice-president (in a college or university), to a training director (in a business or industry), or to a bureau, department, or division head (in a government agency).

In carrying out his responsibilities, the media generalist is usually expected to:

❯ Assess continuously the desirability and feasibility of applying the efficiencies of technology and systematized planning to problems of teaching and learning, with due regard to curricular organization
❯ Organize logistical aspects of educational media so as to facilitate uses that are properly related, varied, timed, located, and presented
❯ Organize information about media so as to assist users in locating and obtaining those best suited to their needs
❯ Establish conditions calculated to stimulate and motivate professional personnel to make appropriate uses of educational media
❯ Measure and evaluate the effects of uses of media and the desirability or undesirability of certain logistical arrangements in their applications to the teaching-learning enterprise
❯ Effect or recommend changes justified by results of such analyses

It is obvious that the educational media generalist must be qualified by education, experience, interests, and personality characteristics. A requirement is that he be generally and broadly familiar through education and experience with the innumerable complexities of the agency in which he works, no matter what his eventual assignment will be. If he is to carry out his responsibilities in a single school, a school system, a college or university, or a county or state department of education, prior certification as a teacher and at least a few years of experience in classroom teaching will be helpful.

He needs additional background on which to base advanced study of the processes of administering and supervising uses of educational media. He must have a broad liberal education, a mature philosophy of education, a general knowledge of the structure and relations of curriculum development and content at appropriate levels, and a familiarity with theoretical and practical aspects of the psychology of learning and instruction.

The generalist must also have a knowledge of administrative theory and an ability to administer that has been developed—preferably—through suitable internship or on-the-job assignments carried out under proper supervision.

Because of the breadth of his responsibilities and the fact that he often works almost singlehandedly in initiating and conducting educational media programs, the generalist must also have considerable familiarity with the full range of educational media, equipment, and processes. Some knowledge of and skills in production processes and techniques, for example, and familiarity with selection standards, distribution and maintenance procedures, technological applications of electronic capabilities to instruction are also needed.

But perhaps above all else the educational media generalist should be a person whose makeup permits him to work easily *with* and *through* others to reach the legitimate goals of his office. He must be quick to recognize and commend quality performances of others, for example, or to share the spotlight of attention or praise, to accept and to delegate responsibility, and to recognize the worth of and inspire those with whom he works. He must be sufficiently secure in the conduct of his office to resist temptations of dictatorial or "lone-wolf" approaches and to use instead the difficult but more effective methods of cooperation and persuasion.

These qualities and accomplishments will permit him to effect a kind of administrative integration of his work, avoid the excesses of gadgetry, and bring his activities into close touch with the total effort of the educational agency of which he is a part. In addition to all these virtues, he must be capable of seeing both the forest *and* the trees—aware of the significance of details but not swamped by them, knowing the important difference between the crucial and the irrelevant.

EDUCATIONAL MEDIA SPECIALISTS

Various specialists perform functions that differ significantly from those of the generalist. In large organizations, for example, specialists may organize and assume supervisory responsibility for selecting, procuring, distributing, and inventorying materials and equipment; stimulating the wider and better use of materials by teachers and others; overseeing and engineering equipment installations; improving the physical environment of media utilization; producing graphic materials (films, charts, transparencies, handbooks, and the like); performing research and evaluation (including experimentation); producing programs and supervising uses of radio and television. Any of these activities may be so important as to require college education and teacher certification. In such cases—and perhaps because of the size of the operation—other less highly qualified specialists may work under his supervision.

Educational media specialists may enter their profession in a number of ways. They may come as art majors (intending to become visual graphics specialists); as journalism or English majors (intending to become curriculum-materials or radio-TV script writers); as librarianship majors (intending to specialize in print media); as business majors (interested in managing media-center operations); as photography majors (interested in specializing in still- and motion-picture production); as public relations majors (interested in audience analysis and public information activities of colleges, universities, school systems, business, industrial, governmental organizations); as psychology majors (interested in designing, controlling, and reporting results of experiments and in recommending courses of action based on such findings); and as engineers or industrial designers (interested in the design and

19

installation of innovational media equipment and facilities, the invention of educational devices, and the general systematization of human communication and instruction).

ADMINISTRATIVE OPPORTUNITIES IN EDUCATION

There are thousands of opportunities for both generalists and specialists in the vast numbers of public and private institutions at various levels in the educational hierarchy—elementary and secondary schools, junior colleges, teachers colleges, colleges and universities, state departments of education, school district offices, or county school units.

There is an obvious need to organize and administer educational media programs at each of these levels. Later chapters will provide considerable detail on opportunities and responsibilities of these assignments; the present discussion identifies in general terms the kinds of work in which educational media personnel engage in single schools, county or district school offices, state departments of education, and colleges and universities.

Single schools

In altogether too many single schools, the educational media staff is either nonexistent or limited to the part-time services of a lone librarian or teacher-librarian who is assisted occasionally by a teacher whose primary concern is for audio-visual materials and equipment. This situation appears less than satisfactory today, and prospects for eventually correcting such deficiencies seem promising indeed. While the scope and complexities of media services in single schools vary in accordance with enrollment, financial capabilities, and characteristics of curriculum, it now seems clear that well-staffed schools of even moderate size will need professional media personnel to:

❯ Study school curriculum organization and recommend ways to improve instruction through applications of educational media
❯ Provide expert assistance, guidance, and evaluation of uses of media in achieving important teaching and learning objectives
❯ Study existing school plant facilities to determine needed improvements to facilitate uses of educational media
❯ Assume principal responsibility for building strong collections of educational media and media equipment closely related to curricular requirements and goals

Contrasts evident in these two classrooms suggest the urgent need for professional assistance of educational media workers in improving the environment for instruction. (*Perkins and Will, Architects; and Kimble Glass Company, Toledo*)

> Develop workable plans and procedures to allow full and proper use of such collections by teachers, students, and others

> Enrich the school's own media collections as necessary and appropriate through recourse to outside sources—district or county media-center collections, museums, sponsoring sources, community agencies, or others

> Train and provide student assistants, as needed, to aid teachers in various tasks related to uses of educational media—operating or monitoring equipment, processing materials, duplicating, others

> Provide first-line assistance in producing appropriate educational media for local school use (copying slides, preparing graphics, making large transparencies, mounting flat pictures, duplicating materials, and the like) and referring more complicated or costly projects to media centers at other levels

> Furnish and monitor the distribution of certain expendable educational supplies (tapes, raw film, art supplies, others)

> Load, monitor, recover and perhaps interpret data from permanently installed teaching machines, self-instruction laboratories, listening laboratories, student-response systems, computer-based instructional devices, and similar installations

It should be quite obvious that no such group of complex services and activities could be performed adequately by one whose education has pointed solely toward classroom teaching. Nor can they be done by even traditionally educated librarians or by those whose backgrounds are limited to audio-visual matters. Rather, what seems to be called for and what more and more school officials are demanding is the employment in each school of at least one educational media generalist. In smaller schools, this individual may work alone, with only the additional help of student assistants; he is responsible for the entire media program. In larger schools, however, the generalist (with a broad background in all aspects of educational media) may be assisted by specialists in librarianship and in audio-visual media.

County and district school units

The many county and district school units throughout the United States frequently provide educational media services that are:

> *Supplemental* Services that are calculated to round out and strengthen services already in effect within single schools, such as short-term loans of enrichment books not part of single-school collections or loans of items too expensive or used too infrequently to merit purchase by one school

> *Experimental* Services that provide opportunities for controlled, small-scale tryouts of materials, equipment, services, or procedures before they are recommended generally

> *Supervisory* Services that seek instances of good utilization, discern problems and areas needing attention or emphasis, and attempt generally to aid in improving instruction

At this level, special attention is given to district-wide or county-wide aspects of educational media. Emphasis is placed upon (1) promoting increased and improved utilization of educational media (often through cooperative relations with other supervisory staff members who have special field responsibilities in art, music, social studies, and the like); (2) budgeting and planning; (3) selecting and purchasing (or producing locally) books, filmstrips, and similar items to be shelved in individual schools; (4) cataloging (often done centrally for all schools in the system or county); (5) inventorying; (6) distributing (on long- or short-term loan basis); (7) maintaining (in good repair); (8) revising or discarding; and (9) continuously evaluating the outcomes of established or new practices.

District- or county-sponsored production programs, especially in television, are also common. In-service staff education in the application of new media to the curriculum is encouraged in various ways (workshops, extension classes, publications, and the like).

State departments of education

The States Audio-Visual Education Study (SAVES), concluded in 1963 by Dr. Francis W. Noel and staff through a National Defense Education Act (NDEA) grant to the University of Southern California,[3] summarized national patterns in new educational media activities in each of the fifty state departments of education. It was pointed out that: [4]

> In the nation as a whole, a total of 75 positions were reported in State departments of education which carry a designated audio-visual title; these occurred in 32 states (64%). Twenty-three states (46%) reported one or more fulltime positions; the total of fulltime positions was 54. Twenty fulltime SDE staff occupied designated audiovisual positions on a part-time basis in 15 states (30%). These states included 7 states (14%) which had already reported fulltime positions, so that in 8 states the full responsibility is carried by a part-time designated person. In the remaining 18 states (36%) which reported no designated audio-visual position, this responsibility is carried by a staff member whose major assignment lies outside the new educational media field. . . . Thus, in 27 states major responsibility for [new educational media] is carried by personnel with other departmental duties.

Typical of the many types of activities performed by new media personnel in state departments of education, as reported in the SAVES study,[5] are the following:

❯ Assisting local schools in new media matters pertaining to curriculum revision

[3] Francis W. Noel and others, *Practices of State Departments of Education in New Educational Media/Audiovisual Education during 1960–61,* University of Southern California, Los Angeles, Calif., 1963.
[4] *Ibid.,* II-3 to II-4.
[5] *Ibid.*

❯ Preparing utilization guides, study resource units, bibliographic materials, and similar publications

❯ Holding conferences and workshops for professional and lay personnel to provide information, stimulation, and guidelines for the use of new media

❯ Developing standards for new media availabilities and utilization (equipment, materials, services) as part of over-all accreditation procedures (forty-four of the fifty states engaged in this activity, although there was great variation in types of services performed)

❯ Developing and enforcing teacher certification standards involving knowledges and skills in utilizing new media and equipment (in six states for classroom teachers; in ten states for supervisory and administrative certification; five states for librarians; seven states for new media supervisors)

❯ Developing and publishing building and facilities standards (usually in cooperation with the state department of education's department of plant planning) as related to new media installations

❯ Conducting research studies and surveys regarding uses and contributions of new media to the school instructional program

❯ Producing various instructional materials (twenty-one states) for use by schools and staff members of state departments of education

❯ Distributing new media on short-term loan bases to schools (fifteen states) or within the state department of education only (twenty-seven states)

❯ Supervising state-wide programs of education television (twenty state departments had some legal responsibilities for this)

Colleges and universities

The urgent need to provide adequate staff, facilities, and resources for the rapidly increasing enrollments in institutions of higher education has stimulated widespread reevaluation of ways of teaching involving applications of new media. A recent report summarizes several significant aspects of this need: [6]

> The communicative process known as higher education has had a long history of gradual and placid evolution, but now it is faced with a series of challenges that appear to call for swift and energetic adaptation. Important questions—questions which undeniably involve the new media—are continuously being raised. Can the valid, traditional purposes of higher education, as well as its new and emerging purposes, continue to be attained economically and effectively by its traditional media of communication? Considering the increasing complexity of interrelationships and abstractions of conceptualization in the several disciplines, will certain forms of nonverbal presentation prove more effective than oral or printed words in transmitting some kinds of ideas? What functional contributions to the learning of certain skills (including the verbal skills of language) can be expected to be derived from use of automated or technological instruction devices and techniques? What changing conditions emphasize the need to speed the process of

[6] James W. Brown, and James W. Thornton, Jr. (eds.), *New Media in Higher Education,* Association for Higher Education and Department of Audio-Visual Instruction, NEA, 1963, pp. 1–2.

evolution in higher education, and how do these changes relate to uses of new media?

One especially interesting plan for providing new media described by President John A. Hannah of Michigan State University in a report to the faculty as he proposed a single comprehensive learning resources center for his campus. He stressed that: [7]

> Such a center would not be a mere re-grouping of forces and facilities. It would—and should—become a dynamic center of experiment and development leading to accomplishments beyond our present power to envisage. Programming for a teaching machine or presentation of a course on television tapes is not a casual undertaking. Such projects entail a great deal of intensive work, minute reexamination and re-arrangement of course content, and intimate familiarity with both the art of teaching and the process of learning. They require substantial investments of effort and money, but experience to date shows that they pay substantial dividends in many ways, including the freeing of the faculty from repetitive teaching and drill in many areas and a speeding up of the learning process.

Educational media services on today's typical college and university campuses are provided most frequently by three separate agencies: the library and library system, the audio-visual center, and the radio-television center. Long considered to be first lines of assistance in providing printed materials to students, professors, and research scientists, many college and university libraries are evolving into centers for more varied collections of teaching and learning resources, many of which were seldom found in libraries until recently—programmed materials, tape and disk recordings, self-instruction carrel facilities with recordings or computer-based instructional devices, and various audio-visual collections. Such changes have brought new requirements for educational media personnel.

The typical college or university audio-visual center now provides new educational media and media services resembling those of similar centers at other levels of education. The most common service is providing 16mm sound films (from college-owned collections or borrowed from off-campus sources) and projectionists. But other more sophisticated programs now exist on campuses all over the country—and more are being established. For example, attention is being given to using new media in collecting and reporting research data, and in many institutions, publishing in film form is as acceptable as it is in print. Radio and television services also involve educational media personnel, who have responsibilties for planning, writing, directing, producing, broadcasting (or distributing by other means), and evaluating general information or educational programs of many different types.

[7] From speech by John A. Hannah, president, Michigan State University, East Lansing, Mich., Mar. 27, 1961.

An important activity that bears on this discussion of opportunities relates to courses in educational media utilization, production, and administration. Most colleges and universities that are engaged in teacher training offer at least a basic course to provide an overview of the range and uses of new educational media in teaching. In many of the larger institutions, additional courses are offered to prepare generalists and specialists in educational media, including those who will function in nonschool assignments in business, journalism, public relations, and others. A growing number of such institutions now offer advanced degrees (to the level of the doctorate) in this field.

OTHER ADMINISTRATIVE OPPORTUNITIES

Administrative opportunities in educational media abound in four other areas: local, state, and Federal government units; various social service agencies; many different fields of business and industry; and the commercial production of educational materials.

Government

A recent collection of leaflets and announcements of the U.S. Civil Service Commission included reference to openings for the following educational media positions:

> Radio broadcast technician
> Exhibits technician and exhibits specialist
> Radio adaptor, radio announcer, radio producer (foreign-language specialists)
> Broadcast recording technician
> Scientific illustrator (medical)
> Medical photographer
> Museum curator
> Filmstrip producer
> Audio-visual producer
> Public information specialist
> Writer and editor
> Visual information specialist; visual information officer
> Librarian
> Photographer

While the above list represents only a few of the many different kinds of media positions, it suggests the range of available opportunities and professional requirements involved. In the foreword to the leaflet describing opportunities in the "Public information specialist" category, for example, appeared the statement: [8]

[8] Public Information Series, Position Classification Standards, GS-1081-0, U.S. Civil Service Commission, April, 1961, p. 1.

This series includes positions engaged in disseminating information about the activities of the Federal Government through the newspapers, radio, television, periodicals, and other information media, or through employee periodicals, and in furnishing advice and consultation to management concerning the information needs of the public. Positions in this series require a knowledge of public information techniques, the ability to utilize communication and informational media effectively, and the ability to evaluate the public information potential of written materials, illustrations, photographs, exhibits, radio, television, and motion picture materials. Employees in these positions must also be able to write and edit effectively.

Typical of the agencies of the Federal government now employing large numbers of media specialists are the following:

> *U.S. Department of Agriculture.* The Office of Information activities involve the production and distribution of films, filmstrips, booklets, charts, flat picture sets, and similar materials on agricultural subjects. The Department now has available more than three hundred 16mm educational films that are distributed through approximately seventy cooperating film libraries throughout the country. Its 35mm filmstrips, for sale to qualified purchasers, treat a variety of home economics and agricultural subjects.

> *U.S. Department of the Interior.* The Division of Information produces audio-visual and printed informational materials of many kinds to inform the public of the continuing need to improve natural resources and recreational facilities and opportunities in the United States. The National Park Service, in particular, finds uses for media specialists of many different kinds. Dissemination of information, one of the basic aims of the service, is carried out through production and distribution of informational leaflets and folders on areas administered, through the presentations of illustrated talks for visitors to national parks and monuments, through the development of museum displays (recently much-expanded with the "Mission 66" program), and others.

> *U.S. Information Agency.* This independent agency has the mission to interpret for the peoples of the world the policies and objectives of the United States government and to increase, in the process, the reciprocal flow of ideas and information and to lessen international tensions through increased understanding. The agency operates the international broadcasting programs of Voice of America. It maintains a large program for producing highly visualized publications, television programs, motion pictures, and similar media, as well as for distributing or displaying them as part of our overseas information efforts.

> *U.S. Department of Defense.* The organization has vast needs for manuals, films, filmstrips, recordings, courses of study, charts, maps, and related instructional materials for the education and training of members of the Armed Forces, for recruitment, or for general information purposes.

Social service agencies

Hundreds of social service agencies, with as many different sets of goals and purposes, also employ educational media specialists in carrying out their programs. Public libraries, in broadening the scope of their services, are often found to be in the audio-visual business, distributing films and related nonbook media on a regular basis. Examples of "new media" activities in four such social service agencies follow:

❯ *Girl Scouts of America* (GSA). The Audiovisual Materials Service at national headquarters produces and distributes motion pictures, filmstrips, charts, 650 TV spots, and similar materials for use by Girl Scout councils all over the country. Requests for production are weighed each year against objectives for the GSA, cost, availability of time of the professional audiovisual staff, and probable salability of proposed items. Production activities are handled either by members of the central audio-visual staff, by free-lance personnel, or by outside production companies. On the permanent professional staff of the Girl Scouts of America central office are the director of Audiovisual Materials Service, a producer-director, a camera assistant, and a film librarian and assistant. In a typical year, GSA sells approximately 800 prints of its films, 1,500 filmstrips, and 1,000 flipcharts; it handles approximately 2,000 rentals.

❯ *Anti-Defamation League of B'nai B'rith* (ADL). The organization has, for more than fifty years, conducted educational programs in the United States to combat discrimination against minorities, to fight the threat of all forms of totalitarianism, and to promote intercultural understanding and cooperation among all religious faiths. Regional offices of the ADL in twenty-five locations maintain audio-visual libraries of films, filmstrips, and dramatic recordings, all of which may be purchased or rented at nominal cost. Many of the items have been cleared for use on television.

❯ *American National Red Cross.* The Office of Public Information in Washington maintains an Audio-Visual Section; it is responsible for various radio and television campaigns, film and other visual-materials production and distribution, and related activities in support of National Red Cross programs throughout the country. Particularly important are its film productions on the subjects of first aid, swimming, and safety education. Recent film releases were titled *People Afloat, Your Breath Can Save a Life, Neighbor to Neighbor,* and *Ice Rescue.* The job description for the audio-visual chief states that he is "responsible for planning and supervising production for national interpretation and promotion of Red Cross activities through radio, television, and motion pictures; for developing and maintaining contacts with radio and television national networks, program producers, and advertising agencies; for providing the areas and chapters with counsel and guidance and materials to assist them in telling the Red Cross story locally through these media. He supervises three audio-visual specialists and one secretary, and assists in supervising the Hollywood representative."

❯ *Public Libraries.* Libraries in all parts of the country are now offering various types of audio-visual services, with special emphasis upon the distribution of 16mm sound films, the organization of special library showings of documentary and other types of films, and the organization and distribution of disk and tape recording collections, principally of musical types. Library positions in the "new media" field have thus become common, particularly in the larger cities.

Business and industry

As in the case of government and social service agencies, opportunities for educational media personnel in business and industry are numerous and varied. They include activities associated with (1) school and college relations, (2) general public relations, (3) employee orientation and training, (4) research and development, (5) commercial production, and (6) distribution and sales. Three examples serve to identify the range of activities in this area:

❯ *American Dental Association.* The Association maintains the Bureau of Audio-Visual Service in its Chicago headquarters, and it handles a number of "new media" activities. In a recent year, approximately 7,500 films were shipped from the center; rental income was $16,000. During this period, approximately 3,500 items were requested by dental societies throughout the country, another 1,000 by dental schools, 900 by government agencies, 1,000

Visualized free and inexpensive materials such as these of the Association of American Railroads shown here, often developed with the professional supervision of educational media specialists, are widely used in the schools. (*Association of American Railroads*)

by nonprofessional groups, 300 by television stations, and 200 by miscellaneous groups. Guidance films to interest high school and college students in careers in dentistry have proved particularly popular.

❯ *National Dairy Council.* The organization is a nonprofit research and educational organization of the dairy industry, with headquarters in Chicago. It operates in cooperation with council-affiliated units throughout the country. The purpose of the organization is "to promote optimum health through the adequate use of milk and its products in accord with current scientific recommendations." In carrying this out, the Council produces and sells a variety of health and nutrition education materials as classroom teaching aids and assists in the health education work of other nonschool organizations. Included in the Council's catalog of available materials are professional source materials, life-size models, posters, displays, booklets, units of work, motion pictures, and filmstrips.

❯ *General Motors Corporation* (GM). The company maintains the Educational Relations Section as part of its public relations program. The office provides various booklets, manuals, charts, films, kits, displays, and other teaching aids for school use. Included in GM collections are more than sixty company-produced free-loan films on such subjects as safety and driver education, industrial processes, home economics, and guidance. Various operating divisions (AC Spark Plug Division, Allison Division, Buick Division, Delco Radio Divison, and others) also produce materals having instructional uses. To assist educators, GM also provides to certain accredited schools and colleges a number of products and product components for instruction and training purposes, including engines, transmissions, and rear axle assemblies. Cutaway models are sometimes provided under this same service.

Commercial producers

Professional opportunities for educational media generalists and specialists are also numerous in areas related to the design, production, and sale of educational materials and equipment. Publishers who once dealt only with books, for example, now require the services of editorial, design, and research specialists who work closely with authors in producing and testing educational products ranging from textbooks and teachers' manuals, on the one hand, to films, filmstrips, charts, transparencies, recordings, workbooks, and programmed books on the other. Many of these materials are produced as kits or "systems." Sales activities for all of these materials require the services of specially trained individuals who combine an intimate knowledge of materials with an acquaintance with problems of teaching.

A relative few producers produce the great majority of educational films now on the market. Three companies are somewhat representative: Encyclopaedia Britannica Films (EBF), Coronet Films, and McGraw-Hill Textfilms. EBF began in 1927 as an experimental adjunct to the Western Electric Company under the name of ERPI. It was the first major company to produce sound films for educational purposes. Its early collaboration with the University of Chicago led first to the production of films in physical and biological sciences and later to other subjects—the social sciences, history, and foreign cultures. The company's collection of film titles now numbers well in excess of 1,000 titles; more are added each year. The professional production staff of the company includes research and writing personnel, directors, cameramen, sound engineers, and other technical personnel. The company's nationwide distribution and sales staff maintains direct contacts with school, college, and library personnel in all major cities and counties. Its film crews often work under free-lance contracts in all parts of the world to produce films about aspects of life on every continent.

As more and more electronic devices (language laboratories, video-tape and audio-tape recorders, closed- and open-circuit TV units, teaching machines) become commonplace in educational and training work in schools and industry, increased numbers of specialized personnel are required to design, produce, and sell them. Activities of architects, electronic designers, educational media specialists, curriculum workers, and engineers in the successful design of modern school facilities emphasize the complementary nature of their contributions to such projects (see Chapter 3).

SUMMARY

This chapter has emphasized opportunities now open to individuals interested in pursuing careers in the educational media field—and they are many: in single schools, county and district schools offices, state departments of education, colleges and universities, various levels of government, social service agencies, and business and industry. It was further pointed out that in nearly all such agencies, there are openings for both generalists and specialists—the former to provide over-all guidance and supervision in large programs or to serve alone in smaller ones, the latter to perform professional tasks of a more specialized nature when the situation permits or requires them.

But whether one is a media generalist or a specialist, and whether he serves education, government, or business, he should be guided by similar fundamental and professional considerations. These requirements were excellently highlighted in David K. Berlo's keynote address to the 1963 national convention of the Department of Audio-Visual Instruction of the NEA. In outlining what he considered to be the desirable relationships of communication theory and applied technology, he emphasized that: [9]

❯ Competence in the technology (of communication) itself must be tied at both ends to the communication process of instruction.
❯ Professionals in educational media are not in "the audiovisual business," not in "the instructional technology business," not in the "message or media

[9] Adapted from David K. Berlo, "You Are in the People Business," *Audiovisual Instruction,* vol. 8, pp. 372–381, June, 1963.

business." They are in "the *people* business." They are paid to affect behavior, to produce information gain, to induce attitude change, and most importantly, to increase the learner's ability to learn without being taught.

❯ To maintain the role of "professional" in the field of educational media requires professional competence in understanding how people behave in the instructional situation. Another name for this is "communication."

❯ The theoretic underpinnings of communication are in psychology, social psychology, sociology, electrical engineering, and quantitative research methodology.

❯ The educational media field needs to emphasize the competence of the rigorous generalist who is capable of grasping the meaning of communication planning and stategy. Media training must emphasize theory and research on the communication process. A competent professional in educational media must be a competent student of human behavior, must be cognizant of relevant theories of human behavior, and must be able, as a minimum, to interpret social theory and research as it applies to instructional communication. And he must be competent to conduct such research and motivated to discover knowledge as well as to apply it.

FOR FURTHER INFORMATION

Berlo, David K.: "You Are in the People Business," *Audiovisual Instruction,* vol. 8, pp. 372–381, June, 1963.

Bern, H. A.: "Audio-Visual Engineers?" *AV Communication Review,* vol. 9, pp. 186–194, July–August, 1961.

Brown, James W., and James W. Thornton, Jr. (eds.): *New Media in Higher Education,* Association for Higher Education and Department of Audio-Visual Instruction, NEA, 1963. 182 pp.

Erickson, Carlton W. H.: *Administering Audio-Visual Services,* Macmillan, New York, 1959.

Films for Libraries, ALA, Chicago, 1962.

Finn, James W.: "Professionalizing the Audiovisual Field," *AV Communication Review,* vol. 1, pp. 9–16, Winter, 1953.

Harcleroad, Fred F.: "The Education of the AV Communication Specialist," *AV Communication Review,* vol. 8, pp. 7–19, September–October, 1960.

Harcleroad, Fred F.: "We Must Base Our Profession on Social Needs," *Audiovisual Instruction,* vol. 8, pp. 382–383, June, 1963.

Holloway, George M.: "Films in the Large Public Library," *Educational Screen and Audiovisual Guide,* vol. 42, pp. 620–621, November, 1963.

Instructional Materials Services for Washington's Schools, Washington State Department of Education, Olympia, Wash., 1960. 56 pp.

Morris, Barry (ed.): "The Function of Media in the Public Schools," *Audiovisual Instruction,* vol. 8, pp. 9–14, January, 1963.

Schuller, Charles F. (ed.): *The School Administrator and His Audio-Visual Program,* Department of Audio-Visual Instruction, NEA, 1954.

"Standards for the Media Specialist: What Are the States Requiring Now?" *Audiovisual Instruction,* vol. 7, pp. 464–467, September, 1962.

United Nations Conference on the Application of Science and Technology for the Benefit of the Less Developed Areas. Bulletin E, Conf. M39/INF. 1/REV. 1. UNESCO, Columbia, New York, 1962.

Witt, Paul W. F.: "Six Steps in Professionalizing the AV Specialist," *Audiovisual Instruction,* vol. 7, pp. 430–432, September, 1962.

chapter 3

Physical facilities
for educational media

Explosive effects of the rising numbers of school-age children, the rapid expansion of knowledge, and the increasing uses of technological devices and other innovations in extending scientific inquiry, and improved educational communication, as outlined in Chapter 1, demand the consideration of physical facilities in relation to uses of educational media.

In the 1950s and 1960s, it became evident that our need was not simply to provide more buildings in which to house a growing school population; it was to plan more buildings constructed according to specifications growing out of changed forms of education. Such plans and specifications continue to occupy the attention of school administrators, architects, board members, and educational media personnel all over the country. Their study has produced remarkable and widespread results, important features of which have been the many experimental validations of school design adapted to changing curriculum requirements. But in altogether too many instances there has been a failure to recognize the need for providing proper facilities for uses of new media.

Foremost among organizations that have aided in dramatizing the need for new approaches to school plant planning are the National Association of Secondary-school Principals, which has emphasized problems and opportunities in reorganizing school curricula and schedules; and the Educational Facilities Laboratories, Inc., which is supported by the Ford Foundation. Effects of the work of these two organizations, as well as that of many other organizations, architects, and planning groups, have been remarkable; together they have produced a series of fundamental changes in the appearance, inner arrangement, construction, and equipment of school buildings all over the country. Especially to the point of this book have been their recommendations concerning facilities, conveniences, and standards relating to uses of educational media.

SCHOOL DESIGN: GENERAL CONSIDERATIONS

Adequate consideration of the physical facilities desired by schools continues to require analysis of (1) educational or training objectives,

(2) characteristics of the groups to be instructed, and (3) kinds of teaching-learning activities to be undertaken. Each bears importantly upon decisions concerning the specialized physical environments in which such instruction and learning are to occur.

In its *Schools for the Sixties,* the NEA Project on the Instructional Program of the Public Schools classified some of the emerging changes in current school programs (many of which bear directly upon problems of school design requirements), as follows:

From	*To*
1. The group	The individual
2. Memory	Inquiry
3. Spiritless climate	Zest for learning
4. The graded school	The non-graded school
5. Self-contained classroom	Self-contained school
6. Scheduled classes	Appointments and independent learning
7. Teacher as a general practitioner	Teacher as a clinical specialist (member of a team)
8. School building use geared to an agrarian society—a 9-month year, limited to children	School building use reflecting urban society—a 12-month year, available to all age groups
9. Classrooms that are like kitchens	Classrooms that are like libraries, living rooms
10. Boxes and egg crates	Clusters and zones of space
11. Teaching as telling	Teaching as guiding
12. A teaching schedule of 30 hours a week with children in class, and 15 hours for planning and correcting	15 hours a week with children in class and 30 hours for research, planning, and development

Source: NEA, Project on Instruction, *Schools for the Sixties,* McGraw-Hill, New York, 1963.

In another analysis of the relationships of instructional goals, experiences, and resources, an "ABC–XYZ" concept is developed.[1] Instructional goals (ABC) are identified as A—knowledge and information; B—attitudes and appreciations; and C—skills and performance. The XYZ aspect of instruction, on the other hand, stresses the varying roles of teachers, learners, and experiences in carrying out the activities through which such goals are achieved. The special point is made that throughout all these activities there is planned variety in the structure (XYZ) of teaching-learning groups—a variety that is functionally related to instructional purposes. With X activities, for example, the *teacher alone* serves as a primary source of information by giving directions or explanations, developing ideas and concepts, or demonstrat-

[1] James W. Brown, Richard B. Lewis, and Fred F. Harcleroad, *A-V Instruction: Materials and Methods,* 2d ed., McGraw-Hill, New York, 1964, pp. 22–26.

ing. Students, in such cases, are "receivers" as they listen, watch, think, or take notes. With Y activities, the teacher and students play *interacting* roles. There is a two-way exchange of ideas and information, a clarification of thinking, opportunity to draw students out—to discover their learning problems and the sources of confusion or misinformation and to provide needed guidance at crucial points. These experiences may come from teacher-and-student or student-and-student exchanges. Finally, with Z activities, the *student works alone* in individual study or practice. He may carry out carefully planned assignments given by the teacher; he may read, take notes, analyze his data, write a report on his findings, or check the accuracy of his conclusions. He may work at a teaching machine or study a programmed book; he may view filmstrips, listen to recordings, see a film, study a chart, or perform an experiment—without help or interference from others.

Trump's suggestions with regard to the administrative organizational aspects of secondary schools provide numerous other considerations to which attention must be given in attempts to design functional school plants. He says: [2]

> A carefully planned instructional system in any subject area, at any grade or level of schooling, varies the educational setting with changes in the purpose and content of what is to be learned. Large group, small group, and independent study arrangements are made to accomplish specific purposes, but also have planned relationships to each other. Diverse pupil talents, motivations, and past achievements are recognized in student grouping and the schedule. Methods of teaching change with the size and make-up of the groups. Curriculum content is altered to serve the needs of basic education for all students and depth education for all students according to his individual talents and interests. *Instructional materials are selected to serve specific purposes in the system, are related to each other, and are readily accessible to teachers and students.* [Italics added.]

Trump's description of one such new learning environment uses as an example the administrative requirements and provisions for social science instruction in a school in which these newly emphasized teaching-learning relationships are encouraged. As usual, provisions are made for (1) *independent study,* (2) listening or watching explanations or demonstrations by others in *large groups,* and (3) *small-group* discussions. In this school: [3]

[2] J. Lloyd Trump, "Places for Learning," *Audiovisual Instruction,* vol. 7, p. 517, October, 1962.
[3] *Ibid.,* pp. 516–517.

The teaching-learning process suggested here stresses the interrelationships of instructional objectives with the structure of teaching-learning groups. (*From James W. Brown, Richard B. Lewis, and Fred F. Harcleroad,* A-V Instruction: Materials and Methods, *2d ed., McGraw-Hill, New York, 1964, p. 22*)

THE TEACHING-LEARNING PROCESS

➡ TOWARD APPROPRIATE CHANGE IN BEHAVIOR ➡

A	B	C
KNOWLEDGE	**ATTITUDES**	**SKILL**
INFORMATION	**APPRECIATION**	**PERFORMANCE**

X	Y	Z
TEACHER ALONE	**INTERACTION**	**STUDENT ALONE**
PLANNING AND COMMUNICATION	**TEACHER AND STUDENT**	**INDIVIDUAL STUDY AND PRACTICE**
	STUDENT AND STUDENT	

In this presentation of the teaching-learning process, above the dotted line are symbolized the *content* and *objectives* of education, and below the dotted line are the *activities* of teachers and learners.

In each relationship between teacher and student, between student and content, different learnings take place at the same time, and the ABC-XYZ arrangement is one of complex and varying relationships:

Both teacher and student have specific roles in each situation for each objective. And, for each situation, there are materials, equipment, and environmental conditions that can most effectively facilitate learning.

Independent study in social science takes place in a social science workroom inside the school and in a variety of locations outside the school. The social science workroom is divided into two rooms, one the size of a conventional classroom, . . . and the other about one-half the size of a conventional classroom.

The larger room contains about ten individual study and writing cubicles. . . . The cubicles are divided by plywood partitions five feet high. The student will find, either in the room or in the cubicle itself, a tote tray to hold the material he is using. In another part of the room he sees at least two tape recorders on a table with earphones so that he can listen to commercially prepared tapes, recordings, or large-group presentations that he has missed or wants to review. In another part of the room he sees a wall screen and projectors on a table nearby with earphones for individual listening. Slide, film, and eight-millimeter sound projectors make a wide variety of presentations available to him.

The room also contains bookshelves on which are located a wide variety of commonly used reading materials in social science. Another part of the room has portable blackboard dividers so that two or three students who are prompted to exchange ideas can easily group themselves for discussion. The room also contains a desk for the instruction assistant who supervises the room and the machine room adjacent to it. . . .

The larger workroom thus provides places for students to think, to write, to listen, to view, to read, and to discuss. A diversity of learning materials are at the student's fingertips. There is no need to travel distances to a library or to go through unnecessary red tape. Students are under the supervision of an instruction assistant who has at least two years of college training in social science, and usually more than that. This is a person who knows when to put the student in touch with the professional teacher or professional librarian.

Adjoining the social science workroom is the social science machine room equipped, among other things, with calculating machines. Good social science instruction includes student surveys and studies in the community with consequent need to tabulate the collected data. The machine room also provides typewriters for writing reports, duplicating machines for preparing them in quantity, and equipment for making maps, charts, and the like. A teletype brings the students the latest information on economics, international affairs, and other local and regional happenings.

Some materials used in independent study and materials rarely used will be stored in the central library. A student doing unusually specialized research will need to go there and to other storehouses of information in the community. The rarely used materials will include not only books and other printed materials, but also recorded and visual materials. . . .

Explanations by others . . . will not take place in conventional classrooms or libraries. Specially designed large-group instruction facilities are required for film showings, telecasts, listening to recordings, transparency projections, work on programed instruction materials, etc. Ways to provide this space in existing buildings or in new buildings are described by this writer in other publications. For example, a wall between two conventional classrooms can be removed and other minor changes made to provide large-group instruction for about 125 students. New buildings will include specially designed spaces for this type of teaching.

Similarly, spaces are needed for *small-group discussion* involving a maximum of 15 students. These spaces can be 250 square feet in size, or approximately one third the size of a conventional classroom. Each school will determine how many days per week and how many minutes per day students will spend in large and small classes and in independent study.

In more and more of today's schools, the planning of new and remodeled plant facilities takes similar requirements into account. Baynham describes such a school (Ridgewood High School in Norridge, Illinois), in which the plan of organization resembles the general recommendations of the Trump plan: [4]

Ridgewood was built with special facilities for three types of learning —*large classrooms* for large, so-called lecture groups; *small classrooms* for small discussion groups; and *individual study areas,* some of which contain individual study booths. . . . The individual study booths . . . are an innovation . . . used to great advantage by the more self-directed students. . . . The school's large classrooms, big enough to hold 125 students, are equipped with rows of auditorium seats with arm rests. Overhead screens, microphones, tape recorders, and curtains to eliminate light are regular equipment. Installations are ready for closed circuit television, but this is a project for the future. Small discussion classrooms are only large enough to seat fifteen students and a teacher around a big discussion table. . . . Ordinarily, students attend large classes first thing in the morning, always reporting to the same room but changing teachers almost daily. For example, 125 students reporting to Room 310 every day at 8.30 a.m. will hear a lecture on English literature on Monday, history on Tuesday, humanities enrichment on Wednesday, English grammar on Thursday, and history again on Friday. Large group lectures mean fairly lock-stepped instruction and are best used for introducing units of work, for explaining fundamental ideas, and for testing. Individual study helps students break out of the lockstep and small group discussion offers the possibility of 100% student participation in learning. . . . In the discussion groups, twelve to fifteen students with an elected chairman develop ideas first encountered in a large class lecture or from individual study. . . . All students, regardless of ability, are provided with opportunities to participate in these seminar groups. In the large group classes, at least two members of a teaching team and sometimes more are always present. In individual study, students may carry out personal study projects or work together in small groups of four to six students.

[4] Dorsey Baynham, "A School of the Future in Operation," *Phi Delta Kappan,* vol. 42, pp. 350–354, May, 1961.

LARGE-GROUP FACILITIES

The recommendation that plans should allow for some instruction in large groups appears to have gained acceptance in all parts of the country. The National Association of Secondary-school Principals suggests that perhaps 40 per cent of a high school student's time might be spent profitably in groups of this size.[5]

Large-group instruction may be carried on, of course, under any one of several plans, including the following suggestions: (1) in a regular auditorium (hopefully one that includes special provisions for working with large groups in face-to-face situations, projection facilities for slides, films, or large transparencies, and student-response systems); (2) in spaces formed by combining two or more ordinary or specially built classrooms or other instructional spaces, using movable or removable walls; (3) by television (open- or closed-circuit); (4) by "wired audio"—as in cases of telephone conference or lecture presentations, channeled listening systems, or special telephone dialing facilities.

Team teaching is often (but not always) used for large-group instruction. Shaplin defines team teaching as: [6]

> A type of instructional organization, involving teaching personnel and the students assigned to them, in which two or more teachers are given responsibility, working together, for all or a significant part of the instruction of the same group of students.

The several examples that follow describe different types of instructional facilities that are intended to aid in solving problems of teaching and learning in large groups. They include (1) a "divisible" auditorium in the Boulder City, Nevada, high school; (2) a teaching auditorium at the University of Texas; (3) a "quad" arrangement in a Michigan elementary school; (4) a flexible multipurpose room in the Ewa Beach, Hawaii, elementary school; (5) an experimental classroom developed at Rensselaer Polytechnic Institute; (6) a centralized instructional-materials facility combined with fold-back walls to provide a flexible-use arrangement in the Lacamas Heights, Camas, Washington, elementary school; (7) large-group instruction by television; and (8) large-group instruction by "wire." The pervading emphasis is flexibility of use and functional adaptation to specialized instructional requirements.

Divisible auditorium

Boulder City's divisible auditorium, developed with the active participation of James D. MacConnell, director of the Western Regional

[5] J. Lloyd Trump, *Images of the Future,* National Association of Secondary-school Principals, Washington, D.C., 1959, p. 8.
[6] Judson T. Shaplin and Henry F. Olds, Jr. (eds.), *Team Teaching,* Harper & Row, New York, 1964, p. 15.

Because Boulder City (Nevada) High School's auditorium may be divided quickly, as the occasion demands, it lends itself to a variety of instructional patterns. Note the arrangements for subdividing the large auditorium into three areas, each sound-insulated from the others. Operable walls are equipped with neoprene pressure gaskets to ensure a tight seal. (A Divisible Auditorium, *Educational Facilities Laboratories, Inc., New York*, 1962, p. 10)

Center of the Educational Facilities Laboratories, Inc., represents a promising model of a facility for redeploying space into the flexible combinations required for certain types of large-group instruction. The drawing on page 41 suggests its principal characteristics: (1) a "nose-cone" shape that focuses on a raised stage at the front, (2) two sound-proof operable walls that permit dividing the auditorium into three isolated rooms, and (3) a complete audio-visual booth installation immediately above the lobby.

In commenting on this installation, the Educational Facilities Laboratories staff emphasizes: [7]

> Because the operable walls add and subtract space quickly and automatically, the auditorium can easily be converted to a flexible combination of large-group instruction spaces. And because the walls block sound as completely as they block sight, these spaces are independent enough of one another so that ordinarily conflicting activities can be carried on in adjoining spaces at the same time. As a result, the school's teaching program can break out of the 30-student boxes in the existing plant. The instructional capacity of the plant itself is increased by the equivalent of at least five classrooms. . . . And the new building, which would stand idle nearly 90 per cent of the time if it were reserved solely for the school-community activities usually conducted in a high school auditorium, is ready for educational use throughout the school day.

The most difficult problem in building the Boulder City auditorium facility was finding a divider that "works." [8] The operable divider partitions finally selected were large folding doors; these were suspended from overhead tracks stretching across openings to the rear alcove areas. These doors, made of rigid panels 3 inches thick, 4 feet wide, and 14 feet 4 inches tall, were joined by continuous hinges such as those used for pianos, top to bottom. When open, the partitions nest in special pockets that are actually outside the building, thus avoiding the usual problems of the bundling of stacked panels and the resulting obstruction of view or passage. All that is required to convert an alcove into a large or very large-group lecture hall is to start a small electric motor that moves the partition along its overhead track. Inflatable rubber gaskets automatically seal sound leakage around all openings.

Various uses to which this divisible auditorium space may be put include:

❯ *Music instruction.* Choral groups, instrumental groups
❯ *General school uses.* Dramatic, public speaking, and assembly programs; class and other large group meetings; large-group testing programs and instruction
❯ *Displays.* Art exhibits, science fairs

[7] *A Divisible Auditorium: Boulder City, Nevada,* Educational Facilities Laboratories, Inc., New York, 1962, p. 5.

[8] *Ibid.,* p. 11.

> *Visual and auditory presentations.* Film showings, demonstrations, re-cording presentations (television in the future)
> *Technical education.* Practice and instruction: Student operation of pro-jectors, amplifiers, stage lighting, and other equipment; trainee instruction in electronic sound control, amplification and recording techniques, equip-ment maintenance, stage management and lighting control
> *Other.* Community uses

University teaching auditorium

A recently built facility at the University of Texas, the Undergraduate Academic Center,[9] includes a teaching auditorium whose function is to permit teaching as many as 300 students as a single group. Original specifications called for a room to be used primarily by professors who wished to meet their regular classes in their regular ways. While it was also expected that some sophisticated large-group teaching and experi-mentation (including use of advanced instructional procedures and re-sources) might be conducted there, the facility was designed to lend itself to traditional lecturing as well.

The resulting building included facilities for the following teaching-learning activities:

> Discursive lectures (voice only)
> Aided lectures (accompanied by correlated visual or audio presentations)
> Demonstrations
> Programmed lectures (multiple projection devices preplanned for maxi-mum impact and most efficient use of time)
> Panel presentations, symposia, or multiple lectures
> Live case studies
> Question-and-answer sessions between students and instructors, using microphones placed around the room
> Student participation in small reaction groups, through use of student-response electrical and other devices
> Presentations of films and slides for large groups
> Observation, by means of a booth facility, of what goes on in large-group auditorium teaching and discussion

This facility is now scheduled principally for regular classes. Addi-tional schedules are made for experiments with multiple instructional media, conferences, small convocations, or special lectures.

Quad arrangement

In Madison Heights, Michigan, a Detroit suburb, the Lessenger Elemen-tary School permits team teaching in what are known as quads, or clusters of four classroom spaces grouped around a central workroom and teaching area.[10] Each pair of classrooms is separated only by a

---

[9] *An Auditorium Teaching Facility,* University of Texas Press, Austin, Tex., 1963. 20 pp.
[10] *Schools for Team Teaching,* Educational Facilities Laboratories, Inc., New York, 1961, pp. 27–28.

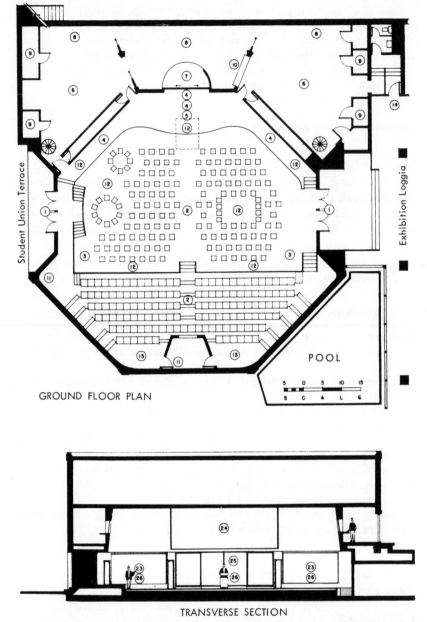

GROUND FLOOR PLAN

TRANSVERSE SECTION

The Undergraduate Academic Center, University of Texas, provides arrangements for effective large-group instruction conducted in any of several ways. Special attention is given here to functional uses of new educational media.

manually operated folding wood partition; when this partition is opened, as many as 120 children may be instructed. The central material-resource, workroom–teaching area is divided into four segments, each equipped for a special subject field; for example, there is a science corner with sinks and demonstration materials and a fine arts corner with easels, paints, and a kiln. The workroom itself is equipped with a raised platform that serves both as a library and a stage. Large- and small-group instruction involving audio-visual materials and devices or television are conducted here. The area is also used by a teacher-technician to prepare teaching materials. Portable walls (held in place by special rubber air-pressure devices and providing as much acoustical privacy as a 3-inch concrete-block wall would give) permit the interconnection of learning areas with workroom areas or the opening up of the interior of the entire learning quad, as desired.

Flexible multipurpose room

The multipurpose room of Ewa Beach Elementary School in Hawaii consists of a circular room surrounded by wedge-shaped units, a stage, and a storage room.[11] The circle is derived from semicircular inside walls that can be moved electrically into an open position, thus exposing a major portion of the large multipurpose room to view of a raised stage. Further flexibility is obtained by folding partition walls that extend from the building's exterior walls toward the center, thus dividing the space for regular classroom use.

Experimental classroom

An experimental classroom designed and tested at Rensselaer Polytechnic Institute for The State University of New York seeks to establish criteria for a large-group facility in which to conduct lectures as well as a variety of other instructional presentations. Criteria for this facility are as follows: [12]

Its chief purpose is to support the utilization of various educational media and devices.

The room is to be multi-discipline in function, suited to use by professors from a number of different subject fields.

The room is intended to have a high utilization rate throughout the school day, thus requiring that materials needed for one class can be readied there while another class is in session.

The room is expected to permit a flexibility of instructional use: for "straight lectures," for highly visualized or sound-supported lectures, for completely automated presentations without the lecturer's presence, for demonstrations, or for other purposes.

While rooms of this type do not readily lend themselves to quick conversion to smaller or larger spaces, flexibility is achieved by con-

[11] Adapted from John Beynon, *Designs for Education: 1963,* Educational Facilities Laboratories, Inc., Western Regional Center, Stanford, Calif., 1963, p. 14.
[12] As reported in Wayne F. Koppes and others, *Design Criteria for Learning Spaces: Seating, Lighting, Acoustics,* Office of Facilities, State University of New York, Albany, N.Y., 1964.

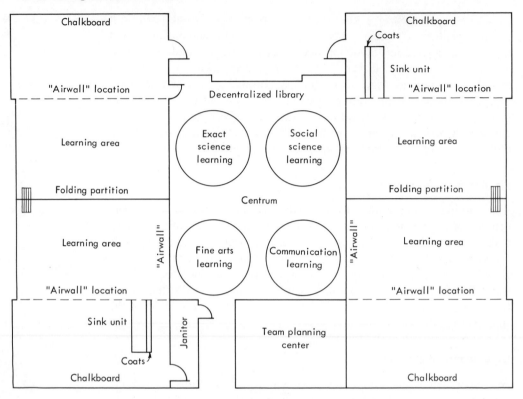

THE LAMPHERE QUAD

The Lessenger Elementary School, Madison Heights (Wisconsin), provides in each four-classroom "quad" facilities for 100–120 students. (*Educational Facilities Laboratories*)

structing a number of such facilities of different sizes and scheduling classes in rooms of appropriate size. Arrangements can also be made to join several such rooms electronically (for television or sound presentations), thus providing means of teaching particularly large groups.

Flexible elementary school

The Lacamas Heights Elementary School in Camas, Washington, was designed to meet the requirements of both present and future instructional programs. A seven-sided circular structure was considered the best means of meeting the following educational requirements:

❯ Use of classrooms for both self-contained and team teaching
❯ Flexibility of space arangement to accommodate and permit the rapid shifting of groups as large as 100
❯ A central area for storage of teaching materials and equipment, as well as a convenient workroom for the preparation of instructional materials

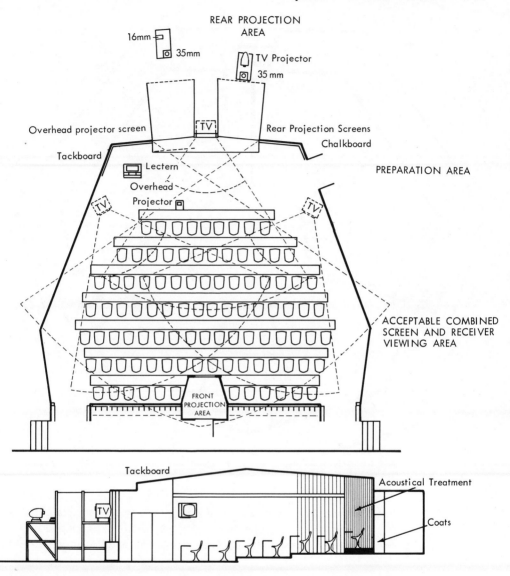

Rensselaer Polytechnic Institute's experimental classroom is intended to establish criteria to guide the design of facilities in which various forms of instruction, many involving uses of new media, may be conducted. (*Rensselaer Polytechnic Institute*)

❯ A private space where teachers can meet and work
❯ Natural areas of separation between the youngest and oldest children attending the school
❯ An adequate amount of covered play space
❯ Ample space for a systematic physical education program
❯ Space for special-service personnel
❯ Space for instrumental music for upper elementary students

47

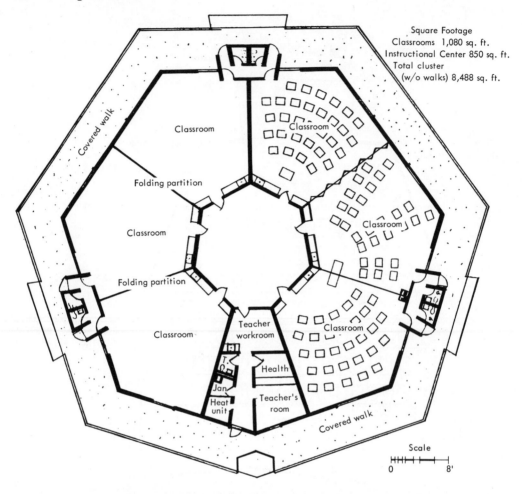

Square Footage
Classrooms 1,080 sq. ft.
Instructional Center 850 sq. ft.
Total cluster
(w/o walks) 8,488 sq. ft.

Covered walk

Classroom

Classroom

Folding partition

Classroom

Classroom

Folding partition

Classroom

Teacher workroom

Classroom

Classroom

T.C.

Jan

Heat unit

Health

Teacher's room

Covered walk

Scale

0   8'

The Lacamas Elementary School (Camas, Washington) features a "cluster" design, each housing six classrooms of 1,080 square feet each and a teacher workroom around a central teacher planning and instructional materials center.

> Space for a central library with an adjoining area for audio-visual media
> A kindergarten area close to the bus loading zone

A "cluster" design eliminated typical long inside hallways and provided usable center space for teacher planning and instructional-materials facilities. Four partitioned walls in each cluster are operable, permitting the combination of as many as three rooms into one for large-group teaching. All classroom storage units (with the exception of the sink and teacher wardrobe units) are equipped with casters to permit easy movement or variation in room arrangements. Several duplicates of the single buildings now form the outlying portions of the school; others may be added as needed to accommodate future enrollments.

The school's kindergarten and multipurpose administrative unit contains offices for the principal, psychologist, speech therapist, health nurse, and librarian. It also contains a central library, which provides audio-visual services and materials; a multipurpose room with showers; and an instrumental-music room. Here again, operable walls are used to permit rearrangement of space.

Facility for television instruction

The educational television programs produced and distributed by the Anaheim school district in California and described in considerable detail in Chapter 10 are part of a highly organized plan for conducting large-group instruction on a system-wide basis. Students in the third and fourth grades receive the programs in their own classrooms; those in the fifth and sixth grades receive them in large, specially equipped classrooms called "audio-visual resource rooms" in groups of approximately seventy-five students. Several uses of television, in addition to presenting programs produced at the central school's offices, include originating programs within a single school, distributing open-circuit (regular broadcast) programs throughout a building, and inviting participation and give and take through intercommunication devices and student-response systems.

In any one of these cases, the students might be placed physically in a single-student, small-classroom, or large-group environment. The numbers to be taught are thus not limited by the usual concept of space.

Facility for instruction by wire

Recent improvements in telephonic services and equipment have led to an increasing number of applications of this medium for instructional purposes. Stephens College, for example, makes effective uses of amplified telephone interviews as a classroom teaching technique.[13] Similar uses have been reported elsewhere, including one involving the interinstitutional cooperation of a number of colleges and universities in various parts of the United States to bring to their campuses the advantages of simultaneous lectures and two-way discussions with outstanding personalities who, for reasons of time or expense, would otherwise be unable to be present in person at even one institution.

With the Stephens College plan, the local telephone company attaches an amplifier to a regular telephone instrument. For the course in American government, arrangements are made in advance to talk with public officials and well-known persons in various parts of the

[13] James A. Burkhardt, "The Use of Amplified Telephone for Interviews and Classroom Teaching," in James W. Brown and James W. Thornton, Jr., (eds.), *New Media in Higher Education,* Association for Higher Education and Department of Audio-Visual Instruction, NEA, 1963, pp. 99–100.

Dr. James A. Burkhardt, Stephens College, experiments with the use of amplified telephone interviews to heighten student interest in his course in American problems. (*Stephens College*)

country. Presentations sometimes involve straight lectures followed by questions; at other times, the method is a give-and-take interview, using questions raised by the students themselves. Burkhardt comments on the program's success: "Students found that ensuing interviews gave issues a ring of reality and a feeling of person-to-person conversation. Insights into personalities, philosophies, and responses of creative minds to current problems were outcomes of these experiences." [14]

Two other uses of wired instruction in large-group teaching should be mentioned. The first is a simple "listening table" arrangement, which could be modified, of course, to include a large number of listening outlets at various stations scattered throughout buildings of an entire school system. The listening table arrangement at Stephens College [15] uses programs originating from tapes or records in the college library as well as from remote sources. Scheduled starting times for various

[14] *Ibid.*, p. 99.
[15] Neal Balanoff, "Listening Table," in *New Media in Higher Education*, pp. 97–98.

programs are posted at tables; it is a standard practice to provide repeated playings. A switching arrangement permits students to select one of several programs that are available at any one time.

A second and more complicated, but potentially valuable, wired-instruction device that also uses telephonic techniques has been developed by F. Rand Morton of the University of Michigan.[16] This unit, which is used in foreign-language instruction, has access to 2,500 or more "audio-lingual frames" (i.e., discrete three-minute work units); these can be dialed at random from student positions that have line access to the device according to a predetermined dial code arrangement. There seem to be possibilities, of course, of extending this mode of selection to the limits of the telephone line itself, thus permitting large numbers of students anywhere on campus or perhaps in even a large school district to dial for "help" or for practice (as in foreign-language study) at the exact time of need.

SMALL-GROUP FACILITIES

The physical facilities for the modern school must also provide opportunities for various forms of interaction and face-to-face activities in small groups (usually defined as containing from five to fifteen students). Bush and Allen say that "the only required physical facilities for small-group instruction are small rooms with flexible tables and movable chairs." [17] The usual size recommended for such rooms is 250 square feet.

Small-group discussion areas can be provided in any one of several ways: (1) as spaces in classrooms that are divided by standing screens or perhaps by movable combination bookshelves and chalkboards or tack boards, (2) as spaces directly off a main classroom, (3) as spaces in the library or instructional-materials center, or (4) as spaces spread throughout a school plant wherever they are available.

Recommendations of Ellsworth and Wagener for the design and equipment of small-group facilities in the library appear to apply equally to similar areas located elsewhere in the school plant: [18]

> Students need to do part of their work in small groups. . . . They like to help one another, discuss ideas found in their reading, and work on group projects. . . . Thus, sprinkled around through the carrels there should be several small rooms . . . [each] with a table and a few chairs. These rooms should have at least one glass wall or window,

[16] F. Rand Morton, "Applications of the Principles of Telephony in the Instrumentation of Language Laboratories," in *New Media in Higher Education,* pp. 90–93.

[17] Robert N. Bush and Dwight W. Allen, *A New Design for High School Education,* McGraw-Hill, New York, 1964, p. 36.

[18] Ralph E. Ellsworth and Hobart D. Wagener, *The School Library,* Educational Facilities Laboratories, Inc., New York, 1963, pp. 70–72.

A VARIETY OF POSSIBLE SHAPES
AND ARRANGEMENTS
FOR SMALL GROUP ROOMS

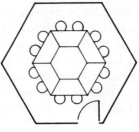

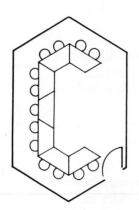
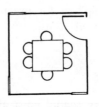
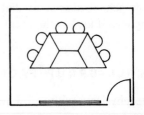
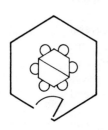
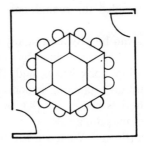
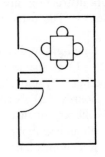
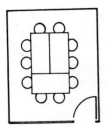
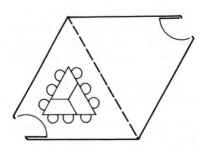
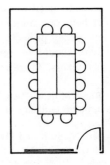

or a window in the door, and be well ventilated. Since they may also serve for use of audio-visual equipment, they should be comparatively sound-proof. Now that earphones are of such high quality, it is no longer necessary to provide individual soundproofed listening booths even for stereo listening. Headphone listening to phonograph records and tapes can be done in a variety of ways. . . . Space for audio-visual displays should be provided.

A variety of possible shapes and arrangements for such small-group rooms is also suggested by Ellsworth and Wagener [19] as shown in the drawings. Note especially the different table shapes (circular, rectangular, and trapezoidal) and the resulting configurations of group arrangements.

LABORATORIES

Various types of laboratories (some of which will be discussed later in connection with language laboratories, listening laboratories, and other self-instruction facilities) must also be mentioned in this general consideration of physical facilities in relation to school utilization of new media.

In their hypothetical 1,200-student secondary school referred to earlier,[20] Trump and Baynham recommend three laboratories for health, physical education, and recreation; three for science; two for mathematics; and one each for English arts, social studies, foreign language, practical arts (homemaking, industrial arts, agriculture, business), and fine arts. Instructional-materials production centers are also recommended by Bush and Allen,[21] as are laboratories for scientific research, the development of reading skills, music, or office-machine practice, and use of various types of machine tools. They define a laboratory as including "those physical facilities provided where specific equipment and tools are needed to enable students to work independently and in small groups to practice skills, to experiment, and to apply ideas suggested in large-group instruction."

INDEPENDENT STUDY FACILITIES

Trump and Baynham indicate that several different kinds of space may be used for independent study.[22] In a typical secondary school enrolling

[19] *Ibid.,* p. 71.
[20] J. Lloyd Trump and Dorsey Baynham, *Focus on Change: Guide to Better Schools,* Rand McNally, Chicago, 1961, p. 4.
[21] Bush and Allen, *op. cit.,* pp. 37, 104.
[22] Trump and Baynham, *op. cit.,* p. 39.

Circular, rectangular, and trapezoidal table shapes, combined with a variety of room dimensions, permit a variety of seating configurations for small-group instruction. (*Educational Facilities Laboratories*)

A "self-paced study station" unit, designed by Sol Cornberg Associates, Inc., provides electronic elements (TV screen, audio speakers, microphone, dialing unit, and others) as parts of a random-access information selection/reception facility. (*Sol Cornberg Associates, Inc.*)

1,200 students, for example, such spaces might include (1) the library reading room, furnished with enough tables and chairs to seat sixty students; (2) a viewing room and a listening room adjacent to the library, each seating up to forty persons; (3) ten conference rooms nearby, each holding up to five persons; (4) five soundproof booths for study with electronic devices, and (5) a 1,200-square-foot room in which to house various teaching machines. Additionally, they recommend at least 300 independent study cubicles or carrels, each occupying approximately 24 square feet, near the library.

Sol Cornberg, one of the country's foremost advocates of electronic versatility in the design of individual carrels refers to his as a "self-paced study station." Its heart is a random-access information selection and reception system capable of employing (1) a telephone dial (various number combinations would produce various kinds of available audio-visual data—TV films, recordings, slides, diagrams); (2) prepunched IBM cards issued to students for a day, week, semester, or year as called for by the instructional program; or (3) other directive possibilities for data retrieval, including mark-sense devices, notched plates, alphanumeric buttons, or other switching systems.

The essential aspect of Cornberg's carrel operation is its ability to retrieve, at the user's command, various kinds of information stored at one or more of several central sources—a county or district instructional-materials center or a state library many miles distant. A cable that is plugged into a wall or floor outlet connects the carrel to central information storage units from which the following information services may be received: (1) live or prerecorded television programs—off the air or originated at some location tied to a closed-circuit system; (2) broadcast radio of all types—shortwave, AM, FM; (3) various audio programs originating within the closed-circuit wire system—including tapes of language lessons, lectures, dramatizations and the like; (4) various visual or audio-visual signals that also originate in the system— slides, motion pictures, filmstrips, microscopic enlargements, enlargements of book pages, charts, microfilms and microcards, and many others.

The actual operation of Cornberg's carrel is described "for the future," as it might be used by a student taking a Russian-language

Recommended reflectable values plotted in this sketch emphasize the varying levels to be encountered in typical classrooms. (*U.S. Office of Education*)

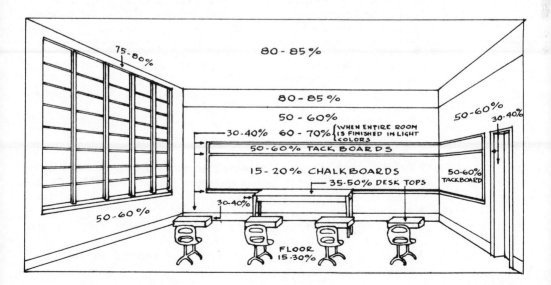

course, who has been assigned by his instructor to prepare a report on Russian idioms: [23]

> First, he may want to review some points made by the instructor at a previous large-group lecture. He dials a number on a dial similar to that of an office telephone. On the small television screen in his carrel will appear a videotape of the last lecture. When the student has refreshed his memory, he will start working on the project assigned in his tutorial session.
>
> He dials another number and on the screen appears a travel film with a narration in idiomatic Russian. After he has absorbed the film, he might dial a third number; through the loudspeaker he will hear a language practice tape. As the announcer speaks the word, the student repeats it into the microphone on his desk. (These responses might also be recorded so that he can replay them to check his own pronunciation.)
>
> Then, for further preparation, the student walks to the library adjacent to his carrel and withdraws a book of contemporary Russian-language short stories.
>
> When he has finished drawing upon these different sources—the audio-visual materials stored in a central electronic library and the books stored in the building library—he writes his report, goes to his seminar, and is prepared to discuss creatively the material he has absorbed in his carrel. The carrel, in short, is not only part of the total program, it is the *integrating factor* of the program.

In recognizing recent increases in independent study requirements in schools all over the country and the resulting need to design suitable facilities and equipment for this activity, MacConnell and his associates recommend carrels with the following somewhat simpler specifications: [24]

❯ A working surface minimally 2 feet deep and encompassing at least 6 square feet of working surface
❯ "Blinders" slightly above the eye level (approximately 20 inches) of the seated student
❯ Extension of the side barriers by 1 foot toward the student (if a 2- by 2-foot rectilinear desk); otherwise to proper dimensions
❯ 10-inch deep bookshelves
❯ Sufficient space to permit two people to sit at one time at a carrel desk
❯ An individual light (controlled by student) and several 110-volt convenience outlets for portable machines
❯ A special jack for closed-circuit TV (if available)
❯ Other facilities, as developed, for multiple channel audio system, or telephone dial system with microphone
❯ Plug-in connections between the carrel itself and the building's intercommunication wiring system

[23] "Space for Individual Learning: The Biography of a Great Idea," by the Editors of *Educational Executives' Overview,* March, 1963.
[24] *Study Carrels: Designs for Independent Study Space,* Educational Facilities Laboratories, Inc., Western Regional Center, Stanford, Calif., 1963. 16 pp.

SPACES FOR TEACHERS

Altogether too few statements on modern educational-facilities planning recognize the special needs of teachers in day-to-day school activities. One recent publication [25] suggests that nearly a third of the typical teacher's time is used for clerical or subprofessional tasks, another third in work that might be done as well with various automated devices, and only a third in the professional work for which he was trained—in planning his teaching and working directly with students.

Important activities in this latter third of a teacher's work are (1) keeping up with developments in his subject-matter area, (2) planning and preparing his daily lessons, (3) developing imaginative instructional materials, and (4) improving the evaluation of students' work. Space in which to perform these activities is therefore a critical factor in today's schools. The report stresses especially the need for space for instructional conferences *between teachers* and *between teachers and administrators*—conferences for the pooling of ideas that focus on educational goals and measurement of educational achievement. In these conference spaces, teachers need convenient access to all kinds of instructional resources (materials, equipment, supplies, devices, professional guides, source books, and the like) as well as assistance from others in the building whose responsibility it is to facilitate instruction. Teaching now appears to be changing from the more or less traditional pattern of one teacher in one room for each period of the day to a staff or team effort in which teachers work *together,* aided by staff specialists, assistants, aides, and consultants.

Required space for teachers is usually provided at several locations throughout the school plant—in the instructional-materials center or library (see Chapter 12), in office suites for teachers of the same subjects, in or near the teachers' lounge facilities, off classrooms, and elsewhere. As much privacy as possible is sought without sacrificing the adavntages of proximity for those who must work together in achieving common goals. At the Flowing Wells Elementary School Number 3 in Tucson, Arizona, for example, the cluster plan used features a central work space for teachers to which each classroom has access. DeBernardis and others recommend placing a preparation and work area in one segment and an office area in another between two or more classrooms. They suggest: [26]

> The preparation and work area should be designed for multi-purpose uses, including materials preparation, conferences, individual or small group study, and classroom library research. It should, if possible, be isolated from the regular classroom and sound-proofed so as not to disturb others in adjacent areas.

[25] Adapted from Raymond C. Schneider, *Space for Teachers,* Educational Facilities Laboratories, Inc., Western Regional Center, Stanford, Calif., no date.
[26] Amo DeBernardis and others, *Planning Schools for New Media,* Division of Education, Portland State College, Portland, Ore., 1961, p. 31.

It should contain a sink and hot and cold running water and two or more electrical convenience outlets.

This area should also be equipped with storage facilities, paper cutters, scissors, art supplies, and necessary audio-visual devices.

It should be convenient to supervise (through windows into adjoining classrooms).

GENERAL REQUIREMENTS FOR PHYSICAL FACILITIES

In the previous discussions, the fact that requirements for physical facilities in education are changing rapidly was emphasized. Now it is quite clear that if all kinds of learning could be achieved simply through having groups of uniform and predetermined size sit quietly at desks listening to lectures, with little or no need for student-teacher inter-communication, the only physical requirements would be a sufficiently large space in which students could hear, take notes, and perhaps see the lecturer's facial expressions. But, as we have seen, this is far from the case in today's educational practice. More and more, schools insist upon a physical environment in which to conduct the variety of teaching-learning activities envisaged and discussed here and in other parts of this book. Such activities involve myriad uses of materials and equipment for which several basic environmental conditions must prevail. Regardless of the type or size of the teaching-learning facility, consideration must be given to:

❯ Controlling and varying light, both artificial and natural, in the teaching-learning area
❯ Providing electrical power in sufficient amperage and voltage with convenience and safety
❯ Controlling sound to eliminate reverberation and unwanted sound transmission between teaching-learning areas, and to "liven" and "deaden" (damp) room areas as required
❯ Providing screens on which to reflect projected still and motion-picture images
❯ Ventilating and heating to provide clean air at controlled temperatures and circulation sufficient to maintain a healthful, invigorating atmosphere for teaching and learning
❯ Seating to provide comfort, convenience, and physical well-being in all the various instructional modes and locations
❯ Displaying instructional materials and products throughout the period of instruction
❯ Storing physical equipment, student products, supplies, and other items needed by students and teachers

LIGHTING

Light control for teaching and learning requires facilities for regulating both natural and artificial light without restricting or adversely affecting other essential environmental conditions. In each case, factors must be adjusted to foster student efficiency in essential learning tasks (reading, viewing, writing, painting, discussion, and the like).

The U.S. Office of Education identifies three terms and their meanings that should be known to those involved with this problem: [27]

❯ *Light quantity or amount of illumination.* Amount of illumination is measured in terms of lumens per square foot or, as they are sometimes called, foot-candles. One foot-candle is the equivalent of 1 lumen per square foot. Unless otherwise required, light values in a room are measured normal to a horizontal plane, 30 inches above the floor.

❯ *Brightness.* Brightness is measured in terms of the foot-lambert. This is closely related to the lumen or foot-candle. A surface has a brightness of 1 foot-lambert if there is 1 lumen per square foot coming from it. Sometimes brightness is also measured in terms of candles per square inch. One candle per square inch is the equivalent of 452 foot-lamberts. The brightness of a nonluminous surface is the result of reflected light.

❯ *Reflector factor or reflectance.* The reflector factor or reflectance is expressed as the percentage of incident light that is reflected by the surface.

It is quite possible for even an inexpert person to determine approximate lighting conditions in classrooms or other teaching-learning spaces by using a simple light meter borrowed from the local power company. Meters of this type employ photoelectric cells to convert light intensity to an electrical impulse; in turn, this impulse actuates a needle moving above a dial calibrated in foot-candles:

❯ *To make brightness readings on nonluminous surfaces,* hold the meter eye directly against the surface to be measured, then slowly draw it back 2 to 6 inches until a constant meter reading is obtained. The surface area to be measured should be at least 12 inches square; its lighting should be diffuse, not focused. To convert the foot-lambert reading to brightness in foot-candles, multiply by a factor of 1.25.

❯ *To estimate the reflectance of a surface,* make (at the same point) two measurements: (1) direct light—with meter eye pointed toward the light source, and (2) reflected light—with meter handled as recommended for brightness reading as above. Divide the latter reading by the first to obtain a reflectance ratio. Thus, a direct reading of 12 foot-candles and a brightness reading of 4, and with 4 divided by 12, would produce a reflectance ratio of .33, or 33 per cent.

Recommended light quantity levels for school lighting, developed by the American Society of Illuminating Engineers and the American

---

[27] *Environmental Engineering for the School: A Manual of Recommended Practice,* U.S. Office of Education, 1961, p. 10.

Institute of Architects and approved by the American Standards Association, are as follows:

Area	Minimum light level in foot-candles
Classrooms—on desks and chalkboards, in study halls, laboratories, offices, libraries, art rooms, and shops	30
Drafting, typing, and sewing rooms	50
Reception rooms, gymnasiums, and swimming areas	20
Auditoriums (not for study), cafeterias, locker areas, washrooms, and corridors containing lockers	10
Corridors	5
Stairways	10

The varying illumination levels encountered in today's schools range between the $\frac{1}{10}$ foot-candle on the screen (the approximate level of light brightness under which it is difficult, but not impossible, to read a newspaper) for projection, the desirable controlled quantity levels mentioned for other activities, and the sometimes excessive levels of uncontrolled intrusions of daylight into the classroom. Ways of achieving proper control under a variety of conditions are discussed in the next section.

Controlling Natural Light

Regulation of natural light entering the classroom is especially important for good projection. Distractions of daylight entering narrow slits or holes and focusing as bright spots in the room are well known. "Washing out" of screen images under such circumstances is usually a problem. Several alternative means of controlling natural light are available:

➤ *Drapes.* Track-mounted transverse drapes completely covering window areas and made of opaque, fire-resistant materials are recommended. Two sets of drapes are sometimes used over the same set of windows—one translucent to diffuse without shutting out light, covered by the other opaque set. This arrangement only partially overcomes the objectionable characteristic of a single set of opaque drapes with which it is difficult to admit partial stages of light with satisfactory distribution or absence of glare. Valances or baffles should be used to eliminate light cracks at the edges. A serious drawback of drapes is their interference with ventilation in classrooms not equipped with air-conditioning facilities.

➤ *Full-closure venetian blinds.* When combined with top light seals and border strips, blinds of this type provide satisfactory natural-light control without restricting window ventilation. Their original installation cost is somewhat higher than the cost for drapes; further, they tend to collect dust and to require regular maintenance to ensure trouble-free operation. But their capability of providing varying degrees of natural lighting without direct glare is a distinct advantage.

❯ *Roller blinds.* Probably the least satisfactory method of controlling natural light is to use cloth roller blinds or shades (often black on one or both sides). Required are: (1) channels and border strips to block out stray light, and (2) a trouble-free roll-up system capable of various adjustments in height. Although initial installation cost of roller blinds is low, they are subject to certain maintenance problems which require time and expense. As with drapes, proper window ventilation is difficult to achieve with roller blinds.

❯ *Underground or windowless classrooms.*[28] Recent experiments with underground classrooms (combining protection from fallout of atomic blast with "perfect" light control) and with total elimination of windows in aboveground classrooms have produced interesting results. Roswell's underground classroom in New Mexico was liked by students and teachers because of (1) elimination of outside noise and sight distractions; (2) freedom from glare and need to adjust window curtains or blinds to outside lighting conditions; (3) consistent, efficient air-conditioning; (4) possible use of every room as an audio-visual room; and (5) extra display or storage space on wall areas usually occupied by windows.

The following additional specifications pertaining to classroom construction relate to the control of natural light:

❯ Windows should be placed only on one wall.
❯ Heating and ventilating units should not interfere with the free opening and closing of drapes, blinds, or other darkening equipment.
❯ Skylights or clerestory and construction (as over doors) should not be used.
❯ Windows should open only toward the outside (not into the classroom) to avoid entangling blinds or drapes.

The Michigan Audio-Visual Association recommends vision strip windows but no skylights: [29]

> Such vision strip windows make light controls less expensive because the actual window surface area is considerably reduced. The installation of skylights should be avoided at all times because they provide a source of light that is costly to control and are unnecessary with modern lighting. Many schools have actually boarded up permanently such

[28] For more complete descriptions of the special problems and advantages of windowless or underground classrooms, see Philip H. Dillard, "No Windows, Please . . . and Put it Underground?" and "Current Study Probes Effects of Windowless Teaching," *Audiovisual Instruction,* vol. 7, pp. 534–538; 539, October, 1962.
[29] "Planning for the Requirements of the Classroom: Minimum Standards for Michigan," *Michigan Education Journal,* vol. 41, p. 23, Dec. 1, 1963.

skylights after the architect completed the building. Lighting engineers state that skylights make it difficult for them to provide uniform lighting even with artificial light.

Controlling artificial light

The many special uses of instructional projection equipment require control of artificial light within the instructional area to permit varying illumination at will from the minimum $\frac{1}{10}$ foot-candle falling on the screen to that sufficent to conduct normal activities without natural light from the outside. Note taking during projection, for example, requires a brightness of at least 1 foot-candle; normal classroom activities (including reading) require at least 30 foot-candles.

Several means may be employed to obtain variable levels of brightness in classrooms:

❯ *Dimmer switches.* A light switch (preferably of the dimmer type) should be located in the rear of the room in a position convenient to the projector position.

❯ *Parallel light circuits.* Two or more separate light circuits permit choice of placement and level of lighting within the instructional area. With such circuits, one may illuminate the front of a classroom with a bank of spotlights, while leaving all other areas dark. Classrooms or demonstration rooms may also be equipped with several banks of special focused lights inset in the ceiling; directed downward, these provide a note-taking beam that does not wash light into screen images. Or a single light behind a screen may be used to provide indirect around-the-screen light, while leaving its surface suitably dark for a high-contrast or true-color image.

WIRING

The many electronic teaching devices used in today's schools and the possibilities of other devices as yet uninvented highlight the need for the special consideration of wiring specifications for existing and future buildings. DeBernardis and others stress that: [30]

❯ The entire wiring system should be adaptable to future needs, capable of alteration without extensive or expensive changes.

❯ Amperage and voltage requirements should be determined by an electrical engineer, based on stated plans for the anticipated use of electrical equipment and circuiting needs in the building. It is much easier to commit the error of providing too little rather than too much capacity. Once circuits are in, it is usually quite expensive to add more.

❯ Receptacle circuits should be no less than 20 amperes at 110 volts AC,

---

[30] DeBernardis and others, *op. cit.,* p. 29. See also "Indiana Regulations Affecting the AV Program," *Audiovisual Instruction,* vol. 7, p. 567, October, 1962.

and more for rooms in which activities will require special load requirements (photographic laboratories, shops, home economics facilities, machine program carrel units, and the like).

❯ Enough circuits should be supplied to permit simultaneous operation of equipment in any or all classrooms.

❯ Three double outlets should be provided on each classroom wall, about 8 feet apart, not more than 36 inches and not less than 18 inches from the floor. If installed in the floor, they should be recessed and properly protected.

❯ Additional outlets should be provided *above* work surfaces on counters or tables.

❯ All outlets should be grounded.

❯ Electrical power conduits should be oversize to permit later alterations and additions. Raceways should be conveniently accessible.

❯ Communication conduits containing lines (or space for them) for intercom units and coaxial cables for TV should also be installed between classrooms and central control facilities in the instructional-materials center and the administrative office area.

❯ Front-to-back communication control conduits should be installed in each classroom and auditorium or large-group facility in which projection or audio equipment will be used.

SOUND (ACOUSTICS)

The increased classroom use of audio materials and devices requires means of controlling sound—of reducing disturbing reverberation or echo or of regulating sound transmission through walls, down corridors, in and out of opened windows, and through heating or ventilating ducts. Several specific planning suggestions for controlling sound are as follows:

❯ Before developing plans or letting bids for new construction, recommend architectural and acoustical engineering consultation with regard to wall and ceiling treatments, baffling, floor covering, partition and joist arrangements, and other crucial details.

❯ Consider installing drapes and/or rugs in either new or old construction to reduce reverberation or echo. Acoustical panels may also be installed for this purpose, but it is usually less expensive in the long run to consult qualified acoustical engineers about such improvements than to resort to trial-and-error methods to correct mistakes.

❯ Classroom sounds transmit readily through open-pipe heating systems. Hot-water or electrical systems largely eliminate this problem.

❯ The *shape* of the room affects its sound and reverberation characteristics. Nonparallel walls produce a better sound environment than the parallel walls of square or rectangular rooms.

❯ Improve a room's sound characteristics by *hard-surfacing* center ceiling portions (with smooth, hard plaster) and treating outer ceiling segments with acoustic tile.

63

The U.S. Office of Education recommends the following as "acceptable noise levels":

Type of room	Acceptable noise levels in decibels
Classrooms	35–40
Cafeterias	50–55
School sites (outdoor noises)	Less than 70
Health rooms	Less than 45
Hearing test rooms	Less than 40
Music rooms	Less than 40

Source: Environmental Engineering for the School: A Manual of Recommended Practice, p. 5.

A general-purpose sound-level meter is rather simple to use to survey sound conditions in various parts of a school plant. Readings made and plotted for various parts of a room provide clues for analyzing noise problems. A band analyzer will indicate frequency ranges of the various sounds and suggest required types of shielding.

SCREENS

Permanently installed wall-type roller, hanging screens (complete with metal dust covers) are essential furnishings for all teaching areas. Several suggestions with respect to their selection and installation are:

❯ The proper size for the room screen should be dictated by room size and shape. Consult screen tables for details concerning screen dimensions for various room sizes or configurations.
❯ Rectangular rooms in which viewing will be done "the long way" are better adapted to the installation of screens having beaded glass surfaces. Squarish rooms in which viewers will be seated far out to the sides of the viewing area should use matte-surfaced screens.
❯ Lenticular screens (with silver or white surfaces) provide, under most circumstances, a fairly uniform 180-degree viewing surface. Their chief drawback is their expense.
❯ Generally speaking, viewers in the rectangular area equipped with a beaded screen should be seated within a line of vision not exceeding 25 degrees (or 30 degrees for a matte-screen surface) to each side of center and no closer than two screen widths (calculated as the width of the screen image itself, not necessarily the white surface of the screen) and no farther away than six screen widths.
❯ Under normal circumstances, hang the screen so that its lower edge is at the viewers' eye level (when seated). In a flat-floored room, this arrangement should provide unobstructed vision for all viewers.

❯ A tilt arrangement to avoid "keystoning" is recommended for screens used with overhead projections from the front of the room. In such cases, the line of sight from the projection lens to the center of the screen should be a right angle (90 degrees).

❯ Screens may be hung at any point where best results are obtained. It may be preferable to suspend the screen in a corner so as not to restrict normal front-of-the-room activities and to provide a better angle of vision.

Portable free-standing screens with tripods may also be used advantageously. They are especially useful for arranging small-group showings (of slides or filmstrips, for example) without interrupting regular activities carried on in other parts of the room.

Satisfactory projections for individuals or very small groups may also be arranged through use of self-standing (easel- or shadow-box types), reflecting or translucent (milky plastic or glass) screens. Sizes as small as 12 by 16 inches will be found useful under certain circumstances. Barron cautions potential users of large rear-projection screens, however, saying: [31]

> Recent claims for rear screen projection stimulate a word of caution to those who consider this device a panacea for audiovisual education. Our careful evaluation of many commercially produced rear projection systems introduced over the past ten years in the Santa Barbara schools indicates that they are no substitute for classroom light control. Rear projection is useful in some applications, but any school board or administrator should consider the total influence on the educational environment before investing in such equipment as an "economy" measure.

VENTILATION AND HEATING

Various and frequent uses of educational media that require the control of light in the teaching area also require adequate and temperature-controlled supplies of clean, properly circulated air. Because of the extreme range of outside temperatures and window space, size of student group, learning activities, and types and amounts of lighting in classrooms in the same building, it is usually impractical to expect adequate servicing of these requirements—short of providing individualized air supplies and adjustments for each room. It is impractical to expect teachers or students to establish their own control procedures by opening or closing windows or heat valves as temperatures rise and fall or as replenishment of air is needed.

The following suggestions offer guidelines for providing for adequate classroom heating and ventilating:

[31] J. Roy Barron, "Rear Screen—Projection Panacea?" *Audiovisual Instruction,* vol. 7, p. 568, October, 1962.

❯ The recommended uniform temperature for study areas is 68 to 70 degrees Fahrenheit or somewhat less (down to 65 degrees) for learning tasks involving considerable physical activity. It is well to remember that each student may emit as much as 500 to 800 Btu's per hour, which alone could cause a considerable rise in room temperature.

❯ The air system should provide individual classroom facilities, automatically controlled, for both heating and cooling.

❯ Special attention should be given in specifications to the noise level of heating-cooling units in operation. Fans and compressors should be sound-proofed.

❯ Air replenishment should be accomplished without opening windows and should provide from six to ten complete changes each hour.

❯ Temperature variations should be minimal throughout the day. A fairly uniform temperature contributes a great deal to bodily comfort and mental efficiency.

SEATING AND TABLES

Seating and table or desk requirements in today's schools reflect the varied character of available learning spaces and the special need to rearrange sizes and positions of student groups in carrying out different kinds of learning activities. There will be occasions, for example, when a film is shown and afterwards the class may be divided into several small discussion groups, or some may search for further information in books in one part of the room while others listen to recorded materials at a special listening table.

DeBernardis and others [32] emphasize four principles in selecting seating facilities:

❯ They should be movable and designed for flexible grouping arrangements.
❯ They should be comfortable and should furnish good posture support.
❯ They should be equipped for note taking where appropriate.
❯ They should be quiet.

Types of movable seating may include (1) regular chairs (they may be folding or stack types); (2) regular armchairs (these provide arm rests but no writing area); (3) tablet armchairs; (4) chairs with attached study tops or book-storage units; or (5) chairs with separate desks.

Movable tables are also available for school use in various shapes; of these the trapezoidal is perhaps the most popular. Rectangular and circular or half-circular tables are also common. Sketches on page 52 suggest many different ways in which these shapes (or combinations of them) may be arranged to provide specialized teaching environments.

[32] DeBernardis and others, *op. cit.,* p. 32.

CHALKBOARDS

Classroom chalkboard requirements vary in accordance with grade level, subject, and teaching activities. While there has been at least one recommendation to do away with the chalkboard and replace it with the overhead projector, an "electronic chalkboard" as it were, it seems clear that some wall writing space will be needed in most, if not all, teaching areas, but that the amount will be determined by the nature of its intended use. In installing chalkboards, the following suggestions apply:

❯ Choose light-colored (not black) chalkboards. Green is recommended.
❯ Choose steel-backed chalkboards for one or more panels to permit use with magnets to hold posters, charts, pictures, and other display items.
❯ Place eraser and chalk tray at the eye level of seated pupils.
❯ Arrange chalkboards to avoid glare from windows and artificial light sources.

DISPLAY

Classroom requirements for display vary according to grade level, subject emphasis, and types of teaching-learning activities. The following general suggestions apply:

❯ Install light-colored tack board or bulletin board (preferably cork-faced to facilitate easy insertion of pins, thumbtacks, or staples).
❯ Provide maximum flexibility in arranging locations of display facilities to allow for future changes in requirements. Reversible boards (tack boards on one side, chalkboards on the other) are recommended. Consider installation of counterbalanced boards to save space.
❯ Install map rails (with cork inserts) above chalkboards. Install track in ceiling across front of classroom to permit suspension of globes or other instructional aids.
❯ Place bottoms of tack boards or bulletin boards at eye level of students when seated.
❯ Provide adjustable shelves on which to display two- and three-dimensional objects. Some of these may be hinged to permit their being raised into position only when needed. Glass-covered display units with locks are also useful.
❯ Consider using some "swinging-leaf" display boards that are hinged at one end to facilitate display of more material than would normally fit available wall space.

STORAGE

The modern classroom should be planned to include considerable storage space that is conveniently and flexibly arranged to meet changing

67

requirements for educational media and equipment. Specific suggestions include the following:

❯ Locate storage facilities in areas of the classroom in which materials, equipment, or supplies are needed.

❯ Determine whether some materials and equipment will require locked storage while others will not.

❯ Place frequently used materials behind folding or sliding doors or single-opening doors or in sliding drawers to avoid an appearance of untidiness. Use open shelves for items presenting a neat appearance and not requiring such protection.

❯ Use adjustable shelving or multiple add-on stacking units to provide flexibility for future requirements.

❯ Consider fire risks in planning storage for volatile or glass-contained liquids.

❯ Plan "walk-in" or "wheel-in" space for storing carts or wheeled projection stands as necessary, thus avoiding the necessity of lifting heavy equipment on and off shelves.

❯ Use wheeled storage units and demonstration tables to provide flexibility in arranging classroom space. Push such units into place to divide rooms into "walled" work or discussion areas.

SUMMARY

The primary aim in designing and constructing schools and colleges has been to provide a pleasant, healthful, and convenient physical environment in which to arrange student groupings and use a variety of instructional resources and tools in order to contribute to the achievement of educational goals. Several trends may be observed:

❯ Construction of facilities to provide meeting and activity spaces for large. medium, and small groups, as well as for independent study

❯ Stress on the development of plant plans having maximum flexibility of arrangement (the combination of one classroom with another, a cafeteria that doubles as an auditorium, a "special" room that is later useful as a "regular" room, for example)

❯ Devotion of less space to specialized auditoriums or study halls

❯ Planning ahead in construction designs so that technological developments of the future may be incorporated

❯ Better control of environmental factors (light, heat, cooling, acoustics) to permit uses of technological devices and related materials in instruction

❯ Design and equipment of instructional areas to make them true "learning laboratories"—places in which learning activities are carried out

❯ Increased attention to the aesthetic appeal of school buildings and grounds through architectural control

One prediction about the school of tomorrow reflects the nature of these trends and the technical suggestions of this chapter: [33]

[33] Paul W. F. Witt, Teachers College, Columbia University, in an address before the International Conference and Exhibition, November, 1963, Paris, France.

The school of tomorrow will be one that serves the educational needs of all people. . . . [It] will provide an appropriate environment for learning. School buildings and physical facilities will facilitate the development of functional curricula and the use of all types of instructional materials and equipment. . . . [The] school of tomorrow will have many resources for teaching and learning. Films, recordings, pictures, programed materials, textbooks, and materials and devices about which we have not heard will be available as needed. Finally, the school of tomorrow will have an adequate staff of well-prepared teachers. It will have classroom teachers and studio teachers. It will have teachers who are specialists in presenting materials to large groups and teachers who are specialists in working with small groups and individual students. Supporting all these teachers there will be curriculum experts and a corps of programers, graphic artists, film, radio, and television producers, consultants on electronic equipment and specialists in the use of media as well as other personnel, some of whom are still unknown to us.

The design, construction, manipulation, and improvement of the physical learning environment clearly require the expert contributions of educational media personnel who are familiar with the educational purposes for which such facilities will be used and with the standards to which they should adhere. The importance of insightful interrelationships of the media staff member with the teacher, the school administrator, the curriculum expert, and various architectural, acoustical, electronic, and other specialists cannot be overemphasized.

FOR FURTHER INFORMATION

Acoustical Environment of School Buildings, Educational Facilities Laboratories, Inc., New York, 1963.

A Divisible Auditorium: Boulder City, Nevada, Educational Facilities Laboratories, Inc., New York, 1962. 24 pp.

Audio-Visual Suggestions for School Building Planners: An Administrator's Check List, Department of Public Instruction, Commonwealth of Pennsylvania, Harrisburg, Pa., 1962. 25 pp.

Baynham, Dorsey: "A School of the Future in Operation," *Phi Delta Kappan,* vol. 42, pp. 350–354, May, 1961.

Cornell, Francis G.: "Plant and Equipment," in Chester W. Harris (ed.), *Encyclopedia of Educational Research,* Macmillan, New York, 1960, pp. 1008–1031.

Cost of a Schoolhouse, Educational Facilities Laboratories, Inc., New York, 1960.

DeBernardis, Amo, and others: *Planning Schools for New Media,* Division of Education, Portland State College, Portland, Ore., 1961. 72 pp.

Design for ETV: Planning for Schools with Television, Educational Facilities Laboratories, Inc., New York, 1960.

Ellsworth, Ralph E., and Hobart D. Wagener: *The School Library,* Educational Facilities Laboratories, Inc., New York, 1963.

Environmental Engineering for the School: A Manual of Recommended Practice, U.S. Office of Education, 1961. 74 pp.

Hauf, Harold D.: *New Spaces for Learning: Designing College Facilities to Utilize Instructional Aids and Media,* Rensselaer Polytechnic Institute, Troy, N. Y., 1961.

High Schools 1962, Educational Facilities Laboratories, Inc., New York, 1962.

"Indiana Regulations Affecting the AV Program," *Audiovisual Instruction,* vol. 7, p. 567, October, 1962.

Instructional Materials Services for Washington's Schools, Washington State Department of Public Instruction, Olympia, Wash., 1960. 56 pp.

Kinne, W. S., Jr.: *Space for Audio-Visual Large Group Instruction,* University Facilities Research Center, The University of Wisconsin Press, Madison, Wis., 1963.

Koppes, Wayne F., Alan C. Green, and M. C. Gassman: *Design Criteria for Learning Spaces: Seating, Lighting, Acoustics,* Office of Facilities, The University of the State of New York, Albany, N.Y., 1964.

Nimnicht, Glendon P., and Arthur R. Partridge: *Designs for Small High Schools,* Colorado State College, Greeley, Colo., 1962. 84 pp.

Palmer, R. Ronald, and William Maxwell Rice: *Laboratories and Classrooms for High School Physics,* Educational Facilities Laboratories, Inc., New York, 1961. 32 pp.

Parsons, James W.: "Roll-on Light Control," *Audiovisual Instruction,* vol. 8, p. 700, November, 1963.

"Planning for the Requirements of the Classroom: Minimum Standards for Michigan," *Michigan Education Journal,* vol. 41, pp. 21–27, Dec. 1, 1963.

Planning Schools for Use of Audiovisual Instructional Materials, The University of the State of New York, New York State Education Department, Albany, N.Y., 1959. 28 pp.

Planning Schools for Use of Audio-visual Materials, No. 1, Classrooms, Department of Audio-visual Instruction, NEA, March, 1958. 64 pp.

Room Darkening for Audio Instruction, Audio-Visual Education Association of California, Southern Section, Los Angeles, Calif., 1960. 14 pp.

Schools for Team Teaching, Educational Facilities Laboratories, Inc., New York, 1961. 36 pp.

Study Carrels: Designs for Independent Study Space, Educational Facilities Laboratories, Inc., Western Regional Center, Stanford, Calif., 1963. 16 pp.

Trow, William Clark: *Teacher and Technology: New Designs for Learning,* Appleton-Century-Crofts, New York, 1963.

Trump, J. Lloyd: "Places for Learning," *Audiovisual Instruction,* vol. 7, pp. 516–517, October, 1962.

Your Audio-Visual Program: A Handbook for Principals, Audio-Visual Education Association of California, Southern Section, Los Angeles, Calif., 1961. 16 pp.

chapter 4

Administering materials

Continuing increases in the variety and quantity of instructional materials point up the need for businesslike and educationally sound administrative procedures

❯ To ensure quality and appropriateness in materials selected
❯ To avoid wasteful duplication and proliferation in curriculum coverage
❯ To effect wise allocations of budgeted funds
❯ To provide widest and longest possible uses of materials for the lowest feasible cost

The fundamental tasks of managing instructional materials to achieve these ends may be discussed generally under the headings of (1) selection criteria, (2) selection process, (3) accessioning, classifying, and cataloging, (4) processing, (5) distribution, and (6) maintenance. Processes, problems, and suggestions with respect to each of these matters will be considered in turn.

DETERMINING SELECTION CRITERIA

Any determination of criteria to guide the selection of educational media should begin with the ultimate goals of the instructional program to which they are intended to contribute. While in most cases these goals will be found to have been developed previously and to be in a state of continuous revision and refinement, they should be reexamined and regularly reconsidered as part of the materials selection process.

One such list of educational goals, as developed by the schools in Montgomery County, Maryland, includes the following: [1]

Competence in the fundamental skills of listening, observing, speaking, reading, writing, spelling, mathematics, and the arts

Recognition of and respect for the worth of each individual

Appreciation for and power in logical, critical, and creative thinking

Understanding and acceptance of the responsibilities and appreciation of the privilege inherent in the American way of life

[1] "Educational Goals for the Montgomery County Public Schools," *Policies and Procedures Handbook,* vol. 1, Public Schools, Montgomery County, Md.

Understanding and evaluations of the cultures and contributions of other peoples

Understanding of scientific truths of the universe and man's relationship to them

Effective human relationships for democratic living, as they apply to the individual in the family, in the school and community, in the country, and in the world

Wise use of human, natural, and material resources

Competence in choosing and pursuing a vocation

Respect for and pride in good workmanship

Values in aesthetic appreciation and creative expression

Ethical behavior based on moral and spiritual values

Although such goals are general, they do provide assistance in formulating criteria to guide the selection of instructional materials. Their influence may be revealed, for example, in preferences expressed for the kinds of materials that stimulate inquiry or problem solving as opposed to materials that give all the answers. They might also be revealed in a policy of weeding out instructional materials that appear to condone discrimination against or belittlement of persons for reasons of race, color, or creed. Or they may be recognized in efforts to obtain instructional materials that dramatize the importance of preserving and making wise use of our country's human, natural, and material resources.

Another special consideration in the formulation of criteria to guide the selection of instructional materials revolves around the question: What particular contributions to achieving instructional goals are to be expected from uses of instructional materials? This question may be answered in part by giving a few specific examples:

❯ The school district that experiences difficulty in hiring qualified foreign-language teachers may obtain expertly prepared, integrated sets of instructional materials (tapes, booklets, sound films, and the like) to *extend teaching abilities* of those who are hired.

❯ The school district seeking to enrich the program of especially able students may choose materials (self-instructional tapes, programmed texts) for individualized, *independent study* activities.

❯ School personnel who are aware that effective instruction is not achieved through unvarying use of "read-discuss-test" procedures will seek to introduce varied approaches to teaching and learning. They will search for materials to whet interest, to present difficult concepts in readily understood form, or to provide springboards to worthwhile learning activities (discussion, experimentation, and the like).

A third special requirement in formulating selection criteria is to provide easily understood standards to facilitate making the necessary discriminative judgments. Several general criteria (stated in question form and applying to *all types* of instructional materials) may be identified:

❯ *Authenticity.*   Is the material factually accurate? Is it up to date? Are author and/or producer well qualified?

❯ *Appropriateness.*   Does the material promote the general educational goals of the school system? Is it in any way objectionable? Is it appropriate (with respect to vocabulary level, difficulty of concepts, methods of development) to the level of instruction intended? If controversial, is the material presented impartially? Is the material basic or supplementary to the curriculum? Does the material present information that presently approved materials do not? Or does it give needed new direction or dimension to currently approved sources?

❯ *Interest.*   Will the material catch and hold the interest of users? Will it stimulate curiosity? Can it be used to satisfy curiosity? Does it raise credible problems that would appeal to intended users?

❯ *Organization and balance.*   Is the material well organized and well balanced? Have principles of learning been followed in its development (e.g., reinforcement, transfer, application)? Is the material presented logically and clearly? Does the material achieve its stated purpose? Are data presented sufficiently comprehensively to be useful? Does the item contain too much extraneous material? Is the material presented imaginatively (not tritely) when imagination is really needed? Is the quality of narration or dialogue satisfactory (content and delivery)? Do the music and background strengthen the presentation? Are titles, labels, or captions appropriate?

❯ *Technical quality.*   Is the technical quality of the material satisfactory? Is the visual image satisfactory (in focus, pleasantly and effectively composed, functionally varied in distance and angle)? Is the sound clear and intelligible? Is color used effectively? Are sound and visual image satisfactorily synchronized?

❯ *Cost.*   Is the cost of the material justified (considering the relative costs of satisfactory substitutes, the money available for new materials)?

Additional supplementary questions may also be needed, of course, to guide the selection of specific kinds of instructional materials—films, filmstrips, recordings, exhibits, maps, supplementary or enrichment books, encyclopedias, models, flat picture sets, and others.

ORGANIZING THE SELECTION PROCESS

Having developed and stated suitable criteria in usable form, the actual materials selection process remains to be organized and administered. It is usually expected that efforts will be made to:

❯ Approach the task systematically, avoiding—in so far as possible—the waste of duplicating appraisals of materials or applying differing sets of criteria, with the result that appraisals cannot be compared or evaluated.

❯ Involve in the appraisal process teachers and other professional personnel whose needs and abilities are similar to those who will eventually use the materials.

❯ Involve students (preferably through classroom tryouts or interviews) in appraisals.

❯ Present resulting data in ways that facilitate their tabulation, interpretation, recording, and use for the purposes intended.

The educational media director may expedite and systematize the materials selection process by having the central administration set up an educational media advisory committee and subcommittees to consider different grade and subject-content requirements. Once such committees have been set up, they may help to refine and restate the selection criteria, as desirable, and to improve selection procedures. A minimum number of easy-to-use appraisal forms must also be developed, as well as a handbook or manual giving details of appraisal and selection criteria and clear instructions concerning their application and interpretation. Such a handbook should reduce both the number and complexity of forms used, since it avoids repetition of explanations and directions. Standardized handbook directions should also lead to increased consistency and reliability of ratings by different committee members.

Examination of forms now used in various parts of the country shows the advisability of seeking to simplify their application in the selection process. If the volume of appraisals is great, for example, serious thought should be given to the possibility of using data-processing techniques. Recommendations of individual committee members may thus be analyzed more thoroughly and in less time than would be possible with traditional hand or calculator methods.

Consideration must also be given to interpretation and use of ratings and recommendations of the subcommittees. Ideally, the media director should receive final purchase recommendations, as individual or combined committee ratings, of the following types:

❯ *Highest priority.*   Purchase immediately, first on the list.

❯ *High priority.*   Purchase first after the highest priority group to the extent that funds continue to be available.

❯ *Valuable.*   Consider for later purchase, but now place in deferred status for reconsideration at some later date along with other new materials.

❯ *Marginal.*   Do not purchase now or probably ever—of doubtful value to the instructional program.

❯ *Unsuitable.*   Do not purchase—unworthy of further consideration, for a variety of reasons.

A number system (1 for highest priority, 2 for high priority, and so forth) is sometimes used to expedite rating summaries. In such cases, a decision must be made as to a method of combining the ratings of individual committee members into a final single rating which is then readily translated into a 'Buy" or "Don't buy" recommendation. It is

This materials evaluation form, as prepared by the Bureau of Teaching Materials, Virginia State Department of Education, is simple to check. Tabulations and interpretations of large amounts of data resulting from selection programs would be facilitated through applications of machine or computer methods.

AUDIO VISUAL TEACHING MATERIALS EVALUATION FORM
Prepared by: Virginia State Department of Education
Bureau of Teaching Materials

Type: (.) 16mm sound ( ) b/w   DATE EVALUATED _____
      ( ) 16mm silent ( ) color   EVALUATED BY _____
      ( ) 35mm filmstrips ____Length COMMITTEE _____
      ( ) Other   ____Cost   SCHOOL ADDRESS _____

TITLE _____
PRODUCER _____

---

1. CORRELATION WITH CURRICULUM   _____   _____   _____
                                     Good   Fair   Poor

2. AUTHENTICITY AND ACCURACY   _____   _____   _____
                                    Accurate Generally   Mis-
                                               True   leading

3. ORGANIZATION   _____   _____   _____
   (Does it tell the story   Well   Fair   Poorly
   simply and effectively?)   organized   Organized

4. IS IT IMPORTANT?   _____   _____   _____
   (Does it make a   Very   Some   Not
   significant contribution   important   important
   to learning?)

5. DOES IT EFFECTIVELY   _____   _____   _____
   DEVELOP CONCEPTS THAT ARE   Very   Uncertain Other
   DIFFICULT TO GET ACROSS   effective   methods
   IN OTHER WAYS?   better

6. ARE THE PICTURES GOOD,   _____   _____   _____
   CLEAR, EFFECTIVE?   Good   Fair   Poor

7. IS THE SOUND GOOD?   _____   _____   _____
                                    Good   Fair   Poor

8. IN WHAT SUBJECT AREAS WOULD YOU RECOMMEND
   USE OF THIS MATERIAL? _____

9. CHECK THE APPROPRIATE GRADE LEVELS FOR WHICH MATERIAL IS
   ADAPTED. DOUBLE CHECK FOR MOST APPROPRIATE GRADE
   LEVEL:

   Primary_____ Elementary_____ Junior High_____
   Senior High_____ College_____ Adult_____

10. CHECK PURCHASE RECOMMENDATION: BASIC_____
    SUPPLEMENTARY_____ DISAPPROVED_____

11. COMMENTS:

---

sometimes considered helpful to know the frequency of final votes (i.e., how many different reviewers rated the same item as 1, 2, 3, 4, or 5). This information permits the media director to judge range and median or modal responses of ratings. If this proves unnecessary, a simple mean or average rating may be used, and items ranked accordingly.

If, as is often the case, available funds are fully spent before reaching the end of the highest-priority or high-priority lists, there is a further complication. A decision must be made concerning the establishment of priorities *within* one or both priority lists. This may be done in either of two ways: (1) by arranging recommended items in order of descending priority, according to committee ratings (average, median, or modal), and then placing orders entirely on this basis; or (2) by reevaluating the rank order of items and making final decisions on the basis of supplementary factors that are held to be important for the final decision though not considered by the original committees. Some items may be recommended, for example, because they are the only ones available or the best of several slightly less than adequate items for an important subject.

Several published guides and source lists are helpful in conducting materials selection programs:

> *Educational Media Index.* Begun in 1964 by the Educational Media Council, this index provides classified, annotated descriptions of instructional materials in subindex form. Items described include educational films and kinescopes; charts, maps, and graphs (in sets); filmstrips; flat pictures (in sets); models and mockups; phonodisks (disk recordings); phonotapes (tape recordings); programmed instructional materials; slides and transparencies; and video tapes. Available from McGraw-Hill Book Company, 330 West 42 Street, New York, New York.

> *National Tape Recording Catalog.* This is a descriptive listing by title and subject of tape recordings available for classroom use. Tapes are contained in a national repository maintained by the University of Colorado in Boulder, Colorado, in cooperation with the National Association of Educational Broadcasters (NAEB) and the Department of Audio-Visual Instruction, NEA, 1201 Sixteenth Street, N.W., Washington, D.C.

> *U.S. Government Films for Public Educational Use.* This is a comprehensive listing of government motion pictures and filmstrips available for use by educational institutions. Order from U.S. Government Printing Office, Washington, D.C.

> *Educators Guides.* This is a series of guides to free instructional materials (curriculum materials; social studies materials; science materials; guidance materials; tapes, scripts and transcriptions; filmstrips). Available from Educators Progress Service, Randolph, Wisconsin.

> *EFLA Cards.* These evaluations in card form are issued by the Educational Film Library Association, New York, New York.

> *Paperbound Books in Print.* This catalog appears monthly, published by R. R. Bowker and Company, 1180 Avenue of the Americas, New York, New York.

❯ *Textbooks in Print.* This appears yearly, in April. Indexed by author, title, and subject, with bibliographic data. It was formerly entitled *The American Educational Catalog* and is published by R. R. Bowker and Company, 1180 Avenue of the Americas, New York, New York.

❯ *The Booklist and Subscription Books Bulletin.* This is published twice monthly and contains general information about subscription books, fiction and nonfiction books, books for young people, children's books, and free or inexpensive materials. It is published by American Library Association, 50 East Huron Street, Chicago, Illinois.

❯ *Children's Catalog.* This is a standard selection guide for children's books through grade 8, containing dictionary catalog of author, title, and subject, as well as annotations of content. It is published by the H. W. Wilson Company, New York, New York.

❯ *Standard Catalog for High School Libraries.* This is a list of nearly 5,000 book titles for junior and senior high school grades. Contains a dictionary catalog and a Dewey arrangement of titles. It is published by the H. W. Wilson Company, New York, New York.

❯ *Library Journal.* This is a monthly magazine, and it is useful here for its critical reviews of books and recorded materials. It is published by American Library Association, 50 East Huron Street, Chicago, Illinois.

ACCESSIONING, CLASSIFYING, AND CATALOGING

Three further procedures—accessioning, classifying, and cataloging—provide other essential bases for systematizing the administration of educational media. The many special administrative problems caused by variations in the shape, size, and complexity of media are reflected to some extent in several current points of view concerning these processes.

Accessioning

As new materials arrive from producers or distributors, they should be checked to ascertain that they are what was originally ordered and in good condition. Only then will it be proper to certify the validity of claims for payment. The *accession record* (a simple ledger file, a card file, or a punched-card or computer-taped file) preserves important data about each item in the materials collections. This record is subdivided into smaller lists, each representing a different item class (films, filmstrips, books, encyclopedias, tape recordings, and the like). The following data appear in the accession record: (1) complete and accurate title—as it appears on the item or (if different) in a standard list, such as the *Educational Media Index;* (2) author or compiler; (3) producer or publisher; (4) production or publication date; (5) purchase date; (6) purchase cost; (7) vendor; and (8) facts about original condition—exact footage for films, number of frames for filmstrips, disk diameter and playing speed, color or black and white, running time, and others.

The accession record provides a simple means of checking the inventory to determine which materials, if any, are missing and the current size of the collection. It also furnishes other data, such as (1) the number of items purchased by years, (2) those purchased from various producers or distributors, (3) the original value (for insurance or statistical purposes) of an entire collection, or (4) the value of different items within the collection.

Shelf arrangement and classification

The usual plan for shelving instructional materials is to place those of the same type together and to arrange them according to accession number or subject classification. Sometimes materials in a category should be subdivided according to size, running time, or other characteristics (for example, 400-, 800-, 1200-, and 1600-foot films; 10- and 12-inch, monaural-stereo, or standard-microgroove disk recordings).

If materials are to be shelved according to accession number, the accession list is subdivided immediately according to categories of materials and used thereafter as a shelf list. In such cases, each sublist is a numerical listing of items in the order of their receipt and in accordance with their actual shelf positions. Filmstrips 1, 2, and 3, for example, will be marked with the call numbers FS-1, FS-2, and FS-3, and placed in the filmstrip drawer by this arrangement.

If subject classification is used, items on the same topic are brought together and placed next to similar subjects according to the Dewey decimal system, Library of Congress, or other classification scheme. With the Dewey decimal plan, for example, all United States history would be in 973, Canadian history in 971, Mexican history in 972, etc. The difficulty of filing several different kinds of materials (ranging from books of fairly uniform size to four sizes of films, bulky kits in various shapes, and models) is quite obvious and helps to explain a usual preference for shelving them separately by type, whether shelf arrangement is by accession number or on a subject basis.

If browsing is permissible or possible, a subject arrangement (generally by types of materials) may be preferred. If there can be no browsing or if housing is fixed and interfiling and shifting are difficult (e.g., filmstrips in numbered drawers), the accession number shelving system is generally preferred.

The Dewey decimal classification system, most widely used in school libraries and educational media centers, was developed in the last century by Melvil Dewey. This system consists essentially of ten main classes, by hundreds, from 000 to 999. The general classes themselves are further subdivided, using a decimal system, to identify finer and finer gradations of the same general subject. As is the case with all classification systems, the constantly enlarging scope of human knowledge presents complications. Dewey's *Abridged Decimal Classification and Relativ Index* [2] is useful in developing a suitable classification plan and procedure. Part I is arranged by classification entries; Part II is a very full alphabetical index. Prefix letters (MP for films, FS for filmstrips, and others) are sometimes added to classification numbers to identify types of media.

Cataloging

The catalog of the instructional media collection consists of a list, usually in card form, of items arranged in one of two ways: (1) in separate sets of cards arranged according to author-and-title and subject, or (2) in "dictionary" form with author, title, and subject in a single alphabet.

Cataloging requires careful consideration of all elements of the educational media program discussed thus far. The basic purpose, of course, is to facilitate matching appropriate instructional media with the expressed needs and purposes of the users. To accomplish this, it is essential to (1) anticipate the most likely needs and purposes of persons consulting the catalogs or descriptive lists, (2) develop catalog card sets which indicate assigned subject, title, author, or other appropriate headings as well as essential technical data about each item, and (3) provide, if feasible, further data on the content of the item as well as its possible contributions to the achievement of established instructional objectives. This last process, known as "descriptive cataloging," especially requires professional insight and knowledge of the educational program generally.

Anticipation of the likely needs and purposes of the users is facilitated, in part, by the analysis of selection criteria discussed earlier. Analyses of curricula for various grade levels or subject fields, for example, will provide lists of topics and subjects in which the achievement of instructional goals may be sought.

While it is not within the scope of this discussion to provide detailed directions for cataloging instructional materials, several general suggestions are presented briefly as an overview of problems likely to be encountered. Shores [3] identifies a minimum of four fundamental elements needed for each main bibliographic entry: (1) author; (2)

[2] Forest Press, Lake Placid Club, N.Y.
[3] Adapted from Louis Shores, *Instructional Materials: An Introduction for Teachers,* Ronald, New York, 1960, pp. 22–23; 25.

This set of cards for the book, *Birds of the United States,* illustrates the numbers and kinds of entries minimally required for such materials. Other media require somewhat different cataloging. (*From Shirley Hopkinson,* The Descriptive Cataloging of Instructional Materials, *Claremont House,* 1963, *p.* 8)

Shelf list card

```
598.2   Watson, H. J.
W338         Birds of the United States.   c1960.

4925    1/10/61    Barton Bookstore    $5.95
```

Title card

```
              Birds of the United States
598.2   Watson, Howard James, 1910-
W338          Birds of the United States, illustrated by
        Frank Martin.   2d ed.   New York, Nature
        Publishers, c1960.
```

Added entry for illustrator

```
              .Martin, Franklin George, 1920-      , illus.
598.2   Watson, Howard James, 1910-
W388          Birds of the United States, illustrated by
        Frank Martin.   2d ed.   New York, Nature
        Publishers, c1960.
```

Subject card

```
              BIRDS - EGGS AND NESTS
598.2   Watson, Howard James, 1910-
W388          Birds of the United States, illustrated by
        Frank Martin.   2d ed.   New York, Nature
```

Subject card

```
              BIRDS - U.S.
598.2   Watson, Howard James, 1910-
W338          Birds of the United States, illustrated by
        Frank Martin.   2d ed.   New York, Nature
        Publishers, c1960.
```

Main entry (author) card

```
598.2   Watson, Howard James, 1910-
W338          Birds of the United States, illustrated by
        Frank Martin.   2d ed.   New York, Nature
        Publishers, c1960.
              xii,297p.   col. illus.   maps.

              Bibliography: p. 295-297.
              Maps in pocket on back cover.


              1. Birds - U. S. 2. Birds - Eggs and nests.
        I. Martin, Franklin George, 1920-      , illus.
        II. Title.
```

title; (3) imprint—or place, publisher, and date of publication; and (4) collation—pages and volumes, total number or inclusive. Materials other than books require other types of entries, as follows:

> *Maps.* (1) Editor, cartographer; (2) title, format; (3) imprint; (4) size (centimeters or inches); (5) color; (6) series and catalog number; (7) scale; (8) projection; (9) relief; (10) special features
> *Slides.* (1) Title, format; (2) imprint; (3) number of slides in set; (4) size; (5) color
> *Filmstrips.* (1) Title, format; (2) imprint; (3) time; (4) sound; (5) color
> *Disk.* Composer, author, poet; (2) title, format; (3) imprint, catalog number; (4) sides, size, rpm or rotation speed; (5) series; (6) performer; (7) notes
> *Tape.* (1) Composer, author, poet; (2) title, format; (3) imprint; (4) playing time; (5) series; (6) performer; (7) source

The size of the set required for adequate cataloging of items in a collection varies by types of materials. The cards required for books, for example, usually will include the following: [4]

> *Main entry (author) card.* Filed by author, this card is the first to be made; it gives complete information concerning the item and provides information about all other cards made for it (thus facilitating tracing these cards upon its withdrawal or for corrections). The main entry card is usually the title card for nonauthored films and other nonbook materials.
> *Title card.* Filed by title, under the first principal word (disregarding, but not excluding, articles and conjunctions). The title is given without inversion, exactly as it appears on the item. The card carries the item title on the top line; the remainder is identical with the main entry card.
> *Subject cards.* Filed alphabetically by subject. Multisubject books have several, each as complete as the main entry card. A subject heading list must be used to ensure uniformity. *List of Subject Headings for Small Libraries* by M. E. Sears [5] is widely used. This list also provides the classification number usually used for the subject.
> *Added entry cards.* Filed by editor, compiler, translator, or illustrator; these separate cards are used primarily by larger libraries and instructional-materials centers.
> *Shelf list card.* Filed by classification call number. This separate card contains essential data of a statistical nature about the item (author, title, call number, accession number, supplier, purchase price, date of purchase, and the like). These cards comprise a catalog that may be substituted for the book or loose-leaf accession record for materials arranged by accession rather than other numbers.

Uniform color-coding and symbol systems are often used to iden-

---

[4] Adapted from Shirley L. Hopkinson, *The Descriptive Cataloging of Library Materials,* Claremont House, San Jose, Calif., 1963, pp. 1–70.
[5] Available from H. W. Wilson, N.Y.

tify cards for different types of media, especially when such cards are to be filed together. Color coding may be accomplished by using vari-colored card stock or cards that have narrow color bands along the top edges. One authority recommends the following color code and symbol systems:

Card or band color	Symbol	Instructional material
Blue	FILM or MP	Motion picture
Green	FS	Filmstrip, silent
	FSS	Filmstrip, sound
Cherry	SL	Slide set
Cherry	VM	"Viewmaster" reel (Sawyer type)
Buff	MAP	Map
Buff	GLOBE	Globe
White or buff	C	Chart
	CP	Poster
Yellow	KIT	Teaching kit
Yellow	TD	Three-dimensional teaching aid
Orange or salmon	PR	Phonograph recording
Orange or salmon	TR	Tape recording
White or buff	AP	Art print
White or buff	PIC	Picture set
White	MF	Microfilm copy
White	MC	Microcard copy

Other color-coding and symbol systems may be used, of course, but they should be applied consistently.

Descriptive material for main card entries should provide bases for determining (1) the type of material (book, film, filmstrip, slide set, disk or tape recording, or other), (2) the general nature of its subject content, (3) the special educational purposes to which the item may be expected to contribute, (4) the grade levels at which its use would be appropriate, (5) the availability of teachers' manual or guide, and (6) other appropriate data that might be considered essential by the user.

Abbreviations commonly used in such entries are shown at the top of page 84.

Catalog distribution

Any suitable catalog of instructional materials to be distributed to off-the-premises users should meet several criteria. It should be (1) reasonably economical to produce and to revise, (2) readily accessible

Abbreviation	*Description*
sd.	Sound
si.	Silent
min.	Minutes (running time)
mm	Millimeter (width)
b & w	Black and white
fr.	Frames (of filmstrips)
2″ x 2″	Slide (transparency)
3¼″ x 4″	Slide (large)
rpm	Revolutions-per-minute (disk recordings)
ips	Inches-per-second (tape recordings)
s	Sides (disk recordings)
″	Inches (disk recording diameter)
p	Primary grades (K-3)
el	Elementary grades (4–6)
jh	Junior high school (7–9)
sh	Senior high school (10–12)
c	College or university
ad	Adult

to users, and (3) sufficiently informative as to the availability, content, characteristics, and applications of media described.

Each of these criteria must thus be examined and evaluated in light of the particular educational situation in which the catalogs are to be prepared, distributed, and used. If that location is a single school and if the number of items and users is small, complex procedures are out of place; a single simple card file (perhaps little more than a shelf list) may be all that is required. If, on the other hand, the number of users is great, and the collection is large and varied, more complex and sophisticated catalogs and many copies of them may be required.

Bound catalogs. These are probably the most widely used type of catalog for nonbook educational media and they may be had in several types. Variations are found in the manner of binding (bookbinding or loose leaf); in completeness (a single catalog listing everything in the collection, or a series of smaller catalogs listing items of interest to different kinds of users—kindergarten teachers, shop instructors, high school social studies teachers, and the like—in the method of reproduction (mimeographed, hectographed, offset- or letterpress-printed); and in the manner of distribution (from one to a building at one extreme to one to each teacher at the other).

Card catalogs. This means of informing users about instructional media is favored by many educational media directors. The usual practice is to set up in each school or using agency one central comprehensive dictionary card catalog. In some cases the central set is supplemented with a smaller set for each instructor; these sets contain only cards related to the individual's special fields of interest.

A principal advantage of the card system is that revision does not require a complete reprinting; it is only necessary to insert or delete cards for newly purchased, withdrawn, or reclassified items. Its chief disadvantages are reflected in (1) high initial preparation costs, (2) the expense and bother of maintaining an inventory of duplicate card sets to provide for an increase in the number of users, and (3) objections of some users to having to consult central card catalogs located at some distances from their offices rather than their own near-at-hand and highly portable bound catalogs.

Cochern [6] studied relative costs, utilization preference, and convenience of bound catalogs and individual card catalogs, and concluded that card catalog costs would be prohibitive for large university and college film libraries, similar in those of moderate size, and considerably cheaper for smaller libraries. However, in the sample tested (twenty-nine institutions returned questionnaires), instructors indicated a preference for the card system.

Preprinted catalog cards are sometimes available for instructional materials of several types, chiefly books and films. Many book publishers and film producers now furnish free several duplicate cards with their titles, but they have a serious disadvantage; so far, they tend to lack the necessary uniformity of content or layout and thus need considerable revision or retyping to make them sufficiently similar to regular cards in the center files. The preprinted cards supplied by the Library of Congress or the H. W. Wilson Company are often easier to use. The well-known *EFLA Film Evaluations,* supplied in 3- by 5-inch card form by the Educational Film Library Association and the Cardalog cards for educational recordings are also widely used and may substitute for locally reproduced cards.

The actual quantity preparation of catalog cards or bound or loose-leaf catalogs (including the necessary writing, editing, and checking of copy and its transformation into type or quality typewriting) is a time-consuming, costly process. The Xerox plate-making process is often used for printing 3- by 5-inch cards in quantity, as are various forms of mimeograph stencil and cardboard plates for offset printing devices. Two promising methods of producing usable copy for cards or printed catalogs are the International Business Machines (IBM) book-catalog and the Econolist sytsems. The IBM system employed in the Berkeley, California, schools [7] provides, in effect, an automatic typewriter, which produces a line of typewritten copy from punched data

[6] George W. Cochern, "A Study of Production Costs and Certain Utilization Problems Involved in the Distribution of Sixteen Millimeter Film Information on File Cards as Compared with Bound Catalogs," doctoral dissertation, Syracuse University, Syracuse, N.Y., 1956.

[7] Information supplied by Lyndon Vivrette, audio-visual director, Berkeley Public Schools, Berkeley, Calif.

on a single IBM card; an average of 8 such cards are required for the typical film description (one each for item numbers, catalog numbers, exact title, producer, production date, running length, color designation, and a content description). The IBM printer prints out one line at a time, about 150 lines per minute, from which more than 500 paper offset master plates may be produced in less than four hours. Once the plates are made, reproduction by offset printing is accomplished in the usual manner. To revise lists, it is only necessary to remove incorrect or outdated cards and interfile corrected or new entries.

The Econolist system also lends itself well to the preparation of catalog paste-up material, producing copy that closely resembles printing and contains heads, spacing, and layout devices commonly associated with more expensive forms of composition and layout. With this interesting technique, each bibliographic item (a single film entry, for example) is typed on an electric accounting-machine card. Upon completion of the file, all cards are loaded onto a specially designed camera, which photographs them at a rate of 7,000 per hour. The result is a series of strips of negative film or positive paper of varying column widths. Offset plates can be made directly from this negative film; the press run is completed in the usual manner.

Still another catalog printing system involves the use of the computer. Programmed data on the computer disk or tape can be printed directly on offset masters and reproduced in catalog form quickly and economically.

PROCESSING MATERIALS

Problems of processing educational media, like those of indexing and cataloging them, are complicated by variations of size, shape, format, and fragility. In readying such materials for shelving and in arranging for their storage, the following conditions must be met: (1) The *system* must be orderly, understandable, and convenient to use—for both borrowers and staff; (2) the physical facilities (shelving, special racks, cabinets, and the like) should be reasonably priced; (3) the system used should make economical use of floor space; and (4) the storage environment should be free from safety hazards or excesses of heat, dust, moisture, or electromagnetic fields.

The several "in-house" labeling and numbering processes that must be performed for the various media should (1) identify them as the property of the circulating center; and (2) facilitate the reading of their titles or numbers by individuals concerned with locating, inspecting, checking, packing, or shelving them.

Books. Open shelving in the reading room is recommended. Shelves should be 3 feet wide (on centers), 8 to 10 inches deep for standard books, 10 to 12 inches deep for oversize books, and 10 to

10½ inches "in the clear" between shelves, with adjustable features to care for oversize books. Collection labels (biography, history, science, etc.) should appear above shelves, as well as call number groupings. Ordinarily, shelves should be kept no more than two-thirds full.

Book processing should include (1) placing a call number on each book spine; (2) identifying the book as the property of the distributing center; (3) affixing a book pocket in the front or back of the book, depending upon practice; (4) pasting a "date-due" slip in the book near the pocket; and (5) inserting a "due-back" book card in the pocket. Both the book pocket and the due-back card should contain the call number, accession number, author, title, and such other data as are required.

Textbooks. The properly processed textbook that is ready for issue to students will be characterized somewhat as follows—subject, of course, to local variations in practice:

➤ *Inventory or accession number.* This includes a number that signifies the book title as well as a series number (91–111, for example, signifies book number 111 in the series identified by the code number 91).
➤ *Card pocket.* This is located on the inside front of the hard cover, and on it is stamped the name of the school or school system as the legal owner.
➤ *Loan card.* This is inserted in the card pocket; on it is printed or stamped the author and title and the inventory or accession number. This card also provides spaces for entering names of (1) responsible teacher, (2) student borrower, (3) date borrowed, and (4) date due back.

While in many instances these are the only preliminary processing requirements, additional precautions may be required to ensure longer textbook life—lacquering covers, attaching kraft paper or plastic jackets, or applying reinforcements.

Films. Open racks are recommended for the storage of films. These may be fabricated locally or purchased ready-made from one of several equipment suppliers. Only in exceptional circumstances is it necessary to store films in closed cabinets because of excessive humidity or dryness. A decision must be made as to whether to assign each film its own numbered space in a rack or return it to a "next-in-line" position, regardless of the number of films normally ahead of it which may be out on loan. Advantages of the former practice are the definiteness of position placement and the consequent ease of locating items on shelves; the principal advantage of the latter is its saving of shelf space. The most common practice is to store each film by a *shelf number* that indicates its position on one of the racks. The first number, in such cases, commonly refers to film length (400, 600, 800, 1200, or 1600 feet); thus MP-4-110 might be used to indicate film 110 in the 400-foot section. The practice of storing films by size provides savings in shelf space.

Open racks, with numbered segments—each for a separate film—are recommended film library equipment.

In processing new films for the shelf (1) place title, call number, and distributing center identification on the edge of the film can lid; (2) attach a colored leader at least 5 feet long on which are lettered "start" or "head," the film title, number code, and identification of the distributing center; (3) attach a trailer of contrasting color that is at least 5 feet long and marked "end" or "tail" at the end of the film; and (4) place a paste-in sheet inside the lid giving additional directions to the film user concerning film care and projection precautions.

Filmstrips.   Probably the simplest and best means of storing filmstrips is to place them in stacks of commercially produced drawer sets made especially for the purpose. Most such drawers are designed to provide permanent numbered positions for the separate filmstrips, thus facilitating pulling or replacing them after use. Homemade boards with rows of holes large enough for filmstrips may also be used. The plastic "one-piece" (lid and can) containers that are now supplied with filmstrips virtually eliminate the possibility of misplacing or "switching" lids.

With sound filmstrips, it is recommended that both the filmstrip

Standardized, pre-fabricated storage units provide efficient housing for film-strips. Note that each filmstrip is numbered in accordance with its drawer position; a label identifies the numbers of those in the drawer. (*San Jose State College*)

and its accompanying tape or disk be stored together in a fiber case and that they be treated thereafter as a single unit.

In processing filmstrips, affix title, call number, and name of the distributing center to the lid of the container only. It is usually considered unnecessary to add special markings to the filmstrip itself.

Slides. Although some instructional-materials centers continue to distribute both single slides and slides in sets, the latter is by far the most common procedure. It is usually recommended that such sets be packaged in boxes of uniform size, folders, or standard reels (such as those which are used with Cavalcade 2- by 2-inch slide projectors).

In processing slide sets (1) label the container with set title, call number, name of distributing center, and total number of slides in the unit, (2) attach a thumb mark to each slide, (3) identify each slide to indicate its unit number and the number of each slide within that unit (thus, SL-2-24 would signify slide 24 in slide unit 2). A decision must be made as to whether to mount slides between clear glass covers or to leave them in the less expensive cardboard mounts.

Disk recordings. Disk recordings are usually stored vertically in segmented racks and arranged according to disk diameter (7, 12, or 16 inches—the latter size being less common than formerly). Segments should be kept fairly compact, since warpage is likely to occur if records are allowed to sag. Corrugated cardboard squares may be inserted to provide the necessary compactness. Care should also be taken not to store records near radiators or heating vents.

In processing disk recordings (1) affix a call number and name of distribution center to each side of the upper edge of the record jacket or album folder to facilitate finding items arranged in vertical storage racks; (2) affix identical data to one side of each record; and (3) affix a book card pocket and due-back slip on the jacket face or inside the album's front cover. Each record in a multiple-record album should be similarly identified to show its position in the series.

Tape recordings. Tape recordings should be stored in the boxes in which they are supplied by the manufacturers, or in round 7-inch metal cans such as those used for 8mm film. It is usually recommended that tapes be stored on edge, rather than flat. Use of segmented shelving will aid in keeping tapes upright while still leaving room to insert new or returned tapes in proper position. Keep tapes from strong magnetic fields, such as those produced by heavy electric motors or transformers.

In processing tape recordings (1) affix title, call number, name of distribution center, playing time, recording speed, type of recording (single or dual track, monophonic or stereophonic) on the face of the tape container; (2) attach a 5-foot paper tape leader containing the word "start" or "head" and repeating the number code, the title, and the name of the distribution center; (3) attach a trailer tape at least 5 feet long, marked "end" or "tail"; and (4) affix a book card pocket and due-back slip on the face of the tape-recording box.

Kits. Kits are best stored and distributed in separate wood or fiber containers especially designed for the purpose. Since shelf or bin storage of boxed kits will be used, some degree of uniformity of shape and size is recommended. Sturdy handles, properly placed for weight balance, facilitate handling; straps or locks reduce danger of loss or breakage from spilling.

When processing kits (1) affix to the outside of the kit case a call number and identifying title (a short title may suffice) and the name of the distribution center, (2) place on the inside of the lid a manual or guide identifying and inventorying items in the kit and suggesting their educational uses, and (3) number each element with the kit call number and the number of the element within that kit (in accordance with the inventory). In the case of a tightly fitted kit, it may also be advisable to supply a visual layout chart to show where each part is to be packed for return to the center.

Maps, charts, and globes.   Store folded maps and charts in regular four-drawer file cabinets; store unfolded ones in special hanging racks, in thin drawers of proper dimensions, on spring rollers, or rolled up separately in mailing tubes.

In processing maps, charts, or globes, affix to each item at some uniform and easily observed position the call number, title, and identification of the distribution center. With unmounted or roller-mounted maps or charts distributed in mailing tubes, mark each container with data suggested above. Identify globes by affixing code numbers to pedestals or hangers. For protection, place them in similarly identified covered containers.

Picture sets.   Picture sets may be stored vertically in regular filing cabinets, or in shelving similar to that regularly used for books. In either case, sets may be placed in large manila envelopes or in heavier cardboard or fiber boxes made especially for the purpose.

In processing picture sets, provide on each envelope or box the call number, title, name of distribution center, and total number of separate pictures in the set; and place on each separate picture the call number and the number of each picture in the set (PIC-3-29, for example, would signify picture 29 in picture set 3).

Specimens.   Specimen collections may be arranged as (1) permanently fixed displays, with each item attached so as to remain in place when displayed or examined (but not handled), or (2) loose displays, with the separate items capable of being handled and examined while out of their containers. As in the case of kits, effort should be made to standardize upon a minimum number of specimen box sizes to facilitate storage and handling.

In processing specimen collections, affix the call number, set title, and name of distribution center on the outside of the container; insert a manual or guide explaining the nature and uses of items in the set; and affix numbers to each item to show its order and place in the set.

DISTRIBUTING MATERIALS

Several basic problems must be considered in developing valid standards and procedures to control the distribution of educational media, of which the following are regarded as typical:

> How to determine which materials should be purchased in sufficient quantities to permit them to be placed in individual classrooms, which

should be placed in individual school collections, and which should be maintained in more remote centralized collections

> How to develop policies and procedures to facilitate the control of distribution to ensure the availability of the right materials for teachers or students when, for as long as, and as often as needed, with minimal loss of effective use time because of transportation or other scheduling difficulties

> How to recover, interpret, and use statistical data pertaining to such distribution in reaching necessary materials management decisions

Placement decisions

Decisions as to where to place educational materials—in individual classrooms, in a special building such as an instructional-materials center or library, in a district or county center, or in a state department of education or university collection—are influenced by (1) the volume of demand for the use of such materials, (2) the size of the materials budget, and (3) the relative convenience and expense of operating centralized and decentralized instructional-materials collections in the educational system.

While there can be no absolute assurance that the frequency or quality of use of instructional materials will rise simply because they are available, it is generally considered desirable to follow the principle of proximity and to place materials as close as possible to intended users.

Ideas concerning the need for permanent educational media collections for *individual classrooms* appear to be changing, largely because of the increasing availability of materials through centralized building or school system media-distribution agencies. It is increasingly common for teachers to rely upon such central agencies to provide educational media in considerable variety on a long-term basis, pending completion of a study unit. Only frequently used items (encyclopedia sets, dictionaries, globes, atlases, basic map and chart sets, chalkboard templates, and the like) are customarily retained permanently in classrooms.

Because of the relatively high initial purchase prices of films and the low cost of direct distribution by mail or school truck, they are usually provided by centralized district or county offices or even by more distant regional or state agencies. It is generally not feasible, however, to provide centralized distribution for heavier or more bulky items (large models, kits, mockups, certain kinds of instructional equipment, and the like) beyond the range of the economical truck transportation that is provided by many district and county school offices.

Booking procedures

The farther removed the source of supply of educational media from eventual users, the greater the need to provide some means of systematically regulating and controlling their distribution. Classroom or single-school materials collections may require no more record keeping than a simple due-back file arranged by date. The district, county, or state center, on the other hand, must develop considerably more elaborate procedures to (1) permit borrowers to indicate in advance the materials they wish to reserve and dates of intended use, (2) inform those making advance reservations that the requests will or will not be filled, (3) ensure an orderly, efficient system for readying materials for shipment on dates indicated, (4) maintain appropriate due-back and use records, and (5) ensure delivery and pickup of materials at appointed dates and times.

Placing advance orders. Placing advance orders with educational media centers is usually done in one of three ways: (1) in person, (2) via telephone, or (3) through the mail. Orders placed in person are often handled directly with the booking clerk, who makes simultaneous bookings and confirmations. In the Montgomery County schools in Maryland, for example, school media coordinators are assigned scheduled times during which to telephone the Instructional Materials Center (IMC) to request reservations of materials for their schools. Under this plan, immediate confirmations or rejections are possible. To complete the transaction, it is only necessary to enter the confirmed date on the booking card and to file the telephone slips under the appropriate shipping date. The school coordinator then notifies the local teacher of the decisions made.

Mail requests for reservations of instructional materials are usually handled as suggested by entries on the film rental order for the Bureau of Audiovisual Instruction of the University of Colorado shown on page 94. The "Do Not Fill In" section contains data signifying actions taken in processing the order. This information is transferred later to shipping, due-back, billing, and statistical record forms.

Bookings. Several files of booking cards are usually maintained for the various types of instructional materials—films, filmstrips, disk and tape recordings, charts, kits, specimen sets, and others—in the center's collections. Control of booking schedules for each of these items is commonly performed manually on a printed booking card containing dates and spaces for all the days and months of one or more years in advance. As in the case of the University of Colorado card for the film *How the Ear Functions,* for example, lines are drawn between the inclusive dates for which the item is reserved, and the name of the institution or individual making the reservation is recorded. Time must be allowed, of course, for transit time going and coming. Duplicate copies of the same media titles are recorded on separate cards, but they are filed together (alphabetically).

Booking card files may be developed in one of several different forms, ranging from those intended only for simple manual operation to files that are more or less automatic. Again, as with so many opera-

UNIVERSITY OF COLORADO
Bureau of Audio-Visual Instruction
BOULDER, COLORADO

1760-020

FILM RENTAL ORDER

Order Date Aug. 23, 1963

SHIP TO:

Lincoln Elementary School
Audiovisual Coordinator
1010 Washington Blvd.
Los Angeles 10, Calif.

CHARGE TO:

P.O.

S451-14

SHIP BY PARCEL POST ☐   TRUCK PICKUP ☐   X Mr. Stansbury   WILL CALL ☐

IF FILMS ARE NOT AVAILABLE FOR DATES LISTED:

Substitutions may be made as to date.   Yes X   No

Substitutions may be made as to title.   Yes   No X

In making substitutions, please observe the following restrictions or schedule:

LIST FILMS CHRONOLOGICALLY BY DATE WANTED. PLEASE DOUBLE SPACE.

	FILM TITLE	Dates Requested			Do Not Fill In			SHIPMENT NUMBER
		1st choice	2nd choice	St.	Ship	Use	Due Back	
	Drums Along The Mohawk	9/12-15	or 9/21-25	4	*available* 10/7-18 or 12/2 on			(9001)
S.H.	Clean Waters	6.00	10/21-25	10/15-19	2	9/9	9/11-15	9/17	8997
S.H.	Winged Scourge	4.50	9/12-15	9/21-25	1	"	"	"	
	War Comes To America I	6.00	9/12-15	4/13-17	1	4/9	4/13-17	4/21	8998
	War Comes To America II	7.50	9/12-15	4/13-17	1	"	"	"	
S.H.	How The Ear Functions	1.25 S	9/12-15	4/13-17	1	9/9	9/11-15	9/17	8997
S.H.	Tuberculosis	3.25	9/12-15	4/13-17	1	"	"	"	
	Divide And Conquor	4.50	4/21-25	2/20-24	2	4/2	4/6-10	4/14	8999
	Heredity & Pre-natal Dev.	4.50	4/21-25	2/20-24	2	"	"	"	
	Automation I		4/ 7-10	Only	4	*available* 4/13 on			(9001)
	Automation II		4/ 7-10	Only	4	"			
	America's Heritage V	(1.25 SDE)	1/10-12	4/20-24	1	4/16	4/2(-24	4/28	9000
	Reproduction Among Mammals	3.25	1/10-12	4/20-24	1	"	"	"	
	Understood Betsy		1/10-12	4/20-24	6				(9001)
	Dr. Pinel Unchains The Insane	6.00	8/27-9/1	9/ 3-7	1	8/23	8/27-9/1	9/5	9001

This mailed-in rental form provides spaces in which to enter essential data for the proper processing of orders. (*University of Colorado*)

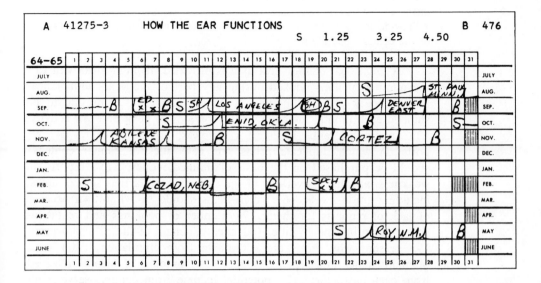

This booking card provides space for a full year's reservations. A duplicate form, printed on the reverse side, makes it suitable for a second year's use. (*University of Colorado*)

tions, the volume of bookings usually determines the most effective booking facilities.

Some media centers place large booking cards (8 by 10 inches or larger) in sunken files that are mounted flush with the counter tops on which the booker processes orders. In such cases, the booking cards are sometimes made more easily accessible by using "repulsion" techniques (i.e., applying tiny bands of magnesium oxide, similar to that on the usual tape recording, capable of holding magnetic charges all of the same polarity which therefore repel each other). Rotary (Wheeldex), visible index (Kardex), and other card systems are also used.

Completely automatic booking and related procedures are being used with increasing frequency, continuing a trend begun several years ago in the Los Angeles Public Schools audio-visual department and in other locations in the United States. At the University of Colorado's Bureau of Audiovisual Instruction,[8] for example, data-processing equipment is used to:

> Print up confirmations of film requests
> Prepare shipping notices
> Handle billing procedures

[8] Adapted from James C. Byrum, "Automation Techniques Applied to Audio-Visual Film Library Operation," unpublished paper, University of Colorado, Boulder, Colo., 1963. 20 pp.

> Prepare reports of circulation, attendance, and the like, for sponsored films in the center's collection

> Provide many useful kinds of statistical data concerning various aspects of the center's operation

A great deal of statistical data is provided. It might deal with (1) the number of films booked during any part of the year, with indications of peak and low periods; (2) the number of films due to be shipped each month, indicating future periods of peak and low activity; (3) anticipated rental income for the year, reported weekly; (4) reports on which duplicate prints (or new titles of similar content) should be purchased on the basis of unfilled requests; (5) reports on weakness, adequacy, overload of the collection in various subject areas, including grade levels; (6) which items should be withdrawn because of lack of requests for them; (7) number of bookings and rental income, per print and by title; (8) average length of life of a film print; (9) reasons why prints are withdrawn from circulation; (10) costs of maintenance and repair of films; (11) amount of income received from each customer; (12) potential income from campus services already booked for which charges will be made; (13) amount of campus service, by department; (14) cost of handling sponsored films; and (15) information as to the need for revising rental rates.

MAINTAINING MATERIALS

The proper maintenance of educational-materials collections is for the dual purposes of (1) preventing their unnecessary physical deterioration and consequent loss of communicative power, and (2) weeding out obsolete items that no longer communicate up-to-date or useful information.

Physical maintenance

An adequate program for the physical maintenance of educational media can do much to lengthen their effective life and to slow or perhaps to prevent their rapid deterioration. Such a program involves:

> Detecting and repairing or replacing damaged or lost portions

> Maintaining cumulative records of condition and maintenance work on individual items

> Cleaning, humidifying or dehumidifying, refinishing, or reboxing items as necessary

Film-handling procedures, using automated methods, provide much essential information for distribution management decisions. This chart shows the flow of activity in an IBM system at the Bureau of Audiovisual Instruction, University of Colorado.

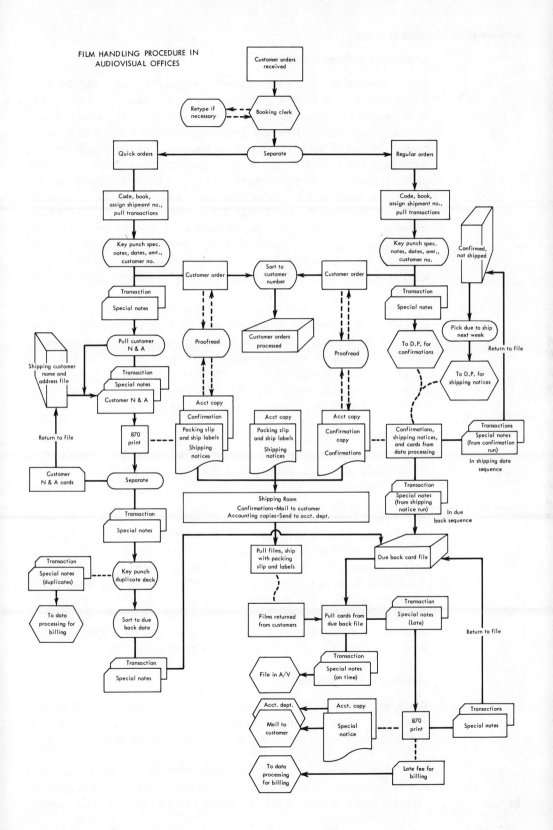

FILM HANDLING PROCEDURE IN
AUDIOVISUAL OFFICES

Sources of maintenance cues

The successful materials-maintenance program requires regular cues, which may be obtained or provided in one or more of several ways. It is usually recommended, for example, that films be inspected each time they are returned by the borrower. Such inspection may reveal broken sprocket holes, damaged perforations, or deep scratches or burns, any one of which could require the item's temporary withdrawal pending insertion of replacement footage. Automatic film inspection units now used widely throughout the country provide a sensitive means of checking the condition of films through counting splices or stopping immediately upon the detection of perforations, tears, or broken sprocket holes. Such units also permit accurate film-footage readings, thus providing bases for comparing present with original lengths and for ascertaining whether portions have been removed without record.

On the other hand, visual inspection provides only a very few cues as to the condition of some items. With tape recordings, for example, it is necessary to depend primarily upon receipt of complaint notes from users or an occasional playing to determine the nature of maintenance work required, if any. And while disk recordings may be checked visually for warpage, deep scratches, or breakage, usually the condition of recording grooves can be noted only through actual playing.

Cues for removing outdated or obsolete items from a collection may also be expected to come most commonly from the users themselves. Especially will this be the case if all users are encouraged to speak freely about the items and if they are also provided with some convenient means of making such reports (a printed form circulated with the item, for example).

Some county and district school systems, university audio-visual centers, and state departments of education also follow the practice of making so-called "close inspections" of educational media at least once each year. By this process, they determine which, if any, of their items need to be repaired or replaced. Close inspections may also be occasions for assessing the currency of items and for nominating for withdrawal (or placement in an archives collection) those failing to measure up to standards. In all such cases, criteria similar to those used in the original selection of *new* materials should be applied.

Maintenance suggestions

While the following are not intended as an exhaustive list of maintenance suggestions, they do indicate some kinds of preventive or corrective activities recommended for different educational media:

Films. When inspecting by hand, allow thumb and index finger to ride lightly on the *sprocketed edge* only to detect broken or punched sprocket holes. Check leader to ascertain that the film title matches the can. Use a film notcher to cut jagged film from around single separated sprocket holes. Check splices to see that they are holding firmly; resplice the ones that have weakened. Visually check portions of film footage to determine whether deep scratches are present. Check film length by use of a footage counter.

However, automatic film inspectors now on the market will do nearly all of these tasks and a few others as well. For example, operating at speeds up to 450 feet per minute and with a maximum film capacity of 2,000 feet, the Harwald Company's Model Q, Mark IV unit will:

❯ Detect sound-track defects (through use of several jeweled "feelers")
❯ Detect thickness discontinuities (extra thick splices, diagonal splices, thin Mylar tape splices, pins)
❯ Detect sprocket punches, enlargements, or other irregularities
❯ Detect broken film or poor splices
❯ Detect and count the number of splices in a film
❯ Clean, lubricate, and polish film
❯ Measure film footage
❯ Provide extremely fast check viewing of long films by sampling segments (both sound and picture) between "fast forward" spurts

Filmstrips. Check each can to ascertain that the proper filmstrip is returned and that it is rewound with "head" out (ready to be inserted for projection the next time it is used). It is usually not recommended that filmstrips be inspected in more detail than this. When they must be handled, do so only by the edges; avoid touching picture surfaces. Also avoid "cinching" loosely wound filmstrips, since such tightening by pulling on the outer end may grind dirt into the emulsion and cause distracting scratches.

Slide sets. Check numerical order of all slides in the set, at the same time determining (1) that the container is the proper one; (2) that all slides are returned; and (3) that they are properly positioned to permit thumb marks and slide numbers or descriptive titles to be read as slides are inserted in the projector or cartridge. Remove finger marks from glass-covered slides by dry-wiping with a clean, soft cloth. Check for cover cracks; if some are found, replace the cover. Brush cardboard-mounted slides with camel's hair brush (do not wipe with cloth).

Disk recordings. Check visually for scratches, worn grooves, cracks, or serious warpage. Listen to selected portions to check sound quality. To clean records, use a soft cloth that has been dipped in cold water and wrung as dry as possible; wipe the record surface gently in the direction of the grooving. Check record containers to ascertain that they are the correct ones for the titles and see that all records are replaced in proper order in albums.

Tape recordings. Check to determine that the tape is packed "head out," ready to be replayed, that the leader is intact, and that the tape title matches the container. It may be possible to detect twisted or creased footage by examining the tape over a strong diffused light. Occasionally, replay the tape in its entirety or make a less detailed check by listening to selected short portions.

Maps. With folded maps, check for tears around grommet holes or creases; check at extreme roll-down points for roller-mounted maps. Repair as necessary. To preserve map surfaces and colors, spray with clear plastic fixative (available in pressurized cans), or store in plastic cans.

SUMMARY

Problems involved in the administration of educational media, although numerous and somewhat specialized in nature, cannot be separated from the mainstream of educational planning. Businesslike and educationally sound procedures are needed to ensure quality and appropriateness in materials selected, to avoid wasteful duplication or proliferation of coverage, to effect wise allocations of budgeted funds, and to provide widest and longest possible use of materials for the lowest possible costs.

Essential elements in the total process of administering instructional materials include (1) the development of appropriate selection criteria; (2) the organization of the selection, ordering, and receiving procedures; (3) accessioning and cataloging; (4) processing and shelving materials; (5) distributing materials; and (6) maintaining the physical condition of materials collections. With all these processes, the educational media director must give highest priority to the needs of those who are to use the materials—the students and teachers served by the school, school system, institution of higher learning, or state of which the media centers are a part.

FOR FURTHER INFORMATION

Allen, William H.: "Audio-Visual Communication—Administration of AV Programs," in Chester W. Harris (ed.), *Encyclopedia of Educational Research,* rev. ed., Macmillan, New York, 1960, pp. 128–130.

Brown, James W.: *The Virginia Plan for Audio-Visual Education,* The University of Chicago Press, Chicago, 1947. 21 pp.

Brown, James W., and John A. Moldstad: "Administration of Instructional Materials," *Review of Educational Research,* vol. 32, pp. 194–209, April, 1962.

Carlin, Kathryn L.: "Distribution Is What Counts," *Audiovisual Instruction,* vol. 5, pp. 334–335, December, 1960.

Cochern, George W.: "A Study of Production Costs and Certain Utilization Problems Involved in the Distribution of Sixteen Millimeter Film Information on File Cards as Compared with Bound Catalogs," doctoral dissertation, Syracuse University, Syracuse, N.Y., 1956. 140 pp.

Durr, William H.: *The School Division Film Library: A Manual of Administrative Procedures.* Virginia State Department of Education, Richmond, Va., December, 1946. 41 pp.

Erickson, Carlton W. H.: *Administering Audio-Visual Services,* Macmillan, New York, 1959, pp. 181–203.

Gerletti, Robert C.: "The Importance of an Evaluation Policy for Instructional Materials," *Audiovisual Instruction,* vol. 7, pp. 289–291, May, 1962.

Hass, Claude W.: "An Investigation of Criteria for the Evaluation of Audio-Visual Services Provided at the County Level in California," master's thesis, College of the Pacific, Stockton, Calif., 1958. 161 pp.

Hopkinson, Shirley L.: *The Descriptive Cataloging of Library Materials,* Claremont House, San Jose, Calif., 1963. 70 pp.

Hyer, Anna L.: "Setting Quantitative Standards," *Audiovisual Instruction,* vol. 6, pp. 506–509, December, 1961.

Roberts, Tom: "An Efficient Film Filing System," *Educational Screen and Audiovisual Guide,* vol. 8, pp. 302–303, March, 1963.

Rufsvold, Margaret: *Audio-Visual School Library Services,* ALA, Chicago, 1949. 116 pp.

Sanborn, William B.: "Someone Has to Mind the Store," *Audiovisual Instruction,* vol. 5, pp. 328–331, December, 1960.

Schuller, Charles F.: *The School Administrator and His Audio-Visual Program,* NEA, 1954. 367 pp.

Shores, Louis: *Instructional Materials: An Introduction for Teachers,* Ronald, New York, 1960. 408 pp.

Skelly, Harry J., "Audio-Visual Services in Counties of Northern California," doctoral dissertation, Stanford University, Stanford, Calif., 1956. 174 pp.

Taba, Hilda: "Evaluation Techniques? First Some Fundamental Questions," *Audiovisual Instruction,* vol. 9, pp. 288–290, May, 1964.

Vivrette, Lyndon: "We Put Our AV Catalog on IBM," *Audiovisual Instruction,* vol. 7, pp. 302–303, May, 1962.

chapter 5

Administering equipment

The recent upsurge in the quantity and variety of instructional materials mentioned in the preceding chapter may also be noted in connection with the administration of new media equipment. Defensible and valid criteria must be developed to guide the selection, purchase, distribution, and maintenance of new media equipment to ensure:

> Quality and usefulness of the items purchased
> Fair value for funds expended
> Fair and adequate distribution of equipment to intended users
> A sufficiently long and useful life of items purchased without excessive maintenance costs

For an organized approach to the administration of equipment supporting educational media programs, there must be answers to numerous questions, of which the following are somewhat typical:

> What must be done to ensure valid determinations of the *types* and *amounts* of equipment that should be purchased? Must something of everything be purchased, or is some restrictive specialization required?
> What are defensible criteria for judging the relative merits of different makes of the same class of equipment? How can such criteria be applied to ensure receiving the best buy?
> Is it wise to follow the cheapest-price policy when purchasing equipment? If not, are there defensible alternatives to this practice?
> To what extent (and how) should teachers, students, administrators, and technical experts be involved in the various processes of choosing and purchasing educational media equipment?
> What are desirable standards for the specification of equipment requirements in the development of bid invitations?
> What standards, policies, and procedures should govern the distribution of educational media equipment within the single school, the district or county system, the college or university, or other administrative unit?
> What standards, policies, and procedures should govern the maintenance of such equipment at these same administrative levels?

EQUIPMENT PROBLEMS

Certain complexities surrounding the administration of audio-visual equipment are due to the fact that the field is at present experiencing:

❯ A rapid increase in the numbers of *new devices* (video-tape recorders, cartridge projectors, printing machines, and others)

❯ A rapid increase in the number of *different manufacturers* of audio-visual devices, which—although not new, since they may have been on the market in one form or another for some time—contain numerous variations of component parts or require new operational techniques

A special panel appointed by the Department of Audio-Visual Instruction of the NEA commented on problems arising from such developments: [1]

A profusion of materials and equipment, almost untried or with peculiar characteristics that add confusion out of all proportion to added flexibility, are cluttering the educational market. The results are waste, frustration, excessive problems of incompatibility of materials with equipment, equipment with equipment, and equipment with building construction. Worse, teachers lose faith in the dependability of equipment available to them.

Should the schools provide a wide-open marketplace for publishers and manufacturers to test their products, or should suppliers be required to give convincing evidence that their products have indeed been developed with attention to the manner in which they will be used and that they do contribute to the advancement of instruction?

Should minor variations built into products for reasons of patent considerations or company distinction—and which are accumulating at a confusing rate—be left to the discretion of companies, or should publishers and manufacturers be made to prove that the variation is justified?

Much of the action regarding these questions must await the future cooperative action of influential national organizations, including those of the manufacturers themselves, but the individual educational media administrator may do much to reduce equipment confusions by increasing his own competence in discharging the technical responsibilities of his position. Wyman comments on this need: [2]

The questions that I am asked today are most often technical, and of a comparative nature. . . . We are deluged today with literature about various makes and models of equipment and materials for doing our work. Some of the specifications are designed to give us the real and important characteristics so that we can make important comparisons and applications intelligently. Others are designed to confuse unknowing purchasers or users—to polish the apple without otherwise improving it.

We are asked to write specifications for equipment, facilities, and materials that will invite competitive bids from a number of possible suppliers. These specifications should indicate acceptable levels of per-

[1] "Panel Summary," *Audiovisual Instruction,* vol. 9, p. 245, April, 1964.
[2] Raymond Wyman, "I Don't Get Asked Much Any More," *Audiovisual Instruction,* vol. 9, p. 350, June, 1964.

formance described in technical terms rather than the usual make and model that we have seen or that is sold by a favored salesman.

When a purchase is pending, we are asked about features on competing brands and models of equipment. What features are really important? Are two machines essentially equal? Do certain terms describe the same performance? Terms such as decibels, frequency response, stroboscope, wow, flutter, rolloff, crossover network, lumens, watts, degrees Kelvin, UL approved, impedance, f number, resolution, foot lamberts, etc., are commonly used and seldom understood by the audio-visual consumer.

GENERAL CRITERIA FOR EQUIPMENT

Several basic criteria may be seen to apply to the assessment of nearly all types of audio-visual equipment, to be supplemented, of course, by other more specific criteria relating to individual items:

> *Usefulness.* How necessary is the item for the educational program in which it will be used? Will it be used with sufficient frequency to justify its purchase?

> *Operability.* Is the item simple and relatively foolproof in its operation? Does it operate much like others of its type, or does it have unique features that will confuse inexpert users? Are operating instructions clearly marked on the equipment and explained more completely in accompanying manuals? Are they complete and easy to follow? If the unit contains automatic operation features, are they dependable and readily used? Is there provision for manual operation as well?

> *Performance.* Will the item perform as necessary in accordance with accepted standards of efficiency for its various optical, electronic, mechanical, or other systems? Is the item acceptably versatile (dual purpose or other capabilities, for example)? Does the item operate at satisfactorily low noise levels? Will it continue to operate over long periods of time without excessive heating or wear?

> *Safety.* Is the item safe? Are turning gears protected? Is the chassis grounded? Do lenses have limit stops to avoid their being dropped accidentally when fully extended? Is the unit equipped with a three-wire grounding U-type plug? Is it equipment with at least a 5-foot power cord? Are cords permanently attached to avoid possibility of loss? Are plugs designed to avoid the possibility of their being inserted in the wrong position or manner, with possibly disastrous results? Is the item properly balanced to reduce hazards of toppling? Are detachable pieces likely to be lost? Do sharp edges or points provide safety hazards? Is the item suitably enclosed in a case or otherwise protected when stored or carried?

> *Compatibility.* Does the item "fit" with others already in the agency's equipment collections? Is there a sufficiently extensive and varied collection of instructional materials to be used with it or will it require special purchase of materials made especially for it? Are its frequently replaced parts (projection bulbs, exciter lamps, tubes, fuses, etc.) interchangeable with other units in existing equipment collections?

❯ *Sturdiness.* Is the item well built, of sufficiently strong materials? Are fittings (handles, knobs, dials, switches) of top quality? If plastics are employed in construction, will they withstand the kinds of normal usage to be expected for the item? Will the plastic deteriorate rapidly with age or upon exposure to heat or sunshine?

❯ *Repairability.* Is the item capable of being repaired without undue expense for parts, labor, or transportation (back to the factory, for example)? May repair parts be purchased locally and at a fair price?

❯ *Portability (if required).* Is the item sufficiently light to be lifted or carried by users (teachers or students, in particular)? Is it so large (even if relatively light) that it is unnecessarily awkward to carry?

❯ *Reputation.* Does the make of the item have an established reputation for quality and utility? Is the dealer's reputation similarly established? Is it likely that claims with regard to price, delivery, warranty, or similar matters will continue to be honored as long as the equipment is in service?

❯ *Cost.* Is the price of the item in line with those of competitive makes of the same type or quality? If higher, is the extra amount justified by superior design, performance, construction, or other features? If trade-ins are involved, are they related realistically to the price of the new items?

❯ *Warranty.* What is the warranty with respect to the number of months of free service (including replacement of defective parts or, when justified, of entire items)?

❯ *Service.* What additional service (beyond the warranty) is offered? Does the dealer agree to unpack and test newly received items? Will he or the manufacturer provide in-service training in its operation or maintenance?

SPECIAL EQUIPMENT CRITERIA

Several additional sets of special criteria should be developed to supplement the more general equipment selection criteria just described. The nature of questions to be asked about several common types of audio-visual equipment (motion-picture projectors, filmstrip and 2- by 2-inch slide projectors, overhead large-transparency projectors, tape recorders, record playbacks, opaque projectors, television receivers, video-tape recorders, and teaching machines) are suggested here.

Motion-picture projectors. Additional questions to be asked concerning 16mm sound motion-picture projectors are: Does the projector operate smoothly and quietly? Or is it so noisy as to interfere with communication for those seated near it? Is the threading process sufficiently clear and simple as to prevent misthreading and consequent film damage? If threaded automatically, can it be manually threaded or unthreaded before the film is completely finished? Is the screen image steady and without distracting flicker? Does the projector provide other special features (if desired and applicable): reverse; two-speed switch (sound-silent); microphone input; zoom lens; permanent oiling system; or time lapse meter? Is the amplifier output adequate for the room or auditorium size in which the projector will be used?

Does the amplifier have a transformer-isolated power supply (one that does not accept AC/DC power inputs)?

The Society of Motion Picture and Television Engineers, 55 West 42 Street, New York, New York, distributes several 16mm test films that provide objective means of checking and comparing performances of various projectors. These films may be used to evaluate such factors as amplifier and speaker response to low and high frequencies, steadiness of screen image, relative distribution of light at various points of the screen, intelligibility of dialogue, reproduction of music without wow or flutter, or other items.

Combination filmstrip and 2- by 2-inch slide projector (manual type). Does the projector design facilitate quick, foolproof changes from film strip to 2- by 2-inch projection or the reverse? Does it accept lamps of sufficiently high wattage for purposes intended (500 watts minimum)? Does the manufacturer offer a selection of projection lenses of different focal lengths to permit use of the projector with different-sized audiences and in different-sized rooms? Is the cooling system sufficiently powerful? Is a heat filter provided in the condensing system to prevent film damage from overheating? Are there separate switches for "lamp" and "fan," thus permitting the fan to be used in cooling the lamp after a projection period?

2- by 2-inch slide projectors (automatic type). Does the unit provide remote controls for slide changing, focus, and reverse? Does it include a special switching arrangement to control "high" and "medium" lamp wattage to adjust screen illumination to slide densities or image sizes? Is a zoom lens available? Does the slide carrier (tray, rotary cartridge, or other) accept the necessary number of slides? Are the slide carriers reasonably priced and easily available? May they also serve a double purpose as storage containers in which to distribute slide units?

Overhead large-transparency projectors. Will the projector platform accept all standard sizes of masks and transparency areas? Does the focusing system permit positive stopping at desired points without "drift," which may cause the screen image to slip out of focus? Is there a separate switch or switch position to permit cooling the unit without at the same time running the projection lamp? Will the unit accept a cellophane roll attachment? Is there excessive light dropoff at the extreme edges or corners of the projected image?

Tape recorders. Will the equipment operate at both 3¾- and 7½-inch-per-second speeds? Is tape threading simple to perform? Is there positive protection against accidental erasure of recordings? Does the equipment contain jacks or connection points for (1) microphone, phonograph, or radio input, at high or low levels; (2) preamplifier output for feeding signal to a second amplifier; or (3) external speaker connections? Does the unit contain a footage counter? Are the recording/playback heads conveniently accessible for cleaning? Is there a switch for cutting off the monitor speaker? Is the amplifier transformer-powered (accepting only AC)?

With stereophonic recorders, other questions may be asked: Does the unit have a separate amplifier for each of the stereo tracks? Does it provide also for making monophonic quarter-track recordings? Does it record in stereo mode or only monophonically? Does it provide for playing half-track monophonic recordings?

One especially effective check of playing quality may be made by recording at both speeds piano notes containing a number of sustained notes (as, for example, undamped piano notes). When playing back such music, pay particular attention to the presence of wow or flutter caused by irregularities of equipment speed. Frequency response of 50 to 14,000 cycles at 7½ inches per second is generally considered a desirable standard for classroom tape recorders.

Record players. Will the equipment reproduce records at 33⅓, 45, and 78 rpm? If required, will it also reproduce at 16⅔ rpm? Both stereophonically and monaurally, if required? If considered essential, are jacks or outlets provided for individual earphone listening? Is there an auxiliary speaker, an output from the pickup cartridge or preamp to an external amplifier unit? Is there a microphone unit? Are separate controls provided for "treble," "bass," and "volume"? Is there a separate "power" switch? If necessary, may the speaker or speakers be detached? Are all cords attached? Is the pickup cartridge easily available and of standard design (interchangeable with those of competitive makes)? Does the pickup cartridge have separate styluses for standard and microgroove records? Does the unit operate manually? (Automatic operation is not recommended for most school uses.) Is the turntable sufficiently heavy (for inertial stability) and rim-driven? Is the motor a four-pole type? Is it equipped with a variable speed control device? (This is recommended.) Is the amplifier transformer-powered (accepting only AC)?

To test record playback equipment for adherence to technical specifications, consider using standard audio test records such as those distributed by Audio-Phile. Give special attention to sustained musical notes (as in slow piano numbers), speech intelligibility, and other factors. For all-purpose listening, it is recommended that the playback frequency response include a range from 50 to 14,000 cps.

Opaque projectors. Does the equipment have at least a 10- by 10-inch opening for reflection of flat picture or other opaque material? Does the lens have a positive stop to avoid accidental dropping? Is focusing accomplished easily by rack and pinion gears? Is the condenser-lens system sufficiently "fast" and the lamp size sufficiently high to produce a satisfactorily brilliant screen image? Is the machine equipped with a built-in light arrow or pointer device? Does it contain an automatic roll feed? Does the copy platform permit height adjustments for projecting thick or thin copy (a page from a bound book or a single loose leaf, for example)? Is the platen equipped with a thick cover glass or pressure plate of the heat-absorption type?

Television receivers. Is the screen size at least 23 inches (measured diagonally across the exposed surface)? Are speakers front-mounted? (Side mounts should be avoided.) Does the unit carry the Underwriters Laboratory seal of approval? Is there a shield at the rear of the unit? Is there an interlocking device that automatically shuts off power to the set whenever this shield is removed? Is the picture tube protected from the danger of implosion? Does the set have a transformer-isolated power supply (accepting only AC)? Does it provide a means of connecting switch-controlled external speakers? Is the audio amplifier rated at not less than 5 watts undistorted output? Does the unit provide both a 300-ohm balanced and a 75-ohm unbalanced VHF antenna input? Does it provide a fine-tuning adjustment? (The latter is desirable but not mandatory.)

Video-tape recorder playbacks. With video-tape recorder playbacks, the all-important selection factor appears to be their degree of compatibility with units being used by other institutions or agencies with whom tape exchanges are anticipated. One recent study of this problem, conducted by William Lewis, developed minimum specifications for helical scan video-tape recorders, as follows: [3]

An overall size of not more than 36″ length, 18″ depth, 18″ height

Weight not exceeding 125 pounds; handles to be provided; light enough for two persons to carry

Capability of accepting up to a maximum of 12½-inch roll of television tape, on a reel of standard National Association of Broadcasters configuration

A requirement of no more than 5 amperes maximum on 102–125 (115-volt nominal) volts, 60-cycle power

Capability of accepting standard baseband video signals, with adjustable video input (75 ohms unbalanced), and any number of scanning lines at a 60 field rate

Video reproduction of a quality acceptable for feeding television display devices directly or through an RF modulator

Provision of one 600 ohm balanced or unbalanced output line, a line input capable of accepting signals from −10 dbm to +8 dbm, and a second low level input for direct connection of a microphone to the television recorder

[3] William C. Lewis, *Television Tape Recorders: A Comparison of Helical Scan Video-tape Recorders,* University of Colorado, Boulder, Colo., April, 1964, Foreword.

Capability of accepting 2-inch wide mylar or polyester base magnetic recording tape, with oxide horizontally oriented

A reel-to-reel tape speed of 3.7 inches per second; a head-to-tape speed of 641 inches per second

A minimum video response of ±3 db, 10 cycles to 3 megacycles, signal-to-noise 38 db or better; a minimum audio response of ±3 db, 100 to 8,000 cycles-per-second; a signal-to-noise ratio of 40 decibels at 500 cycles per second with less than 3% distortion; less than 3% RMS at +10 dbm

Manufacturer-guaranteed interchangeability with tapes made on other machines of his manufacture as well as with machines of other manufacturers using the same standards

Teaching machines.[4]   Is the use of teaching machines justified? Is there available a considerable supply of adequately tested and otherwise suitable programmed materials to be used with the machine? Are programmed materials presented in the device in a manner that is consistent with the teaching philosophy of those who will use it? Is the machine easily operated by students? Does its operation offer any motivation in itself? Will the device stand up under extreme use? Is it the right size for the area in which it will be used? Is it sufficiently flexible or versatile to be used with more than one type of programmed material? Are the placement and design of its control mechanisms convenient and logical from the viewpoint of users? Can the teacher easily replace or modify the program to adapt it to a particular student's problem? Will the machine function consistently under all possible sequences of control manipulation? Is the machine sufficiently tamper-proof to discourage vandalism or cheating? Does it have an automatic shutoff to provide "fail-safe" operation?

ORGANIZING EQUIPMENT SELECTION

Here we shall consider the *process* of organizing equipment selection. Budget planning—continuity budgeting, incremental budgeting, and developmental budgeting—although it bears upon the selection and purchase of instructional equipment, will be discussed later in Chapter 7.

Personnel for selection

It was mentioned earlier that all individuals importantly involved in the use of equipment—educational media specialists, teachers, students,

[4] Adapted in part from Leonard W. Ingraham, writing in *Social Education,* January, 1964, and a joint statement by the American Educational Research Association, the American Psychological Association, and the Department of Audio-Visual Instruction, NEA, *Audiovisual Instruction,* vol. 6, pp. 358–359, April, 1961.

technicians, and others—should participate in the processes of equipment selection. To conserve time and to ensure greatest efficiency, it is to be hoped that each individual's consideration will provide new (not duplicating) data on which to base final purchase decisions.

The *educational media director's* chief responsibilities with regard to equipment selection are to obtain and interpret data concerning the current status of equipment inventories in his organization or institution and to seek the advice and guidance of appropriate individuals and groups concerning standards (qualitative and quantitative) to be applied. It is his further responsibility, of course, to organize equipment selection activities to reach desired conclusions within the limits of time and funds available. In initiating this work, the media director will often seek the help of colleagues in other institutions who have faced problems similar to his, who have made their decisions, and who have already had time to discover their validity.

Technical personnel (central office engineers and equipment maintenance technicians, purchasing specialists in electronic equipment, and others) should also provide valuable assistance at various stages of the selection process. They may be asked to run preliminary tests, for example, and thus save valuable time by eliminating at the outset equipment that fails to measure up to previously established technical standards. In the process, they may give special attention to such objective factors as (1) weight, (2) dimensions, (3) sturdiness of construction, (4) safety features, (5) wattage and screen illumination, (6) power requirements, (7) Underwriters Laboratory seals of approval, (8) serial and model numbers, (9) frequency response, (10) wiring quality, and (11) warranty and service provisions. By disassembling or by conducting "run-in" operating tests over an extended period and using one or more units of the type under consideration, the technical staff may also obtain much useful data to aid in making recommendations for or against purchase.

Teachers may contribute valuable assistance in deciding upon equipment purchases by serving on selection committees. Their special areas of competence may be tapped by inviting them to thread or operate equipment as part of a competitive tryout or demonstration program. In doing this, they will give particular attention to ease of operation, volume, intelligibility and faithfulness of reproduction, convenience of handling, and similar "consumer" matters. Science teachers, audio-visual specialists, and others who are familiar with technical and scientific matters pertaining to the equipment being considered may give especially helpful suggestions and recommendations.

Students (particularly those who may be asked to serve as operators or instructional-materials center assistants) should also be asked for their reactions to the operability, safety, portability, and other features of equipment that are clearly within their sphere of competence.

Competitive testing of equipment

In setting up competitive tryouts of various makes of the same class of equipment, an effort should be made to establish conditions that permit true comparisons; results should not be invalidated by dissimilarities or inconsistencies of environmental or administrative conditions. The recommendations of Cross and others appear to retain validity: [5]

Plan to have the demonstration in a room which will be typical of the room in which such equipment is used.

Use the same screen for all comparative demonstrations of similar projection equipment.

Use the same materials (i.e., film or record) for all comparative demonstrations of projection or playback equipment.

Use new lamps of the same wattage for all comparative demonstrations of projectors.

Allow the same amount of time for each demonstration or for each sales representative to present his equipment.

Make provisions for equipment to be left after the demonstration so that committee members may examine it at their leisure.

Provide each committee member with equipment appraisal forms.

Exceptionally useful as a checklist of the availability, cost, and characteristics of principal items of audio-visual equipment to be evaluated is the *Audio-Visual Equipment Directory*.[6] This publication provides more than fifty different classifications of items of concern to those involved with the selection of audio-visual equipment, including such varied items as "repetitive" motion-picture projectors, splicers, projection tables and stands, teaching machines, tachistoscopic and reading devices, film cleaners, power megaphones, reels and cans, slide sorting equipment, synchronizers, test scoring machines, voltage regulators, and presentation boards and supplies.

SPECIFICATIONS AND BIDS

For several reasons, writing down specifications is considered an administrative essential whenever plans are made to purchase instructional equipment. When public monies are being spent, of course, there is nearly always the requirement that proof be furnished (or available) to show that contracts provide for the purchase of items meeting speci-

[5] A. J. Foy Cross and others, "Provision of Audio-Visual Materials, Equipment, and Building Facilities," in Charles F. Schuller (ed.), *The School Administrator and His Audio-Visual Program,* Department of Audio-Visual Instruction, NEA, 1954, p. 74.
[6] Published annually by the National Audio-Visual Association, Inc., 1201 Spring Street, Fairfax, Va. The usual selling price is $6 per copy.

fied minimal standards for the lowest acceptable price, and that other important factors (warranty, trade-ins, terms of service) have also been considered. But probably the best justification for detailed specifications is to ensure delivery of items of the quality and characteristics originally desired, not some less suitable substitutes.

It is a frequent practice to specify the make and model of some suitable equipment item "or equal" and indicate the lowest acceptable serial numbers of such equipment to preclude delivery of superseded units of earlier manufacture in the same model year. But a generally more satisfactory procedure is to specify minimally acceptable levels of performance in technical terms as represented by the following factors:

❯ *Technical features.* Amplifier output wattage, distortion limits, power requirements, speeds of operation, frequency response, speaker size and type, flutter and wow, signal-to-noise ratio, input and output provisions, types of wiring, transistor or tube complements, lens and condenser quality and treatment

❯ *Accessories.* Accompanying reels, microphones, cords, plugs, repair kits, replacement belts, bulbs, speaker cords, or stands for the unit to be furnished at the price stipulated

❯ *Construction.* Weight, dimensions, quality of cover or other finish, quality of hardware, colors

❯ *Guaranty.* Agreement with regard to free service, explanation of further service (as, for example, free replacement of defective parts "during the life of the item")

❯ *Other service.* Agreements with regard to unpacking, checking, and installing equipment; providing in-service training for teachers or technicians in operating or maintaining equipment; delivery to desired point of use

The State of Missouri recommends the following standard specification, or some suitable variation of it, as a means of obtaining equipment as desired and ordered: [7]

> The vendor must deliver the equipment unpacked, set up and ready to operate, and must check to make sure that all accessories, spare reels, line cords, etc., are present and in working order.
>
> He must check the equipment at time of delivery to determine that it operates properly in the location where it is to be used.
>
> The vendor must be prepared to furnish authorized factory repair service for the equipment within the state of Missouri or city of [to be filled in].
>
> He must maintain in stock such consumable items (lamps, tubes, belts, etc.) as are necessary to provide for the normal operation of the equipment.

[7] Hubert Wheeler (Missouri State Commissioner of Education), *Audio-Visual Instruction, An Administrative Handbook: 1961 Tentative Report,* Publication 21-H, 1961, p. 38.

The vendor must maintain or have immediately available within the state of Missouri or city of _____ a reasonabe stock of spare mechanical parts for the equipment.

The vendor must be prepared to furnish rental (or loan) equipment upon reasonable notice for use while this equipment is undergoing repairs.

MAINTAINING EQUIPMENT

Problems involved in maintaining educational media equipment grow more complex with the increasing numbers and types of items on the educational market and their expanded use in schools. This point is emphasized by Ruark: [8]

> Without qualified or contracted maintenance service on increasingly complex audio-visual equipment, the local district often finds itself stymied in the use of materials for lack of simple *preventative* maintenance or not-so-simple *basic* maintenance; it is not only the downtime of equipment, the loss in materials rentals, and the cost of repairs which must be totted up, but also the lost learning opportunities and teaching time, which simply cannot be replaced.

Several questions related to problems of equipment maintenance are often raised:

What are the pros and cons of operating an institutional equipment repair service as compared with contracting for such service through outside commercial agencies?

What is the optimum amount of decentralization for equipment maintenance and repair services? Which services should be provided at the school level, which at the district or county level? Which should not be provided at all? By whom should these services be provided at each of these levels?

When and how should it be decided to discard or to trade in equipment rather than to continue to service it?

What general administrative provisions may be put into effect to ensure systematic and adequate preventative maintenance of instructional equipment?

The *budgetary* aspects of these questions are discussed in more detail in Chapter 7, where attention is given to such matters as probable costs of equipment purchases for varying standards and varying types of instructional situations, costs of providing equipment servicing and purchasing necessary equipment maintenance supplies, and costs of replacing worn-out items in accordance with anticipated life spans for different types of equipment.

[8] Henry C. Ruark, Jr. (ed.), *Douglas County Instructional Materials Center Survey,* Division of Instruction, Oregon State Department of Education, Salem, Ore., October, 1963, p. 10.

Echelons of equipment maintenance

The work of maintaining the operating efficiency and dependability of instructional equipment is generally thought to be something which should be conducted, in part, at each of several different administrative levels. The principle is clear: Carry out simple maintenance procedures as close as feasible to the point of actual equipment use (at the single-school level, for example); refer to some central office (district, county, or contract agency) those requiring more complex analysis, replacement, or servicing.

Appropriate maintenance tasks for the single school (to be carried out by qualified instructional materials center student corps members, by a large-school maintenance technician, or by a qualified and willing faculty member) are often considered as consisting of the following:

Equipment tear-downs are ordinarily conducted by the district, county, state, or college audiovisual facility or by outside agencies contracting for repair services. Special training and tools are required.

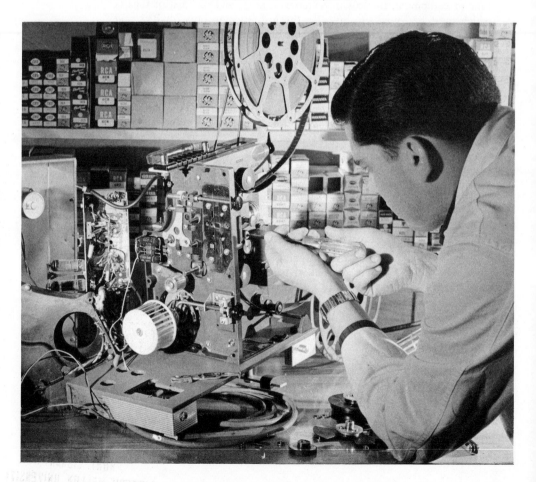

(1) regularly cleaning and oiling equipment, according to schedule; (2) replacing bulbs, belts, exciter lamps, fuses, and similar items; and (3) performing minor adjustments as needed. Other tasks suggested as being more appropriate for the central system or commercial repair service are: (1) replacing motor brushes; (2) checking and replacing amplifier tubes and parts; (3) replacing machine elements (tilt gears, lens rack-and-pinion assemblies, condensers, and the like); and (4) completely tearing down, cleaning, oiling, and adjusting equipment on a once-a-year or some other regular basis.

Commercial versus institutional services

Various factors must be considered in deciding whether to set up a centralized institutional maintenance service, staffed with its own personnel and providing its own stock of spare parts and supplies, or to enter into contractual agreements with one or more commercial equipment dealers or electronics shops to supply such services. These factors are related to (1) the actual or anticipated volume of repair and maintenance services, (2) costs of providing them on a contract basis as compared with costs of providing them through one's own organization, and (3) the value of certain worthwhile fringe benefits that might accrue from either plan for providing maintenance services—the convenience and security of having someone always available when needed and the possibilities of having maintenance personnel perform other services, such as surveying the needs for the improvement of classroom facilities or similar projects.

The most obvious basis for determining whether to set up an institutional maintenance service or to rely on some commercial agency is to estimate relative costs. The discussion of budgeting in connection with equipment maintenance and replacement that is included in Chapter 7 provides a model procedure by which to obtain this estimate. If, after analysis, turning to a commercial agency is agreed on, special help should be sought in drawing up a contract containing detailed specifications as to the kinds and frequency of services to be provided, the limitations on costs, the contractor's responsibility with respect to such matters as completing repairs within a specified time, providing replacement equipment loans while items are in the shop, and other related services.

Maintenance records

Cumulative records should be kept to show details of maintenance and repair work conducted on various items of instructional equipment. These records will provide a basis for estimating (1) the dependability or durability of different makes and types of equipment; (2) costs of repairing and maintaining them; (3) the frequency with which certain parts require replacement, adjustment, or repair; and (4) the volume of maintenance work conducted during any particular period. Such cumulative records may also form a basis for determining when a certain equipment item has reached the point of being excessively costly to maintain and ready to be junked, traded, or replaced.

If developed in loose-leaf or card file form, cumulative records may also be used selectively to control and schedule preventive maintenance work (weekly, monthly, yearly checks) for equipment items in or out of the shop area.

The maintenance of instructional equipment will also be facilitated by a systematic inventory system that provides a classified listing of information about all items on hand in the organization. Data concerning equipment items are often placed on the cumulative record cards referred to above, thus offering the convenience of having all required information in a place where it is most frequently needed and used.

Classification of different types of equipment can be handled simply through the assignment of code letters and accession numbers in accordance with some such system as the following:

Classification	Equipment
MP	16mm motion-picture projector
FS	Filmstrip projector (nonautomatic)
FS(A)	Filmstrip projector (automatic)
SL	2- by 2-inch slide projector (nonautomatic)
SL(A)	2- by 2-inch slide projector (automatic)
OH	Overhead transparency projector
OP	Opaque projector
TR	Tape recorder
PH	Phonograph playback
TM	Teaching machine
VR	Video-tape recorder

By filing cumulative maintenance record cards of the same classification together and numerically under that heading, the equipment collection records become easily understandable and convenient to use.

SUMMARY

The selection, inventorying, distribution, and maintenance of instructional equipment represent especially important aspects of the work of educational media personnel for, without proper attention to the details of these processes, uses of instructional materials will be seriously hampered. As was true in the case of our previous discussion of instructional materials, the selection of equipment requires full and responsible participation of several types of people—materials specialists, technicians, purchasing staff members, teachers, and students—each contributing his own special knowledge of needs and requirements involved. General criteria pertaining to all instructional equipment, as well as special criteria related to various specific types, must give attention to significant technical, human, and financial factors, no one of which may be ignored. The proper maintenance of these items is also essential; without it, the quality of learning experiences will be reduced by inefficient performance of equipment.

FOR FURTHER INFORMATION

"Audio-Visual Equipment Standards Recommended by AVEAC-SS, 1961," *Educational Screen and Audiovisual Guide,* vol. 41, pp. 373–375, July, 1962.

Baker, Joseph J., and Jon S. Peters: *School Maintenance and Operation,* Interstate Publishers, Danville, Ill., 1963. 278 pp.

Brown, James W., and Richard B. Lewis: "Experiences, Materials, and Equipment for Learning," *The National Elementary Principal,* vol. 40, pp. 15–17, January, 1961.

Brown, James W., and Richard B. Lewis (eds.): *A-V Instructional Materials Manual,* 2d ed., McGraw-Hill, New York, 1964. 192 pp.

Brown, James W., Richard B. Lewis, and Fred F. Harcleroad: *A-V Instruction: Materials and Methods,* 2d ed., McGraw-Hill, New York, 1964, p. 56. (See also Reference Section II on equipment operation.)

Browning, Robert E.: "The Case for Upgrading of Equipment Standards," *Educational Screen and Audiovisual Guide,* vol. 41, pp. 372–373, July, 1962.

Eboch, Sidney C.: *Operating Audio-Visual Equipment,* Chandler Publishers, San Francisco, Calif., 1960. 73 pp.

Erickson, Carlton W. H.: *Administering Audio-Visual Services,* Macmillan, New York, 1959, pp. 293–306.

Finn, James D.: *Audio-Visual Equipment Manual,* Holt, New York, 1959. 363 pp.

Finstad, Allen: "Where Is the Switch?" *Audiovisual Instruction,* vol. 6, pp. 196–198, May, 1961.

Leverenz, Humboldt W., and Malcolm Townley: *The Design of Instructional Equipment: Two Views,* Occasional Paper 8, Technological Development Project, NEA, 1963. 51 pp.

Lewis, William C.: *Television Tape Recorders: A Comparison of Helical Scan Video-tape Recorders,* University of Colorado, Boulder, Colo., April, 1964. 52 pp.

Purchase Guide for Programs in Science, Mathematics, Modern Foreign Language, Ginn, Boston, 1959. 336 pp.

Schuller, Charles F. (ed.): *The School Administrator and His Audio-Visual Program,* Department of Audio-Visual Instruction, NEA, 1954, pp. 60–82.

"Speedy Repair Equals Good Utilization," *Audiovisual Instruction,* p. 153, March, 1963.

White, Lawrence B.: "Analysis of Problems of Maintenance and Operation of Language Laboratories in California High Schools," *California Schools,* vol. 32, pp. 437–455, November, 1961.

Wyman, Raymond: "I Don't Get Asked Much Any More," *Audiovisual Instruction,* vol. 9, p. 350, June, 1964.

chapter 6

Administering
production services

The well-balanced, comprehensive educational media program requires significant quantities of locally produced materials to supplement and round out its offerings of commercially produced items. Some support for this claim is reflected in the Illinois Curriculum Program statement: [1]

> The curriculum should determine the types of instructional materials needed for effective teaching. To accomplish a specific learning objective, teachers often rely upon instructional materials which they prepare locally. There are many instances in the classroom where communication between the teacher and the student becomes difficult because the verbal presentation is inadequate to stimulate a response from each student because of his lack of association between a mental picture and verbal symbols. While there is a multitude of commercially prepared audio and visual instructional materials one must realize that commercially-produced materials cannot possibly fit every teaching situation or answer every teaching need.

Kemp also identifies several reasons to support programs for the local preparation of instructional materials. He says: [2]

> Commercially produced audiovisual materials are, of necessity, general in their treatment of their subject since they must interest widespread audiences. The preparation of materials having a local emphasis is often up to . . . the persons most interested in using them. Such specialized audiovisual materials, prepared locally, help . . . bring meaningful local applications and observations to your class or group. . . .
> The success of such new developments as team teaching, large-group instruction, instructional television, and self-instruction is due in part to the local planning and preparation of creatively conceived audiovisual materials. . . . Because "mass" educational methods promote impersonal teaching, it becomes highly essential to achieve good understanding between instructor and student, to make sure that com-

[1] *Instructional Materials,* Illinois Curriculum Program, Office of the Superintendent of Instruction Administration and Supervision Series, Bulletin A-3, Springfield, Ill., 1961, p. 83.
[2] Jerrold E. Kemp, *Planning and Producing Audiovisual Materials,* Chandler Publishers, San Francisco, Calif., 1963, p. 4.

munciation takes place. And to communicate effectively . . . requires you to develop, prepare, and use appropriate instructional materials of many types in association with the best modern-day teaching methods available to you. . . .

[Most] people—adults and children alike—enjoy preparing audio-visual materials. The learning and the related experiences resulting from such activity easily justify the time and expense involved.

VALUES OF LOCAL PRODUCTION

In their study of practices throughout the United States, Faris, Moldstad, and Frye [3] identified several general values of local production and categorized them under headings of currency, flexibility, and adaptability. In the opinion of these investigators, the currency of locally produced materials derives from their up-to-dateness, their recentness, and their capabilities of "using yesterday's data as part of today's communication." Their flexibility is reflected in the capacity for being reproduced and used in many different forms and ways. A diagram of an organ of the body, for example, might be used first as a large transparency for large-group study via the overhead projector, as an individualized study sheet reproduced through offset printing, as a large wall chart, or in any one of several other forms—each suited to some special teaching requirement. Finally, the adaptability of locally produced materials may be recognized in their uses under various physical and environmental conditions and in the characteristics of the different kinds of audiences or classes to whom their communication is directed.

Local preparation of instructional materials thus may be seen to have several potential values for teachers and students. As one plans or creates a teaching device, for example, he is forced to evaluate the content of his presentation; he becomes more critical of his approach to the communication problem; and he profits from seeing the subject from a new point of view. The planner or creator of an instructional medium or device is also in a position to evaluate its effectiveness as he uses it and to determine ways of improving its content or utilization pattern. The person who receives satisfaction from having planned or produced a valuable instructional device tends to take pride in using it well, just as the student who receives instruction through its use may be especially interested by the personalized presentation and the knowledge that the item was made by the person who uses it. Finally, it should be pointed out that local production frequently provides instructional materials or devices that are otherwise unavailable—perhaps because they are too local in nature to interest commercial producers, who could not expect to recoup production costs by selling only a few copies of them.

[3] Gene Faris, John Moldstad, and Harvey Frye, *Improving the Learning Environment: A Study on the Local Preparation of Visual Instructional Materials,* U.S. Office of Education, 1963. 148 pp.

PRINCIPAL PRODUCTION ACTIVITIES

The most common local production activities for educational purposes and the materials or products of local utility that grow out of them are of the following types:

> *Mounting.* Dry mounting pictures and similar flat materials (with tissue, Chartex); wet mounting (with liquid adhesives); framing (wood, tape, glass); installing three-dimensional objects (in specially designed and labeled cases for display and shipment); laminating (between plastic sheets or in plastic blocks, as in the case of fragile specimens); binding booklets, reports

> *Lettering.* Charts, posters, or display items by freehand brushwork, with lettering guides (stencil types and others), with paste-on or ceramic letters, with various kinds of typewriters or with Embossograph or Line-o-Scribe equipment, or similar means

> *Coloring.* Charts, posters display items with airbrush, commercial adhesives, plastic inks, crayons, tempera, water colors, papers, cellophanes, and similar materials

> *Photographing.* Copying original or textbook drawings; making original black-and-white or color photographs; copying slides; enlarging still pictures (principally black-and-white) to "study print" sizes (and larger); photographing 16mm and 8mm motion pictures; photographing filmstrips from local copy

> *Writing and editing.* Preparing script and storyboard presentations; outlining and writing study guides, booklets and brochures; information leaflets, reports of various kinds, and the like

> *Recording.* Taping radio broadcasts; video-taping TV presentations; recording original sound (concerts, student dramatizations, language exercises, speeches, lectures); video taping original sound and pictures; editing taped materials; duplicating (multiple copies) tapes

> *Reproducing.* Printing press, spirit, stencil and ink, offset (multilith), diazo, thermal (thermofax), liquid developer (verifax), silk screen

> *Constructing.* Felt boards and felt-board materials, dioramas, displays and display boards, special boards (magnetic, peg, plastic insert, and other), puppet and marionette theaters and characters, working models and mockups

It will be noted, of course, that one other highly important production activity—television—is omitted from the above listing. It is treated separately in Chapter 10, "Administering Educational Television."

Faris, Moldstad, and Frye [4] determined in their study of school practices with respect to the local preparation of *visual* instructional materials, that:

> *In individual schools,* the six most frequently produced items were (in this order) graphic materials (charts, posters, etc.), large transparencies (7 by 7 inches and 10 by 10 inches), 2- by 2-inch slides, mounted pictures, photographs, and flannel boards.

[4] *Ibid.,* pp. 21–25.

> *In educational television stations,* the rank order for the top seven items was graphic materials, photographs, mounted pictures, models, exhibits-dioramas-murals, 2- by 2-inch slides, and large transparencies.
> *In school systems,* the rank order for the top six items was 2- by 2-inch slides, photographs, mounted pictures, graphic materials, large transparencies, and flannel boards.

It should be remembered, however, that no effort was made in their study to determine instances and volume of production of many *nonvisual* items contained in the list of principal production activities discussed previously, such as those mentioned under "writing and editing," or "recording."

LOCAL PRODUCTION CRITERIA

Several basic criteria should be considered in appraising the suitability or desirability of proposed local production projects, as suggested by the following:

> *Need.* Is there an important need for instructional materials or devices? May it be satisfied only through some appropriate local production activity? Or is it likely that some already available commercially produced item would serve equally well?
> *Suitability of content.* Will the item's content be appropriate for the group for which it is intended? If the group's previous acquaintance with the subject is advanced and sophisticated, will a locally produced visualization really satisfy the need? Or might it actually contribute negatively toward achievement of goals? Is there evidence that the item, as conceived and executed, does facilitate and develop desirable reactions?
> *Suitability of medium.* Is the visualization, recording, or print presentation medium suitable for the ideas and concepts to be developed as well as for the *conditions* of communication (the physical environment, the psychological setting of the process) involved? Will charted relationships, rather than strictly verbal statements, be needed, for example, to simplify essentially abstract or complicated ideas? And if the communication is to be conducted for large groups rather than small groups, must such visualizations be produced as transparencies for projection rather than as small drawings or charts?
> *Feasibility.* If it is determined that the item is needed and worth producing, do local resources, staff, and facilities suggest that the production is feasible? Is there sufficient time to produce it? Can it be carried through to completion?
> *Practicality.* Is the educational return from the item likely to be sufficient (for the producer, the students, the instructor, the system) to justify the expenditure of time, effort, materials, equipment depreciation?

Quite obviously, the foregoing questions lead inevitably to the more fundamental three-pronged query: *What* instructional materials should be prepared, by *whom,* and *where?* Answers will vary, of course, according to the special purposes, circumstances, and administrative levels involved. Some production activities might be well suited to requirements of a large county or district, for example, but inappropriately expensive or time-consuming for the staff of a single school. Therefore, in the interests of economy and efficiency, the essential task is to determine which activities are appropriate to the unit involved, omitting or leaving to others those which are not.

PRODUCTION WITHIN A SINGLE SCHOOL

Within the single school, it is logical to provide local materials preparation services and facilities that are simple, inexpensive, and "first echelon" in nature, for which needs are immediate and personal, and which cannot be performed so well by others. Such activities are usually of three types:

❯ *Those undertaken by students themselves* as vehicles for significant learning experiences in classrooms or shops or as photographic, artistic, dramatic, audio-visual, or library club activities, and the like
❯ *Those undertaken by teachers* in individual classrooms, in special preparation rooms, or in workshops to provide instructional materials urgently and immediately needed for use in their own classes, as for hallway displays, or similar purposes
❯ *Those undertaken by educational media center personnel* for production within the school building or elsewhere (the district or county media center or through contracts with photo shops, commercial artists, or other outside agencies)

Recommended facilities, supplies, and services

In the typical single elementary school (enrolling perhaps 200 to 400 students), it is reasonable to expect that teachers and, to some extent, students will have access to a materials production room that provides facilities, supplies, and services of the following types:

❯ Mimeograph and spirit duplicators and supplies
❯ One or more drafting tables (tilt-top), suitably lighted, equipped with T-squares and parallel rulers
❯ A light table (with a surface of at least 3 by 4 feet) on which to inspect and sort negatives, slides, and transparencies, and do tracing
❯ Thermal and/or diazo devices (such as thermofax or Ozalid) to be used in producing paper or transparency reproductions of typed, printed, or line-drawn materials
❯ Recording facilities (a special soundproofed, acousticized room in which instructors, technicians, or students may record, duplicate or edit tapes, or record disk to tape live or in a combination of these forms). This room should contain at least two tape recorders, one or more disk playbacks, a mixing panel, and suitable microphone equipment

❯ Paper-cutting equipment, preferably one printshop type, heavy-duty cutter capable of trimming or cutting the equivalent thickness of at least 500 sheets of typing paper at a time, as well as other smaller hand-operated cutting boards

❯ Paper-punching equipment (three-hole and two-hole; perhaps spiral binding types)

❯ One or more large work table areas on which charts or picture materials may be processed for dry or wet mounting

❯ A dry mounting press (preferably one capable of accepting 16- by 20-inch mounts) and tacking iron

❯ One or more 35mm cameras, 8mm or 16mm motion-picture cameras, and Polaroid cameras to be used by teachers in connection with field trips or other special assignments

❯ Various tools (hammers, small saws, pliers, squares, yardsticks, tape measures, staplers and stapler guns, files)

❯ Storage and check-out facilities for local preparation materials and supplies (crayons, precut letters, lettering pens, inks, tagboard, mounting board, pressed board, veneer board, tapes, raw film, felt-board materials, muslin, dry-mount tissue, Chartex, thermo or diazo reproduction sheets and supplies, carbons)

Facilities such as those described above for the typical elementary school should, of course, be supplemented for secondary schools. In such institutions, the preparation room must usually be larger and more adequately equipped and supplied and have, in addition:

❯ Photographic copying equipment, including a copy stand on which is mounted a good 35mm camera (such as the Contaflex), appropriate copying lights, and controls

❯ Simple motion picture (8mm and 16mm) editing equipment, including rewinds, splicers, viewer-editor, editing rack

❯ Photographic darkroom containing developing tanks, trays, contact printer, enlarger, timing devices

❯ Multilith or other offset printing—duplicating equipment

Further information is given in Chapter 12, "Media Services in the Single School," concerning the physical arrangement and administration of the materials preparation activity in the typical single-school instructional materials center. It is the usual practice to encourage students as well as faculty members to use the facilities.

Wayland High School

Production activities for the local preparation of various types of instructional materials at this Massachusetts high school were described by Faris, Moldstad, and Frye.[5] The school has been cited as a pioneer

---

[5] *Ibid.*, p. 65. A further physical description of this school is contained in *Profiles of Significant Schools: Wayland Senior High School, Wayland, Massachusetts,* Educational Facilities Laboratories, Inc., New York, 1963. 28 pp.

in physical plant design and in the dedication of its staff to the critical use and evaluation of innovations in teaching method, curriculum organization, and program administration. Special emphasis is given to team-teaching patterns involving large- and small-group instruction. A full-time staff of approximately thirty-five teachers, supplemented by a number of student teachers from Boston University, are employed in teaching a four-year program for some 600 students.

Early in the present experimental program, Gerald McVey, a "communications specialist," was added to the staff to work as part of a teaching team to suggest effective means and methods of informing and instructing student groups of various sizes, to supply expert advice on sources of appropriate materials, and to assist in producing various required audio-visual materials for instructional presentations. Characteristics of his work are suggested by the following description of typical activities: [6]

> Last fall the team of teachers responsible for the course in American history wanted to develop the best unit possible on the Civil War. The American history teachers collaborated with the music instructor, the art instructor, the instructor of American literature, and Mr. McVey to plan an integrated presentation they thought would best communicate the essential understandings and appreciations of this important period in our country's development. Related films, specially taped musical selections, colored slides, projected maps, etc., were all programmed into this series of presentations to approximately 150 students enrolled in American history. Other instructional materials were developed for use in the follow-up small group discussions. Twelve student assistants, working under the instructional coordinator's direction, assisted in the actual production of many of the locally developed teaching materials.

To facilitate these local production activities, a special 8- by 14-foot production or preparation room was equipped in the school. In it were placed:

Dry mount press
Laminating equipment
Cloth mounting facilities
Various lettering devices and supplies
Coloring equipment (including airbrush) and supplies
Several still cameras (35mm, 4 by 5 inches, 2¼ by 2¼ inches, Polaroid)
Photographic enlarger and darkroom equipment
Copy camera equipment
16mm movie camera, tripods, etc.
Reflex copy (thermal, wet) devices
Ditto and mimeograph equipment
Diazo reproduction equipment (especially for overhead transparency productions)
Silk screen equipment
Supplies of paper, inks, tagboard, etc.

[6] Faris, Moldstad, and Frye, *op. cit.,* p. 66.

A special budget was set aside in the high school to provide supplies and to contract services for the production of needed teaching materials.

PRODUCTION AT THE COUNTY OR DISTRICT LEVEL

The county or district educational media center is said to serve best in supplementing or complementing the materials preparation activities of the single school by producing items that (1) do not require close personal contact between teacher and graphic or audio specialist; (2) may be developed jointly through cooperative efforts of individuals in several schools or on the staff of the central administrative office; or (3) merit standardized duplication (as in the case of tape recordings, slide sets, photographic study print sets, and the like) into multiple sets for use throughout the system. Media centers at this level also function appropriately in developing specifications and inviting bids from commercial agencies for special film productions, "outside" processing (commercial photographic services for copying, printing, and mounting slide or transparency materials, mounting flat pictures, enlarging pictures for study print sets, and others), or design and artwork (chart making, bulletin layout, display design).

Alameda County Schools

The Alameda County (California) schools maintain a Division of Curricular Services. It is comprised of an audio-visual section, a library for the schools, a curriculum library of professional materials, and an audiovisual production laboratory. Activities of the production laboratory are intended "to meet specific needs of the local curriculum [and] to meet general needs of the curriculum where materials are not available from commercial sources." [7] Activities of this center include preparation of the following instructional materials:

❯ *Study print packets.* These are specially edited collections of 11- by 14-inch photographs by the center's staff photographer or purchased from commercial suppliers. Collections are packaged in special tied folders, complete with study guides and utilization suggestions. Local productions emphasize activities and landmarks of Alameda County and the Bay Area.
❯ *Slide units, 2 by 2 inches.* Units are specially planned and photographed by the staff photographer and edited for continuity and emphasis. Study and utilization guides are included.
❯ *Duplicated tapes.* These are copies of original tape recordings of speeches, conferences, discussions, dramatizations and of noncopyrighted

[7] Rock LaFleche, Superintendent of schools, Alameda County Schools, Hayward, Calif. *Curriculum Materials Center,* 1960, p. 10.

tapes (such as those from the DAVI collection, which are distributed by the University of Colorado) in a master tape file.

> *Charts.* Original layout and artwork is provided by the center, including professional suggestions on visualization possibilities; special applications to the work of central office staff members in the schools.

> *Pictorial resource material for teacher education.* Still pictures (principally black and white) illustrating county office publications for use in displays and for other informational purposes are produced.

> *Kits.* Specimens and artifacts boxed to facilitate shipment to county schools, with accompanying study and utilization guides are prepared.

The photographic staff for local materials preparation consists of two photographers and one photographic clerk. Services of a graphics artist are also available from another of the county schools offices.

The production unit maintains an indexed file of negatives and positive proof prints for all staff photographs. Positive prints not used for a period of five years are destroyed, but all negatives are indexed and kept indefinitely. A principal activity of the unit is making black-and-white photographs for various school districts within the county. Costs of this service are defrayed from the regular curriculum-materials contracts between the county and the districts. All photographic work done must make an educational contribution for the district involved; no work is done on a personal basis.

The unit's facilities include (1) two darkrooms; (2) a production room, in which are contained mounts, presses, copying racks, lighting stands, and similar equipment; and (3) an art room for the preparation of graphics.

San Diego County Schools

The schools in San Diego County, California, recently undertook a rather unusual community educational resources project to "discover men, materials, and ideas" within the local community to "reduce the time lag between the development of new knowledge and its availability to the teacher and learner . . . and to identify and organize the community resources . . . so as to bring about their most effective and efficient utilization in the instructional program." [8] A central staff, headed by Ronald L. Hunt, coordinates the project, which seeks to enrich the curriculum of schools in the San Diego region, and improve instruction in the main subject areas. Special materials and resources of interest include (1) films, filmstrips, slides, and other photographic and printed materials; (2) manpower for preparation of instructional materials, in-service education of teachers, and consultation; (3) visits to local industrial and government plants and seminars for students, teachers, and administrators; (4) collections and catalogs of specimens or equip-

[8] Ronald L. Hunt, *Discovering Men, Materials, and Ideas,* Community Educational Resources Project, San Diego County Department of Education, San Diego, Calif., 1961, p. 1.

ment for experiments, with supplementary information; (5) demonstrations and supplementary teaching by experts in the area during regular class hours or after school; and (6) opportunities for students to obtain useful experience on a first-hand basis while engaging in various activities in selected industrial and other situations.

Task groups of teachers, administrators, and representatives of community agencies and organizations often cooperate on specific projects, many of which eventuate in kits of study materials concerning the curriculum and including such items as films, filmstrips, slides, study prints, resource lists of people, program and activities descriptions, manuals, and guides.

The educational value of these activities may be judged from a partial listing of projects undertaken or completed within the past few years: (1) establishment of a common area directory for the more than seventy special libraries maintained by industrial, commercial, education, and local-county-state-Federal agencies in the region; (2) development for school use of a botanical garden containing rare live plants in an ecological situation; (3) organization and dissemination of information about space and space problems, utilizing sound filmstrips, educational films, information pamphlets, and picture sets; (4) preparation of large study prints and a filmstrip for groups visiting the San Diego Zoo; and (5) production of sets of biology slides from a local United States Navy hospital, as well as tissue cultures, X-ray films, and materials for radioisotope experiments. Still other materials have been developed to aid studies of nuclear energy, plasma physics, cyrogenics, human communication, oceanographic research, modern medicine, and computers.

PRODUCTION AT THE STATE LEVEL

Noel and others [9] reported materials production activities by educational media personnel during the year 1960–1961 in twenty-one of fifty state departments of education. Thirty 16mm films were produced by eight states; one state produced one 8mm sound film. Thirty-three filmstrips were produced in four states; nine states produced relatively small numbers of slides; seven were involved in producing overhead transparencies. Magnetic tape recordings produced or duplicated (including language tapes) totaled approximately 58,000, but no disk recordings were produced; video tapes were produced in only two states. Only one state reported production of a programmed textbook, but five had produced numbers of graphic materials (charts) larger than 18 by 24 inches and four reported smaller charts.

[9] Francis W. Noel and others, *Practices of State Departments of Education in New Educational Media/Audiovisual Education During 1960-61,* University of Southern California, Los Angeles, Calif., 1963, II-72-74.

Summarizing the findings, Noel observes: [10]

> If number of states engaged in production [national spread] is the
> [criterion] . . ., slides are the most common items produced [by
> state departments of education] for public school use; 16mm sound
> motion pictures and magnetic tapes are second in importance. . . .
> If numbers of materials produced [is the criterion], the most important
> production activity . . . would be that of production of magnetic
> tapes. Radio broadcasts were second in importance; television, when
> combined with video tapes, was third. Production of graphic materials
> was fourth in importance throughout the nation.

Virginia State Department of Education

The department's Education Film Production Service has been headed
since 1946 by J. E. Oglesby and is somewhat unique among state departments. In its first fifteen years, it produced more than sixty 16mm sound
films as well as large numbers of 35mm filmstrips, 2- by 2-inch slides
and slide sets, and tape recordings. Although its films are intended
primarily for instructional uses in Virginia schools, prints have been
sold throughout the United States. Film production services of the unit
are also available to other Virginia agencies.

Film production requests usually originate with professional personnel in a county or city school division, the Virginia State Department
of Education, or with the heads of state agencies. Approval by the
state superintendent of public instruction and the Governor on subject-
matter content and purpose of the film is required before a production
is authorized.

The supervisor of the Film Production Service is directly responsible to the head of the Division of Publications and Teaching Materials,
which also contains the Library Section and the Film Distribution Section. Additional staff members are two film specialists, who do research,
write scripts, and direct and edit films; one assistant supervisor, who is
responsible for camera and sound; and a stenographer-clerk, who is
responsible for typing and handling records pertaining to sales and
distribution.

The Service has a budget of $50,000 per year from the Virginia
State Department of Education. This sum covers costs of production
of from four to six reels of sound-color 16mm film, black-and-white
photographs for publicity and general information, conference recording, and miscellaneous functions, such as advising and conferring with
school personnel and various state agencies on production problems.
Prints of films and other productions are available to Virginia schools
and state agencies at actual cost. By 1962, more than 1,400 film prints
were in use in Virginia.

The Service estimates its sound-color film production costs to be
approximately $700 per ten-minute reel for materials and $2,000 for

[10] *Ibid.*, II-74.

salaries, or $2,700 per reel in all, as compared with the usual estimated cost of $12,000 per reel for comparable commercial productions. Some appreciation of the range and character of subjects covered may be had from the selected in-print titles now circulated: *The Elementary School (Three Parts); Field Trip; Teaching Materials Center; Tippecanoe and Tyler Too; James Monroe; George Mason of Gunston Hall; Jamestown: Place of Beginnings; Captain John Smith: Explorer; Jefferson of Monticello; Common Law; Modern World of Industrial Arts; Distributive Education; School Bus Safety; Mosquito Control; Commercial Fishing in the Chesapeake; Virginia's Fishing Industry; Natural Wonders of Virginia; Maps and Pioneers; Dismal Swamp; The Character of Lee; Inauguration of the Governor of Virginia;* and *Marine Animals on the Virignia Coast.*

PRODUCTION IN HIGHER EDUCATION

Local production activities at the higher educational level show interesting developments which have been stimulated, in part, by rapidly increasing college enrollments, shortages of qualified faculty, inadequate facilities, and budgetary restrictions. The college instructor has often seemed the least willing of all educators to make "standardized" presentations of course materials through "systems," interinstitutional television networks, large-group instruction, programmed instruction, or team teaching. But there are promising and hopeful signs of change. The pressure of numbers alone demands serious consideration of procedures and resources suited to teaching large groups in appropriate circumstances. Thus there is frequent use of locally prepared instructional materials—the large transparencies (for the overhead projector), short film clips, 2- by 2-inch slides, and charts—in large-group instruction particularly.

In response to such needs, most colleges and universities now attempt to provide local preparation services through their educational media centers.

San Jose State College

San Jose State College enrolls some 20,000 students and has a faculty of approximately 1,200. Its Materials Preparation Service is part of the Division of Audio-Visual Services, and its purpose is "to assist faculty members by preparing teaching materials not available commercially for specific instructional needs." The staff numbers five: (1) a coordinator, who is of professional level and has a doctorate in education and a specialty in the production field; (2) two photographers, who are qualified to do still and motion-picture photographic work; and (3) two graphic artists, who are skilled in a variety of graphic arts techniques.

Production requests go first to the coordinator, who is responsible for discussing plans and needs with faculty members, assessing priority ratings, and advising on the selection of the most suitable medium. The coordinator encourages the faculty member to analyze his instructional problem and to ask: What do I want to achieve? What behavioral changes do I wish to bring about in my students? What particular characteristics of the student audience must I consider in preparing the proposed materials? Under what environmental conditions will they be used—in a large auditorium, in a small classroom, under conditions rated "good" or "poor" for auditioning or viewing? What particular characteristics of the "message" to be communicated must be given special consideration? Will it be necessary, for example, to show actual motion? Must natural sound be available? Is color essential? Will juxtaposed scenes be needed for comparison purposes? [11]

Principal production activities, in rank order of volume, are:

➤ Copying 2- by 2-inch slide materials (from textbooks, charts, photographs, other slides)
➤ Taking black-and-white pictures and preparing 8- by 10-inch glossies
➤ Preparing visualized chart and diagrammatic materials (usually in 20- by 30-inch format)
➤ Preparing large transparencies for use in overhead projectors
➤ Taking or rephotographing 35mm color pictures (photographing original works of art for the art department) to be used as 2- by 2-inch slides
➤ Photographing and editing 8mm and 16mm silent-film footage for specialized teaching problems (relatively infrequent)

Recording services, administratively related to the Division, also account for a considerable volume of local production activity. Original recording and tape duplication services are provided.

ADMINISTERING LOCAL PRODUCTION

Various procedures are needed to ensure satisfactory interpretation and application of the local production criteria discussed earlier. Each is intended to make sure of the approval and execution of projects that are needed, suitable as to content and medium selected, feasible for the situation, and practical—worth the money, time, and effort and not already on hand or available through commercial sources.

Advisory committee

A small group of people who have a broad knowledge of curriculum or training problems is sometimes helpful to the educational media

[11] These and other related ideas are developed at more length in Jerrold E. Kemp, "Planning for Local Production," *Audiovisual Instruction*, vol. 8, pp. 296–298, May, 1963.

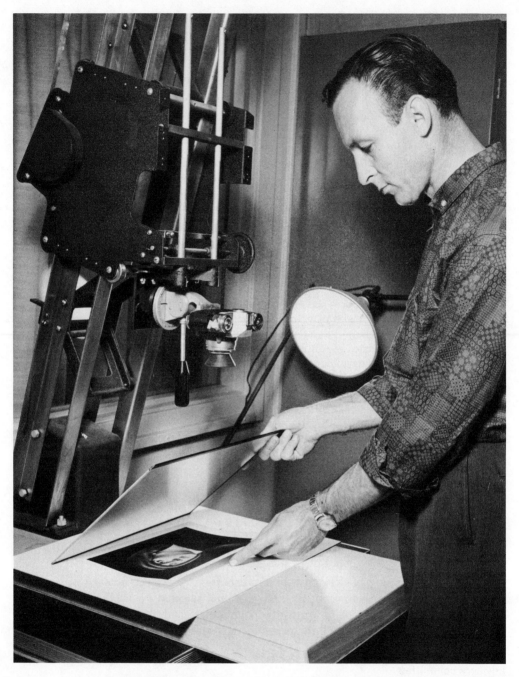

A single-lens reflex 35mm camera provides a simple means of reproducing photographs and drawings as 2-inch by 2-inch transparencies. (*San Jose State College*)

Local production of simple charts often does much to improve the quality of teaching. (*San Diego County Schools*)

administrator who must decide whether or not to produce the proposed item. Other specialists may serve with the committee on an *ad hoc* basis as the need arises. The production service head may serve as its chairman and executive head of the committee.

One of the first activities of such a committee should be proposing for official approval a preliminary set of policy statements to guide its deliberations and work. Many proposed projects may be approved or rejected on the basis of such a guide without any reference to the full committee; some may be referred to a smaller subcommittee; and some may require the consideration of the full committee.

Perhaps the greatest contribution of this committee is strengthening the unit's resolution to produce only projects that have been carefully thought out and to reject those proposed prematurely, with only off-the-cuff thinking.

Some form of centralized control of local production activities, however simple, is needed to avoid confusion, wasted effort, inaccuracies, misunderstandings, or careless approval of unnecessary projects. The following control procedures are recommended:

❯ *Assign a project number* to the original proposal. Place it on all records pertaining to the project to facilitate collating data.

❯ *Discuss the proposal* with its author, referring to established policies and criteria. If they are met, agree on additional data or actions needed to proceed with the recommendation; if they are not, recommend appropriate action, such as referral to the policy committee, or disapproval.

❯ *Develop an accurate* over-all statement of project specifications and requirements. Deadlines should also be estimated and noted.

❯ *Organize assignments* and distribute to various responsible personnel (photography, art, etc.).

❯ *Enter appropriate data on a* project progress chart or file board to facilitate checking on the current status of all projects.

❯ *Require progress reports* including data on time spent, materials, and other items. These progress reports may prompt the production supervisor to check the adequacy, suitability, or expense of work periodically.

❯ *Collate and summarize records* upon completion of the project.

❯ *Discuss finished project* with its sponsor, noting positive or negative reactions, and if necessary, correcting or adjusting the production before its release.

❯ *Establish a follow-up date* or schedule to obtain feedback as to its eventual use and value.

❯ *Summarize and evaluate* production records regularly (weekly, monthly, yearly) to appraise the scope and worth of production activities and to determine activities or functions needing strengthening or improvement.

Production contracts and specifications

The local production supervisor sometimes needs to use the services and facilities of commercial photographers, artists, motion-picture or recording studios, and record-pressing or tape duplicating laboratories of private organizations. He is often required to develop detailed specifications and bid proposals that have the force of business agreements, with the help of the business management officials in his organization. The expert assistance of the institution's purchasing agent should be sought in wording such contracts or bid invitations. In their preparation, special attention should be given to such matters as time of delivery, length, format and quality, specific costs for the first and subsequent copies, assurance of freedom from copyright infringement or suit for plagiarism, invasion of privacy, or libel.

Copyrights and permissions

Local production activities sometimes include two practices that have legal significance. The first and probably most common is taking pictures of individuals without their permission, with the subsequent possibility of suit on grounds of invasion of privacy; the second is reproducing copyrighted materials.

In his production guidebook, Kemp says: [12]

> Everyone has the right to control the use of pictures of himself or his property. If you are making audiovisual materials you must respect this right. If you fail to do so, you may expose yourself to personal, professional, or financial embarrassment. Specifically, a person may either permit you or forbid you to show pictures of himself, his children, or his property. It does not matter whether you show them free, or for a compensation, to a large or small audience, or whether you show them yourself or turn them over to someone else to be shown.
>
> Most people readily agree to being filmed and to having the pictures used, but you should protect yourself and your associates by having them *sign a release form.* . . . The release authorizing the use of pictures of a minor child must be signed by the parent.
>
> A special kind of property that must be covered in a signed release is the property in copyrighted materials—commonly books, magazines, and other printed matter, and commercial films. In this case, you must get the clearance from owner of the *copyright,* not the owner of the *object.* (You may own this book; but you do not own the copyright in it—see the back of the title page.) You will be wise if you assume that books and the like are copyrighted, and seek clearance before you use pictures from them or parts of them in your audiovisual materials.

Notice of copyright, giving date of copyright and its holder, must appear on printed items. The copyright date, the year of publication,

---

[12] Kemp, *Planning and Producing Audiovisual Materials,* pp. 22–23.

PERMISSION FORM

Date_____

I hereby give permission to (Insert name of individual, group, or institution) to make pictures of me, of my minor child (Insert name of child), or of materials owned by me and to put the finished pictures to any legitimate use without limitation or reservation.

Signature_____
Name (printed)_____
Address_____
City_____ State_____

Project_____
Project Director_____

```
              PERMISSION REQUEST (COPYRIGHTED MATERIALS)

                                       Date_____
TO:  _____
     _____
FROM:_____
     _____


   I should appreciate receiving your permission to reproduce
without fee the material(s) itemized below for use as
indicated:
   (In this space, cite volume, page numbers, picture or
   chart title, or other data to serve to identify the
   item.)




The item(s) will be used as follows:

(In this space, describe specifically the manner in which
the items will be reproduced, the number of copies to be
made, and the manner and circumstances under which they
will be used.)

                         Your signature_____
                         Title_____
                         Institution_____
                         Address_____
- - - - - - - - - - - - - - - - - - - - - - - - - - - - - - - - -
(Please sign one copy and return in enclosed self-addressed,
stamped envelope.)
Permission is hereby granted to use the material(s) described
above in the manner you have specified.

                         Signature_____
                         Official Title_____
                         Organization_____
```

---

appears in books on the title page or page following. On works of art, a symbol (a circled letter "c") accompanied by initials, monogram, trademark, or other symbol denoting the copyright holder may be used. It should be remembered that under the present law the first copyright remains in force for twenty-eight years and that one renewal is allowed —making the protected period fifty-six years in all. For further information concerning copyrights or restrictions pertaining to them, write to the Register of Copyrights, Library of Congress, Washington, D.C.

SUMMARY

The well-balanced educational program provides for the local production of various types of instructional materials to supplement commercial products, which—since they are designed to have wide market appeal—cannot always satisfy the unique demands of all teaching-learning activities. Locally produced materials can often meet such unique requirements without great expense, and thus enrich the school program in important ways.

Principal local production activities have been identified in this chapter as (1) mounting pictures, charts, and other flat materials; (2) lettering and coloring charts, posters, and display items; (3) photographing; (4) writing and editing; (5) recording—largely of tapes; and (6) constructing displays and models.

Recommended criteria for approving local production projects are based on (1) curricular need, (2) suitability of content, (3) suitability of medium, and (4) feasibility and practicality of production. The single most important question related to application of these criteria is: *What* instructional materials should be prepared locally, *for whom,* and *where?* It has been emphasized here that such production may be undertaken in the single school by both teachers and students, as well as by specialized personnel in the educational media center of the school, school district, county schools office, the state department of education, a university or college, or other agency. Similar criteria guide production policies at each of these levels.

FOR FURTHER INFORMATION

Bridges for Ideas, University of Texas Extension Division, Visual Instruction Bureau Series, Austin, Tex.

Brown, James W., and Richard B. Lewis (eds.): *A-V Instructional Materials Manual,* 2d ed., McGraw-Hill, New York, 1964.

Brown, James W., Richard B. Lewis, and Fred F. Harcleroad: *A-V Instruction: Materials and Methods,* 2d ed., McGraw-Hill, New York, 1964.

DeJean, Jean: *Visual Presentation Handbook for Business and Industry,* Oravisual Company, Inc., St. Petersburg, Fla., 1959.

Faris, Gene, John Moldstad, and Harvey Frye: *Improving the Learning Environment: A Study on the Local Preparation of Visual Instructional Materials,* U.S. Office of Education, 1963. 148 pp.

Frye, Roy A.: *Graphic Tools for Teachers,* 2d ed., E. and I. Printing Company, Austin, Tex., 1963.

Frye, Roy A.: "Take-home Workshops for In-service Training," *Audiovisual Instruction,* vol. 8, pp. 314–315, May, 1963.

Haas, Kenneth Robert, and Harry Q. Packer: *The Preparation and Use of Audiovisual Aids,* 3d ed., Prentice-Hall, Englewood Cliffs, N.J., 1955.

Hines, Robert: "Skill Training via Tapes and Transparencies," *Audiovisual Instruction,* vol. 8, pp. 311–313, May, 1963.

Kemp, Jerrold E.: *Planning and Producing Audiovisual Materials,* Chandler Publishers, San Francisco, Calif., 1963.

Kemp, Jerrold E.: "Planning for Local Production," *Audiovisual Instruction,* vol. 8, pp. 296–298, May, 1963.

LeMay, James E., and Eric F. Burtis: *They See What You Mean: Visual Communication with the Overhead Projector,* Audio-Visual Department, General Aniline and Film Corporation, Johnson City, N.Y., 1959. 88 pp.

Melcher, Daniel, and Nancy Larrick: *Printing and Promotion Handbook,* McGraw-Hill, New York, 1956. 438 pp.

Minor, Ed: *Simplified Techniques for Preparing Visual Instructional Materials,* McGraw-Hill, New York, 1962.

Morlan, John E.: *Preparation of Inexpensive Teaching Materials,* Chandler Publishers, San Francisco, Calif., 1963. 102 pp.

Veenendaal, W. L.: "The Literature of Local Production," *Audiovisual Instruction,* vol. 8, pp. 324–330, May, 1963.

Weisgerber, Robert A.: "Educational Film Production: Profiles of a Process," *Audiovisual Instruction,* vol. 8, pp. 299–303, May, 1963.

Whitney, Elwood: *Symbology: Report on the Fourth Communications Conference of the Art Directors Club of New York,* Hastings House, New York, 1960.

Williams, Don G., and Luella Snyder: *Motion Picture Production Facilities of Selected Colleges and Universities,* U.S. Department of Health, Education, and Welfare Bulletin no. 15, OE-51005, 1963.

chapter 7

Budgeting

In a limited sense, the budget of any enterprise is simply a formal statement of anticipated revenues and expenditures for a given period. In public school systems or institutions of higher education, budget proposals are drawn up for adoption by a legally constituted authority that has the power to authorize appropriation of public funds. A similar procedure is followed in the case of private institutions, whose budgets are subject to approval by their own boards. Hence, it is hardly surprising that an educational budget is sometimes regarded as a document put together primarily to satisfy certain legal, control, and accounting purposes. This it is, but it is also a great deal more.

Although the budget serves as a kind of formal contractual instrument that sets financial conditions and limits, its fundamental meaning and validity can only be determined with regard to the goals of the program it is intended to implement. Basically, a budget is the financial aspect of a plan. The larger view of educational budget making is described by Osview and Castetter as:[1]

A process that emphasizes means by which a community's educational aspirations may be achieved

A process of planning educational policy which is then brought into existence through the mechanical facilities of the budget

A process which is viewed as an indispensable tool of good management, rather than as a legal burden

A process which encourages wide involvement of people, the side effects of which may be nearly as important as the budget document itself.

According to an old saying, "if wishes were horses, beggars would ride." Budget making is a sometimes painful reminder that wishes are not horses. Yet the first requirement of a good budget is a good wish. The second, perhaps, is that we know something about horses or the means of making the wish come true and assess their relative value and availability in comparison with alternative means of reaching the goal. An educational budget can be only as good as the community's

[1] Leon Osview and William B. Castetter, *Budgeting for Better Schools,* Prentice-Hall, Englewood Cliffs, N.J., 1960, pp. 11–12.

aspirations for the education of its people, the young and the old. But aspirations are only daydreams until they are translated into specific aims and plans. One of the most critical tasks of the chief administrative officer of an educational program is seeing that the goals of the enterprise are properly reflected in budgetary planning for departmental activities; in addition, he must see that departmental budgets are developed at the proper levels of administrative responsibility and with suitable coordination by those who must administer and coordinate them. Let us see how this applies to the development of the educational media budget.

BUDGETING FOR EDUCATIONAL MEDIA SERVICES: SOME GENERAL CONSIDERATIONS

Most school systems and institutions of higher education do not have a single department or administrative unit that is responsible for the organization and use of all media. In some cases, an instructional-materials or learning resources center may have such an inclusive jurisdiction; the more typical situation involves some separation of media functions. More often than not, the separation results in two, three, four, or even more discrete departments or programs. Many modern school systems have a library, an audio-visual program, language laboratories, a television and/or radio instruction division, and each may go its own separate way. Very often the administration of textbooks constitutes still another separate element. In higher education, the case is essentially the same. It becomes necessary, therefore, to ask what an educational media budget is and who should have the responsibility for planning and administering it.

Planning the total educational media budget

One aspect of the budgetary problem concerns the extent to which the various media services can or should be separate for purposes of administration and/or budget planning and how such separation (or integration) may affect the operation and economy of the whole instructional system.

Theoretically, it could be argued that all instructional media—print and nonprint—should be administered as a unified program and that one departmental administrator should coordinate the development of its budget. This would make for economy by reducing unnecessary duplication of facilities, equipment, and personnel. It would also allow for thorough and systematic coordination of various instructional resources, which becomes increasingly important as technology accelerates. Contrary arguments could be advanced on the grounds that departmental programs tend to become less efficient if they are too large and inclusive or that individual programs get more support from separate budgets than from a combined budget. In addition, it could be said that unified programs may become extremely complex and that properly qualified administrators to head such programs and provide effective and impartial leadership are rare. The question of integration or non-integration of the various media is, of course, not the subject of this chapter. For the present, it is sufficient to point out that the problem exists and has important implications for budget planning.

Returning to one of the basic assumptions outlined in the opening chapter, the authors propose that—regardless of administrative arrangements in any particular case—the various facets of all educational media resources be viewed as a unitary system or a closely related cluster of departmental operations *at some level,* especially in certain critical phases of administrative planning. When library, audio-visual, and other media services are administered as separate departments, each having its own budget-making procedures, the development of the several budgets must be properly coordinated and viewed from a common perspective at the next higher level of administrative authority.

In a public school system, an assistant superintendent in charge of instruction might act as chairman of a central planning group and represent *all* media services, including audio-visual, library, television and radio, textbooks, or any combination of them. This central planning group would relate the media services to the system's total instructional objectives and plans; it would thus provide an overview of media functions and tasks that would serve as a point of departure for departmental budgets. In addition, the central planning group (possibly called the educational media council) could review tentative drafts of departmental budgets to ensure coordination of resources and the development of articulated and complementary services. Similar procedures could be followed in a college or university under the direction of the chief administrative officer for the academic program.

Planning and administering the departmental media budget

In educational administration, the so-called "unit type" of organization is generally accepted as the desirable pattern. One person, the chief administrative officer, is responsible for the total educational enterprise, including the instructional program and its related business or financial affairs. The latter usually fall under the direct control of an assistant superintendent, vice-president, or business manager. Usually, the organization of media services, such as a library, audio-visual center, or instructional-materials center, is similar; one person has full responsibility for the program, including the development and administration of the departmental budget. This is desirable and consistent with the notion of centrally coordinated planning of all media services as discussed in the preceding section.

In most large school systems, colleges, and universities, modern education requires a central department or departments of media services combined with related decentralized services. Here we shall deal almost exclusively with budgeting for centralized media programs. Such programs, of course, usually include provisions for decentralized facilities in individual schools or sectors of an institution of higher education.

Budget planning is sometimes complicated by the fact that some systems and institutions still fail either to centralize media services that should be centrally administered or to follow consistently the principle of unit organization of media services that are administered as a centralized departmental operation.

At first glance, it might appear that media services that have not been centrally organized do not represent a budgetary problem. This is partially true, since the nonexistence of a centralized program or organization often limits or drastically inhibits the use of the media. Of course, a nonexistent department has no budget problem—but the institution has—it is simply suppressed, clouded, and dispersed. The problem is that instructional services related to the use of certain media —say, audio-visual instructional materials—are not properly organized and discharged by some appropriate central agency. Thus, they are thrust like unwanted and deprived stepchildren upon inhospitable agencies or departments that were not constituted to take care of them in the first place and would rather not have to bother with them at all.

Another type of administrative budgetary problem exists in some cases—mostly public school systems—where technical and clerical personnel performing audio-visual or other media services report to an administrator who is not "in charge" of the departmental services. In such cases, it is questionable whether the head of the media program has adequate administrative control to properly discharge his responsibilities. Even though he develops the departmental budget, he must rely upon clerical assistants who are not responsible to him to process purchase orders, keep accounts and records, and carry out other functions that may not be under his surveillance and control. Such a system *can* work reasonably well, but it appears to be wrong in principle. In time, it tends to lead to results at the departmental level similar to those growing out of the multiple type of administrative organization for the educational program as a whole.

Conversely, it might be argued that the head of an educational media department is a professional and that he should be concerned primarily with supervisory and consultative activities and that he should be relieved of fiscal or business concerns in order to properly discharge his professional functions. Support for this argument can be found in many situations, and some textbooks on school administration (even recent ones!) propose that the purchasing of all equipment and supplies, including instructional materials, should be centralized. This is a perfectly sound notion from the standpoint of good business practice; in the modern school, however, it may run counter to expanding departmental programs, such as new media services, which require a rather high degree of autonomy and flexibility in planning, selecting, and acquiring facilities, equipment, and materials that do not necessarily fit into comprehensive standard lists and must be put together as an integrated package of instructional resources.

"Performance budgeting" versus "object budgeting"

It may be economical and desirable in some situations to centralize certain fiscal procedures, such as purchasing and accounting, but there are definite disadvantages and dangers in lumping together all materials, supplies, and equipment for general budget-planning purposes without regard to function. The problem is brought into focus in discussions of performance budgeting as opposed to the more conventional object budget.[2]

> The school budget today is usually an object classification which shows what education buys (teacher time, books, chairs), not what it does (teach math, science, history). An object classification fails to show the nature of the educational program or the accomplishments under the program. No doubt the object-centered budget is necessary for many reasons, but a systems analysis approach requires a more useful and probably an additional, accumulation of costs—an accumulation which collects and assigns costs to major inputs in combinations that carry out tasks or functions.

The school or college budget is an expression of educational policy and a tool of management that should reflect thorough and systematic planning. Planning for educational media at the departmental level must begin with the objectives of the entire instructional program and a definite conception of the part that the media will play in achieving those objectives. Since media are, by definition, means of reaching goals, the use of any particular medium or combination of media can be justified only as a selection from a set of alternatives. Selecting from a set of alternative means is implicit in all educational budget planning, but it tends to remain implicit once a system of operations has been established. A functional or "systems" approach, beginning with objectives and tasks to be performed, rather than a list of objects used or customary annual expenditures, helps to keep this fact in view. This is not to deny the necessity or importance of budget categories that are uniform from period to period or from one institution to another. A system of budget categories, such as that given in the U.S. Office of Education publication *Financial Accounting for Local and State School Systems*,[3] has great value in facilitating accounting procedures or serving as a basis of compiling data for comparisons. The fault or the problem lies not in their formal use as an accounting device,

[2] James Mauch, "A Systems Analysis Approach to Education," *Phi Delta Kappan*, vol. 43, p. 159, January, 1962.
[3] Available from U.S. Government Printing Office, Washington, D.C.

but in allowing such formal categories to get in the way of an analysis of needs as the basis for planning.

THREE LEVELS OF BUDGETING

The basic elements of budget planning are these: surveying the task to be done; ascertaining the tools and services required; determining what resources are already at hand; and deciding what additional resources will be required, taking into account their relative effectiveness and possibility of assembling and paying for them. Budgets vary with changing goals and plans for achieving them. If goals and procedures remained unaltered from year to year, the same budget could be used over and over again, with allowance for replacement and changing costs of goods and labor. But if goals are altered, if sights are raised, or if present means for achieving goals are considered inadequate or out of date, then budget changes must be made to support improvements, new functions, or different means. The degree to which budget making is governed by present goals and norms or seeks to establish some higher standard can be described in terms of three levels of planning.

Level 1, or continuity budgeting is budget planning in its simplest aspect, and it is demonstrated when a program is already under way and is to be continued "as is" and without any important modifications, except to provide for increased student enrollment and faculty membership. In such cases, needs can be plotted readily for facilities, salaries, equipment, materials, supplies, etc., making due allowance for replacement and gradually increasing expenditures in all categories to keep pace with enrollment. Actually, this kind of planning for simple continuation of established services or functions is central to a great deal of routine budget making. The validity of this kind of budget development lies in the fact that sound programs typically show continuity and gradual growth. On the other hand, budgeting on the basis of continuity can become a trap if planners are not sufficiently sensitive to possible deficiencies or changing conditions.

Sensitive planning for long-term growth and change can bring continuity budgeting into line with current reality, changing conditions, and emerging needs. There are two approaches to this problem, and both are necessary. One is to take a hard look at the adequacy of the present program in terms of local needs and recognized standards, if they exist. The other is to scrutinize and analyze the program constantly as a system that operates within the total instructional system, and to make the adjustments necessary to allow for effective functioning, recognizing that such adjustments may lead to profound reorganization. These two approaches may be described as budget planning at levels 2 and 3, respectively.

Level 2, or incremental budgeting is concerned primarily with the adequacy of means *in use* to implement an established program. Goals and established functions or procedures for reaching them are not at issue in any important sense. The question is only whether the present means or tools are sufficient. There are two common ways of dealing with this problem. One is to determine whether the supply of materials, equipment, and services presently afforded is equal to the demands. (This is relatively simple if requests or demonstrated needs are taken at face value. It becomes more complicated if the awareness and active interest of teachers and students in the potential of the various media and related services are considered.) Another possibly complementary way of dealing with the question of adequacy is to apply standards developed by an authoritative source to set minimum requirements for equipment, staff, facilities, and other factors in consideration of the number of students, faculty, or classrooms being served. When a program is found to be deficient, the incremental expenditures required to correct the deficiency may be spread over a period of years.

A method for combining continuity and incremental budgeting to bring an audio-visual program up to a given standard in terms of equipment and materials over a period of five years is shown later in this chapter. Erickson has outlined a somewhat similar method, showing how systematic long-term budget planning could bring an audio-visual program up to a given norm over a ten-year period.[4] His plan involves a one-year jump to a "desirable minimum" level, followed by a more gradual and evenly spread increase over the remainder of the ten-year period to reach a level of "high adequacy."

In practice, most budgeting for educational media programs is carried on at level 1 and, to some extent, at level 2. Level 2 budgeting may be intermittent or sporadic, depending on fiscal circumstances and the climate of support. Two points should be noted: Mere expansion of facilities to keep pace with expanding enrollments is still level 1 budgeting, since it does not entail an increase in the ratio of instructional resources to the size of the operation; and also, level 2 budgeting becomes self-terminating when the desired standard is attained.

Level 3, or expansion or creative budgeting involves expansion of the educational media program in terms of goals and related functions, reorganization, creative innovation, or any combination of such changes. Level 3 budgeting usually occurs as a result of technological developments or administrative decision to enlarge or reorganize existing programs. It is also prominent in budgeting for media programs in newly formed systems or institutions, where initial planning of resources is involved. Once a program has been formed, once the new pattern has been established, level 3 planning tends to recede into the background, but in these years of stress and change it is hardly ever completely dormant. Of course, the fundamental questions that surround level 3 budgeting are not primarily fiscal problems at all; they are ques-

[4] Carlton W. H. Erickson, *Administering Audio-Visual Services,* Macmillan, New York, 1959, chap. 7.

A summary of the major quantitative standards for school library programs

Type of collection	Delegated administrative responsibility	Location in the school
The collections of printed materials		
The collections in the school library	Head School Librarian	1. School library area or areas, with seating space for at least 45–55 in schools with 200–550 students or fewer and for 10 per cent of the student enrollment in schools having 551 or more students. 2. Classroom collections on short- or long-term loans from the school library.
The collection of professional materials for the school faculty	Head School Librarian	A separate room, either as part of the school library suite or in another part of the school
The collection of supplementary materials (Sets of supplementary texts; classroom reference materials)	Head School Librarian	1. May be housed in a separate area, in the textbook room, or in storage-stack space of the school library. 2. Classroom collections on short- or long-term loans.
The collection of audio-visual materials		
	Head School Librarian or Co-ordinator of Audio-Visual Materials, depending on local school policy and organization	1. The audio-visual center (may be part of the school library suite or a separate center near the library). 2. Classroom collections on short- or long-term loans.

Annual expenditures	*Size of the collections*	*Personnel*
1. Funds for regular library books: in schools having 200–249 students . . . at least $1,000–$1,500. In schools having 250 or more students . . . at least $4.00–$6.00 per student. 2. Additional funds as required for: Encyclopedias, unabridged dictionaries, magazines, newspapers, pamphlets. Rebinding Supplies and equipment.	1. Books: Minimum size of the collections in schools having 200–999 students . . . 6,000–10,000 or more students . . . 10 books per student. 2. Magazines: a. At least the following number of titles in the general magazine collection in Schools having Grades K-6 . . 25 Schools having Grades K-8 . . 50 Junior high schools . . . 70 Senior high schools . . . 120 b. Plus at least 5 titles in the area of librarianship and instructional materials. 3. At least 3–6 newspapers. 4. An extensive collection of pamphlets covering a wide range of subjects.	1. Librarians: For the first 900 students or fraction thereof: 1 librarian for each 300 students or major fraction thereof. For each additional 400 students or major fraction thereof: 1 librarian. 2. Clerks: 1 clerk for each 600 students or major fraction thereof.
For materials, a minimum of $200–$800, depending on the needs and size of the faculty and the availability of other collections of professional materials in the community. Funds for supplies and equipment.	1. Books: At least 200–1,000 titles, the number depending on the needs and size of the faculty and the availability of other collections of professional materials in the community. 2. At least 25–50 professional magazine titles. 3. Other instructional materials as needed.	
1. Funds allocated as needed. These funds are in addition to those recommended above for the school library and for the faculty collection. 2. Funds for supplies and equipment.	1. The size of the collection depends on the needs and enrollment of the school. (Extensive use of school library materials and individualized reading and instructional programs tend to reduce the size of these collections considerably.) 2. The type and number of reference materials purchased for classroom use depend on local school policy.	1. Library clerks as needed in addition to those provided for the school library and audio-visual collections.
1. Not less than 1 per cent of the total per pupil instructional cost ($2.00–$6.00) for the acquisition of audio-visual materials. 2. Funds for supplies and equipment.	1. A sufficient number of all types of audio-visual materials for use in the classrooms, in the school library, and for home use. 2. Films used six or more times a year are purchased. 3. Filmstrips and recordings used more than once a year are purchased.	1. When the head school librarian has partial administrative responsibility for audio-visual materials, the number of librarians and the number of clerks are each increased by 25 per cent. 2. When the head school librarian has full administrative responsibility for audio-visual materials, the number of librarians and the number of clerks are each increased by 50 per cent.

tions of analysis, evaluation, and judgment, which are contextual to all budget planning.

Level 3 budgeting is necessarily involved in taking a fresh look at goals and the organization of technical and human resources used to achieve them. Such an effort, sometimes called the "systems approach to instructional planning," is discussed in the final chapter of this book.

STANDARDS FOR EDUCATIONAL MEDIA PROGRAMS

Budgeting at any level involves a set of standards, implicit or otherwise. The use of objective norms as a basis for incremental budgeting has already been mentioned. Their value is perhaps less obvious for continuity budgeting, which tends to make the going program its own standard, or for level 3 budgeting, which may involve new functions or innovations not covered by existing standards. However, "official" standards from authoritative sources can be very helpful as long as they are used judiciously and applied flexibly. Unfortunately, sets of standards for equipment, materials, staff, etc., are not available for all types of programs. Those discussed here were developed by the American Library Association (ALA) and the Department of Audio-Visual Instruction of the NEA.

In 1960, the ALA published the well-known *Standards for School Library Programs.*[5] A summary of quantitative standards for materials, equipment, facilities, and staff is given in the table. The fact that this publication included standards for audio-visual materials and services was significant both as an expression of ALA policy and because it afforded the first combined set of standards developed by a national organization which could be applied to instructional-materials centers, including both print and audio-visual services. However, it should be noted that these standards were developed from a librarian's viewpoint and on the assumption that audio-visual services could be simply added to the conventional library or not, as the local situation might warrant.

Standards for providing schools with audio-visual equipment and facilities have been developed by the Department of Audio-Visual Instruction of the NEA. The organization recommends a starter set for a typical school of about 500 students:

Equipment or facility	*Where and how many needed*
Projection:	
16mm sound motion-picture projector	One per building; increase with demand for use.
Filmstrip projector and/or 2- by 2-in. slide projector	One per ten classrooms or less; increase with demand for use.
Opaque projector	One per building, if classrooms can be well darkened.

[5] *Standards for School Library Programs,* ALA, Chicago, 1960.

Equipment or facility	Where and how many needed
Overhead projector	One per building; increase with teacher demand.
Microprojector	One per building; only in junior and senior high schools.
Screens (wall)	One per projector (50 by 50 in.); matte white or beaded; less expensive material may suffice.
Screens (portable)	One per building (60 by 60 in.); for auditorium and community use.
Portable equipment stands	One for each projector (roll-away).

Audio:

Record players (10 in. and 12 in.)	One per five classrooms or less; new equipment should be three-speed.
Transcription players (taking 16-in. records)	One per building; should be equipment that can also serve as public-address system.
Radios	One per five classrooms (FM, where FM programs are available); where suitable programs are broadcast daily and where reception is good.
Television receivers	Variable; as required for instruction.
Sound recording device (disk or tape)	One per building; tape only on new purchases; disk for special purposes only.
Public-address system (portable)	One per building; for auditorium or outside uses.
Microphone and floor stand	One per public-address system.

Production: *

2- by 2-in. slide camera	One per district of 1,000 or more pupils; teacher-owned equipment may be adequate.
Motion-picture camera	One per 1,000 or more pupils, if used for instructional purposes and by competent persons.
Photographic darkroom	One per building, if supervised.
Photocopying device	One per 1,000 or more pupils, for making transparencies and photographic aids.

Classroom:

Room darkening equipment	Classrooms in which regular use of projected aids is called for.
Electrical outlets	One at front and rear of all classrooms and on or near all laboratory or workshop tables.

* Production equipment and facilities for the local production of teaching aids are recommended where skilled personnel is available for production or for the supervision of production.

Equipment or facility	*Where and how many needed*
Bulletin boards	Covering approximately one-third of free wall space; interchangeable panels preferred.
Chalkboard	Approximately one-third of free wall space; flexibility in amount and distribution of chalkboard and bulletin board space is desirable.
Filing cabinet	Four-drawer file cabinet in each classroom, to be used in filing flat pictures, pupil records, and other teaching materials.
Exhibit space	Shelf space desirable for exhibits, in addition to the necessary book shelves.
School or educational system:	
Instructional-materials center	One per building and/or floor, one per county or school system desirable; for storage of equipment and materials and as a circulation center for all instructional materials.
Special projection or audio-visual room	Desirable for each school, if not taken as a substitute for darkening of individual classrooms; if construction costs can be justified by uses other than the showing of motion pictures. If acoustically treated, the room can double as a recording studio or little theater.

Source: Jack Tanzman, "An Audio-Visual Program: What You Need Beyond Equipment," *School Management,* vol. 8, p. 131, April, 1963.

For those budgeting audio-visual programs in the schools, the *Guide for Cooperative Evaluation of County and District Audio-Visual Programs,* as developed for the Bureau of Audio-Visual and School Library Education of the California State Department of Education, may be helpful.[6] This publication contains a set of quantitative standards, as well as guidelines for evaluating centralized audio-visual programs.

As a general rule of thumb for budgeting instructional materials and related services, the Department of Audio-Visual Instruction of the NEA, has recommended an annual expenditure of $2 to $6 per student, or about 1 per cent of the annual instructional budget. This corresponds to the audio-visual figure given in the ALA standards for school libraries.

---

[6] *A Guide for Cooperative Evaluation of County and District Audio-Visual Programs,* Bureau of Audio-Visual and School Library Education, California State Department of Education, Sacramento, Calif., 1965.

It should be noted that the 1 per cent recommendation pertains to the conventional audio-visual program and is not intended to cover such media services as television, language laboratories, programmed instruction, etc.

The standards cited thus far pertain to instruction at the high school level and below. The national organizations have not proposed detailed standards for audio-visual programs in higher education in recent years. The ALA *Standards for College Libraries* [7] provides guidelines that emphasize four-year undergraduate instruction; however, the section that deals with audio-visual materials, which are sometimes administered by the library, is cursory and stated in the most general terms. Actually, it would be difficult and somewhat hazardous to develop comprehensive standards for media services in colleges and universities for the middle 1960s. The reasons for this include the rapidly changing technology; changing instructional needs and demands; the new and still exploratory character of developments, such as television, programmed instruction, etc.; and the wide variety of ways in which educational media services are organized and administered. Standards would, of course, be useful to institutions that are developing new media programs or trying to change and improve what they already have; however, standards tend to age very rapidly and sometimes produce rigidity when flexibility and growth potential are needed. Needless to say, the same qualifications should be kept in mind when using the standards for elementary and secondary schools.

A BUDGET–MAKING PROCEDURE

The actual preparation of budgets for educational media programs could be discussed under a variety of headings—audio-visual services, libraries, instructional-materials centers, instructional-resources programs, and television and radio—and some integrated media programs combine some or all of them. A detailed discussion of budgets for all possible media programs would be cumbersome and repetitive. Budgeting for conventional libraries is adequately covered in other publications and need not be considered here. Budgeting for television and radio is highly specialized and rather complicated and will not be treated in this chapter. Some general comments on costs of equipment and other factors involved in budgeting for instructional television are given in Chapter 10. In this section, we will confine the more detailed discussion of budgeting to the audio-visual program.

The following discussion outlines steps for arriving at estimates of actual costs of implementing the audio-visual media program in a school whose objectives, standards, and present resources are known.

[7] *Standards for College Libraries* (adopted by ACRL, a division of ALA), Association of College and Research Libraries, Chicago, 1959. (Reprinted from *College and Research Libraries,* vol. 20, pp. 274–280, July, 1959.)

The procedure is taken from an article by Durr,[8] which is based on an "average" school in the state of Hawaii in 1963. The significance of this material is not in the actual figures, but in the simple and straightforward method of arriving at costs of maintaining and expanding quotas of materials and equipment to bring them up to given standards [9] and to ensure satisfactory use of resources.

Present status. Durr's analysis begins with a description of the "average" school and what is available (statistically) in this hypothetical school. It has an enrollment of 750 and 26 teachers; 4 classrooms have light control.

This school also has the following equipment:

Equipment of an average school

Equipment	Average number *	Unit cost	Total replacement cost
16mm projectors	2.4	$600	$1,440.00
Filmstrip projectors	2.8	115	322.00
Micro projectors	.5	125	62.50
Opaque projectors	.4	350	140.00
Overhead projectors	1.0	200	200.00
Screens	5.0	40	200.00
Movie movers	.7	160	112.00
Radios	6.0	100	600.00
Record players	16.0	75	1,200.00
Headphones	6.0	6	36.00
Tape recorders	3.4	150	510.00
			$4,822.50

* This figure was obtained by dividing the total amount of equipment reported in schools by the number of public schools in the state.
Source: William Henry Durr, "Hawaii's Public School Audiovisual Program," *Educational Screen and Audiovisual Guide,* vol. 42, pp. 670–673, December, 1963.

Equipment servicing and supplies. Next, Durr asks what it will cost to service and maintain the equipment and to provide necessary supplies for operating it. Assuming that projectors (16mm and filmstrip), tape recorders, and record players should be checked and

[8] William Henry Durr, "Hawaii's Public School Audiovisual Program," *Educational Screen and Audiovisual Guide,* vol. 42, pp. 670–673, December, 1963.
[9] The standards referred to are those recommended to the State Department of Education following a survey of audio-visual education in Hawaii conducted in 1960. See *Audio-Visual Education in Hawaii: Report of the Survey, May 1–21, 1960,* U.S. Office of Education, 1960.

serviced annually, he arrives at the following estimated annual expenses for equipment servicing and supplies, based on the then current prices in Honolulu.

Annual servicing costs

Equipment	Cost per unit	Average number	Total cost
16mm projectors	$15.00–$20.00	2.4	$ 36.00–$ 48.00
Filmstrip projectors	3.50– 5.75	1.4	4.90– 8.05
Record players	3.50– 6.50	16.0	56.00– 104.00
Tape recorders	5.00– 7.50	3.4	17.00– 25.50
Radios, screens, etc.	20.00– 50.00		20.00– 50.00
Totals *			$133.90–$235.55

* Equipment servicing will cost between $134 and $235 annually. Probably $185 would be a good average figure.

Source: William Henry Durr, "Hawaii's Public School Audiovisual Program," *Educational Screen and Audiovisual Guide,* vol. 42, pp. 670–673, December, 1963.

As equipment is used, parts will wear out or burn out and must be replaced. This includes such items as projection lamps (normal life 25 projection hours), exciter lamps, tubes, belts, shuttles, etc. The following is a conservative estimate of the number of such replacement items that will be required on an annual basis for our average school.

Annual replacement costs

Replacement items	Number of units	Cost per unit	Total replacement cost
16mm projector lamps (4 per projector)	10	$6.50	$ 65.00
Filmstrip projector lamps (3 per projector)	8	4.60	36.80
Record player pickup cartridges (.5 per player)	8	5.00	40.00
Overhead projector lamps (3 per projector)	1	6.75	6.75
"Take-up" belts (1 set per projector)	2.4	1.50	3.60
Tubes for radios, tape recorders, projectors			30.00 (estimated)
Total			$182.15

Source: William Henry Durr, "Hawaii's Public School Audiovisual Program," *Educational Screen and Audiovisual Guide,* vol. 42, pp. 670–673, December, 1963.

Equipment replacement. An important factor in audio-visual budgeting is the replacement of equipment as it wears out or becomes obsolete. Durr's analysis is based on an average life of ten years for all categories of equipment, as listed below. The ten-year figure is used for making a rough estimate. Others might prefer to use a life-span based on local experience or a variable scale that provides a life-span figure for each type of equipment. The method used by Durr has the advantage of simplicity. Since the average life-span of all equipment is assumed to be ten years, he simply takes the total cost of equipment in the average school, $4,820, and divides it by 10, thus obtaining $482, the amount that should be budgeted each year for replacement. One remaining comment may be appropriate. As the pace of technological change continues to accelerate, and more new types of equipment are introduced in audio-visual programs, budget makers will have to give more consideration to obsolescence in planning for equipment replacement, as well as to the acquisition of new equipment.

New equipment purchase. Next, Durr deals with the problem of bringing equipment up to standard. Since this would entail very heavy additional expenditures if limited to a single year's budget, the incremental costs for additional equipment, filmstrips, and classroom light control facilities are spread over a period of five years. Thus he arrives at an annual budget that is divided into two parts: one to maintain the level of the program; the other to bring it up to standard over a five-year period. (This involves a combination of continuity and incremental budgeting.) Each item listed represents a computation based

Equipment purchase to achieve standard in five years

Equipment items	Number needed	Total cost of equipment needed	Annual budget for equipment (⅕ of total)
16mm projector	.6	$ 360.00 =	$ 72.00
Filmstrip projector	2.2	220.00 =	44.00
Microprojector	.5	62.50 =	12.50
Opaque projector	1.7	595.00 =	119.00
Overhead projector	1.0	200.00 =	40.00
Screens	8.0	320.00 =	64.00
Radios	1.5	150.00 =	30.00
Tape recorders	1.6	208.00 =	41.60
Totals		$2,115.50	$423.10

Source: William Henry Durr, "Hawaii's Public School Audiovisual Program," *Educational Screen and Audiovisual Guide,* vol. 42, pp. 670–673, December, 1963.

on the difference between the present complement of equipment in the average school and the standard. Thus, the first item indicates that the school is short on 16mm projectors by .6 or three-fifths of a projector. Since the cost of .6 of a new projector is $360, one-fifth of this figure becomes the annual budget for new motion-picture projectors that is required to bring this category up to standard over a period of five years. A similar formula is used for the other items.

Audio-visual materials. Durr deals with the budgeting of audio-visual materials in a very similar manner. First he establishes the present status of the program. Then he calculates what is required to maintain the collection of materials at its present level. After this, he projects a five-year budgetary program to bring the supply of materials up to standard. After ruling out maps, globes, and felt boards, which are budgeted as "classroom equipment" in Hawaii, he finds that the present complement of audio-visual materials in the "average" school is as follows:

Present supply of audio-visual materials

Item	Number in school	Approximate unit cost	Value
Filmstrips	170	$5.00	$ 850.00
Slides (2 by 2 in.)	13	.50	6.50
Microslides (science)	22	.50	11.00
Records	180	3.00	540.00
Flat pictures	120	.50	60.00
Total value of materials			$1,467.50

Source: William Henry Durr, "Hawaii's Public School Audiovisual Program," *Educational Screen and Audiovisual Guide,* vol. 42, pp. 670–673, December, 1963.

Postulating an average life-span of five years for materials, Durr estimates that roughly 20 per cent of the total value of materials ($1,467.50) or a rounded figure of $300 should be budgeted each year for replacement.

In dealing with the problem of bringing quotas of instructional materials up to standard, Durr's discussion is limited to filmstrips, for which the standard was 420 filmstrips per elementary school.

Since the school now has 170 filmstrips on hand, we can say that it needs to purchase 250 additional prints. These would cost, at an average of $5.00 per filmstrip, $1,250.00. If these were purchased over a five-year period, we should budget $250.00 per year for this purpose.

With respect to other materials, he makes this added comment:

> We have not included funds for purchase of additional recordings, slides, tapes, transparencies and transparency making materials since we have not as yet developed agreed upon standards for such materials. However, we can assume that such need to be purchased and should be included in future budgets as needs are more specifically determined.

Light control facilities.　Again, using the "average" school as a base, Durr finds that only four out of twenty-two classrooms have facilities for light control adequate to permit clear and effective projection of films, filmstrips, opaque materials, and microslides. Estimating the average cost of light control at $150 per room, he arrives at a total cost of $3,300. Prorated over a five-year period, this amounts to an annual budget figure of $660.

Budget summary.　In view of the foregoing analysis, Durr summarizes the total proposed audio-visual budget for the "average" school as follows:

Average annual school audio-visual budget *

	Investments	*Expenditures*
A. To maintain present level:		
Equipment servicing (conservative figure)	$133.90	
Equipment supplies (lamps, belts, tubes, etc.)	182.15	
Equipment replacement (ten-year life)	482.25	
Materials replacement (five-year life)	300.00	
Total A		$1,098.30
B. To achieve minimum standard in five years:		
Equipment purchase (additional items)	$423.10	
Filmstrip purchase (additional items)	250.00	
Classroom light control facilities	660.00	
Total B		$1,333.10
Total A and B		$2,431.40

* Since our average school has an enrollment of 750 pupils, we see that the budget as set forth above would break down to an average of roughly $3.25 *per pupil*. It must be noted, however, that several of the items are nonrecurring expenditures. For example, when light control facilities were provided in the classrooms, this item could be dropped other than a nominal amount for servicing and repair. Also, when additional equipment is purchased to the point where standards are achieved, future purchase would be required only for replacement.

Source: William Henry Durr, "Hawaii's Public School Audiovisual Program," *Educational Screen and Audiovisual Guide,* vol. 42, pp. 670–673, December, 1963.

It should be noted that the preceding discussion deals only with equipment, materials, and facilities for individual schools. It does not contain allowances for centralized services at the county or district level: these would include costs of staff salaries, motion pictures and other centrally circulated materials, central broadcast services, and central equipment, including production facilities.

GENERATING SUPPORT FOR EDUCATIONAL MEDIA PROGRAMS

Perhaps the single most striking trend in the changing pattern of educational expenditures in recent years is the sharply rising proportion of the instructional budget that is spent on teaching materials. In the six-year period from 1958 to 1964, for example, expenditures for instructional materials rose twice as fast as the total instructional budget for the public schools.[10] Probably somewhat similar increases in expenditures have taken place in higher education.

But while these changes are impressive, they do not warrant the conclusion that a full-scale instructional-media revolution has come about in education—yet. To improve media services in education, it is necessary to provide more and better materials, but it is also necessary to provide ample technical instrumentation. It is in this latter respect that we are still moving slowly. A number of important technological innovations have occurred, and more are in process, as we have seen; but the total effect is still quite limited when judged on a comparative scale. Clark has pointed out the still rather trival impact of technology upon education in the following interesting comparison: [11]

In 1890 the average manufacturing plant in the United States spent most of its building and equipment money on the building. The best figures available would indicate that about 75 per cent of the total building and equipment money in 1890 manufacturing plants went into the building itself. About 25 per cent went into machinery or equipment. It is fairly obvious that the building simply supplied a place for the work to go on, and that the efficiency of the process was determined in a very large degree by the equipment and the machinery to carry on the process. This became increasingly clear to American businessmen during the next two generations, but those responsible for school construction and operation did not learn this lesson.

By 1960 American business had completely reversed the figures of 1890. The average industrial plant in the United States spent most of its building and equipment money on the manufacturing equipment. The best figures available would indicate that of the total building and equipment expenditure in 1960 approximately 25 per cent went

---

[10] Based on information taken from a national survey of public school budgets in the United States from 1957–1958 to 1963–1964.
[11] Harold F. Clark, *Cost and Quality in Public Education,* Syracuse University Press, Syracuse, N.Y., 1963, pp. 8–9.

into the building, and approximately 75 per cent went into the machinery. Business had made the discovery that efficiency depended far more upon better tools and equipment than on more expensive and elaborate buildings to house the equipment.

The best estimate available would indicate that in 1890 the average school spent well over 90 per cent of its buildings and educational equipment money on the building; less than 10 per cent went into the educational equipment. The figures seem to be roughly the same for schools in 1960.

These figures become of even greater significance when it is realized that the total amount of capital expenditure on building and equipment per teacher averages out about the same as it does in a new manufacturing establishment. The average investment for building and educational equipment in a new school in the United States comes close to $30,000 per teacher.

The average investment in building and equipment in a wide range of new manufacturing plants will also average close to $30,000 per worker. In industry most of the $30,000 is spent on tools and machinery; in education most of the money is spent on the building. Output per man-hour in manufacturing has doubled since 1930, and probably doubled between 1890 and 1930. It would be extraordinarily difficult to prove that there have been any very great increases in output per man-hour in the schools since 1890.

There have doubtless been many other factors contributing to the rapid increase in output per man-hour in industry. But certainly a major factor has been the enormous increase in the amount and quality of the tools and equipment available to the average worker. Although there has been some slight change in the schools, the basic technology of the school of today is approximately the same as it was in 1890.

Why has the rate of technological advance in education trailed so far behind industry or professional services, such as medicine? There are a variety of reasons—some of them apparent and some not so apparent. The following suggestions are given because they have a direct bearing upon budget making and the problem of generating support for the use of newer media in education.

❯ Fearful resistance to technological change is based partly on the questionable notion that machines will displace teachers. This is perhaps the crudest and most superficial of the negative arguments, and it is usually countered by pointing out that we already have a shortage of well-qualified teachers or that teaching requires endless amounts of creative human energy, which should be released from bondage to mechanical and repetitive tasks by appropriate applications of the most advanced technological resources available.

❯ Another source of resistance stems from the related notions that the newer media tend to promote mechanization of the instructional process and loss of feedback from learner to teacher. Both allegations contain some measure of truth. The problem is not to refute such statements, but to find out what they mean and to evaluate that meaning. Mechanization and loss of feedback may be permissible, even desirable, in some contexts or during some phases of the instructional process. Also, it may be that technological factors produce some opposing or mutually corrective effects. Technological systems are used not only for mass instruction, but also for independent study and for student response capabilities that can augment student-instructor feedback in some instructional situations. Moreover, technology can release more teacher time for work with small groups and individuals, thus reducing mechanization and improving feedback.

❯ The initial and operating costs of some newer technological devices are high, and the gain in effectiveness and/or economy of instruction is not always immediate or immediately apparent.

❯ Both education and technology are becoming more complex and more costly. As a result, it is becoming evident that the introduction of new technological resources is no longer simply a matter of piecemeal adding of new "aids" to instruction. Rather, a comprehensive and penetrating analysis of the total instructional enterprise as a system is needed, and this poses a difficult and time-consuming problem. Educators and laymen are not yet accustomed to a systems approach to instructional planning and budget making, but there are signs of increasing interest in this difficult and critical problem. They will be discussed in the final chapter of this book.

In recent years, the introduction of new technological resources in education has been stimulated and supported in part by Federal funds and by some of the private foundations. The National Defense Education Act (NDEA) of 1958 occasioned at the outset a series of appropriations amounting to $47 million annually for the purchase of audio-visual equipment, plus an additional initial appropriation of $18 million for research in the use of new media in education. The Educational Television Facilities Act, mentioned in Chapter 10, provided for a Federal appropriation of $32 million to be used by the states on a matching-funds basis to expand and improve educational television broadcasting facilities. Large expenditures by the Ford Foundation were an important factor in the growth of educational television, especially during the critical 1950s.

Thus it has been demonstrated that the Federal government and private organizations can assume an important function as a stimulant of growth in education. If the continuing interest of the Federal government is demonstrated by further extensions of media-oriented programs such as those initiated by the NDEA, the present rate of growth of technological resources in education may be sustained or even increased. However, the major burden of support still lies at the local level with local school districts and the states and the private agencies that support their own educational programs. In the long run, adequate support for the educational media must come from a higher degree of support for the total educational program (from whatever sources and levels), and this will be generated by public understanding and appreciation of the total instructional program and the part that the media play in it. One implication appears to be clear: In the late 1960s and 1970s, it should become increasingly apparent that the investment in better teachers and buildings will pay off best if accompanied by increased funds for the modern materials that will make teachers and facilities maximally effective. Not only must we spend more for education—we must also be prepared to spend more of the education dollar for media and materials, including the new technological resources. We must be willing to pay for good teachers and supply them with twentieth-century tools to teach effectively and efficiently.

SUMMARY

Educational budgeting in the best sense is a focal point in the development of policies and plans by which a community fulfills its aspirations for the development of its youth. Departmental budgets for educational media services should be developed by those who administer them, in proper accord with the goals of the total instructional program. Clusters of media services administered as separate departmental functions should be coordinated for planning and budgetary purposes at the next higher level of administration. Generally speaking, educational media services are best conducted under a type of administrative organization in which one person has full responsibility for the program, including the development and administration of the departmental budget. Centralization of some fiscal procedures is often necessary, but it should not obscure the need for a sufficient departmental autonomy in functional budgetary planning and administration.

There are three levels of budget planning: (1) continuity budgeting for simple continuation of an established program at its present level; (2) incremental budgeting to bring an established program up to some norm of adequacy; and (3) expansion or creative budgeting to support new goals, expanded functions, more highly developed means of implementation in an existing program, or a new program. Standards such as those developed by the Department of Audio-Visual Instruction of the NEA and the ALA can be helpful as guides, suggesting minimums for certain categories of equipment, materials, facilities, and staff; but they should be used carefully and selectively in this period of rapid change and technological development.

A sample budget-making procedure outlined in this chapter illustrates how level 1 and level 2 budgeting can be applied to audio-visual equipment, materials, and facilities for a public school system.

A concluding discussion of the matter of support for educational media programs emphasizes the discrepancy between the stage of technological advance in industry on the one hand and education on the other. Reasons for this technological delay in education may be due, in part, to the resistance and doubts of some teachers and laymen—as well as to the higher cost and complex problems of planning involved in the full-scale introduction of a modern technology of instruction. The Federal government and some private foundations have assisted the introduction of new technological resources in education, but the long-range problem of generating a higher level of support for the contemporary educational media program remains to be solved.

FOR FURTHER INFORMATION

Audio-Visual Education in Hawaii: Report of the Survey, May 1–21, 1960, U.S. Office of Education, 1960.

Clark, H. F.: *Cost and Quality in Public Education,* Syracuse University Press, Syracuse, N.Y., 1963.

The Cooperative Approach to Audio-Visual Programs, Department of Audio-Visual Instruction, NEA, 1959.

Durr, William Henry: "Hawaii's Public School Audiovisual Program," *Educational Screen and Audiovisual Guide,* vol. 42, pp. 670–673, December, 1963.

Erickson, Carlton W. H.: *Administering Audio-Visual Services,* Macmillan, New York, 1959.

Financial Accounting for Local and State School Systems, U.S. Government Printing Office, Washington, D.C.

A Guide for Cooperative Evaluation of County and District Audio-Visual Programs, Bureau of Audio-Visual and School Library Education, California State Department of Education, Sacramento, Calif., 1964.

Mauch, James: "A Systems Analysis Approach to Education," *Phi Delta Kappan,* vol. 43, pp. 158–162, January, 1962.

Osview, Leon, and William B. Castetter: *Budgeting for Better Schools,* Prentice-Hall, Englewood Cliffs, N.J., 1960.

Rugg, K. C.: *Improving Instruction: Budgeting Your Audio-Visual Program,* Indiana University, Bloomington, Ind., 1960.

Standards for School Library Programs, ALA, Chicago, 1960.

Tanzman, Jack: "An Audio-Visual Program: What You Need Beyond Equipment," *School Management,* vol. 8, p. 131, April, 1963.

chapter 8

Improving utilization practices

Good utilization of educational media is primarily a matter of human understanding, skill, and motivation. It requires well-trained, competent teachers who know media and materials and how to arrange the conditions of their use for optimum results. Of course, highly qualified teachers alone will not suffice.

No matter how well trained or how experienced and skilled teachers may be, they obviously cannot make effective use of the media unless the instruments of instruction are available and usable. The proper media and materials must be *there*—in the right place at the right time. If materials are to be projected, broadcast, played, or displayed, the teacher must have the necessary equipment in good working order, the confidence to use it, and technical assistance when needed. Moreover, buildings and classrooms must be designed and constructed so that they are truly functional in a technological sense and not obstacles to modern techniques of instruction. All of this is obvious, but frequently neglected or overlooked.

The organization of media services and facilities will be discussed at length in other chapters. Here we will deal with the utilization problem as it involves teacher behavior and the means for helping teachers improve their instructional practices.

TEACHER COMPETENCIES

Important teacher competencies required for effective utilization of educational media include the following: (1) understanding of the behavioral processes involved in communication and learning, (2) knowledge of media characteristics and capacities, (3) ability to evaluate and conduct or participate in experimental studies of teaching and learning, (4) familiarity with appropriate materials and their sources, and (5) command of necessary mechanical skills.

Understanding behavioral processes

The need for understanding the psychological factors involved in communication and learning is so apparent and so readily accepted that it is sometimes not given sufficient scrutiny. More precisely, the need is taken for granted, but the difficulties involved in meeting it are not brought clearly and emphatically into view. Most teachers have been exposed to a course in educational psychology—relatively few have had similar work in the field of communication theory. The application of such sparse psychological training to the utilization of audio-visual and other media in teaching is often inadequate, since many teachers do not receive courses in audio-visual education or the communication of information and ideas by various means. And these courses are sometimes deficient in their treatment of the psychological factors involved in teaching as communicating. The problem is complicated further by the fact that there is no fully developed science of learning or communicating to provide ready-made answers to all instructional-media problems.[1] The important implication is this: Teachers must be made aware of the limitations (as well as the strengths) of present knowledge and theory in the fields of learning and communication; they should also have selective exposure to the vast array of research findings that provide clues and leads, if not final answers, to so many instructional problems. Teachers thus instructed should also be oriented to research methodology so that they can not only keep up with and evaluate new findings, but so that they can also participate effectively in the continuing effort to develop a science of instructional technology.

Knowledge of media characteristics

Obviously, knowledge of the media is of critical importance in using them effectively. The characteristics to be considered relate to (1) the sheer physical capacities and peculiarities of the stimulus output and the technological means required to produce it, and (2) the social and psychological factors that control the impact of the medium. Knowledge of the social and psychological characteristics of the media is most needed and most difficult to obtain. By and large, experimental studies of instructional media in education have concerned gross learning effects rather than highly refined and specific intermedia comparisons or analysis of particular media. The relatively few studies of the latter type are not widely known among teachers. Moreover, the implications of existing research are not yet highly developed or widely disseminated. Obviously, there are serious limitations in our knowledge and understanding of the media, just as there are in the psychological foundations of their use. Alert teachers—with the assistance of knowledgeable supervisors and administrators—can compensate, in part, for the deficiencies of present scientific knowledge by practical experience and careful observation of the results of various "cut-and-try" procedures. To extend their understanding and competence, they should also become conversant with the present state of the experimental knowledge and active participants in its further development.

[1] Arthur W. Melton, "The Science of Learning and the Technology of Educational Methods," *Harvard Educational Review,* vol. 29, pp. 96–106, 1959.

Research skills

A wise and capable teacher must know the limitations of present knowledge of human behavior and thus understand the necessity of working out experimental solutions to many instructional problems as he goes along. This suggests that pedagogical know-how should be linked with a method of testing and enlarging itself. What does this entail?

In a dynamic society with an expanding technology, teachers who try to work effectively and creatively will have increasing opportunities to engage in the experimental trial, development, and evaluation of new practices and the uses of both old and new media. To face this challenge with professional skill and confidence, they should have some grasp of research methods and an experimental approach to their work. This does not mean that every classroom teacher should be fully versed in formal research methods and statistical procedures or that all teachers should be able to design a controlled research study; it does mean that they should understand the place and value of experimental procedures in developing and refining instructional practices, should not be afraid to try new or alternative techniques on a provisional basis, and should be ready and able to participate in both formal and informal research activities. Moreover, teachers should be aware of research findings that are relevant to their own instructional tasks and ready to learn from the experience of others.

Teachers experiment not merely to compensate for lack of complete knowledge regarding communication and learning or because of the novelty of much of the present paraphernalia of instruction. They also experiment to keep alive and sensitive to the constantly changing conditions and demands of their work. Teaching is an art, with aspects that lend themselves to scientific study. Much current instructional practice is well established and productive. Teachers should not be encouraged to try new things or new ways just because they are new nor merely for the sake of change. But what teacher, what administrator, what student or parent is fully satisfied with all that goes on in the classroom now? Teachers try new things and new ways because they must make changes and seek better ways of getting the job done. In this context of urgent awareness of need for better methods of teaching, the experimental approach can demonstrate its worth.

Familiarity with materials

Another competency required for effective utilization—and a simple one—is knowledge of what media and materials are available. This entails an acquaintance with information concerning instructional materials and where they may be found. The teacher's competency must be matched with adequate cataloging and other means for facilitating the flow of information from those who store and circulate the materials to those who use them. Conversely, there must also be an adequate flow of information from those who use the media and materials to those who obtain them and make them available for classroom use. These important aspects of the organization of media services are discussed in detail in Chapter 4.

Mechanical skills

Finally, teachers must have the necessary mechanical skills to operate certain kinds of instructional devices with efficiency and confidence. When teachers are on their own, they are more likely to use appropriate media if they are confident they can operate the equipment or supervise its operation by students without undue risk of human or mechanical failure and the embarrassment that results when things break down.

Mechanical skills are becoming somewhat less critical because of two separate but concurrent trends: (1) Engineers are designing instructional devices that are lighter in weight, more compact, and easier to operate; and (2) schools and colleges are making more use of complex technical systems that are often operated by technicians. In some respects, the teacher of the 1970s may encounter fewer mechanical difficulties than today's teacher. In the place of mechanics, however, will be more fundamental and more complex problems, such as those indicated in the following section.

CHANGING ASPECTS OF THE UTILIZATION PROBLEM

A changing technology has altered the problem of using instructional media. The increasing use of a more powerful and more highly centralized technology of instruction has created the need for a new order of knowledge and skills in the organization and conduct of teaching.

In the first fifty years of this century, technological trends in education augmented problems of utilization mostly by increasing the number of tools or devices with which the teacher was required to deal. In the 1940s and early 1950s, the growing use of audio-visual instructional devices and materials was paralleled by an increasing emphasis upon audio-visual and other methods courses designed to help teachers master these new tools of the trade. Such courses contained varying amounts of background psychological material and discussion of media characteristics, usually combined with a heavy emphasis on techniques of use, demonstrations, preparation of materials, and laboratory practice in the operation of motion-picture projectors, tape recorders, and various other devices that the teacher could operate in his own classroom. Such training will continue to play an important role in the preparation of teachers in the future, but with gradual and important modifications.

165

Beginning in the late 1950s and in the 1960s, teachers began to find themselves involved in using complicated technical systems that often could not be operated on an independent basis. Television systems usually required centralized studio equipment operated by technicians and frequently involved the teacher in some sort of group instructional procedure that was not subject to his personal control. Similarly, language laboratories, teaching machines, and other automated instructional systems tended to become centralized instructional facilities. Although still far from practical application in the classroom, the experimental use of computers in programmed instruction was just one more development that dramatized the changing shape of the problem of utilization.

The independent use of some media in individual classrooms will not disappear or even become less important. The equipment used by individual teachers and students will no doubt continue the trend toward reduction of size and weight and greater simplicity of operation. For example, the cartridge-loading projector, and tape recorder, will simplify manual operation. However, as the teacher is relieved of mechanical risks and difficulties in operating technical devices, he encounters new and more complicated utilization problems that result from more highly integrated instructional procedures. Often he will give up some control of the total instructional process and accept a more specialized role in the joint use of complex technological systems by groups or teams. And although he may find it easier to operate a modern 16mm or 8mm projector or prepare a color transparency, he may find it much more difficult to discover his proper role as a television teacher, as an instructor using programmed materials, or as a member of an instructional team that is using various media with the aid of technical assistants.

In tomorrow's schools, the teacher's difficulties in using the technology of instruction will arise mainly out of the formidable task of understanding the place of the media and the changing role of the teacher. The skills needed to solve these contemporary problems lie primarily in the areas of experimentation, planning, and human relations. Good utilization has never been an easy goal. It is significant that this challenge becomes even more difficult as teachers are relieved of the mechanical operation of the instructional tools—a convincing demonstration that effective teaching depends primarily upon more fundamental understandings and skills.

IMPROVING UTILIZATION THROUGH SUPERVISION AND CONSULTATION

Supervisory and consultative services are generally considered critical functions of the professional administrative personnel who are involved in educational media programs. However, the discharge of such functions is often severely limited in terms of staff. Typically, the full-time head of an educational media program has a crowded schedule that makes visits to schools or classrooms or conferences with individual teachers difficult. The larger the educational system or institution, the greater the problem. For this reason, educational media administrators must exert their instructional leadership in the most efficient and telling ways. Even the busiest administrator should reserve some time for occasional visits to classrooms and conferences with teachers, but his instructional leadership will reach much further if he obtains the cooperation of school principals and supervisors, who are closer to the classroom.

A centralized educational media program that serves one of the world's largest metropolitan areas was operating recently with a supervisory staff of five consultants. Many other large metropolitan areas are even less well served, and many medium-sized and smaller educational media programs have no supervisory staff at all, aside from the head. On the other hand, most school systems have a better supply of general and special (subject-matter) supervisors, and they are in key positions to help teachers make effective use of instructional media. Realization of this opportunity, unfortunately, is not always easy; sometimes there are serious obstacles—obstacles resulting from threats to the role and status of the supervisor in the changing school.

In recent years, the functions and concerns of supervisors have been profoundly affected by sweeping changes in education. Much of the curriculum and instruction philosophy that dominated supervisory practice in the 1930s and 1940s has been subjected to highly publicized critical attacks. Criticisms mounted during the 1950s and continued into the 1960s, long after the demise of progressive education, which was held accountable by some for so many educational ills. During the same period, sources of curriculum change shifted from teachers and supervisors to the public and professors in the academic disciplines—a shift dramatized by the work of the School Mathematics Study Group, the Physical Science Study Committee, and the Chemical Education Materials Study, for example. Such projects resulted from an increasing demand for mastery of subject matter and a keen interest in reorganizing academic disciplines to bring them abreast of current scientific and cultural developments. At the same time, concern over mounting enrollments and teacher shortages was reflected in growing interest in organization and method as related to the technical instruments of instruction. The Federal government and private foundations entered into the discipline-oriented efforts to modify curricula and supported the implementation of proposals for sweeping technological changes in education.

MacKenzie has pointed out the net result of these events: "Many supervisors felt by-passed. They had lost the initiative and frequently found themselves in the defensive position of justifying already existing instructional practices or trying to keep the vigorous critics and reformers from 'throwing out the baby with the bath.' " [2] No wonder that many felt threatened by technological changes in education. Frequently these changes did not involve them at the planning stage. Some were linked with a psychology of learning that was alien and suspect to many supervisors and teachers. On the whole, the growth of technology in education seemed to represent a trend toward uniformity—toward greater centralization of initiation and determination of curriculum and instructional practices. All of this was in apparent conflict with traditional notions of supervision and local control in education.

Supervisors working in the general area of instruction or specific subject-matter areas represent a great potential for improving media utilization in teaching. Full realization of this potential will require better communication between media administrators and supervisors than there has been in the past. It must be apparent that unless those who administer educational media and those who supervise teachers have some common views, they cannot work effectively toward common goals. Supervisors are already contributing substantially to better use of media in many schools. These contributions should grow to the extent that supervisors are involved in planning media developments in teaching and that media personnel participate in the planning and development of the instructional program as a whole.

Instructional leadership involves administrative, supervisory, media-related, and other personnel, including the teachers themselves, and that fact should not be overlooked. In September, 1962, the NEA Department of Audio-Visual Instruction sponsored a six-state conference on better utilization and evaluation of television in education. The conference involved the cooperation of affiliated organizations of the Association for Supervision and Curriculum Development and DAVI in the states concerned: Illinois, Indiana, Kentucky, Michigan, Ohio, and Wisconsin. A distinctive feature of this conference was that the planners invited *teams* representing classroom teachers, television teachers, audio-visual-materials and television directors, supervisors of instruction, principals, school superintendents, and school board members. This is a good example of one kind of effort that might help raise the level of communication and cooperation among the various parties who are concerned with better utilization of educational media.

IN–SERVICE TRAINING

Today's teachers need to know how to use the tools of their profession. Many are competent to do so when they begin to teach, but many are prepared poorly or not at all. A national NEA survey conducted in 1963 revealed that many classroom teachers felt that they had received too little preparation for using audio-visual equipment and materials. In

[2] Gordon N. MacKenzie, "Role of the Supervisor," *Educational Leadership,* vol. 19, pp. 86–90, November, 1961.

fact, they identified this area as the one *most* lacking in their professional training.[3]

Some states require an audio-visual course for teacher certification. Many colleges and universities have similar requirements. On the other hand, recent emphasis on subject-matter preparation of teachers has changed certification patterns in some states, tending to compress or reduce the required methods courses, including special courses in using the media. Whatever the general impact of these changes, one unfortunate fact is clear: Many teachers are still entering jobs without adequate orientation to the technological facts and demands of their profession.

In-service training is not a substitute for adequate preparation, but it can be an important compensating factor. It can also make a vital contribution to better utilization of the media by upgrading and updating the instructional practices of experienced teachers. In-service training can do these things, but only if it is effective.

What makes in-service training effective?

The point of in-service training is to bring about desirable changes in teacher behavior. The extent to which programs accomplish this varies greatly. Every year, huge amounts of money and teaching effort are poured into in-service procedures that probably leave teachers and teaching practices very much as they were before the programs began. To reach and change teacher behavior, Flanders has suggested that: [4]

Proposed ideas about teaching and learning must be organized into concepts which have meaning in terms of overt behavior

Concepts about teaching and learning become useful to the extent that they can be applied personally—related to the teacher's own behavior, his own pupils, his own classroom

Insight into principles of effective teaching comes about through personal inquiry

Teachers should have opportunities to practice or try out techniques or procedures *during* the in-service program

Emphasis should be placed on *resources* that enable teachers to implement the trial of new concepts and methods

Teacher participation in the in-service program should be voluntary

Teachers should have ample opportunity to evaluate the in-service training program

Faculty meetings, workshops, and other in-service training procedures can be interesting, stimulating, provocative—and still fail. Good,

[3] Reported in *NEA Journal,* vol. 9, p. 34, December, 1963.
[4] Ned A. Flanders, "Teacher Behavior and In-service Programs," *Educational Leadership,* vol. 21, pp. 25–29, October, 1963.

well-presented ideas are not enough, even when the presentation is made by authorities and experts. Even demonstrations, which at least translate the idea clearly into overt behavioral terms, may lead nowhere if the teacher has not adequate motivation or resources to take the proposed practice into his own classroom and try it out. Finally, actual classroom trial may abort unless there is a *sustained* effort to provide support; to encourage repeated trials and experimentation; to allow the teacher to feed back his early disappointments, failures, and frustrations; and to help him correct errors and gradually refine his techniques. When these things are done, it is much more likely that the teacher will gain the experience and success that lead to some lasting change in his behavior.

Use of media in in-service training

Using educational media to implement in-service training objectives is psychologically sound, economical, and effective for a variety of purposes. The adage that "teachers teach not as they are taught to teach, but as they are taught" has a great deal to it. There is sound logic in the idea of making use of modern communication devices in order to teach others to use them.

There are limits to the amount of time that teachers can give to faculty meetings, workshops, and conferences. And there are limits to the human resources required to arrange and conduct such activities. To support and augment in-service training, printed materials, television, motion pictures, and other media can be used to:

❯ Describe and illustrate new instructional practices
❯ Televise the lecture-demonstration part of college-originated educational media courses on a service-area basis
❯ Report experimental research findings
❯ Bring new materials to teacher's attention by television motion-picture previews or evaluative reports
❯ Present teachers, supervisors, and resource persons in panel discussions, demonstrations, or other television or radio presentations to reach widely diffused audiences by broadcast or more closely defined audiences by closed-circuit transmission

State departments of education have made particularly effective use of printed publications to disseminate new information on media, materials, and techniques. One recent publication, prepared under the direction of the Bureau of Audio-Visual and School Library Education of the California State Department of Education, had an initial distribution of 12,500 copies to school administrators, supervisors, audio-visual directors, and schools of education throughout the state.[5]

[5] William H. Allen (ed.), *Improving Instruction through Audio-Visual Media,* California State Department of Education, Sacramento, Calif., 1964. (Prepared under the direction of Harry J. Skelly, Chief, Bureau of Audio-Visual and School Library Education)

DISCOVERING AND ANALYZING
THE FACTS

Improvement of media utilization practices begins with two simple questions: What is being done? How well is it being done? Answers depend upon these additional questions: What teachers are using what media and materials for what areas of instruction? How many teachers are making adequate use of available resources? What media and materials are being put to effective use? Which are being used poorly, infrequently, or not at all? Some of these questions involve simple counting. Some require evaluation, which is more difficult.

Quantitative data gathering

Ordinary accounting and reporting procedures can be used to compile periodic quantitative data regarding utilization on a systematic basis. Gathering such information need not entail laborious or highly complex bookkeeping chores. Most schools using instructional materials from a central source employ some sort of order form, such as the one shown below. Similar forms used in colleges and universities may resemble the service record for Sacramento State College. Such records, typically printed for duplicate copies, may be accumulated to provide the raw information necessary for a complete statistical account of the utilization of equipment and materials. This form is filled out in triplicate when the equipment and materials are booked for use. A copy of each booking is retained as a record. The accumulated copies may then be tabulated periodically to show quantitative use of equip-

Records of uses made of materials, as derived from copies of forms similar to that shown here, provide data for evaluating educational media programs. (*Tulare County, California, Schools*)

To Be Shipped	Due Back in Office

(DO NOT WRITE ABOVE THIS LINE)

REQUEST FOR MATERIALS

TULARE COUNTY SCHOOLS
AUDIO-VISUAL DEPARTMENT
COURT HOUSE
Visalia, California
Phone RE 2-5511 Ext. 327

SCHOOL

STREET ROUTE OR BOX

CITY   STATE

TEACHER   ☐ DELIVER BY TRUCK   ☐ WE WILL CALL

PLEASE SEND THE FOLLOWING ITEM FOR USE ON DATE INDICATED	DATE WANTED	CANNOT BE USED AFTER
TYPE FIRST CHOICE (Write only one title in this space.)		
SECOND CHOICE (Write only one title in this space.)		

ment and materials by categories; by specific items, such as titles of motion pictures or tape recordings; or by users.

Data-gathering procedures such as those just described are not difficult to administer, and the added cost is negligible. The information produced can be used to:

❯ Determine what media and materials are used in what areas of teaching
❯ Determine the extent to which existing facilities and resources are used
❯ Identify teachers who make use of the various media, those who may make excessive or indiscriminate use of some media or materials, and those whose repertoire of instructional techniques may be unduly restricted
❯ Provide information for organizing and staffing administrative and service operations, thus ensuring adequate facilities, equipment, materials, and services for good utilization.

Subjective reporting

Interview reporting by supervisors and principals can supplement statistical information and assist in forming judgments regarding the state and quality of instructional practices. Conferences with teachers—held individually or in small groups—help to reveal attitudes toward instructional uses of the media, the quality of their motivation, and their evaluation of the informational, supervisory, research, and service efforts to help them make more effective use of the tools of teaching. Typical questions might include:

❯ What types of materials (and media) other than those owned by individual students do you utilize in teaching?
❯ How do you make decisions regarding the use of media and materials, and what resources are helpful in making such decisions?
❯ What instructional resources have been most useful? Least useful?
❯ What media and/or materials would you like to use that are now lacking?
❯ What media and/or materials are denied to you because of inadequate service or inconvenience?
❯ What are your most difficult problems in using media and materials, and how can they be corrected?
❯ Are catalogs, bulletins, and other sources of information adequate? How might they be improved?
❯ What additions to (or changes in) consultative and in-service training procedures would help you to use the media effectively and creatively in your teaching?
❯ What can research contribute to the evaluation of your own teaching practices and their improvement?
❯ How can the efforts of school principals, general and special supervisors, and educational media personnel best be coordinated to provide maximum assistance to teachers?

Subjective reporting is most productive when it is used to supplement and help interpret statistical and other more objective information.

Teachers reporting directly on their own practices and problems or supervisors and principals reporting their observations may be more candid in spoken interviews or small-group discussions than in formal written reports. Also, much useful information can be obtained from facial expressions, voice inflections, and off-hand remarks that would never show up in statistical information or formal written statements. Finally, the direct human contacts involved in subjective reporting may be invaluable as a means of developing mutual understanding and rapport.

Further sources of information

Once the elementary information has been assembled from statistical sources and subjective reports, the stage is set for analysis of the data; but this, of course, is only a good beginning. Further and more reliable information will be required to determine the effectiveness of the media and ways of using them. Ordinarily, this entails some kind of experimental procedure. In some cases, desirable alternatives to existing practices can be identified rather easily on the basis of well-established norms of instructional method and known media characteristics or capacities. At other times, firm reference points are lacking, and the quest for better utilization must be carried on through research. This may vary over a wide range—from informal trial and appraisal of results to "action" and "developmental" research to highly controlled research studies.

A good example of the more formal experimental approach is the study conducted by Gropper, Lumsdaine, and Shipman on the improvement of televised instruction based on student responses to achievement tests.[6] This interesting study, which was conducted in Pittsburgh, compared the results of simultaneous telecasts of two versions of a series of instructional presentations in general science for junior high school students. In each case, one version was shown earlier to a preview audience of students, and they were then tested on the presentation. The results of this test were used to produce the modified version. Results on objective and essay test items showed an average gain or advantage of 12 to 26 per cent for students who watched the revised versions over those who watched the original preview versions. Such research studies have wide implications for teaching and for getting reliable information for improving media utilization practices.

[6] George L. Gropper, Arthur A. Lumsdaine, and Virginia Shipman, *Improvement of Televised Instruction Based on Student Responses to Achievement Tests,* Metropolitan Pittsburgh Educational Television Stations WQED–WQEX and American Institute for Research, studies in Televised Instruction, Report 1, Pittsburgh, Pa., March, 1961. 67 pp. (USOE project no. 336; University Microfilms pub. no. 62–1079)

SUMMARY

In brief summary, effective utilization of educational media requires:

> Carefully selected instructional materials and equipment, reliably and conveniently available and in good supply
> Adequate space and facilities providing convenient location and operation of equipment, as well as sufficient control over physical conditions such as light, acoustics, and ventilation
> Teachers who have the requisite knowledge of behavioral processes and media characteristics
> Teachers who have the skills to work effectively with an enlarged repertoire of devices and techniques and with personnel involved in joint instructional procedures
> Teachers who have the motivation to cope with technological change and to experiment with new ways of teaching in a continuing search for better results
> Consultative services drawing upon a wide range of supervisory and administrative personnel who look upon utilization of media as an integral aspect of the total problem of good teaching, but one that requires constant and serious attention
> Preservice training geared to the demands of modern teaching
> In-service training that emphasizes meaningful and voluntary teacher involvement in a "try-it-out-and-evaluate" approach to better instruction
> Appropriate use of various communication media to support and augment in-service training for utilization of instructional media
> Adequate information to determine and evaluate current utilization practices and explore ways of improving them

This is a formidable task; it calls for careful planning and organization, vigorous promotion, and sound professional leadership. The administrator of the educational media program has many other jobs to perform, but unless this one succeeds, the others will fail. Leaders of educational media programs need to improve the quantity and strength of their own supervisory personnel. They must also build a broad base of communication and cooperative effort that involves general and special supervisors and school principals, in a joint effort to foster and improve the use of modern technological resources in education.

FOR FURTHER INFORMATION

Allen, William H. (ed.): *Improving Instruction through Audio-Visual Media,* California State Department of Education, Sacramento, Calif., 1964. (Prepared under the direction of Harry J. Skelly, Chief, Bureau of Audio-Visual and School Library Education)

Berlo, David K.: "You Are in the People Business," *Audiovisual Instruction,* vol. 8, pp. 373–381, June, 1963.

Brown, James W., Richard B. Lewis, and Fred F. Harcleroad: *A-V Instruction: Materials and Methods,* 2d ed., McGraw-Hill, New York, 1964.

Brown, James W., and James W. Thornton, Jr.: *College Teaching: Perspectives and Guidelines,* McGraw-Hill, New York, 1963.

Erickson, Carlton W. H.: *Administering Audio-Visual Services,* Macmillan, New York, 1959.

Flanders, Ned A.: "Teacher Behavior and In-service Programs," *Educational Leadership,* vol. 21, pp. 25–29, October, 1963.

Knowlton, James, and Ernest Hawes: "Attitude: Helpful Predictor of Audiovisual Usage," *AV Communication Review,* vol. 10, pp. 147–157, May–June, 1962.

Meierhenry, Wesley C. (ed.): "Learning Theory and AV Utilization," *AV Communication Review,* vol. 9, supplement 4, September–October, 1961. (Entire issue)

Melton, Arthur W.: "The Science of Learning and the Technology of Educational Methods," *Harvard Educational Review,* vol. 29, pp. 96–106, 1959.

Nordberg, H. Orville, James M. Bradfield, and William C. Odell: *Secondary School Teaching,* Macmillan, New York, 1962.

chapter 9

Textbook administration

Although in some ways the United States textbook industry must be regarded as rather small—at least in comparison with such behemoths as steel, automobiles, or refrigerators—it is, nonetheless, a highly important, influential educational activity.

Each year in this country, for example, approximately one hundred seventy textbook publishing companies turn out a product that retails for more than $300 million. Their printed books come in various sizes, shapes, and colors—as basal (basic) or supplementary textbooks, programmed books, teachers' manuals, workbooks, encyclopedias or reference books, anthologies, dictionaries, and thesauri. They also come in hardbound or paperback editions, as originals or reprints, as unadorned black and white or multichromed wonders of the printing trade.

The value attached by educators to these products is reflected in a report of the NEA Project on Instruction on selected instructional practices, on the basis of returns of 1,442 questionnaires from elementary- and secondary-school principals scattered throughout the country. It was concluded that "the textbook was the resource listed . . . as the one recently most useful for a teaching program (1960–1961). What the publishers printed for school use was indicated as a strong determinant of what the students had studied." [1]

It has also been estimated that "95 per cent of text time in American public schools is spent on print and that 90 per cent of this printed material is in the form of textbooks." [2]

The special advantages claimed for textbooks in the conduct of education are so well known as to require only brief restatement here:

❯ Textbooks help to organize and unify instruction, providing in the process a common set of learning experiences on which still other learning activities such as seeing films, listening to recorded dramatizations, hearing lectures, and the like, may be based.

❯ Textbooks permit a needed individualization of instruction. Within limits, each student in a class may read what he wants to read, at times convenient to him, under the circumstances he chooses, as quickly or slowly as he

---

[1] *The Principals Look at the Schools: A Status Study of Selected Instructional Practices,* Project on Instruction, NEA, 1962, pp. 23–24.

[2] Wilbur Schramm, "The Publishing Process," in Lee J. Cronbach (ed.), *Text Materials in Modern Education,* the University of Illinois Press, Urbana, Ill., 1955, p. 143.

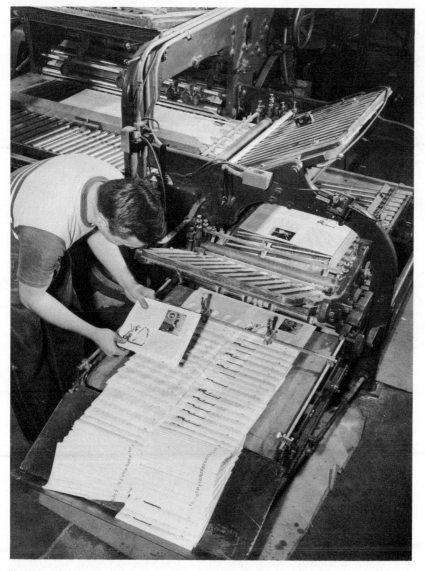

Today's highly mechanized book publishing industry continues to turn out useful, well-written, and sturdily bound products that meet varied school requirements. (*Rand McNally and Company*)

wishes and with whatever skipping or repetition he considers necessary or desirable. Textbooks may be carried home, studied en route, or taken to the library or to a study carrel. The teacher may vary textbook assignments for students in the same class, requiring some to read all of topical presentations, some only portions of them.

❯ Textbooks permit scientifically graded introductions of expertly prepared instructional content that build on concepts, skills, and information introduced previously or that lead to those to be introduced later in a series.

177

The county or district media center usually warehouses quantity orders of textbooks and monitors their distribution to schools. (*Alameda County, California, Schools*)

❯ Textbooks and accompanying manuals provide helpful and detailed suggestions to teachers concerning ways of introducing and capitalizing upon their content. School administrators and others believe that such materials can improve teacher performance in the classroom, especially the performance of those who are new to the profession.

Quite obviously, then, the school textbook program is seen to require professional consideration. In more and more situations, the responsibility for coordinating activities related to their appraisal, selection, purchase, processing, distribution, and maintenance are delegated to educational media center personnel whose duties encompass the total educational media field.

CURRENT TEXTBOOK TRENDS

Several significant developments in the textbook industry reflect its response to current educational trends, which has led to different ways of producing, publishing, and distributing its products. Some of the more important of these developments—developments of which educational media personnel must be aware—are as follows:

> Less reliance on a single textbook and the use of a principal text and a number of supporting supplementary texts, pamphlets, and periodicals instead
> Increased availabilities of paperbacked materials, especially the classics
> Continuance of the move away from the practice of large-scale, single-book adoptions and toward more permissive arrangements that encourage selection of books geared to local needs and interests
> Increased textbook sales, due to generally increasing school enrollments, the improved economic status of school patrons, and decisions by more and more school boards to enrich textbook and supplementary book offerings
> Demand for innovations in textbook content brought on by curriculum reforms and the increasing rapidity with which new knowledge is discovered and old knowledge outdated
> Production of books that are increasingly attractive and functional from the viewpoints of typography, layout, illustration, and color combining better appearance with improved readability and idea communication
> Correlation of systems of materials (including films, filmstrips, recordings, workbooks, programmed materials, models, specimens, charts, etc., in one kit or package), each planned to contribute maximally and sometimes uniquely to communication
> Growing emphasis upon inquiry (problem-oriented instruction) rather than telling or "acquiry" as a rationale for organizing and presenting textbook content
> Production of textbooks for students on two or more "tracks," adapting difficulty or concept density to students of varying abilities
> Continuous collaboration on a large scale of nationally known experts (who may not be teachers) with superior classroom teachers in writing and trying out textbook materials (e.g., projects of the Biological Sciences Curriculum Study, the Physical Science Study Committee, the School Mathematics Study Group, or others)
> Entry of foundation- and government-supported organizations into the preparation, validation, and editing of text materials (sometimes in competition with commercial publishers)

Implications of the two last trends (large-scale collaboration by subject experts and classroom teachers and the entry of foundation- and government-supported groups into the preparation of textbook materials) are of concern to many observers in the field. In his *Revolution in the Textbook Industry,* for example, M. Frank Redding pointed out at least two problems. Concerning the first—that of maintaining editorial freedom and integrity for the publishers—he said: [3]

From the first, Government and foundations made it clear that the fruits of these labors would, eventually, come to publishing—either

---

[3] Frank M. Redding, *Revolution in the Textbook Publishing Industry,* Occasional Paper 9, Technological Development Project, NEA, 1963, pp. 18–19.

through being placed in public domain (and thus given freely to all), or by being offered up for competitive bids by the publishers. . . .

And here the critical debate ensued. It can be argued, of course, that so long as these materials came to the schools and classrooms in the traditional manner of textbooks (i.e., offered for sale by publishers' representatives) the safeguards of the American publishing process were in place. Presumably these sponsored creatures would have to compete with those offerings of other publishers which had come into being through a more normal process of birth. Selection committees would still be privileged to choose from a wide variety of published offerings. Where was the problem?

The problem, came the answer, lies at the very heart of the publishing process. For if a publisher is to be a publisher, he must retain final authority in the creating and developing of his product. To take over a "finished" project, bring it out as a book, and sell it to the schools reduces the function of the publishing house to that of a printer or distributor. That revered phrase, "editorial integrity" comes under fire.

In continuing, Redding expressed even more serious concern with the potentially restrictive influences of large-scale indoctrination and training upon the traditionally diversified approaches to American education, saying: [4]

It is clear that when "courses" developed by foundations or Government carry with them funds for subsidizing the retraining of teachers on a mass scale, a new problem is created for educational publishing. . . . [It] must be remembered that a standard definition of a textbook is simply "a course of study in print." That is, the function of the textbook author is so to shape and structure the basic content of a subject area as to give it beginning, middle, and end—in short, prepare a *course*. Traditionally, then, the variety of textbooks available in a subject at a given grade-level has existed because it was understood that some teachers preferred a course organized one way, others preferred it in another. Such preference generally grew out of the differences in background and training (especially *training*) among teachers. So varied are these differences that eight, ten, or twelve text offerings may exist for one course at one grade level.

Now something new has been added. Many thousands of teachers are being trained in the conduct of *one* kind of course, *one* point of view, *one* methodology, *one* set of materials. Over a period of years, then, we may conceivably expect to see *one course* in a given discipline. (Did someone say "brainwashing"? The word has been used— and in precisely this context!). . . .

Aside from the philosophic implications of this unprecedented development in American Education, many publishers foresee certain quite real threats to established competition within the textbook industry. As it is, published offerings to the schools are rich and diverse chiefly because a wide variety of opinion concerning *content* and

[4] *Ibid.,* pp. 19–22.

method exists within the teaching profession. . . . Basic to the whole system is the existence of an educational market with many and varied points-of-view on book content. *Substitute for this a kind of academic single-mindedness and the whole structure collapses.* . . . *[If] teachers in critical subject areas are to be indoctrinated with one point of view in teaching one kind of course with one set of materials, diversity is at an end.* [Italics added.]

TEXTBOOK ADOPTION PRACTICES

The adoption of textbooks for use by schools continues to be a complex process fraught with legal technicalities and opportunities for misunderstanding. A host of complications arises from the sheer numbers of good and not-so-good textbooks from which to choose, from the competition between publishers, and from the increasing sophistication of teachers and students.

Variations in adoption practices

Various textbook adoption practices are in effect in schools and school systems throughout the United States. There are, for example, situations in which:

> Individual teachers adopt their own books without reference to other authority (seldom used).
> Individual school staff members develop, with the assistance of the principal or others, a list of recommended books for approval and action by the superintendent.
> There is centralized system-wide (district or county) selection of books on the basis of recommendations of special evaluation committees, supervisors, or other responsible individuals.
> There is state-wide adoption by the state board of education, usually with direct participation of special textbook selection committees representing different interests.

With most such forms there is the further possibility of variations known as "basal," "co-basal," and "multiple." With basal adoptions, the single book or series chosen for a grade must be used by all schools; the adoption period generally ranges from one to six years. With co-basal listings, two such books or series are chosen to compete for use in the schools. The multiple adoption system involves the listing of three or more books or series for each grade or subject. Only three states—Alabama, California, and North Carolina—use basal or co-basal adoptions (and then not for all levels or subjects). When adoptions are made at the state level, the more common practice throughout the United States is to follow the policy of multiple listings.

A trend toward more local control of book adoptions may be observed in several current practices. Increasingly common, for example, is the use of the so-called "open system," a plan that places no special limits on the list of approved textbooks; rather, it permits books of all recognized publishers to be made available if they fit school requirements. In some cases, the open system applies equally to all schools in a district or county unit; more commonly, however, the schools of various districts within such administrative units make their own basal, co-basal, or multiple selections from these open lists.

Several variations in textbook adoption policies at the state level may be discerned in the programs of Virginia, California, and Georgia:

> *Virginia.* The State Board of Education adopts a multiple list of textbooks for each grade or basic subject area. Schools choose from this list. Local school officials then may make use of it for single or multiple adoptions. The purchase by any pupil of more than one basal textbook for a subject is discouraged except in schools having limited library facilities.

> *California.* The *Education Code* requires uniform use of state-adopted basic textbooks in all elementary schools. While it permits adoption of one or more basic texts, the usual practice is to adopt only one, along with various supplementary texts, and textbooks are furnished without direct cost to children. It also requires that adopted books be continued in use for not less than four years. When an original adoption period has expired, the State Board of Education may extend it for one to four years. Possible overemphasis on uniformity resulting from this procedure is relieved by the right of the local school districts to purchase supplementary books that do not appear on the list with local funds. The governing board of each California high school district is also empowered to adopt textbooks of recognized publishers who file bonds with the State Board of Education. Adoption periods must be for not less than three years. Adopted books are supplied free (on a loan basis) to all appropriate students.

> *Georgia.* The state maintains a free textbook system under which the State Board of Education is authorized to prescribe textbooks for use in elementary and secondary schools. Multiple listings of books for use in each grade are supplied. School systems may then make single adoptions from this list to meet local and individual needs.

Evaluating and selecting textbooks

Despite the complexities of textbook selection, there is surprising unanimity among professional educators as to administrative policies and procedures needed to guide the process. In one report developed by the Joint Committee of the NEA and the American Textbook Publishers Institute, for example, the following evaluation and selection procedures were recommended: [5]

> *A written policy.* The school system should have a written policy to govern evaluation and selection procedures. The written policy should be made available to all administrators and classroom teachers, to textbook

[5] *Guidelines for Textbook Selection,* Joint Committee of the NEA and the American Textbook Publishers Institute, New York, 1963.

publishers and their representatives, and to any members of the school community upon request.

> *Two-way communication.* The procedures should provide two-way communication between publishers' representatives and members of the adoption committee. Publishers' representatives should, upon invitation, present their textbooks to the committee as a whole.

> *Continuing communication.* The procedures should also provide the publishers' representatives with the opportunity to confer with principals, department heads, supervisors, and key teachers not only during an adoption period but on a continuing basis.

> *A systematic review.* The procedures should include, subject to revision, annual plans for reviewing the textbook list and adoption schedule.

> *Composition of committees.* The procedures should establish the size of the various committees and prescribe their membership.

> *Mailing examination copies.* The procedures should provide publishers' representatives with the opportunity to send examination copies directly to the committee which evaluates books and to other advisers of the committee.

> *Mailing advertising and promotional materials.* Procedures should permit publishers' representatives to send circulars and other descriptive materials directly to the textbook committee and its advisers.

> *Sales interviews.* Procedures in cities adopting multiple lists should permit publishers' representatives to interview not only textbook committees that select books for listing but also the teachers in each school who are responsible for selecting titles from the approved list, if this conforms with the adoption policy in the school system.

> *Announcing pending adoptions.* Procedures should describe school administration policy in announcing adoptions. The administrator should make clear whether the announcement is to be mailed to all textbook publishers and their representatives or to be available for the representatives' information at the administration office.

> *Providing time for the selection committee.* Procedures should provide selection committees and teachers with the time they need to evaluate and recommend titles for adoption.

Adoption at the state level: California

Procedures for selecting elementary-school textbooks to be used in grades 1 through 8 of the California public schools are based on legislative statutes, although final responsibility for the process rests with a ten-member State Board of Education that is appointed by the governor. A board-appointed group of eleven professional educators, known as the Curriculum Commission, is assigned major resonsibilities for textbook adoptions. It operates as follows: [6]

> Working from a calendar that shows termination dates of adoption periods of existing books, the Commission determines when it must begin study of conditions which should surround the selection of new books. With

[6] Adapted from various materials supplied the authors by the California State Department of Education.

available information about current school needs, the Commission then appoints subcommittees to draw up criteria governing the call for bids and the judging of books. These criteria are recommended to the State Board of Education, which in turn directs that a call for bids be issued by the Bureau of Textbooks and Publications of the State Department of Education. The approved criteria statement accompanies the call for bids. In a large adoption which involves quite a number of books, a preliminary study is sometimes made to eliminate those with obviously least merit. Intensive study is then concentrated on those remaining.

❯ The call for bids specifies when and how books and sealed bids shall be submitted. Each publisher is required to provide free samples of books to be evaluated. For a 1964 adoption, for example, each book publisher was required to submit 350 copies of each book to be considered. These were sent directly to individual Commission members who were to conduct the evaluative studies. Members of the State Curriculum Commission may also request still other books for classroom tryouts or other purposes.

❯ In the meantime, the Commission has met and agreed upon major outlines of the evaluative studies to be conducted. These vary in nature from adoption to adoption according to kinds of material considered or conditions under which evaluations are to be made.

❯ Individual Commission members usually secure the additional cooperation of other groups of educators who represent school districts and county offices. In a normal adoption, the number of teachers, principals, supervisors, college professors, or lay citizens involved in the studies ranges from 300 to more than 2,000.

❯ Upon completing the individual studies and gathering the necessary facts, Commission members meet to agree upon books to be recommended to the State Board of Education. When the Commission has agreed upon its recommendations, the successful books are exhibited for a 30-day period in public libraries for examination before the Board makes a final adoption. Written recommendations and copies of all recommended books are then transmitted by the Curriculum Commission to the State Board of Education. When the Curriculum Commission has agreed upon its recommendations, bids (which had previously been submitted by publishers) are opened. When making their original recommendations, Commission members are purposely unaware of the nature of the bid prices.

❯ On the appointed date, the State Board of Education receives official recommendations of the Commission together with bid summaries and cost analyses for the various books involved. This discussion, open to the public, provides opportunity for interested individuals to react to the recommendations in accordance with procedures prescribed by the State Board of Education.

❯ The final stage in the process is the formal adoption of the textbooks by the State Board of Education. This may result from one of several types of recommendations which the Commission has made. In some instances, the Commission will transmit a recommendation of a single book or series, in which case it usually specifies that after examination of all the books submitted, the one recommended is so clearly outstanding that it should be adopted unless an unreasonable difference in cost exists between it and the other books for which bids have been received. When two or more textbooks are given equal rattings of educational quality, the Commission normally recommends the one most economically priced. If one book recommended by the Commission should happen to cost considerably more than others, the State Board of Education may return the recommendation to the Curriculum Commission for further study. This same procedure may also be used when some objectionable feature becomes apparent to the Board, or if serious objections to the adoption are received from outside sources.

Local textbook adoptions

Although the laws of the several states place final responsibility for the approval and adoption of textbooks in the hands of state, county, and local boards of education, the usual practice at the local level is to authorize the superintendent to appoint a textbook selection committee to recommend specific adoptions—whether from multiple or open listings.

The composition and conduct of the work of this committee are of crucial importance, for it is through such efforts that the full intent of textbook laws are put into effect. A number of questions pertain to such appointments:

❯ What should the qualifications of committee members be (personal, professional, other)?

❯ Should there be one or more lay representatives as well as professional school personnel on the committee?

❯ Should there be just *one* system-wide committee? Or would it be preferable to have a main coordinating committee that receives assistance from other subcommittees, each involved with some specific tasks (e.g., recommending adoptions for sixth-grade science)?

In selecting and organizing the local textbook selection committee, the superintendent or other appointing official should:

❯ Consult supervisors, principals, and others in the system to recommend especially well-qualified individuals as its members. Classroom teachers who will use the textbooks should certainly be represented, as should curriculum specialists, educational media generalists, and librarians. Special subject experts and outside lay consultants also should be added to the committee or consulted, as appropriate.

❯ From those so qualified, choose an appropriate number (from seven to eleven are recommended). The size of the committee will be determined, in part, by the nature of its responsibilities and assignments.

❯ In the appointment letter, indicate specifically the functions of the committee, name its chairman or indicate procedures to be followed in having the committee choose its own, and list and supply copies of official rules, regulations, forms, and other materials with which committee members should be familiar. If deadline dates and schedules are involved, these should be spelled out. Indicate the nature of expected final committee actions and the form in which results should be presented.

❯ Publicize committee appointments to inform school personnel and others about the composition and responsibilities of the group.

185

DEVELOPING AND USING SELECTION CRITERIA

Various pros and cons have been and continue to be expressed about what constitutes an effective means of judging textbooks. Rating charts (score cards) are widely supported, yet many claim that they over-emphasize the purely mechanical aspects of books and substitute analysis of such features for the more desirable understanding of their true educational worth.

It has also been recommended that textbooks be rated on the basis of their own aims, rather than aims that appear to be so general that they might apply to nearly any book. In judging in this way, a teacher may try the book in question on himself, seeking to estimate the validity of the author's approach, the suitability of the difficulty level, or the appropriateness of suggested student activities and assignments.

A third and highly recommended means of developing textbook ratings is organizing a program for their controlled use in classrooms. Under this plan, students actually use the books to study materials related to some topic or special purpose. Such tryouts provide bases for measuring the extent to which students understand the ideas and vocabulary of the text, follow its directions, and perform the assignments.

There are other procedures, of course, and they might be used to obtain textbook evaluations, but neither they nor those just described can be considered completely objective or foolproof. In consequence, it can only be recommended that one seek as much objectivity as possible: a multiple approach to evaluation, utilizing several sources of data, usually results. The approach involves (1) *semiobjective analyses* of content, using a suitable rating-card device that contains statements of generalized criteria and detailed subquestions or comments to aid in standardizing examinations; (2) *introspective analyses,* through which evaluators seek to understand and rate books in terms of the authors' purposes; and (3) *controlled classroom tryouts.*

The following criteria for evaluating basal textbooks in grade 6 social studies are abstracted from a statement adopted by the California State Curriculum Commission in 1961 (and submitted with an advance "call for bids" to publishers of books to be evaluated):

> ❯ *Introduction.* The social studies, including history, geography, civics, and related subjects, occupy a most important position in the curriculum of the California schools. The major purpose of the social studies is the development of the well-informed patriotic American citizenry. Textbooks in these subjects are important because they provide information and help to develop skills essential for responsible citizenship. Such textbooks affect the ideals, loyalties, and attitudes of pupils. The utmost care will be exercised to select textbooks that (1) are factually accurate; (2) are up to date; (3)

develop appreciation of and loyalty to our basic American ideals and institutions; (4) are written objectively and in good taste; and (5) are written by authors who are competent and are loyal to American ideals and principles.

❯ *Scope of content (weighting: 325).* Basic texts shall cover the complete content outlined for the grade or give adequate coverage to a major portion of the content. (The theme for grade 6 is an overview of global geography and study of life in Latin America.) (There follows a complete statement of areas of emphasis in "Global Geography and Study of Life in Latin America," describing generalized understanding concerning the effects of scientific discovery on life in the world today, interrelationships among countries of the Americas, and how people live in various Latin American countries.)

❯ *Point of view and nature of content (weighting: 150).* The book shall stress the interrelationships and contributions of all the social sciences that are significant in developing appreciation and understanding of the content for the grade (see *Report of California State Central Committee on Social Studies*); develop concepts in ways appropriate to the characterictics of child growth and development and to principles of learning presented in the report; emphasize desirable social attitudes; interpret the present in terms of the past; stress the movements, principles, and facts generally considered to be of greatest significance; emphasize movements and trends rather than isolated events; emphasize meaning, interpretation, and use of facts; emphasize wise use and conservation of human and natural resources; be written with consideration of definitely known interests of pupils and in an interesting manner; be accurate and fair in its treatment of issues; be up to date; contribute to the development of critical thinking and problem solving; stimulate interests that will lead to further study; be of acceptable literary quality.

❯ *Appropriateness to grade level (weighting: 150).* The concepts treated shall be appropriate for and within the understanding of pupils of the grades for which the material is intended. The reading difficulty of the materials, including vocabulary, sentence structure, and organization, shall be appropriate for the grade.

❯ *Organization (weighting: 100).* The materials shall be organized and presented so as to facilitate correlation with other subjects; to encourage flexibility of use; and in comprehensive units dealing with topics or problems.

❯ *Illustrations (weighting: 100).* The book shall include an appropriate number and variety of up-to-date illustrative materials, including pictures, maps, charts, graphs, and diagrams, that definitely contribute to the understanding of basic relationships and clarify the text and enrich the content.

❯ *Aids to learning (weighting: 100).* The book shall contain an appropriate number and variety of suggestions and directions for study; exercises, questions, problems, and activities that are organized and presented to provide for individual differences; selected references, including bibliographies and sources of audio-visual materials. The book shall also contain an index, glossaries, appendixes, etc., appropriate to its nature.

❯ *Physical features (weighting: 75).* The book shall conform to generally accepted standards of appearance; size, style, and spacing of type; margins and arrangement of materials on page and sheets; cover design; and size.

TEXTBOOK PURCHASING PATTERNS

Free distribution of textbooks is required in many states and permissive in others. But even when textbooks are described as "free," they must be accounted for—there must be a calling for bids and handling of matters related to ordering, shipping, and billing. The nature of these several operations may be made clear by reference to procedures now employed in several representative states.

In Georgia, for example, money is appropriated annually for the purchase of textbooks; the law stipulates that it "shall not be less than $3 per child per year." These funds are then credited by the State Department of Education to the account of each school system in the state. Textbook orders (made up from the approved multiple adoptions list mentioned previously) are forwarded by the system superintendent to the State Division of Instructional Materials and Library Services for checking and approval. Approved orders are then sent directly to the Georgia office of the publisher involved or to the Georgia School Book Depository, a privately operated facility that handles materials on contract with individual publishers. As orders are filled, charges are credited against the system's account in the State Department of Education.

Actual shipments or deliveries of textbooks from publishers or contractual distributors are usually made directly to schools or to centralized county or district textbook depositories. If the former, individual school personnel are expected to provide the necessary processing required to maintain later distribution control over the books. If the latter, centalized processing is often completed before books are redistributed to individual schools.

In some cases, counties and districts combine centralized processing with a plan for maintaining their own warehouse inventories of the textbooks ordered most frequently, issuing them to schools as requested and restocking as necessary, thus avoiding shipping delays that often occur with orders filled from more distant points.

In Indiana, the Commission on Textbook Adoptions of the State Board of Education receives sealed bids from publishers of approved textbooks prior to the deadline date expressed in a formal "notice to publishers" that is issued each year according to schedule. Prices for accepted titles are then published in the *Administrative Handbook for Indiana Schools* for the guidance of school and district personnel in placing future orders. Prior to July 15 each year, the schools notify authorized dealers of the titles and probable numbers of books they will require for the ensuing year. The dealer agrees that he will deliver them during the month of August, unless other arrangements are mutually agreed upon.

In Florida, the usual procedure is to develop contracts with textbook publishers for a period of five years; during this time, publishers guarantee to deliver adopted books at the contract price, regardless of interim advances in costs. Purchase and distribution of textbooks are financed through annual general revenue appropriations made biennially by the Florida State Legislature. County textbook allocations are made on a uniform principle prescribed by the State Board of Education. The amount of money allocated to counties ordinarily sets the ceiling for textbook expenditures for that year, although balances may be increased through unexpended funds that are carried over from preceding years. Additional funds may also be granted counties that are experiencing marked increases in enrollment, losses by fire or storm, or facing unexpected expenses.

Florida law requires that every textbook publisher to whom a contract is issued must maintain a depository in which sufficient books are kept to permit filling orders without delay at a convenient distribution point. Such depositories may be maintained jointly; currently, all publishers ship through a single depository, the Florida School Book Depository in Jacksonville. Books are sold to the state at a price that is f.o.b. the depository.

Florida also maintains the State Textbook Exchange in Tallahassee, which is used primarily for collecting and redistributing surplus textbooks. The program has been credited with saving thousands of dollars.

TEXTBOOK ECONOMICS

Many questions arise in any consideration of the economics of textbook purchases and use: What must schools budget as a minimum to obtain and maintain an adequate supply of excellent and up-to-date textbooks? What are recommended ways of developing and arranging the budgets? How can budget allocations be made to reflect needs for additions of new titles, replacements, and purchase of extra sets to provide for increased enrollments? The NEA recently reported: [7]

> The cost of textbooks is a small item in the total cost of education. And today there is real danger that the percent of the school budget which goes into books may decrease. There is great need for better salaries. Expensive technological equipment which introduces other media into the processes of teaching and learning is being purchased. Other costs are also rising.
>
> In 1958–59, expenditures per pupil for textbooks were at a median level of $3.48 in the largest city school systems (100,000 and over in population) and $4.02 in the smallest systems (2,500–9,999 in population) studied. Costs per pupil ranged from less than $1 in some systems to more than $12.
>
> At present the American Library Association recommends a bare minimum of $4 per pupil per year, for library purchase only, to procure books nominally classified as trade books, rather than text-

[7] *NEA Research Memo, Textbook Selection,* Research Division, NEA, July, 1962, p. 9.

books. This allows nothing for magazines, pamphlets, newspapers, encyclopedias and dictionaries. This is a budget which will add one book each year to the school library for each pupil in that school.

Obviously, textbook purchases should be at the rate of several books per pupil per year. The committee should never reject an excellent book on the basis of cost alone. What costs the most in the operation of a school system is the salaries of its employees. To save money on the less than 2 per cent of current expenditures used for textbooks is a pennywise and pound-foolish policy.[8]

The American Textbook Publishers Institute, a professional and trade association for publishers of textbooks, reference books, test materials, and workbooks, stresses that the *per capita* supply of textbooks has dwindled by 20 per cent during the past ten years and points to a need for better knowledge on the part of school personnel as to how textbook needs should be projected and budgeted. In a statement on this subject,[8] the executive secretary, Austin J. McCaffrey, pointed out that on a national basis, the expenditures for textbooks on the elementary and secondary levels average less than $5 per pupil—about $3.50 at the elementary level and $6.50 at the secondary.

Faulty budgeting practices were believed by McCaffrey to constitute the greatest threat to adequate supplies of textbooks in the school: [9]

Our pupil population is growing so fast, that administrators can't keep on top of their problem. . . . Take this example. School A with 1,000 pupils spends $3 per pupil each year on textbooks. That's $3,000. The average life of these books is five years. That gives you a total of $15,000 worth of books in use—or $15 per pupil for the period. Now let's say that enrollment in that school increases to 1,200 the fifth year and the school still spends only $3 per pupil. It will than have only $15,600 worth of books available for 1,200 pupils—an average of $13 per pupil. In other words, in order to maintain its supply at $15 per pupil, it will have to budget the usual $3 per pupil for the 1,000 older pupils and $15 for each of the additional 200. That's the only way to give this new 200 its own complete set of books.

The problems of maintaining textbooks in good repair throughout their period of adoption and determining and requiring proper reimbursement by users who damage or lose them are related economic aspects. With reasonable care, textbooks should last throughout the adoption period and if one is lost or damaged beyond the limits of "reasonable wear and tear," either the student or his parents is usually asked to make proper reimbursement to the issuing authority.

The Florida schools are required to collect the value of lost or damaged textbooks and turn over such collections to the state superintendent; eventually, they are allocated to the textbook credits of the

[8] Austin J. McCaffrey, "How to Select and Budget for Textbooks," *School Management,* vol. 2, pp. 26–30, September, 1958.
[9] *Ibid.,* p. 30.

county involved. In all such cases, the value of books that have been used for a year or more is left to the discretion of the person assessing charges (within a variable of 50 to 75 per cent of original cost), although it is assumed that any book still suitable for distribution should be valued at at least 50 per cent of its original cost.

The importance of replacement charges in relation to pupil attitudes is stressed in a Florida State Department of Education publication: [10]

It is highly important that collections be made for loss and careless or malicious abuse of books. The value of these collections is not primarily preservation of the State's investment in books or in the replenishment of inventories, however important these may be; the fundamental value of emphasis on collection for lost and damaged books is essentially the development in the pupil of an appreciation of public property, the promotion of a sense of responsibility, and the encouragement of behavior appropriate to a well-oriented growing personality.

INFORMATION ABOUT TEXTBOOKS

Useful information about textbooks, their availability, content, publishers, and prices may be obtained from the following sources:

Textbooks in Print. Issued yearly (in April); indexed according to author, title, and subject; contains bibliographic data. Available from R. R. Bowker and Company, 1180 Avenue of The Americas, New York, New York. *American Textbook Publishers Institute.* Write to 432 Park Avenue South, New York, New York.
Paperbound Books in Print. Issued semiannually; lists several thousand inexpensive paperbacks (reprints and originals) with subject guides. Published by R. R. Bowker and Company, 1180 Avenue of The Americas, New York, New York.
Books in Print. Issued annually; lists reprints of catalogs issued by various publishers. Available from R. R. Bowker and Company, 1180 Avenue of The Americas, New York, New York. See also *Subject Guide to Books in Print* by the same publishers.

SUMMARY

In American education the textbook—unlike its counterparts in many other parts of the world—occupies a significant and influential role. While there are predictions that this influence will wane and perhaps disappear almost entirely with increased use of electronic, audio-visual, and other forms of information retrieval, this view is far from universal.

[10] "General Policies and Suggestions: Administration of the Textbook Program," *Florida School Bulletin,* vol. 25, p. 12, June, 1963. (Textbook issue)

It seems reasonable to expect that textbooks will continue to be planned, written, published, and used; it is also reasonable to expect that their content and presentation in the future will be considerably improved over what we have today. The effects of various national efforts at improving textbooks are already being observed in publications that have grown out of programs such as those of the Biological Sciences Curriculum Study, the Physical Science Study Committee, the School Mathematics Study Group, and others. Indeed, the activities of such groups—many of them financed and underwritten by government and foundations—have caused concern on the part of some observers as to whether it will be possible to continue the editorial integrity of private publishers who contract to print, bind, and distribute products over whose content and treatment they have no control.

Variations in textbook adoption and distribution practices reflect, in large part, other differences in administrative practices found in school systems throughout the country. Today's trends in practices are toward greater breadth of selection and toward more open listings and multiple adoptions.

FOR FURTHER INFORMATION

Alm, Richard S.: "Textbooks: The Problems of Choice," *Educational Administration and Supervision,* vol. 42, pp. 353–357, October, 1956.

Booher, Edward E.: "Textbook Publishing: An Art Extended," *Audiovisual Instruction,* vol. 6, pp. 16–18, January, 1961.

Cronbach, Lee J. (ed.): *Text Materials in Modern Education,* The University of Illinois Press, Urbana, Ill., 1955. 216 pp.

Cummings, Howard H., and Helen K. Mackintosh: *Curriculum Responsibilities of State Departments of Education,* U.S. Office of Education, Misc. no. 30, 1958, chap. 4, "Textbook Selection and State Requirements," pp. 20–26.

Davis, O. L., Jr.: "Textbooks and Other Printed Materials," *Review of Educational Research,* vol. 32, pp. 127–140, April, 1962.

Faison, Edmund W. J.: "Readability of Children's Textbooks," *Journal of Educational Psychology,* vol. 42, pp. 43–51, January, 1951.

Jennings, Frank G.: "Textbooks and Trapped Idealists," *Saturday Review,* pp. 57–59, Jan. 18, 1964.

McCaffrey, Austin J.: "How to Select and Budget for Textbooks," *School Management,* vol. 2, pp. 26–30, September, 1958.

McLuhan, Marshall: "Electronics and the Changing Role of Print," *Audiovisual Communication Review,* vol. 8, pp. 74–83, September–October, 1960.

Mellott, Malcolm E.: "What to Look for in Choosing a Textbook," *NEA Journal,* vol. 44, pp. 158–159, March, 1955.

Spaulding, William E.: *How Shall We Judge Them?* Houghton Mifflin, Boston, 1961. 24 pp.

Vartanian, Pershing: "Criteria and Techniques for Textbook Evaluation," *Social Studies,* vol. 53, pp. 123–127, April, 1962.

chapter 10

Administering
educational television

Of all the new media in education, none is growing so rapidly or in so many directions as educational television. New administrative arrangements are constantly being developed to meet new and often unique instructional problems, and new uses for the medium are still being uncovered. This combination of diversity and rapid growth has resulted in a variety of patterns of organization. There is no single standard for the administration of ETV to serve as the basis for this discussion. Instead, we will look at television as a resource to be combined with others in solving certain kinds of instructional problems, at the development of the medium into its present varied forms, and at a few specific examples of station and closed-circuit administrative structures.

Both television and its counterpart, radio, have important roles in educational broadcasting. Both are vigorous today, and both will undoubtedly continue to play vital roles in education. As of 1964, educational radio stations (mostly FM) were still being licensed at a steady rate of about two per month. However, television has unquestionably become the dominant medium, towering far above radio in its impact on education. For this reason and because of space limitations, the discussion of educational broadcasting in this chapter will be confined almost entirely to television. Only brief attention will be given to radio in the following section on the development of educational broadcasting.

BACKGROUND: DEVELOPMENT OF
EDUCATIONAL BROADCASTING

The year usually chosen to mark the beginning of commercial broadcasting in the United States, 1920, may be used for educational broadcasting as well. The first university-owned radio station, Wisconsin's WHA, was licensed in that year, although experimental broadcasts had begun earlier.[1] From that time until all new-station construction was

---

[1] The early years of radio's history are well covered by Gleason L. Archer, *History of Radio to 1926,* The American Historical Co., New York, 1938. The growth of educational radio is traced by John Walker Powell, *Channels of Learning,* Public Affairs Press, Washington, D.C., 1962, pp. 28–40.

Educational television continues to play an increasingly important role in American education. Here a Swiss-developed rear-view television projector, the "Eidophor," is used in an experimental sociology course taught at Pennsylvania State University. (*Pennsylvania State University*)

halted at the beginning of World War II, more than 200 licenses for radio stations were issued to educational institutions, but few of these stations survived for many years. Those which did, particularly those in the northern sections of the Midwest, successfully demonstrated the teaching value of radio, and most of them also have survived the shift of emphasis in educational broadcasting toward television. Today only 30 educational AM radio stations still operate, and most of them were originally licensed in the 1920s and early 1930s.

Two new forms of broadcasting that were to become more important educationally than AM radio were just coming out of the experimental stage when the United States entered World War II. After the war, television and FM radio quickly became major commercial broadcast services, and their potential as transmitters of education was recognized as it had never been with AM radio. In 1945, the Federal Communications Commission (FCC) set aside 20 FM channels specifically for educational use, an action that had long been urged for AM without success. This set an important precedent for educational television channel reservations, which were to come later.

The FCC's table of TV channel allocations, set up originally in 1941, had not contained specific provisions for educational stations.

By 1948, most of the channels had been assigned. The story of the FCC "freeze" on new-station construction (1948–1952), the original reservation of 242 channels for ETV,[2] and the subsequent rather plodding growth is well known and need not be recounted here. For purposes of summarization, the pattern of growth of ETV stations during their first decade or so will suffice.

The slow start of educational television was due partly to the cost, since the original capital outlay requirements frequently ranged upward from $200,000. Because ETV stations were required to operate on a noncommercial basis, they often had to look to outside agencies for support, particularly during the difficult period of initial construction. Certainly, the slow beginning of ETV would have been even slower had it not been for the generous help of agencies of the Ford Foundation, and more recently, the Federal government.

In the decade from 1951 to 1961, the Ford Foundation spent $50 million on ETV activities. These included (1) supporting the Joint Committee on Educational Television, the agency through which educators lobbied for the reservation of ETV channels and which later assisted local groups in activating those channels; (2) establishing and maintaining a center for ETV program production and distribution, which is now—after several name changes—called National Educational Television (NET); and (3) assisting in the construction of thirty-five ETV stations in key cities by granting $3.5 million on a matching basis to educational institutions or community groups.

In 1962, after several earlier attempts to get legislation past the House of Representatives, Congress passed the Educational Television Facilities Act aud authorized expenditures of $32 million over a five-year period. After some delay, the first funds were appropriated in 1963, and the first grants were made that year. Appropriations are made on a matching basis for the construction of ETV broadcasting facilities or for additions to the service of existing stations, with no more than $1 million to be allocated in any one state.

Another serious obstacle to ETV's early growth was the fact that the FCC had placed 162 of the 242 original reservations in the ultra-high-frequency (UHF) band, which was opened in 1952 to make space for more stations. But stations assigned in the UHF band were at a disadvantage because most receivers manufactured and sold could receive only Channels 2 to 13, which are in the very-high-frequency (VHF) band. All-channel receivers were more expensive, and few people purchased them. In Los Angeles, for example, a UHF educational station could not get an audience sufficient to justify continued programming when the potential audience already had a choice of programs originating from seven VHF stations. Only in 1962 were steps taken to correct this imbalance between the VHF and UHF bands. Legislation that became effective in 1964 requires that all new television receivers be capable of receiving all channels in both bands. But this

[2] FCC, *Sixth Report and Order,* Apr. 14, 1952.

law will have effect only as older models are replaced with all-channel sets.

In 1964, a further revision of the allocation of UHF channels was proposed by the FCC to accommodate still more commercial and educational stations. It would increase the total number of ETV reservations to about 700. The National Association of Educational Broadcasters (NAEB) replied to the FCC's plan with two studies. One showed that educational interests would need 1,200 channels in the next ten to fifteen years; the other used computer data to show how 1,000 of these channels could be incorporated into the revised table.

During these years of educational television expansion, educational radio has also been growing, although the number of AM stations has somewhat decreased. The upsurge has come in FM radio, for FCC regulations have made it very easy for educational institutions to start low-power stations. In less than ten years, nearly two hundred educational FM stations have begun to operate, and expansion is continuing. However, this expansion does not really reflect an increase in

Educational uses of closed-circuit television facilities have increased greatly with the development of simple-to-operate, relatively inexpensive camera units similar to that shown here. (*San Jose State College*)

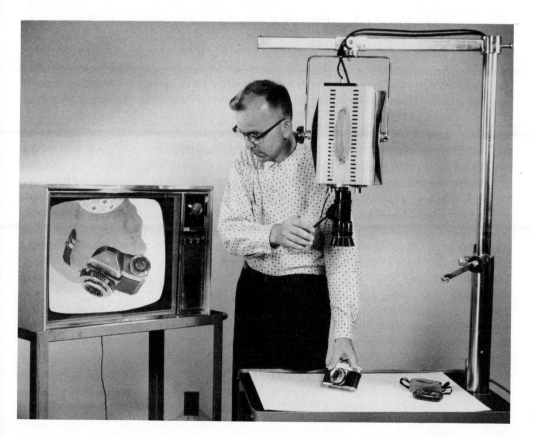

the use of radio for instruction, with a few exceptions. Most of the stations are operated by college students as an extracurricular activity or broadcasting laboratory, with programs of a general cultural nature rather than a means of implementing an instructional program.

So far, this overview has concentrated on broadcast stations, but the greatest growth—as least in terms of the number of installations —has been in closed-circuit television (CCTV).[3] Accurate count of CCTV installations is difficult to obtain, since these systems are not accountable to any regulatory agency, and figures obtained through surveys, go rapidly out of date. The Technological Development Project of the NEA published a directory in mid-1963 that showed over 400 installations, including 98 in school districts, 266 in higher educational institutions, and 78 in medical and dental schools.[4]

The dimensions of CCTV are further confused because of the widely different uses to which the systems are put and the variations in the extent and complexity of the distribution systems used to disseminate programs—ranging from occasional use in a lecture hall to magnify the instructor's demonstrations to complete formal courses broadcast by a state-wide system. A closer look at the various forms of CCTV will be provided later in this chapter.

ETV: NEW PROBLEMS AND NEW PROMISES

Administrators considering possible uses of instructional television must (1) determine whether its demonstrated values are applicable to their particular instructional requirements, (2) gain acceptance and support for its use, and (3) analyze and justify the costs that such a program is likely to involve.[5]

Advantages and capacities

The advantages of broadcasting for education have been enumerated by a number of authors, and the list expands or contracts with the author's viewpoint and the form of broadcasting discussed. As superintendent of schools in Pittsburgh, Calvin Gross listed the advantages (here paraphrased, in part) that his district derived from open-circuit telecasts: [6]

[3] There is no comparable "closed-circuit radio," except the carrier-current radio stations operated at some colleges as a student activity. Recordings have taken over this function, permitting greater flexibility.

[4] *Studies in the Growth of Instructional Technology, II: A Directory of Closed-circuit Television Installations in American Education with a Pattern of Growth,* Department of Audio-Visual Education, NEA, May, 1963.

[5] We discuss television exclusively here because it is of paramount interest to most educators. Radio should not be forgotten, however, as it can also serve important educational purposes, and at far less cost than television.

[6] Calvin E. Gross, in *The Superintendent's Viewpoint on Educational Television: A Panel Discussion before the Region I Conference of the National Association of Educational Broadcasters,* Thomas Alva Edison Foundation, March, 1959.

❯ *Television can bring to the classroom certain courses that, for one reason or another, the school does not offer.* For example, there has been a growing interest in the teaching of foreign languages in the elementary grades, but frequently financial considerations and lack of trained teachers have prevented widespread adoption. Television offers a means by which schools can present a first-rate course in elementary foreign language to its students.

❯ *Television can satisfy certain special needs of a school.* Many school districts are unable to offer a course in high school physics because of the lack of trained teachers. Now any student within the range of stations telecasting the films can have a first-rate course in physics, however limited the budget, the teacher supply, or the school equipment.

❯ *Television can bring enrichment to a course already offered in the school.* Television can bring outstanding guests and unusual experiences to the students—enrichment far beyond what could ever be offered in any classroom.

❯ *Quality instruction can be spread on a broad base.* When an especially selected teacher has the opportunity to give full time to the production of one television lesson each day and has the assistance of several specialists, he can produce first-rate lessons. These lessons excel in the use of visual and enriched materials, smoothness and clarity of presentation, and effective transition.

❯ *Television lessons can provide in-service training for participating teachers.* No matter how expert a teacher may be, he can learn through the observation of another expert teacher at work. Television provides ample opportunity for such observation.

❯ *Television can stimulate students to greater activity.* When one visits classrooms that have been using television lessons, he notes a tremendous growth in materials and projects that have developed as a result of viewing. This is concrete evidence of the stimulation and motivation of the youngsters.

❯ *Television can be a powerful public relations adjunct.* When parents can see what their children are being taught and how, they become more interested in the schools. It takes the school to the parents.

A different type of categorization of television capacities was developed by the California state college system as part of a report seeking legislative support for ETV. It identifies a series of separate "operational objectives" for which television may be used by higher educational institutions: [7]

The planning and development of an instructional television service

The production of instructional TV presentations in conjunction with existing television stations in the area of the college

Closed-circuit instructional television services

Operation of an educational television broadcast station

Interinstitutional exchange of televised instruction

[7] Marvin Laser, *Television for the California State Colleges: A Report to the Chancellor and the Trustees,* April, 1963.

Observation services for teacher education

Image magnification and other related TV teaching aids

Curriculums in broadcasting

Other uses, such as development of a CCTV system solely for the distribution of pre-recorded audio-visual materials, or for courses in broadcasting amounting to less than a full curriculum in that area, etc.

Despite the inclusiveness of these arguments (and it is difficult to conceive of situations in which some form of TV could not be used effectively) it remains for the administrator of each school, district, or college to consider TV in relation to his own instructional program and its problems. The particular pattern of development will depend upon the characteristics of both the medium itself and the school situation. Whatever the specific purposes for which broadcasting may be used, systematic planning for television in education entails a consideration of such common problems as acceptance, cost, and choice of facilities. These will be discussed in the following pages of this section and in the next section.

Acceptance

During the past decade, there have been a number of instances in which instructional TV projects have faltered because of resistance by members of the faculty and/or administration. Any widespread use of TV to attempt to solve instructional problems requires the cooperation of many people throughout the staff—studio teachers, production personnel, classroom teachers, business and personnel officers—so a broad base of support is necessary. Often resistance comes when teachers, department heads, or principals feel that they have not had adequate opportunity to participate in the planning of TV instruction. The solution to the problem is to get all concerned involved in policy making and planning at the appropriate stages of development. Instructional television cannot be introduced or implemented by administrative fiat. On the other hand, nurturing a vigorous program probably will not be facilitated by a timid or vacillating attitude on administration's part. Strong leadership is not inconsistent with the democratic development of clear-cut policies that represent teachers, students, and administration alike, but constant two-way communication and give and take are required.

A further resistance arises out of the apprehensions of teachers who are afraid to appear on TV, those who regard TV as a competitor, those who are afraid of being displaced, and those who fear that TV will destroy the values of small-group face-to-face instruction. There is no simple or magical answer to these doubts and fears. By appropriate orientation or experience, teachers should come to know that they will not be forced on camera, that they can teach with better preparation, more support, and optimum effectiveness on television, if they are so inclined. Teachers who at first fear the competition may learn that classroom TV frees them to give more time to other more personal aspects of instruction. The fear of displacement or loss of job is real in a psychological sense, but it tends to disappear when teachers are oriented to the facts or involved in the planning and use of television as a teaching tool, but not as a supposed total answer to the complicated and varied tasks of instruction. Finally, teachers who fear that the medium will dehumanize the instructional process may feel reassured when they are exposed to various limited, partial, and special applications or to instructional plans that balance large-group TV presentations against small group face-to-face teaching in the same course. Of course, there is no assurance that any of the common negative attitudes or fears of teachers will be quickly dispelled by information, involvement in planning, or direct participation. Familiarity with television frequently leads to changes in attitude; quite often it is in a positive direction, but sometimes not. In the long run, much depends upon the further development of use of the medium and the way in which it is administered in any particular case.

Cost

Another important concern to those who plan and administer instructional television is the matter of cost—not merely the formidable outlays for initial installations and operation—but the problem of analyzing costs. The costs of television—equipment, personnel, etc.—cannot merely be added to existing figures, but must be computed in such a way as to allow comparison with alternative methods of instruction: [8]

> In order to arrive at an understanding of the cost of TV teaching and any possible financial benefits that may accrue (aside from the possible educational values), it is necessary to make comparisons with the costs of conventional teaching. Although there is a widespread view—perhaps a universal view—in the academic community that educational values may be imperiled if they are made subsidiary to economic considerations, there is also recognition of the sobering reality that adequacy of financial provisions also has a direct bearing on the potential quality of educational programs.

> *Television for the California State Colleges,* the report quoted here, goes on to show methods by which the costs of conventional and TV teaching can be computed. *The procedure is shown here only as an example of the method of computation. The method can be applied in any situation, but the figures, will vary considerably, of course.*[9]

> The costs of conventional teaching may be stated in a number of different ways. One way is to calculate the separate costs of teaching

[8] *Ibid.,* p. 59.
[9] *Ibid.,* pp. 60–61.

Sample analysis of estimated costs for TV teaching (using video tape repeats for three additional semesters) *

Step 1

Calculating the television production costs per student unit per semester

a. Annual production cost

TV equipment ($18,324 amortized over 5 years)	$21,665
TV staff salaries	28,000
Operating expenses budget	31,000
Total	$80,665

b. Cost per production hour (6 hours of new live production per week, 45 weeks per year: 270 hours): $80,665/270 $299.00

c. Production hour cost pro-rated over 4 semesters in which tapes are used: $299/4 (per hour, pro-rated)   75.00

d. Tape playback and student proctor cost: $12.00 per hour

Playback cost	3.00
Proctor cost (6 student proctors @ $1.50 per hour)	9.00

e. Total cost per hour, pro-rated ($75 + $12)   87.00

f. Cost per student per hour ($87/number of students) e.g., $87/265 : 33¢ per student class hour   0.33

g. Cost per student per unit (15 class hours per semester equals 1 unit) 15 × 33¢ : $4.95 per student unit   4.95

Step 2

Calculating the cost of television teacher per student unit, per semester (Illustration based on ⅔ configuration)

a. Total cost of TV teacher for course (3 units preparatory released time, 12 units for semester of taping course, 3 units for next three semesters of tape playbacks), for 24 units $9,215

b. Salary per semester, pro-rated over 4 semesters   2,304

c. Salary cost per TV unit taught ($2,304/2)   1,152

d. Cost per student unit per semester for 265 students ($1,152/265)   4.36

Step 3

Calculating cost for non-TV teachers for 1-unit discussion section which accompanies 2 units taught on TV

a. Cost per 1-unit discussion group per semester ($9,215/24) $384

b. Discussion groups needed @ 1 per 40 students: 265 students, 7 discussion groups (6.6 to be exact, but must be rounded off at next higher number)

c. Cost of seven 1-unit discussion groups ($384 × 7)   2,688

d. Cost per student unit per semester for discussion group ($2,688/265) $10.14

(NOTE: If exact multiples of 40 students are involved, cost per student unit per semester would be $9.60.)

* Adapted from Marvin Laser, *Television for the California State Colleges: A Report to the Chancellor and the Trustees,* April 1963.

Step 4

Calculating total cost, including subcosts of Steps 1, 2, 3 (TV
production, salary of TV teachers, salaries of non-TV teachers
for discussion groups)

a. Production costs (2 units @ $4.95 each)	$9.90
b. TV teacher (2 units @ $4.36 each)	8.72
c. Non-TV teacher (1 unit @ $10.14)	10.14
Total cost per student for course	$28.76
d. Cost per student unit ($28.76/3)	$9.58

expense, departmental expense, and institutional expense, to total these
expenses, and then to arrive at the "total expense per student credit-
hour" (or, student-unit). . . . These figures, however, do not afford
a basis for accurate comparison with estimated costs of teaching by
television. Items which include the costs of clerical salaries, supplies,
and equipment related to teaching, general administration, student
services, libraries, maintenance and operation of plant, etc., are not
affected by television teaching since they remain as more or less fixed
costs even when television teaching is under way. Since the only portion
of expenses per student unit which might be directly affected by television teaching—to be called *direct instructional expense*—is faculty
salaries, this figure must be isolated from the other expenses.

Because of the variability of teacher unit-load factor in different
categories of courses, variations in assigned student-teacher ratios,
and differences in actual class size the *exact* direct instructional expense per student in all sections of all courses shows considerable
variations. However, an *average direct instructional expense* can be
calculated as follows: The present average (mean) faculty salary for
the State College system is $9,215. The most typical undergraduate
course in the State Colleges (the type enrolling by far the largest number of individual students) is a lecture-discussion course meeting
three hours per week for three units of credit and enrolling up to a
maximum of 40 students per section. . . . A State College faculty
member has a teaching load of 24 units per year. . . . Although not
all of his courses will be of this category, nor will all sections necessarily
enroll 40 students, the average cost per student unit per semester can
be calculated. The cost for direct instructional expense *only* comes to
$9.60.

Step 1

To determine teaching cost per unit taught per semester divide
$9,215 by 24 = $384.

Step 2

To determine cost per student unit (assuming 40 students per class)
divide $384 by 40 = $9.60.

Then the costs of television teaching are computed: [10]

In calculating the costs of direct teaching by television, four groups
of sub-costs are involved: the cost of television equipment, the cost of

[10] *Ibid.,* pp. 61–63.

television production staff, the operating expenses of the television service, the salaries of faculty members who teach by television. The total cost of television equipment will depend on [its selection] according to local campus requirements. However, in the cost calculations that follow *all TV equipment is amortized over a period of five years,* and the costs apportioned to the production hours (units taught). . . . The total annual salaries and wages for the television operations staff will also depend on the total complement of staff employed, and again this will vary according to the phase of the operational plan. However, all TV staff annual salaries and wages are calculated as a part of production costs and pro-rated for production hours (units taught). The annual operating expenses are also variable according to the phase, but include such items as production expenses, spare parts, supplies of all kinds, and—as a major item if tape recording is done —video tape. In the cost calculations all TV operating expenses are also figured as a part of production costs and pro-rated for production hours (units taught).

Faculty salaries involve both the salaries for the TV teacher or teachers and the salaries for the non-TV teachers who are assigned discussion groups which accompany a course taught in the ⅔ or ⅓ configuration. [A configuration means that one-third of the course hours are taught via TV, with the remaining time in other activities— discussion, laboratory, etc. A two-third configuration would have two or three hours weekly via TV.] The faculty salaries for the TV teachers have been calculated according to the base figure ($9,215) with unit load figured as full load (normally 12 units) for teaching a 3-unit TV course, with released time of 3 units in the preceding semester for preparation, and with released time of 3 units per semester in subsequent semesters when video tapes are repeated. Faculty salaries are then pro-rated for the units taught. Salaries for teachers of the non-TV discussion groups are also pro-rated per unit taught. . . . A sample cost analysis showing details of procedures used is included.

TYPES OF TELEVISION FACILITIES

The decision to use television in an instructional program cannot be resolved by a simple "yes" answer. What it comes down to, in the end, is what type of facility will best serve the purposes of the program, giving due attention to its cost and relative economy as compared with alternatives. Should an open- or closed-circuit system be used? Should the school system or college provide its own or make use of other facilities? Some basic features of the main alternatives—their various advantages and disadvantages—are considered in the following discussion.

Open-circuit systems

Broadcast (open-circuit) television makes use of a system by which signals broadcast from a tower and antenna can be received by television receivers within range of the station and equipped with suitable receiving antennae. This is the most powerful and most expensive use of the medium. A major problem at the outset is obtaining a channel (by FCC license), which can be difficult, particularly in or near major cities. If a channel is available, transmitting equipment, a tower, and an antenna must be purchased, and licensed engineering personnel must be hired to operate the station. With such a station, only one program may be transmitted at any one time.

Broadcast stations may reach many people in widely scattered locations, including homes and offices. This takes in people who find it impossible or inconvenient to get to a school; or it might preclude their having to come to a school regularly if facilities were not available for them there.

Broadcast audiences, although they may be quite large in the aggregate, are often composed of individuals—just one person, perhaps —watching single sets. In-school broadcasts, on the other hand, are directed to classroom audiences. The type of audience, of course, has implications for program preparation. Broadcast audiences, for example, are nonselective—i.e., anyone may "tune in" so long as he is within range of the station, and this may preclude the discussion of certain topics intended for specialized audiences.

Closed-circuit systems

The basic definition of a closed-circuit system is that the signal orig-inated must be carried by cable or microwave relay directly from the originating point to every intended reception point. Instead of a trans-mitter, tower, and antenna, a distribution system is needed. A con-tinuous and selective physical connection must be maintained between the central point of transmission and all receivers. Microwave relays can serve as a "wireless wire" between selected points of transmission and reception in the system without destroying the concept of private communication.

Closed-circuit systems do not require the availability of a television channel, nor is a license required to operate. Technical personnel need not be licensed. However, the requirements for operational and main-tenance personnel, which vary with the amount and extent of use of the equipment, may be similar to those in a broadcast station. Because of this "direct connection," CCTV systems do provide for selective audi-ences. Only receivers connected to the system may receive the program.

In contrast to broadcast systems, the audiences for CCTV almost always are gathered in groups, although the degree of "captive-ness" may depend upon the extent to which classes viewing the lesson are monitored.

CCTV systems permit multiple programs to be distributed simul-taneously. Engineering considerations determine the precise number of signals that can be sent, but some systems allow a number of radio and television signals to be sent on the same cable or a pair of cables, and in either direction, so that what are reception points at one time may become originating points later.

CCTV systems are also capable of great flexibility and lend themselves to a "building-block" approach. For example, a system might start with a single camera and one or more receivers in a classroom and be used to magnify science demonstrations. Later the system could be extended to several classrooms in the same building. The next step might be to procure additional cameras and construct a studio, so that a wider range of materials and more elaborate presentations could be accommodated. Then the distribution system might be extended to nearby schools, to surrounding districts or counties, finally state-wide or even nationally.

Wiring and maintaining many and widely scattered locations can be costly via closed circuit. Of particular interest here is a July, 1963, ruling of the FCC; it is known thus far only as operation in the 2,500-megacycle band, and it permits educational broadcasters to combine many of the advantages of both open- and closed-circuit systems. From a central transmitter, programs can be sent to scattered schools and other reception points where these high-frequency transmissions are converted for regular channels and reception by conventional receivers. Since the broadcasting is on frequencies that the ordinary set cannot receive, the private quality of the broadcast is preserved. Also, multiple channels are provided in this band.

Use of commercial facilities

Thus far, discussion has concerned matters that are relevant if you provide your own TV facilities. Some of the problems and costs of "do-it-yourself" TV may be avoided by using commercial or ETV facilities, by purchasing or renting prerecorded materials, or by contracting for services. The first alternative will be considered here, the others in the following brief sections.

Using commercial facilities obviously elimates the need to own equipment or to hire operating personnel. The facilities are often better than most educational institutions could provide, but on the other hand, there may not be much opportunity to use them for preparation and rehearsal. Station schedules are crowded, and time means money, so the visiting producer should be prepared to do all but final run-throughs before coming to the studio.

Costs may be nothing or may include a "facilities charge" with no charge for airtime, or they may be full commercial rates. All TV stations are required by FCC regulations to provide time for education, but the definition of education is loose, and if a number of educational organizations are interested in having broadcast time, free time may not be available. However, even paying commercial rates may be cheaper than purchasing and maintaining facilities in some cases.

Frequently, the free time made available for educational use is limited to hours that the station cannot sell readily to advertisers, such as early mornings. And the schedule may get moved around if the station finds an advertiser who wants the time originally allotted for the educational program.

In any event, arrangement with commercial stations should be based on a clear understanding regarding the facilities, production assistance, and time available, and some formal agreement should be drawn up. A good deal of bitterness has been generated unintentionally between educators and commercial broadcasters when conditions were not clearly spelled out and recorded.

Use of ETV station facilities

Some schools and colleges that do not own their own television equipment may find it possible to make use of the facilities controlled by some other educational agency, such as a community corporation. A single college or university may use such facilities for broadcasting public relations or instructional programs or work out an arrangement where broadcasting students may train at the station. Usually, a single public school or district does not seek such facilities. More commonly, school districts in the station's coverage area cooperate in preparing and broadcasting instructional programs, paying for production and use of facilities by a fee for which the participating districts have been assessed. An example of this is included later in this chapter. Of course, under such an arrangement a district has only a partial voice in the choice, preparation, and scheduling of programs.

Purchase of rental or prerecorded materials

Another way to avoid the costs of a television production studio is by purchasing and renting prerecorded materials. These may be broadcast by educational or commercial stations or over a CCTV system. Of course, control over the content is lost, and there is no opportunity to give the materials a local flavor. However, there are sources from which a wide range of excellent materials is now available. The Instructional Television Library Project, which is described later in this chapter, is one example.

Contracting services

As ETV continues to expand, various kinds of contract services also are becoming available. Consulting firms are available to do the basic planning. Local telephone companies install and maintain CCTV distribution systems just as they do telephones; only the program origination —either from a studio or from prerecorded sources—and the receivers are required. In some communities, school districts have been able to get free distribution services through a community antenna company. Community antennas are established to provide TV distribution to homes in towns cut off by mountains from regular broadcast signals, and often spare channels are available for education.

PATTERNS OF ORGANIZATION

It should be no surprise that there are few rules for organizing and operating television services for education—the concerns of each school district, college, or university are unique and preclude any indication of one best method of approach. We can, however, look at some of the organizational patterns that have evolved and examine a few specific examples in more detail as case studies.

National

Generally speaking, it has been conceded that most educational materials do not have the immediacy and urgency that would justify the tremendous costs of a "live," interconnected educational network, and that distribution on tape and film is sufficient. Consequently, the simultaneous distribution of educational material has been left up to those who already have the facilities, the commercial networks. However, the possibility of joining existing regional educational systems makes the ultimate existence of a true national network seem at least more feasible, if not urgently necessary at this time.

The commercial networks broadcast regularly scheduled educational material, including weekly programs of general interest such as the series produced by Johns Hopkins University and broadcast on stations of various networks, beginning in 1948, and daily programs of direct instruction such as "Continental Classroom," "College of the Air," and "Sunrise Semester." These have been carried in the early morning, usually from 6 to 7 A.M. College-level courses are broadcast in half-hour segments for a semester. Local institutions may make their own arrangements for supplementing the telecasts and providing credit for completing a course in which the telecast provides the basic content.

In addition, several organizations that support various ETV activities operate on a national scale.

❯ *National Educational Television.* The organization is supported largely by the Ford Foundation and provides program services to the nation's ETV stations. NET (formerly National Educational Television and Radio Center —NETRC) also was active in the development of new stations, but since 1964 has concentrated on "that continuing major task of providing a strong national cultural and public affairs program service."

❯ *National Association of Educational Broadcasters.* The association provides representation for educational broadcasters before the Federal government, has legal and engineering counsel available, conducts conferences and studies, publishes research and periodicals, and operates a placement service. The organization was reorganized in late 1963 in an attempt to provide specialized services for broadcast stations, closed-circuit systems, and individuals. Semiautonomous divisions were established for (1) ETV stations; (2) educational radio stations, including a tape network for the distribution of prerecorded programs; (3) instructional systems, primarily CCTV operations; (4) individual members; (5) institutional affiliates.

❯ *Department of Audio-Visual Instruction, NEA.* This is the department through which the organization maintains its interest in broadcasting as one important sector of the total spectrum of the educational media. The subject of instructional broadcasting is covered in the reports and periodicals of the organization.

❯ *Educational Media Council.* The council provides a cross-media approach to broad educational problems. Broadcasters are represented by the NAEB.

❯ *National Instructional Television Library.* The library, together with two affiliated regional libraries were set up in 1962 to explore methods of interchange of recorded instructional programs and series. The libraries publish catalogs of materials that may be obtained either from the producer directly or from the library. The 1964 edition of the national library catalog, for example, lists approximately 150 different series of programs for elementary school use, 60 for secondary schools, 50 for college, 45 for adult viewing, and 10 for in-service training for teachers.

The Federal government also lends support nationally to educational broadcasting through the National Defense Education Act and the Educational Television Facilities Act, both of which were mentioned earlier.

Regional

Several educational broadcasting systems are regional and cut across one or more state lines. Regional networks provide for program exchange, for organized growth of ETV throughout an area, and assist in the activation of new channels. The Eastern Educational Network, for example, is a cooperative, self-supporting group composed of stations, state departments of education, and production centers in New England, New York, Pennsylvania, New Jersey, Delaware, Maryland, and the District of Columbia. The network stations exchange about one thousand hours of instructional and adult programs annually.[11]

Other regional groups include organizations that were specifically developed to serve educational broadcasting and organizations that have added broadcasting to other activities. In the former category are the Great Plains and Northeastern Regional Instructional Television Libraries (affiliated with and serving the same purpose as the National Instructional Television Library). Perhaps the best-known regional organization is the Midwest Program on Airborne Television Instruction

[11] Michael Ambrosino, "Eastern Educational Network," *NAEB Journal,* pp. 24–25, March–April, 1963.

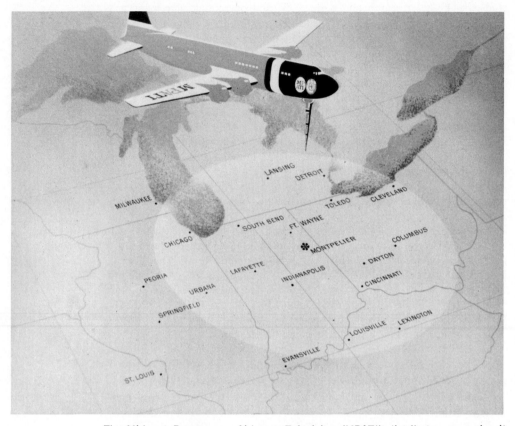

The Midwest Program on Airborne Television (MPATI) distributes open-circuit programs to classrooms in 17,000 schools serving nearly 7 million students. (*MPATI*)

(MPATI), which broadcasts ETV programs to schools in parts of six states from its flying transmitters.

Among organizations that have added ETV to other activities are the Western Interstate Compact on Higher Education and the Southern Regional Educational Board (SREB). The SREB has established a regional administrative and consultative office to help clusters of states develop and use recorded instructional materials. The SREB office will, for example: [12]

❯ Help the state clusters to develop their own vital patterns of interinstitutional cooperation in the planning, production, use and revision of ETV recorded materials, such patterns to be sufficiently individualized to meet needs of individual state clusters, but at the same time sufficiently related for region-wide use.

[12] William L. Bowden, "Regional Cooperation in the Utilization of Recorded Materials for Educational Television in the South," *Audiovisual Instruction,* vol. 8, no. 6, p. 408, June, 1963.

❯ Help departments in the colleges and universities to plan, produce, use, and revise recorded materials of unquestioned excellence which SREB identifies as critically needed. The SREB then uses them extensively in all or most of the seven subregional clusters of states. Disciplines that have indicated interest include teacher education, psychiatric education, nursing education, architecture, and agricultural sciences.

❯ Gather information about the status and use of new instructional media (with emphasis on closed-circuit television in higher education) that will be useful for the planning and developmental needs of interinstitutional and interdisciplinary groups in the subregions and in the region as a whole.

State

State organizations show great diversity, and a sequence of events rather than a pattern of organization is all that can be identified here. At least half a dozen states have made no effort in educational broadcasting. In others, Governors have called state-wide conferences or appointed study committees, but taken no formal action.

In some, state-wide plans have been prepared for ETV station construction and/or an ETV office at the state level. Such a plan may have been prepared at the request of the state legislature or prepared by the executive branch in support of a request to the legislature for funds to construct and operate ETV facilities. An example of state-wide planning is the program initiated by the Ohio Educational Television Network Commission, which was established by the Ohio Legislature in 1961. The commission was created as an independent agency of the state government. The commission has been directed to establish a network of educational television transmitting stations, including the construction of new stations and interconnecting them all. The commission will develop an operations plan for the network and supervise the development and scheduling of programs. An engineering survey proposed development in four phases, each requiring approximately two years to complete. The survey suggested building the network from the existing four (1960) ETV stations in the state into a complex that would include twenty-nine transmitting stations of various types and eleven producing studios.[13]

The next step has been activation of one or more ETV stations under the state plan or gathering existing ETV stations under some sort of umbrella commission. A difficult problem may arise in the latter case, where community or university stations operated by different administrations are to be brought together into a single organizational unit.

Finally comes full implementation of a state ETV network or system. In most states, TV plans have been concerned primarily with broadcast stations and connecting links between stat ons. But some closed-circuit facilities are also administered by state-level agencies.

[13] *Educational Television in Ohio—1963,* Ohio Educational Television Network Commission. 4 pp. (Mimeographed)

Although state-wide planning has existed in some states for a number of years, the greatest interest in state-wide organization has come as a result of the Federal government's Educational Television Facilities Act. Under this act, construction grants are made directly to individual applicants, but the law requires that a state ETV agency must be in existence and must be kept informed of all applications for Federal funds.

Local

Examples are widely diversified—a community ETV station serving several counties, a school district closed-circuit system, or a simple system for image magnification in a single classroom. The following cases include such local organizations as a maximum-power community broadcast station, a station operated by a university, and finally, a low-power station operated by a school district. We will deal first with educational TV systems organized at the state level.

CASE STUDIES: ETV AT THE STATE LEVEL

The following examples of state-level ETV organizations are selected to show different types of programs utilizing open-circuit, closed-circuit, and microwave-relay systems and combinations of these, serving various levels of education. In two instances, the network conveys televised instruction to schools throughout the state. The other two involve networks linking institutions of higher education for cooperative programming among campuses.

State-wide network

With the establishment of the Alabama ETV Commission (AETC) and an appropriation by its Legislature in June, 1953, Alabama became the first state to start a state-wide ETV network. The commission is charged by law with the control and supervision of all ETV stations in the state. Five members are appointed by the Governor with the consent of the Senate for staggered terms of ten years each.

Three stations began broadcasting in 1955 and 1956, a fourth in 1962, and a fifth in 1964. The stations are joined by microwave relay. Eight additional channels have been allocated by the FCC for future use. Programs originate from three sources—the University of Alabama, Auburn University, and the Birmingham Area ETV Association. Each of the three sources operates its own studios, contracting with the AETC to provide an equal share of the total programming. The interpretation of programming policy and implementation of production for the network have been delegated by the AETC to a program board composed of five members. Specific coordination is provided by a director of coordination and information who is responsible to the general manager.

The Alabama stations reach nearly 80 per cent of the potential audience in the state with broadcasts for in-school viewing, college and other adult courses, and general-interest viewing. Programs of special interest include a precollege English course that is broadcast every semester in an attempt to circumvent the necessity for college freshmen to take remedial courses, basic literacy courses aimed at the 60,000 Alabama adults who cannot read or write, and programs originated by state agencies to explain their services.

The network is operated on an annual appropriation of about $200,000 from the Legislature. Total appropriations for ETV, including the operation of the participating studio production centers, approximate $450,000 annually.

State-wide CCTV system

The Texas Educational Microwave Project (TEMP) is a demonstration project which was initiated under a Title VII grant of the National Defense Education Act (NDEA), with additional support by the Ford Foundation's College Faculty Released Time Program for Television Instruction. Eleven institutions of higher learning in the central Texas area are linked together by microwave transmitters in a single closed-circuit system. The institutions represent several types of colleges and universities—public and private, Protestant and Catholic, senior and junior.

The idea of TEMP came in 1957 from the presidents of most of the eleven institutions that eventually made up the system. The actual development fell largely upon the television staff at the University of Texas, which was the only school with prior TV experience. Several phases of planning, including consultation with foundations, securing FCC authorizations for the microwave system, and pilot programming, were undertaken; full operation began in September, 1961. Eight courses were supplied by TEMP to the participating institutions, and nearly 4,000 students enrolled in them on their own campuses. Since that time, additional courses have been added, enrollments have increased, and greater acceptance has been gained—all pointing to the continued growth of the project.

TEMP itself operates with a minimum staff and budget and with a very informal organizational structure. An administrative council is composed of representatives of the participating institutions. The administrative staff of six have responsibilities to their own colleges in addition to their work for TEMP. The participating colleges each contribute around $40,000 for operation, which provides salaries for three engineers; power, maintenance, operation, and improvement of the tape-recording and microwave equipment; office supplies and duplication; travel; tape amortization; and new course development. The main microwave system was purchased with NDEA funds, and the development costs and faculty salaries for preparing the initial taped courses were also paid by NDEA and the Ford Foundation's College Faculty Released Time Program for Television Instruction.

Developers of the project readily admit that it was undertaken at the initiative of the outside supporters and not because of any pressure for TV cooperation among the institutions. Further, it is not self-supporting, although an attempt is being made to make it so. Nevertheless the project has indicated that: [14]

> Disparate institutions can organize a project of this character. Religious affiliation, size, traditions, concept of mission, and symbols of status had to be considered, but offered no serious barriers to effective organization.

> The network can operate with shoestring facilities, but such operation has more crises in it than are good for well-ordered academic pursuits.

> The intercollege setting causes relatively few significant changes in course content, but leads to a standardized pattern of presentation (two TV lectures, plus one discussion group weekly).

> No new utilization problems are encountered in the interinstitutional system, but utilization remains the greatest problem to effective TV teaching.

> Intercollege network, generally speaking, is desirable financially. Even with the costs of microwave, studio operation, etc., the ability to reach large numbers of students and to re-use tapes can reduce costs below the traditional forms of instruction.

Other Plans

Two other state plans will be mentioned briefly. The Oregon interinstitutional approach to college-level teaching used an open-circuit approach (as contrasted with Texas's closed circuit). Several colleges, both state operated and private, within the coverage area of stations in Corvallis and Portland used courses originated at one of the participating institutions. The stations were operated by the state's division of higher education.

In South Carolina, a TV system is progressing through various phases until it reaches every public high and elementary school in the state. Closed-circuit television was chosen originally because of the need to transmit multiple programs simultaneously, but broadcast facilities are being added as well, and saturation coverage is anticipated.

CASE STUDIES: ETV AT THE LOCAL LEVEL

Because of the range of a high-power television transmitter (with suitable tower and antenna) a locally operated ETV station can have more

[14] Extracted from R. C. Norris and others, *Texas Educational Microwave Project,* final report submitted to the U.S. Office of Education, Washington, July, 1963.

The South Carolina closed-circuit educational television network, state-wide in scope, provided multichannel facilities that permit the simultaneous production of programs for several grade levels or subjects. (*South Carolina Educational Television Center*)

than merely local effect, in the usual sense. The community ETV station described in the next case study, for instance, reaches into fifteen counties in California. Similarly, ETV broadcast stations operated by universities, such as the one described in the second case study, may serve not only their own campuses, but also the schools, other institutions of higher education, and the adult community of a large metropolitan or rural area. The limitations of this type of service are more likely to be the hours available for programming than the physical limitations of the transmitting equipment. The two case studies devoted to school districts operating their own television facilities are selected to illustrate an open-circuit system in the one instance, a closed-circuit system in the other.

Community station

KVIE is a community station operating on Channel 6 in Sacramento, California. Three commercial stations, also on VHF channels, also serve the area. Some local programming is done, but most evening programs come from NET. The daytime school programs broadcast by KVIE are a major source of its support. Additional voluntary pub-

215

lic support is received from community patrons. Since the station reaches into fifteen counties and potentially serves 250 school districts, the school programs are prepared by a broadly based committee. The Valley Instructional Television Association (VITA) is composed of administrative representatives of the fifteen county superintendents of schools. These representatives are empowered to commit their counties to the support of VITA.

The VITA committee meets monthly to discuss the financing of the school service, programming needs, and other matters of policy. It hires a director to serve as coordinator of the service and as liaison between VITA and the station. He is responsible for negotiating the needed time on the station, for scheduling instructional programs in accordance with the committee's suggestions, for planning and contracting for the production of new programs and series, and for the dissemination of teaching materials to participating districts.

A recent change in policy at the state level indicates recognition of the multicounty function of VITA. Formerly, state-aid funds were apportioned directly to counties for audio-visual services, including TV; now state support for the administrative expenses of VITA is given directly, before the remaining audio-visual funds are disbursed to the counties.

School districts purchase the ETV service on the basis of 50 cents per pupil in average daily attendance, with a ceiling of $15,000 annually, which is a concession to the larger districts. Although districts that do not contribute financially to the support of programs do not receive any of the prepared teaching materials, they cannot be prevented from watching them. A typical year's service (1964–1965) includes:

❯ Eighteen series of supplementary instructional programs for elementary school
❯ Three series for high school supplemental instruction. In an attempt to solve the problem of the different schedules of high schools throughout the viewing area, one program, *The Communists,* is broadcast ten times in a single day
❯ In-service programs

University station

KCTS-TV, licensed to the University of Washington, is a pioneer ETV station—one of the first ten—and represents a truly cooperative community effort to get a station on the air. A sizable grant of studio and transmitting equipment from a local commercial station, studios supplied by the university, transmitter operation by a technical school, plus financial assistance from the city and county schools, public contributions, and a Fund for Adult Education matching grant have been combined to result in a station that has an $850,000 physical plant and a current annual operating budget in excess of $250,000. About two-thirds of the budget is provided by the public schools, which pay $1 per pupil for in-school broadcasts. Most of the remaining funds come from the university.

Employees generally spend full time with the station (in many such stations, faculty members may regularly have part-teaching and part-station responsibilities). The station manager reports to the academic vice-president of the university, who also serves as chairman of the station's advisory board. This board of twelve members has six representatives from the public schools, two from other universities, a representative of the Seattle Public Library, two public members, and the university-appointed chairman.

School district station

When it is possible to concentrate the viewing audience within a single district or county, administrative problems are simplified. So far, because of the problem of providing a sufficiently large financial base, few stations operated by single districts are on the air; but more are expected as districts qualify for Federal matching funds for construction.

KDPS-TV, Des Moines, Iowa, represents an emerging development, the broadcast station operated directly by a local school agency. The station began broadcasting in 1959, with financial support from the Ford Foundation. Since June, 1962, however, it has been supported completely by local funds. (The TV station was preceded by KDPS-FM, which also provides instructional and cultural programs in Des Moines.) KDPS-TV is licensed to the Des Moines Independent Community School

KDPS - TV ORGANIZATION

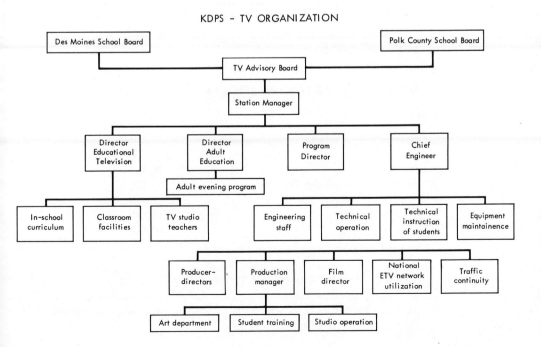

District and is operated in association with the Polk County Board of Education. The organization of the station is charted on page 217.

Like most ETV stations, KDPS programs for in-school use are broadcast during school hours; programs for general audiences are scheduled in the evenings. A recent programming summary shows:

Program information	Hours weekly	Per cent of schedule
Type of broadcast:		
Elementary courses	11½	25
Secondary courses	5⅙	11
College and in-service	1	4
Informal children's (daytime)	6¾	15
Informal adult	13½	30
Evening, children's	3½	8
Other	3⅓	7
Totals	44	100
Originating source:		
KDPS studios	21¾	49
NET	12	27
Other (film, tape)	10¼	24
Totals	44	100
Live programs	11⅔	26
Recorded programs	32⅓	74
Totals	44	100

Some additional dimensions of the KDPS-TV operation can be seen in the following:

Audience for KDPS-TV school programs

Area	Number viewing	Per cent of enrollment
Des Moines Community School District	28,300	66
Polk County (outside Des Moines):	8,320	55
Guthrie County	2,019	50
Boone County	1,686	32
Total	40,325	

The budget on page 219 has an unusually small amount listed for new equipment, which may indicate that the station has settled into a pattern of operation in which there will be only normal growth of its existing activities with no major new demands.

Annual budget for KDPS-TV *

Expense	Budget	
Operation:		
In-school programming	$46,000	
Evening programming	14,586	
Teaching supplies and equipment	8,342	
Salaries—studio personnel	77,000	
General	11,600	
All operating costs		$158,000
Supplies (office, art, mailing)		3,000
Maintenance and replacement		27,500
New equipment		2,991
Total		$191,491

* The operating expenses of the station are borne largely by the Polk County Board of Education, which levies a .5-mill property tax. This tax provides about $160,000 annually. Two other counties and several small districts contribute small sums, based on the number of pupils enrolled (at 75 cents per pupil). The remainder of the cost is subsidized by the Des Moines district.

School district CCTV system

The following description of Anaheim, California, is extracted from a 1963 report by Robert E. Shanks, superintendent of schools.

In September, 1959, following more than two years of study and consideration, some eighty teachers in fourth and fifth grade classrooms, together with six carefully selected television teachers, began providing regularly scheduled, related classroom and televised learning experiences for approximately 2,600 pupils in the Anaheim City School District.

From these beginnings the program was continued during the next school year for pupils in grade four and five and was also expanded at the start of that year to include classroom and televised teaching for a majority of the third and sixth grade pupils throughout the District.

During these two school years the extensive testing and evaluation program provided much useful test data which could be used to make statistical comparisons of pupil achievement in the "television" and "non-television," or "control," classes. These comparisons, on the whole, definitely favored the concept of related classroom and televised teaching. Pupils receiving both classroom and televised teaching in social studies, science, arithmetic enrichment, and music appeared, on the whole, to have a definite advantage in the learning situation over those pupils who received all their instruction in these subjects in the "control classes."

At about this same time a surprising number of requests were received from parents of "control class" pupils asking that their children be included in the classes to receive televised instruction during the coming school year. It was therefore decided to eliminate the "control classes" completely, effective at the beginning of the 1961–62 school year.

Thus the Anaheim District has, since September, 1961, been utilizing its own district-wide closed-circuit television network and facilities, television teachers and studio production staff, to provide televised teaching as an integral part of its overall instructional program for all pupils in grades three, four, five, and six. More than 8,000 pupils attending the District's twenty-one elementary schools are regularly receiving related classroom and televised teaching in selected subject-matter areas.

Anaheim city school district ETV program weekly schedule, school year 1963–1964

Channel 3	Monday	Tuesday	Wednesday	Thursday	Friday
Grade 3					
10:45	Social Studies	Science	Social Studies	Science	Social Studies
1:20	Music		Arithmetic	Arithmetic	
Grade 4					
11:10		Music			
12:55	Spanish I		Spanish I	Literature	Spanish I
2:10	Science	Social Studies	Science	Social Studies	Social Studies

Channel 6	Monday	Tuesday	Wednesday	Thursday	Friday
Grade 5					
12:55	Science	Social Studies	Science	Social Studies	Social Studies
1:45			Music		
2:30	Spanish II	Spanish II		Spanish II	Spanish II
Grade 6					
9:15	Social Studies	Science	Social Studies	Science	Social Studies
10:00				Music	
11:15	Spanish III	Spanish III	Spanish III		Spanish III

The average daily viewing time for pupils is about twenty-five minutes at the third grade level, and about thirty-five minutes for pupils at the fourth, fifth, and sixth grade levels. This means that about twelve per cent of the instructional day is spent receiving televised teaching in the classroom. The televised lessons range from ten to twenty minutes in length, depending upon the lesson content to be presented.

All of the third and fourth grade pupils receive the televised lessons in their own conventionally organized, "self-contained" classrooms. About 60% of the fifth and sixth graders throughout the

District are currently receiving their televised instruction in the same manner.

The same televised lessons are also being received by the other 40% of the fifth and sixth graders grouped together in large class groups, averaging about seventy-five pupils per class. These groups are housed in specially equipped, larger classrooms, called audio-visual resource rooms, at twelve of the District's twenty-one schools; and these pupils are participants in the District's "Redeployment Plan."

This plan involves a regrouping and redeployment of pupils and teachers for instructional purposes. It departs decidedly from the conventional arrangement of the school day for elementary school pupils and their teachers. It makes use of the televised lesson presentations as a regularly scheduled aid to teachers of large classes, and as an integral part of the total instructional program in large classes where pupils spend half their school day. It also makes possible the establishment of unusually small instructional groups (or "skills classes") in order to provide more individualized instruction in the basic elementary school subjects for these same pupils.

The school day for these pupils is divided into two equal parts, separated by the lunch period. During the morning all of the sixth graders receive instruction together as a large class group in the audio-visual resource room where two resource room teachers are assigned. Meanwhile the seventy-five fifth graders are divided into three small groups (of about twenty-five each) and are assigned to three different skills teachers in separate skills classrooms. After lunch the pupils trade places, the entire fifth grade group meeting together as a large class group in the audio-visual resource room while the sixth graders are divided into three small groups for instruction in the three skills classrooms.

The resource room teachers, using the televised lesson presentations as a regularly scheduled aid, are responsible for providing the fifth and sixth grade instruction in social studies, science, conversational Spanish, physical education, health, safety, fire prevention, art, and music.

In the skills classrooms the three skills teachers provide instruction in the basic elementary school subjects: reading, spelling, handwriting, written and oral language, and arithmetic.

Test results obtained as a part of the District's continuing evaluation of its entire program indicate that pupils in the redeployment plan, particularly in those subject-matter areas taught in the large class group with the aid of televised lessons, often excel the achievement of pupils receiving similar instruction in conventionally organized classrooms.

The redeployment plan has made it possible for the District to provide a substantially smaller pupil-teacher ratio for a large number of its upper grade pupils for the teaching of the basic three R's without an appreciable increase in per-pupil costs for current expenditures. At the same time, this has been done without creating a need for a large number of additional classrooms, as would have been required by maintaining the traditional "self-contained"· classroom pattern and reducing the pupil-teacher ratio so substantially for the same number of pupils.

The redeployment plan divides almost in half the number of subjects for which the teacher is expected to make adequate daily or weekly lesson preparations. Thus it solves, at least to some extent, a very real problem of teacher planning-load and work-load at the elementary school level. The redeployment plan provides opportunity for a teacher to concentrate her efforts in those subject-matter areas in which she has special talents. Moreover, the redeployment plan, or any similar plan involving team teaching, brings teachers together far more effectively to exchange ideas and learn from one another as they team together to make the most of their particular teaching abilities for the benefit of their pupils.

Net operational expenditures for the instructional television program from the District's regular sources of operational revenue during the school years 1959–60, 1960–61, and 1961–62, amounted to $442,069, or about three and one-half per cent of the total current operational expenditures for all school district purposes during these first three years of the program. In addition, during these years, $94,000 was received and expended in three separate grants from the Ford Foundation in support of operational expenditures of the redeployment plan. Also, in 1959, the District received $50,000 in matching funds for purchase of television equipment under the terms of Title III of the National Defense Education Act, and this additional amount was expended during that year for television capital outlay purposes from the general fund budget. Total capital outlay expenditures charged to the District's building fund budget for the program during these three years amounted to $555,079, not including $79,852 received in 1960–61 and 1961–62 as Title III, NDEA matching funds. Operational expenditures for the television program in 1962–63 amounted to about four per cent of total general fund expenditures, while capital outlay expenditures were minor, the major expenditures to establish the district-wide TV network having been completed.

SOME GUIDELINES FOR ADMINISTERING EDUCATIONAL TELEVISION

From the foregoing discussion and case studies of educational television in its varied forms, it should be apparent that there can be no simple formula for the administrator who must cope with planning and developing this medium in a particular setting. Only general guidelines can be suggested with regard to facilities and equipment, personnel, and administrative structure. Each of these three areas will be treated briefly.

Facilities and equipment

A convenient way of discussing the problem of facilities and equipment is in terms of the three functions: origination, distribution, and reception. Obviously, any use of television in teaching involves at least some receivers. Some form of origination equipment will be needed unless the TV activity is limited to the use of off-the-air programs from local broadcast stations. Distribution needs hinge upon the forms of origination on the one hand; the location, spread, and size of the target audience on the other.

Origination

TV cameras for live origination vary a great deal in cost and in the applications to which they can be put. Most schools purchase vidicon cameras, which are less expensive to purchase and operate than are the image-orthicon cameras used by most commercial stations; probably those ETV stations that devote a large share of their programming to home audiences could justify the high cost of image-orthicon equipment. Even vidicon cameras range in price from under $1,000 for industrial cameras with limited capabilities to over $10,000 for the best studio cameras, with viewfinders and multiple lenses. Minimum cost camera chains should be considered only for strictly limited or specific applications, and should be tried out even then, for many cameras lack desirable features that may be needed for general studio production, such as adjustments for varying light levels, etc. For image-magnification uses, a single camera may be sufficient, but for studio presentations, lecture-demonstrations, etc., at least two cameras will be needed, and a third is recommended for exclusive use in integrating films and 2- by 2-inch slides into the presentations.

Some schools find it advantageous to use TV for showing motion pictures, instead of moving separate motion-picture projectors into each classroom. Although this can be an expensive use of TV and may require additional cameras and additional channels on a distribution system, there may be strong compensating advantages, in some cases, such as economies effected through lower requirements for audio-visual equipment and multiple copies of films, as well as diminution of delivery-service costs.

While most ETV planners think of cameras and possibly a studio first, it may be that in some cases the top-priority item for origination should be a tape recorder. Studio space and camera equipment can be rented or contracted for if need be, and prerecorded tapes can be borrowed or leased as well. The critical advantage of video tape is that it permits flexibility by making it possible to schedule different sections of the same course at different times.

In the early 1960s, advances in TV tape-recorder design considerably lowered their initial and operating costs, but also resulted in a series of machines that all operated on different standards. For most applications, probably the most suitable video-tape recorder is a transverse-scan machine, the type used by commercial and ETV stations, on which standard most prerecorded materials are available. Such machines facilitate the interchange of programs, but recorders of this type cost $35,000 or more.

For many applications, a lower-cost helical-scan machine may suffice. Its disadvantages are that its recordings can be used only on machines of the same manufacture, and several models are limited to closed-circuit use since they do not meet FCC broadcast standards. Nevertheless, the helical recorder provides satisfactory pictures for most educational purposes and it does have several advantages over the transverse-scan type: it is cheaper and simpler to operate, for example, and most models are highly portable.

Distribution

The distribution system serves only to get the instructional material from its point of origin—studio, tape, or a broadcast signal—to the classroom where it is to be used. It can range from a master antenna on the school roof connected to a few sets in various rooms to a state or even national network. Some comparative considerations on broadcast and closed-circuit distribution were mentioned earlier; here are a few additional suggestions:

❯ When planning the construction of buildings and the preparation of grounds surrounding them, provisions for television should be included just as they are for power, telephone, etc. It is much less expensive and troublesome to lay conduits and make other necessary installations in new buildings during construction than to add them later. Even if a complete system is not to be put in use immediately, it may be wise to at least provide conduit for a possible later installation. Also, electrical outlets should be provided generously where they will be needed.

❯ In science lecture halls and laboratories, clinical testing areas, and auditoriums, either or both, TV reception or origination may be needed. For these areas, a two-way distribution system should be installed. Although the two-way system is more expensive than one designed for reception only, it is less costly than adding a second distribution system to originate from these points. Multiple channels for television, as well as circuits for intercommunication and radio, may also be included in such systems, thus providing considerable flexibility.

❯ For scattered locations, as throughout a school district, a 2,500-megacycle system should be considered. This combines many of the advantages of both open- and closed-circuit systems.

Reception

One of the advantages of instructional television is its capacity to make a variety of locations into "classrooms," both in and out of school and college buildings. While almost any room can become a TV reception area, much of the benefit may be lost unless optimum conditions are provided for viewing and listening. Specifications for television receivers are discussed in Chapter 5. A good general discussion of the physical aspects of reception is found in *Design for ETV,* a publication of the Educational Facilities Laboratory, Inc.[15]

[15] *Design for ETV,* Educational Facilities Laboratory, Inc., New York, 1960.

Personnel

Once a school system or institution of higher education has made the decision to enter the field of educational television, a full-time professional person to head the program should be employed as soon as possible to assist in the early planning and development. Qualifications and other considerations are briefly indicated in the following personnel categories, which are listed in a more or less typical sequence for hiring.

Project director: Ideally, the administrative head of ETV would be experienced both in television production and administration, in teaching, and possibly in educational administration as well. The combination is rare; it usually becomes necessary to look for some approximation to the desired set of competencies. Some universities now have graduate programs to produce trained candidates for positions of leadership in educational television. Such candidates may be particularly strong when they have had prior experience in education and/or television.

Engineer: Specific qualifications for an ETV engineer depend to some extent upon the size and character of the operation. If only one man is to be hired, it is important to find someone who is capable of installation and design as well as operations and maintenance, and to pay the salary necessary to hire a man with those qualifications.

Secretarial assistance: In a small operation particularly, this position demands a versatile person who can work under pressure, meet deadlines, and cope with a variety of crises without undue emotional strain.

Television teachers: Two approaches may be considered in the assignment of TV teachers: (1) They may be assigned on a full-time basis to the TV project and be responsible to the project director; or (2) they may be released only temporarily or part time from regular assignments. Both approaches are used in public schools, but colleges usually follow the second pattern.

Graphics-photography: Almost any schedule of instructional television will soon require at least one full-time person in graphics-photography. A versatile person is needed—layout, design, cartooning, lettering, and photography will all be called for.

Production crew: In colleges, camera operators, floor directors, and other technicians needed for actual production are often recruited from among students who are studying broadcasting or related subjects. Even high school students can perform well in these jobs with practice and supervision. Otherwise, additional staff will have to be considered to cover these positions.

Producer-director: As the project grows and the director becomes more concerned with administration and planning, the telecasts themselves will be assigned to producer-directors. Eventually a production manager may be needed to coordinate the productions.

Additional personnel: Additional staff will fall within the categories already mentioned in most cases: more and specialized engineers for recording and transmitter operation; additional office help; department heads to assist the project director (or station manager) with public relations, research, and so on.

Administrative structure

When used as a medium of instruction, television should be administered in accordance with the precepts given at the opening of this book. Primarily, this means that the ETV head should report to an officer who is in the direct line of administrative responsibility for the total instructional program. An effective TV teaching program will require changes in traditional scheduling patterns, room assignments, teaching assignments and loads, budgeting, etc. These problems relate to all aspects of the use of instructional media and services. Thus it is most important that the instructional-television program be contained in an administrative structure that coordinates all instructional-media services and integrates them into the instructional program as a whole. If ETV is administratively separate from other media services, it is desirable to have the heads of the various services, including television, report to the same academic administrative officer at the next higher level. While these rules of administrative organization are recommended for general practice, some circumstances may dictate entirely different—and quite workable—arrangements.

An added consideration and qualification is that the purposes of educational television, which serves the total educational enterprise or community, are broader than formal classroom instruction (possibly including cultural programs for the general public, for instance); thus a somewhat different concept of administration is needed. This is true especially in the case of community ETV stations.

Finally, careful distinctions should be drawn between college and university programs that serve the total instructional program and those having a more limited function, such as training media personnel. Sometimes the same television facilities may be used for both purposes. If the potential conflict of interests is recognized in such cases, policies and rules may be developed to govern the scheduling of facilities and personnel and to prevent confusion and misunderstanding.

SUMMARY

The development of educational television in a wide variety of forms, slow at first, has been facilitated by the assistance of private foundations and the Federal government. Early difficulties associated with the lack of a balanced use of VHF and UHF channels have been recognized; the reservation of additional channels for education and legislation requiring manufacturers to equip sets for UHF reception have greatly reduced this problem. Although television has already become a significant factor in education at national, regional, state, and local levels, a period of continued expansion appears to lie ahead.

Television is a powerful medium with many potentials, including the diffusion of outstanding teaching to large numbers of viewers, the supplementation and enrichment of the curriculum, observation experiences, image amplification, and others. Balanced against these strengths are the difficulties that educational planners and administrators face in using a new medium—especially the problems of acceptance and cost, in this case. The use of television also involves a choice of facilities appropriate to the situation and the job to be done. The alternatives include broadcast or open- and closed-circuit systems, the use of commercial facilities, the use of ETV facilities not owned by the educational agency in question, or even the use of facilities made available through contracted services.

A wide variety of patterns of organization at the various levels (partially illustrated by a series of case studies) demonstrates the versatility of the medium on the one hand and the absence of any simple formula for the ETV or educational media administrator on the other. Still there is an accumulation of experience with more or less typical uses of television from which general administrative guidelines can be drawn concerning such matters as facilities and equipment, personnel, and administrative structure.

FOR FURTHER INFORMATION

Campion, Lee, and Clarice Kelley: *Studies in the Growth of Instructional Technology, II: A Directory of Closed-circuit Television Installations in American Education with a Pattern of Growth,* Department of Audio-visual Instruction, NEA, 1963.

Cassirer, H. R.: *Television Teaching Today,* UNESCO, Paris, France, 1960.

Design for ETV: Educational Facilities Laboratories, Inc., New York, 1960.

Diamond, Robert M. (ed.): *A Guide to Instructional Television,* McGraw-Hill, New York, 1964.

Educational Television: The Next Ten Years, The Institute for Communication Research, Stanford University, Stanford, Calif., 1962.

"The Feasibility and Role of State and Regional Networks in Educational Broadcasting," *Proceedings of the NAEB Conference,* National Association of Educational Broadcasters, Washington, September, 1959.

"Instructional Broadcasting," *Proceedings of the NAEB Conference,* National Association of Educational Broadcasters, Washington, D.C., May, 1963.

Lewis, Philip: *Educational Television Guidebook,* McGraw-Hill, New York, 1961.

Powell, John: *Channels of Learning,* Public Affairs Press, Washington, 1962.

Schramm, Wilbur (ed.): *The Impact of Educational Television,* The University of Illinois Press, Urbana, Ill., 1960.

Schramm, Wilbur, and others: *Television in the Lives of Our Children,* Stanford University Press, Stanford, Calif., 1961.

Sources of Information on Educational Media, U.S. Office of Education Bulletin 1963, no. 2, 1963.

Television's Uses in Education: A Functional Analysis, Western Interstate Commission for Higher Education, Boulder, Colo., April, 1962.

chapter 11

Administering programmed learning and other types of independent study

The problem of providing appropriate conditions for independent study is as old as education itself. The Socratic dialogue, the "don" system of tutorial instruction long practiced at Oxford and Cambridge, the Winnetka Plan of the 1920s, the Dalton School program of the 1930s, and the Trump plan of the early 1960s all contain one common element: They are concerned with individualized instruction coupled with opportunities for self-paced, self-monitored learning.

Recently, the mounting pressures of rapidly increasing school and college enrollments have stimulated new interest in problems of the individual student who is unable to chart and pursue an educational path suited to his unique interests and potential because he is submerged in large classes, isolated from an overextended teacher, or caught in the lockstep of rigid, regimented instruction. Though ability grouping has been tried frequently as a partial answer to such problems and with varying degrees of favor and success, not even its strongest proponents would argue that this is independent study. And while the library and such related facilities as the home room and study hall also have afforded places and materials for students engaged in individual study tasks, lack of adequate materials or other conditions frequently have prevented their optimum use.

More recently, the problem and potential of independent study have been cast in a somewhat new perspective by the advent of programmed instruction, oral-lingual laboratory approaches to language teaching, and various technological developments that help to make these and other forms of self-instruction feasible and effective under present conditions of enrollment and staffing in our schools.

PROGRAMMED INSTRUCTION AND TEACHING MACHINES

Of all the various new media of instruction, programmed materials and related teaching machines are perhaps the most revolutionary; certainly they are the most controversial. They raise a number of difficult

Today's sophisticated teaching machines find increasing use in the schools and introduce problems pertaining to their proper administration. (*San Jose State College*)

questions for school and college administrators; these range from deciding on the place and validity of programmed materials in teaching generally, through selecting and evaluating programs and machines, to organizing and administering a plan to use them. While these and other matters will be considered later in this chapter, attention will be given first to the nature of programmed instruction and its rapid growth during recent years.

The character of programmed instruction

Programmed instruction represents a concept of rather highly structured independent study by which the student is guided through a sequence of carefully controlled responses that are intended to modify his behavior toward rather specific goals. So-called "instructional programs," sometimes known as "autoinstructional materials," are put together according to a well-defined set of principles and conventions: carefully organized series of "items" or "frames" break the subject matter down into small bits or "steps"; each step requires a response, and the response is followed by immediate confirmation. In other words, each item in the program presents some information, and each item is followed by a question. The student responds to the question (usually in writing) and immediately checks his answer against the confirmation answer given in the program. If the student is using a teaching machine, certain aspects of the programmed learning process can be automated.

The character of the possible benefits of programmed techniques and materials in teaching and learning were emphasized by Hilgard: [1]

❯ Programmed learning recognizes *individual differences* by beginning where the learner is and by permitting him to proceed at his own pace. It is possible that programmed learning may succeed in reducing individual differences because of these features.

❯ Programmed learning requires that the learner be *active*. Learning by doing is an old educational adage, and it is still a good one. The teaching machine (or program in book form) fights the tendency for the student to be passive and inattentive by requiring his participation if the lesson is to move.

❯ Programmed learning provides immediate *knowledge of results*. Whether because it provides reinforcement, reward, or cognitive feedback (to use some of the words that experts use in talking about these matters), there is abundant testimony that an instantaneous report of results is important in learning.

❯ Programmed learning emphasizes the *organized nature of knowledge* because it requires continuity between the easier (earlier) concepts and the harder (later) ones.

❯ Programmed learning provides *spaced review* in order to guarantee the high order of success that has become a standard requirement of good programs. Review with applications, if properly arranged, permits a high order of learning on the first run through the program.

❯ Programmed learning reduces anxiety because the learner is not threatened by the task: *he knows he is learning* what is required and gains the satisfaction that this knowledge brings.

The development of programmed instruction

Programmed instruction has so far had a remarkably rapid, but still rather tentative and scattered development. The start of this development may be traced from the publication of B. F. Skinner's now historic paper on the subject, which appeared in 1954.[2] The resulting interest in

[1] Abstracted from Ernest R. Hilgard, "Teaching Machines and Creativity," *Stanford Today,* vol. 1, Autumn, 1963.
[2] B. F. Skinner, "The Science of Learning and the Art of Teaching," *Harvard Educational Review,* vol. 24, pp. 99–113, Spring, 1954.

the subject in the late 1950s and early 1960s began to have tangible effects in terms of commercial production; by 1963, 352 programs were listed in the U.S. Office of Education catalog *Programs '63*. This commercial activity was both preceded and accompanied by considerable experimental development and testing of programs and teaching machines by psychologists and educators in the military services, in industry, and in various educational institutions.

A national survey revealed that several hundred United States schools were using programmed instruction in 1961–1962, although in many instances this use was on a trial or experimental basis.[3] In California, surveys by the Bureau of Audiovisual and School Library Services in 1962–1963 and 1963–1964 showed a similar pattern of expansion. In the latter year, 149 schools and college or university campuses reported some use of programmed instruction, as compared with a figure of 73 for the preceding year—an increase of more than 100 per cent. Still another index of mounting interest in programmed instruction was the rapid increase in the number of colleges and universities that offer specialized courses in the field.

Looking at the actual implementation of programmed instruction in the schools, however, one must agree with one observer who characterizes it as having reached "a stage of cautious trial and limited use." [4] Still, there are signs of growing acceptance and a realization that programmed instruction is a significant educational innovation. While the direction of future growth is uncertain, there is increasing evidence that its impact on the schools will be important and lasting.

By no means all of the opinion on programmed instruction is positive. A substantial segment of the current literature voices misgivings and doubts, pointing up the fear of the mechanization or dehumanization of teaching and learning, the discouragement of creativity and discovery, and the substitution of a system that only provides ready-made answers.[5] The broad controversy over programmed instruction—its values, limitations, and proper uses—will no doubt persist. In the meantime, however, teachers and administrators must deal with specific problems such as selecting programmed materials and devices, to be discussed next.

Selecting programmed instructional materials

A decision to use or not to use programmed instructional materials is neither primarily nor exclusively an administrative concern. Nevertheless, persons who have administrative responsibilities for educational

[3] Center for Programed Instruction, *The Use of Programed Instruction in U.S. Schools,* U.S. Office of Education Publication OE 34022, 1963.

[4] Wilbur Schramm, *Programed Instruction Today and Tomorrow,* The Fund for the Advancement of Education, New York, 1962, p. 5.

[5] For further discussion of such attitudes, see Hilda Taba's discussion of "errorless learning" in "Evaluation Techniques? First Some Fundamental Questions," *Audiovisual Instruction,* vol. 9, pp. 271–272, May, 1964. See also Wilbur Schramm's discussion of the hardening of programming techniques, *op. cit.*

media should be expected to assist teachers, supervisors, and administrators as they approach the unfamiliar problems of evaluating and selecting these new (and for many, still untried) instructional materials. The following criteria, taken from the 1962 Interim Report of the Joint Committee on Programed Instruction and Teaching Machines, provide a starting point for such evaluation and selection activities: [6]

Criteria for Assessing Programs

"Internal" and "External" Sources
of Information About Programs

A useful distinction can be made between "internal" and "external" characteristics which might serve as possible criteria for program evaluation.

"*Internal*" characteristics refer to features that can be revealed through visual inspection of the program. These include both the content of the program and the way the program is constructed. Content might be described in terms of relative emphasis given to various topics as well as general organization of the material. Descriptive characteristics of program construction might include information about the length of frames, use of branching sequences, techniques of prompting, patterns of repetition and review, modes and frequency of response called for, procedures and scheduling of reinforcement, and the like.

"*External*" information about a program refers to features which cannot be observed merely by inspecting the program itself, such as the way it was developed and characteristics of its performance as a teaching instrument. External information of interest to a potential purchaser could include such things as the source of program content, qualifications of authors, history of the program's development, tryout and revisions, and test data indicating gains in achievement produced by the use of the program. This information, as indicated more fully below, may be presented in a descriptive manual supplied by the program publisher.

Critical reviews of programs may furnish an additional basis for evaluation. Such reviews are beginning to appear in professional journals along with reviews of textbooks. (Some reviews include data on achievement attained by using the program as well as the reviewer's opinion about program content and style.)

Programs as Related to
Textbooks and to Tests

The applicability of internal and external kinds of information as possible criteria for evaluating programs may in part be seen by

[6] "Criteria for Assessing Programed Instructional Materials: 1962 Interim Report of the Joint Committee on Programed Instruction and Teaching Machines" (American Educational Research Association; American Psychological Association; Department of Audio-Visual Instruction, NEA), *Audiovisual Instruction,* vol. 8, pp. 86–88, February, 1963. (Prepared with the cooperation and support of the Educational Media Branch, U.S. Office of Education, under NDEA Title VII)

comparing programs with textbooks and also with educational or psychological tests.

Programs as compared with textbooks. Both programs and textbooks may be inspected to determine what topics are covered and the relative amount of attention given to each. Such inspection would also indicate whether the subject matter is factually correct, whether it is current, etc. However, despite their similarities, programs differ from textbooks in several important respects that may affect their evaluation. A program's requirement for frequent student response generates a special source of data useful for revising the program in detail. The tendency to empirically guided development of programs is coupled with an orientation toward testing the specific effects produced by a program, and toward more sharply focused objectives defined in terms of specified behavioral outcomes. In addition, the program is intended to generate a more predictable pattern of student behavior than does the study of a textbook, which generally has a less specialized purpose in aiming to serve as a reference source as well as a sequence of instruction.

Programs compared with psychological and educational tests. Although programs aim primarily to instruct students rather than to test them, programs and tests share some important attributes. Since both generate student-response data as an inherent feature, both tend to be developed in terms of empirical procedures. The difficulty of each item in a program, as in a test, can be investigated by presenting the program to appropriate samples of students and recording their responses. Both the program and the test have limited ranges of usefulness that can be described to the potential user in terms of empirical evidence; and in both cases it is possible to specify an external criterion to indicate the extent to which some intended outcome is achieved, as evidenced by the kinds of behavior that have been developed or differentiated.

*Uses of Internal and External Information
for Assessing Programs*

Inspecting the subject-matter content of programs. At the present time, the principal recommended use of internal data obtained from inspection of the programed materials is for determining whether program *content* is appropriate to the educator's objectives. As with other educational materials, program titles often are not definitive. Programs labeled with the name of a particular subject matter can vary widely in terms of content and associated instructional objectives. The prospective purchaser of a program should, therefore, inspect the content of the program at least as carefully as he would that of a textbook. Preferably he should go through the entire program to determine what aspects of the subject are treated or omitted, and the extent ·to which particular sub-topics are developed.

Limitations of program inspection. A risk in relying on inspection for evaluating a program is that one's perception of its value may be inappropriately influenced by his reaction to particular structural features of the program. For example, certain frames or items may seem too difficult or too easy. However, the difficulty and appropriateness of items in a program, like those in a test, generally cannot be judged accurately by inspection alone. External data are needed—data from an actual tryout of the program on students who are representative of the population of intended users.

The need for test data to assess a program's effectiveness. Empirical evidence on what is learned from the program can also be a better basis than mere inspection for answering such questions as whether program sequences have too much or too little repetition, review, prompting, overlap of steps, etc. At present, the scientific evidence is not considered sufficient to permit accurate prediction in these respects or to justify recommendation that adherence to specific rules of program construction be used as a basis for program evaluation. External evidence is recommended as the main basis for the evaluation of program effectiveness—in particular, test data obtained from using a program under specified conditions which provide dependable measures of gains produced in student achievement and of the time students require to achieve these gains.

Uses and assessment of programs. Programs may have a variety of uses. For example, they may be intended to provide the main source from which students are expected to learn facts, principles or skills—or they may be intended only to review or introduce other instruction. In most schools, programs will probably be used in conjunction with other media of instruction. However, no matter what eventual use is contemplated for a program, it will generally help a prospective user to know what the program *itself* actually contributes to the students' knowledge or proficiency—in addition to what is contributed by other elements in the instructional situation.

The kinds of effects that can be revealed through empirical tryouts are limited by the content of the achievement tests or other measures used to assess these effects. Inspection of the program by the prospective purchaser, supplemented by independent professional reviews (when available), may sometimes suggest additional uses for which a program might be suitable, or kinds of program effects which are not indicated by field-test data because they were not contemplated in the programer's original purpose.

Inspection of achievement-test content. Aside from the data obtained in testing a program's use under laboratory or field conditions, inspection of the program itself as a basis for appraisal can be supplemented if the author or publisher has spelled out the program's purpose by describing and exhibiting in full the achievement-test items which purport to exemplify what the program is intended to teach. These criterion-test items, as well as responses called for by the program and test, can be examined to see what the learner is required to be able to do, and whether this reflects the kind of competence which the educator wishes to achieve. Such an analysis of test content as a basis for determining a program's objectives may be particularly helpful for programs which are intended to serve as a primary source of instruction rather than merely as an adjunct to other instructional material.

The foregoing criteria suggest that proper evaluation of programs requires highly specific and detailed information. For this reason, the

1962 Interim Report [7] recommends that producers of programs provide manuals containing information about such matters as (1) the program's purpose and intended use, (2) the source of program content, (3) the manner in which the program was developed, including tryout and revision, and (4) the conduct and results of tests to determine empirically its effectiveness or "performance characteristics." The implication of this recommendation is that users of programs should persistently seek such information and that publishers of programs should be encouraged to develop and provide these necessary data in some suitable form, such as a manual.

Of course, publishers' information does not do away entirely with the need to engage in local tryouts and experimentation, which are also useful means of assessing materials. It is usually good administrative practice to allow teachers to experiment with any new and/or controversial materials; this is especially recommended in the case of programmed items. Such experimentation might well focus on their application to local instructional objectives, thus preventing unnecessary and wasteful replication of research already completed by producers or others users.

Scheduling and programmed instruction

From an administrative point of view, perhaps the most distinctive aspect of programmed instruction is that it permits each student to work independently and to proceed at his own pace. This suggests a relationship between programmed instruction and other recent efforts to break the lockstep of the traditional structure of education. Programmed instruction emerges as a potential boon to the administrator who seeks to build a more flexible school program—a search that has led to such recent developments as multiple-track instruction, the ungraded school, and others. While the specifics of such plans are not important to this discussion, the point should be made that each of them provides for varying rates of student progress, to some extent. Similarly, each presents severe administrative problems—particularly problems of scheduling.

Schramm has suggested that the ideal way to solve scheduling problems while at the same time ministering to the needs of individual students "is to have one teacher per subject level. *And the nearest approximation we can make to that ideal arrangement is to let programed instruction, where possible and appropriate, sit in for some of the teachers we don't have.*" [8] He adds the further comment: [9]

We probably have no teacher we can turn loose for ten hours of tutorial work to guide that bright third grader through the Boolean

[7] *Ibid.*
[8] Schramm, *op. cit.*, p. 31.
[9] *Ibid.*, pp. 31–32.

algebra which has excited and challenged him. But a program can do it. . . .

I am not suggesting that students working at their own rate will do all their work in programed instruction. Far from it. They ought to read voraciously, and write, and explore, and discuss, and experiment. But they will find many topics where they need more help than a book will give them. . . .

In fact it may be only through the wise use of programed instruction that the administrative difficulties of the ungraded school and the dual progress plan can be overcome with sufficient ease as to make the plans widely feasible. It would seem that a selection of excellent programs would be equivalent to adding expert and specialist teachers to the team. In particular, schools which are not ready to go to one of these advanced patterns can add excellent visiting teachers in the form of programed instruction, without any risk to the relationships in the one-teacher classroom.

In short, the advent of programed instruction, just at this time, may administer the coup de grace to the old dragon of progress-by-yearly-lockstep in the closed classroom.

It should be noted that while programmed instruction can implement a flexible pattern of teaching, it also introduces additional scheduling difficulties. Such problems are multiplied by the number of students who are pursuing independent courses of study. The ultimate outcome of this trend is the so-called "continuous-progress" school in which each student can enter at any time, proceed on his own unique path of instruction and at his own rate (linking in with appropriate group activities as he goes along), and complete his studies whenever his efforts and capabilities permit. Thus, in the continuous-progress school (described in more detail in Chapter 16), the task of scheduling individual student activities goes well beyond conventional methods, but it can be handled quite satisfactorily with the aid of a computer.

Programs versus machines

An additional problem in the administration of programmed instruction relates to the issue of the program versus the so-called "teaching machine." Some programs require machines for their presentation; others are presented in book form. Still others appear in both versions —as an independent book or manual and in a form for use in a machine. The machine program itself may be prepared as (1) a text or sheaf of printed sheets, (2) a scroll, (3) a filmstrip, (4) a motion picture, (5) another form of transparency suitable for projection, (6) a sound or video-tape recording, or (7) some combination of these. It may even be stored in the "memory" of a computer. The vast majority of programs now available are produced as printed texts.

Obviously, the machine alone does not teach; it only dispenses the program. The use of machines adds materially to the cost of programmed instruction, although some of the simpler machines of a box type are quite inexpensive. What, then, can be said for the relative advantages of nonmachine book-type programs as compared with those requiring machines?

The official position taken with regard to this question by the Joint Committee on Programed Instruction and Teaching Machines in 1962 was that: [10]

> The comparative merits of machine and non-machine presentation of printed programs for use in schools is as yet an unresolved issue. Any advantage for machine over book presentation cannot be tested in the abstract but would depend on the characteristics of a particular machine. Some machines have demonstrable advantages for certain uses, including research; and suitable machines are required for programs that utilize audio materials.

Several research studies have reported "no significant differences" in student learning from either printed texts or machines, when equivalent programmed materials were presented. Some studies showed a time-completion factor in favor of the textbook method. Commenting on this situation, Gotkin expressed the view that for literate subjects, using standard linear programs present machinery may be "more of a hindrance than a help." [11] At the same time, he pointed out that machinery is essential for preliterate subjects who are not using written verbal materials. Also, he stressed the unique functions of computerized teaching machines, which "provide the programer with far greater flexibility than is available in textbook programing." [12]

To this discussion, Finn adds the important observation that programming, thus far, has been confined largely to verbal materials. His view that programming should be expanded to include more audio-visual stimulus materials has obvious implications for the wider use of machines. He argues that machines never should have been taken seriously as dispensers of verbal materials in the first place, that "they represent a means of increasing the communication band-width, of manipulating a little larger chunk of experience. Nothing in this concept diminishes verbal programing; it merely expands the challenge to the programer and makes the oft-quoted statement that books are better than machines completely irrelevant." [13] (Finn also directs attention to the teaching-machine capabilities of the language laboratory, a subject that will be discussed later in this chapter.)

What are the administrative implications of the foregoing discussion? Apparently, machines have a secure place in the future of programmed instruction, but the additional cost of some of those of the box type should be carefully examined when equivalent programs are

[10] "Criteria for Assessing Programed Instructional Materials . . . ," *op. cit.,* p. 85.
[11] Lassar D. Gotkin and James D. Finn, "Machines Revisited," *Programed Instruction,* vol. 3, pp. 1–2, October, 1963.
[12] *Ibid.,* p. 1.
[13] *Ibid.,* p. 2.

available in less expensive book form. When there is a choice, competing claims should be checked against experimental evidence—or lack of it. In the light of Finn's comments, administrators might encourage exploration and experimentation for the further development of the audio-visual capacities of teaching machines. Efforts of this sort can be pursued in both the industrial and educational contexts. A good example is the growing use in universities and colleges of programmed audio-visual laboratory instruction in operating audio-visual equipment.

From the standpoint of cost, it may be that relatively expensive machines with audio-visual or multi-media capacities and systems involving computers will prove economical in situations where their unique characteristics are desirable and can be put to good use for a sufficient number of students.

Information about programs and machines. Satisfactory solutions to problems involved in administering programmed instruction rely heavily upon contact with suitable sources of information. Two journals that are devoted exclusively to programmed instruction and teaching machines are *The Journal of Programed Instruction,* and *Programed Instruction.* Both are published by the Center for Programed Instruction of the Institute of Educational Technology, Teachers College, Columbia University, New York, New York. The *AV Communication Review* (Department of Audio-Visual Instruction, NEA, 1201 Sixteenth Avenue, N.W., Washington, D.C.) publishes articles dealing with research and theory. The Center for Programed Instruction, under contract with the U.S. Office of Education, publishes an annual catalog of programs (*Programs '63* and *Programs '64,* etc.).

For further information regarding specific types of teaching machines, the reader may wish to consult the Technological Development Project report on teaching machines and programmed learning by Finn and Perrin.[14] (Reference works on the use of computerized teaching machines and the use of computers as teaching machines are listed in the bibliography at the close of this chapter.)

LANGUAGE LABORATORIES

Regardless of the form by which it is dispensed (book, machine, or computer), the program represents a distinct advance in the development of resources for independent study. Thus far, we have considered programmed materials and teaching machines only in the strict sense of these terms. The many other new technological devices that enable individual students to work with auditory and visual recorded materials also can be considered as forms of "teaching machines" or "programs." In the broad sense, language laboratories represent one such form.

[14] James D. Finn and Donald G. Perrin, *Teaching Machines and Programed Learning, 1962: A Survey of the Industry,* U.S. Office of Education Publication OE 34019, 1962.

In the thirty years prior to 1950, foreign-language enrollments in the nation's high schools dropped from 27 to 14 per cent. Enrollments at the college level also decreased, and many institutions of higher education eliminated their foreign-language entrance requirements. A strong resurgence of interest in foreign-language teaching was marked by the following events in the 1950s:

> *1952.* At a meeting of the Central States Modern Language Association there was a strong proposal that the place of the foreign languages in the educational program be reexamined from the standpoint of the national interest. This proposal attracted national attention and was endorsed by prominent national figures. The Rockefeller Foundation issued a widely publicized report stressing the need for more Americans to know foreign languages and cultures. The foundation also made a large grant to the Modern Language Association to conduct a three-year study of the role that foreign languages and literature should play in American life.

> *1953.* The U.S. Office of Education called a conference on the role of foreign languages in American schools. The Commissioner of Education, then Earl McGrath, used this occasion to urge educators at all levels to give more attention to the teaching of foreign languages as a means of making Americans more conscious of other nationalities and cultures.

> *1954.* A widely publicized report, *The National Interest and the Foreign Languages,* prepared by Dr. William L. Parker and published in 1954, proposed that the study of foreign languages should begin in the elementary grades.

> *1958.* Continued and mounting interest in the teaching of foreign languages was given further impetus through the enactment of the 1958 National Defense Education Act, which specifically recognized foreign languages as one of three academic areas requiring expansion and improvement to meet critical national needs. Title VI authorized the establishment of summer and full-year institutes to train teachers in the audio-lingual approach to the teaching of foreign languages. Additional funds were made available to schools to assist in the purchase of audio-visual equipment, including language laboratories. The research program set up under Title VII made it possible for schools and colleges to conduct experimental studies exploring the relative effectiveness of various instructional methods, including the popular audio-lingual technique, which came into growing use along with electronically equipped language laboratories.

A survey made in the school year 1957–1958 revealed that 64 high schools in the United States were using electronic installations for teaching foreign languages. By 1961, this number had increased to 2,500, and by late 1962, it was estimated that language laboratories were being used in 5,000 secondary schools and about 800 colleges and universities in the country. It was observed that: [15]

[15] James D. Finn, Donald G. Perrin, and Lee E. Campion, *Studies in the Growth of Instructional Technology. I: Audiovisual Instrumentation for Instruction in the Public Schools, 1930–1960; A Basis for Take-off,* Occasional Paper 6, Technological Development Project, NEA, 1962.

Never before in the history of American education has this kind of investment been made in so short a time for technical equipment to be used in instruction. Almost overnight, the American educational system has acquired a whole new technique of instruction which begins with a new theory of teaching languages, extends through the preparation of all kinds of new materials (tapes, books, films) and ends in a laboratory loaded with electronic gear.

Administrative implications

Developments of the scope, scale, and momentum of the language laboratory obviously involve a host of new problems, many of them administrative in nature. Unlike some other recent technological developments in education, this one serves primarily a single field of study. For administrative purposes, language-laboratory facilities are not readily identified with others that serve the instructional program as a whole. Yet the planning, design, installation, operation, maintenance, and scheduling of the language-laboratory facility involve a mixture of administrative, technical, and instructional functions carried

Competent personnel must be found and trained to operate and maintain language and listening laboratory equipment. (*San Jose State College*)

out by several different offices and people who are in varying lines of administrative authority.

In smaller schools and school systems, the chief administrative officer is ordinarily directly involved in planning, budgeting, and contracting for the installation of language-laboratory facilities, in cooperation with the appropriate department head and educational media administrator. In larger school systems and institutions of higher learning, on the other hand, an assistant superintendent of instruction or academic dean is likely to be involved, rather than the heads of the institutions. After installation, scheduling is influenced by the character of departmental use. Arrangements for technical operation and maintenance vary considerably; some directly involve the educational media administrator and his staff, and some do not.

Even more trying—from an administrative point of view—are instances in which administrative arrangements must provide for multiple use of language-laboratory facilities to serve instructional needs above and beyond those of the language program. It is not so important that there be a strict uniformity of administrative control from one instance to the other: it is important that administrative responsibilities be discharged effectively and economically, with full participation of the educational media director to ensure attention to technical features, educational requirements, operation and maintenance, and cost to balance and effectively integrate the expanded use of facilities as part of the total instructional-materials program.

Types and capacities

A language laboratory has been defined as "a classroom or other area containing electronic and mechanical equipment designed and arranged to make foreign-language learning more effective than is usually possible without it." [16] Broadly speaking, there are two types: (1) the *class* system, which is operated by a teacher and scheduled for use by class groups, and (2) the *library* system, which is designed for students working independently and at their own convenience. With both types, students sit at tables or individual counters; they may be partially isolated from one another by dividing partitions. [17]

Language laboratories are frequently divided into three classes or "levels," in accordance with performance capacities of equipment and the manner in which students use it, as follows:

❯ *Level 1* installations provide a phonograph or tape recorder by means of which students listen to a master recording on a disk or tape. Such systems

[16] Alfred S. Hayes, *Language Laboratory Facilities: Technical Guide for the Selection, Purchase, Use, and Maintenance,* U.S. Government Printing Office, 1963, p. 1.

[17] Because this chapter is concerned primarily with *self-instructional* systems, the following discussion of language laboratories will be confined mainly to their use by individual students, as in the case of library installations.

may or may not provide headphones for individual students. This "audio-passive" type of laboratory provides only for listening.

> *Level 2* facilities provide both headphones and microphones in addition to the master playback unit, which may be a phonograph, a tape recorder, or both. The student listens to the master recording, responds into the microphone, and instantly hears his own voice through his headphones. This unit is sometimes called an "audio-active" laboratory.

> *Level 3* installations provide for access to a tape-recording device that can be used by individual students. A student listens to a master recording through headphones, responds into a microphone, and then hears a recording of both the master voice and his own. Obviously, the level 3 laboratory is best suited for individual study because the individual has access to a tape recorder that he may operate at his own pace and convenience to play prerecorded materials, as well as to record and play back his own voice.

Equipment specifications

Plans and designs for language-laboratory systems are complicated; they need not be discussed in complete detail here. Some general guidelines and cautions will be given, however; for further detailed information, the reader is referred to the publications of Hayes and Hutchinson, which are listed in the bibliography for this chapter.

It is important to recognize at the outset that suitable language-laboratory equipment must provide adequate sound reproduction at a fidelity level higher than that needed in ordinary applications, where the primary requirement is merely the intelligible reproduction of native-language speech. Suppliers of equipment and even engineers may be unaware of the system-performance characteristics necessary to enable the students to actually hear and differentiate various recorded speech sounds to the degree required for effectively learning an unfamiliar language. Hence it is important to be able to provide proper and precise specifications, including those for frequency response, noise, and distortion.

Over-all specifications. For the system as a whole, Hayes's guide which is published by the U.S. Office of Education, recommends the following, in terms of frequency response and intensity variations: [18, 19]

> At the "low end" of the human voice sound range (60–250 cps), the response should rise from −15 db at 120 cps to 0 db at 250 cps.

[18] Hayes, *op. cit.,* chap. 5.

[19] The technical terms describing fidelity of sound reproduction, such as "frequency response," "intensity variation," "noise," distortion," "cps," and "db," that occur in these specifications cannot be defined and discussed adequately in this text. If the reader is not already familiar with them, he can find a suitable background discussion in Hayes, *op. cit.,* chap. 5. This source contains the complete and detailed specifications from which those given here are adapted.

❯ In the "middle range" (250–6,000 cps), the response curve should be flat (no peaks or valleys greater than 1 db), or it may rise on a straight line to 3 db at 6,000 cps, but it must not fall.

❯ At the "top end" of the range (6,000 cps and upward), intensity variations should not exceed ± a few db to 8,500 cps.

❯ Above 8,500 cps, frequencies should be attenuated as rapidly as is possible and consistent with economical design.

Hayes also emphasizes the importance of very low distortion and noise factors in the good language-laboratory facility. His discussion, quite technical in nature, need not be reproduced here. The requirements given for the amplifier are indicative of the general level of performance sought: [20]

Total harmonic distortion (measured by standard wave-analyzer techniques)	25%
Intermodulation distortion (using 60 and 6,000 cps, four-to-one ratio)	2%
Signal-to-noise ratio	60 db below 6 milliwatts

A language-laboratory system consists of various components, each having its own performance capacities and limitations. But in thinking of the performance of the system as a whole, it is obvious that any single component is capable of setting a limit upon the quality of sound delivered to the student's ears. And since the system as a whole is no better than its weakest element, it is highly important to select individual components with greatest care.

Amplifier. The amplifier is the heart of any sound system. Since its cost is determined largely by power requirements (relatively low for language laboratories), a language-laboratory amplifier can be built to optimum specifications at quite a low cost. A good rule is to select an amplifier with characteristics that exceed the desired performance standards for the system as a whole by a good margin, thus setting a high potential for the system and helping to compensate for the unavoidable deficiencies of other components, such as headphones.

Headphones and microphones. Headphones are likely to be the weakest link of the total language-laboratory system. Since they are the final "screen" through which the sound reaches the student's ears, what he actually hears can be no better than the performance of these critical and somewhat limited instruments. The problem of selecting headphones is complicated by the facts that: (1) present testing methods provide no satisfactory indication of performance above 6,000 cps; and (2) frequency-response ratings are often stated without indication of intensity deviation (± x db) over the range. For these two reasons,

[20] *Ibid.*, p. 80.

Hayes suggests that it is important to specify brand names and model numbers of known quality or their equivalent when ordering headphones.[21] The same rule should be followed in the case of microphones, which usually present similar problems.

Tape recorders.   The tape recorder (or disk-recording player) should also provide sound reproduction that meets the system requirements mentioned above. Tape recorders that are equipped with dual recording heads are generally considered desirable for use in a level 3 system because they enable one simultaneously to record and play back two separate tracks: one for the master and one for the student's recording of his own voice. This arrangement facilitates the comparison of student speech with that on the master recording. Also, many laboratories use tape recorders that will operate at two speeds ($7\frac{1}{2}$ inches per second and $3\frac{3}{4}$ inches per second).

Other specifications.   In addition to requirements just discussed, specifications for any language laboratory must provide a general description of the proposed system, including (1) the teacher's console or central recording unit, (2) the number and type of student stations, and (3) the actual equipment installations, including headphones, microphones, tape recorders, student-teacher intercommunication facilities, and other features desired. While it is important to stress sound fidelity, specifications should also call for a system that has heavy-duty mechanical features to ensure long wear and satisfactory operation without undue maintenance problems under conditions of constant or even abusive use. A complete sample procurement specification meeting most of these requirements is included in the appendix of Hayes's guide.[22]

Visuals in the language laboratory.   Specifications in the preceding section are of the sort usually given. They pertain chiefly to the "audio" features of the unit. Many consider an audio facility to be sufficient for most needs because language is composed of sounds only and is a matter of hearing and speaking—hence, they feel that little or nothing is required in the way of visual materials. On the other hand, some language teachers believe that visual materials (pictures, slides, filmstrips, motion pictures, maps, and realia) are distinct and significant assets in teaching any foreign language and that language laboratories should have special facilities for their regular use in connection with the audio system.[23] To meet this requirement, a few integrated sets of materials for the teaching of foreign languages thus began to appear in the early 1960s, although most language laboratories were still limited to recording and reproducing voice sounds only.

[21] *Ibid.*, pp. 84–85.
[22] *Ibid.*, p. 106ff.
[23] Elton Hocking, "It's Time to Join Forces," *Audiovisual Instruction,* pp. 642–643, November, 1962.

Steps in planning

Although most language laboratories are administered primarily on a departmental basis, this administration entails questions of planning, design, budget, operation, and maintenance that reach well beyond the usual resources of a single department. In all such cases, the importance of planning as a "team" procedure must be emphasized. The following guidelines, taken from a publication of the New York State Education Department, are oriented toward this point of view: [24]

> Pre-planning should start with a well-organized study to determine: (1) the present and anticipated enrollment in each language offered, (2) which languages will be offered in future to meet pupil needs and interests, and at what grade level they will be introduced, (3) the number and kinds of classrooms that will be needed to carry out the program, (4) the immediate and projected need for properly trained teaching personnel, and the procedures to be followed in orienting teachers and training them to use the audio-lingual approach, (5) the goals for each year of language study, and plans for acquiring or developing needed teaching materials (tapes, records, films, filmstrips, texts, reference books, etc.), and (6) ways for evaluating student achievement, suitability of teaching materials used, equipment performance, teaching effectiveness.
>
> Planning should be a team activity. The team should include: foreign language teachers, the audio-visual coordinator, the school administrator, and the business manager.
>
> Visits to electronic classrooms that are operating satisfactorily in other schools will be of great help in planning. Visits should include time to observe the facilities in use, and to discuss them with the people who planned and are using them.
>
> Planners should get to know about the equipment units which can be used in an electronic classroom facility; the strengths and weaknesses of units produced by different manufacturers; and the type of installation that seems to be most useful for the school concerned.
>
> Planning should result in a set of written specifications which clearly state the operational requirements and standards for the electronic facilities desired. Such specifications are essential in obtaining satisfactory equipment from suppliers.
>
> Bear in mind that a fully equipped electronic classroom is a complex operation, and may be rather expensive. It must be operated efficiently; otherwise the cost will be too high for the results obtained.
>
> Choose a level of audio-lingual activity suited to the teacher(s) and pupils who will use it. Planners may wish to start with rather simple

---

[24] Thomas D. Paolucci, "Developing an Electronic Language Classroom," The University of the State of New York, State Education Department, Albany, N.Y., pp. 4–5. (No date) (Prepared in cooperation with NDEA, Title III)

equipment as a first step, adding to their facilities as the teaching staff learns how to make fuller utilization of them.

While negotiations for a laboratory are under way, a committee of teachers should be listing and ordering blank tape, taped series of lessons and drills, records for special lessons and such manuals and supplementary materials as will be needed when the laboratory is completed.

THE ELECTRONIC STUDY CENTER

The concept of a system designed to facilitate independent study with the use of modern electronic devices flows readily from the modern language laboratory with its private booths equipped for listening, responding, and recording. Numerous observers have already noted the broader self-instructional potential of the language laboratory, which has become an almost standard feature in schools and colleges throughout the nation.

In an article entitled "Why Stop at Language Labs?" Regenstreif [25] proposes that the existing language-laboratory facility might well serve additional functions as an electronic study center to benefit instruction in other areas of the curriculum. He recognizes serious problems involved in extending the use of language laboratories, including the reluctance of language teachers who tend to guard against incursions that might restrict their own programs, but he believes that such difficulties can be overcome. He also suggests that a demonstration of positive results could lead to the development of additional facilities or the conversion of old-style study spaces into electronic study centers.

The suggestion can be carried still further. Multiple use of language laboratories or similar facilities comes to mind simply because such installations are currently available. But there is no logical reason to stop there. A really modern and fully equipped independent study facility that includes viewing as well as listening and recording devices has been proposed by various authorities, including the Educational Facilities Laboratories. Such installations have appeared in a few schools and colleges as prototypes of an optimum-learning facility—the independent study space or carrel that is equipped to supply all types of materials—from print or projected materials to video image with sound. To make it fully effective and complete, the multi-media carrel may be linked with a central information "bank," which stores and on demand instantly supplies several kinds of printed, audio, and visual information.

The following description of a multi-media study carrel and its contributions to the instructional program is oriented toward the secondary school. But the concept presented is equally applicable to insti-

[25] Harry Regenstreif, "Why Stop at Language Labs?" *Audiovisual Instruction,* vol. 7, pp. 282–283, May, 1962.

Light strip
Speaker
Control and vision panel

Multi-media carrel units permit various kinds of visual, audio, and printed data to be brought from remote sources to the student's place of study. (*From Ralph E. Ellsworth and Hobart D. Wagener,* The School Library, *Educational Facilities Laboratories, Inc., New York,* 1964, *p.* 67.)

tutions of higher education and—perhaps in a more limited way—to elementary schools as well: [26]

> Unless independent study is made possible by giving youngsters the time and the place to work on their own, it becomes a matter of mere lip service. Today the student's typical day consists of six hourly periods. For each of these he goes to different classrooms and laboratories, to the gymnasium, and to the library for a study period. To accomplish practically the revised patterns of time and study proposed here, we would start by providing each student with a study carrel base. From this he would go to the other activities of his school day, some of which might be large group lectures, committee work, special projects, laboratory work, and sports. The youngster would spend part of his day at his study carrel where he would work with all types of carriers—books, teaching machines, records, tapes, radio, and individual television, movie, or slide projectors. When he needed guidance he would go to the teachers and teaching assistants who would be in charge, as they are now, of his learning progress. That progress would be judged on the basis of evidence submitted in regular examinations, oral and written reports, personal conferences, and teaching machine scores. When he needed study materials or bibliographic guidance he would go directly to the materials or to the library staff, which has the same relation to the materials of instruction

[26] Ralph E. Ellsworth and Hobart D. Wagener, *The School Library: Facilities for Independent Study in the Secondary School,* Educational Facilities Laboratories, Inc., New York, 1963, pp. 32–33.

as the teachers do to the content of instruction. Each is master of his part of the learning situation.

In the beginning stages of such a program, both machines and materials might be checked out at the library's circulation desk, just as books and printed materials are checked out. The student would carry the equipment to his carrel, use it there, and return it to the desk when finished.

Should the media program and collection grow extensively to the point where it might involve thousands of tapes, records, kinescopes, films, and the like—and should the size of the student body warrant it—the school might consider some means for transmitting information electronically from a central storage bank. There is a variety of such systems, some simple and others highly sophisticated, but their common denominator is that the student or teacher can recover information without handling the hardware in which it is stored. Rather, he signals an electronic control room where materials are kept, and the program of his choice is transmitted to him. In that case the carrel is fitted with a television screen for the reception of visual materials, headphones for sound, and a telephone mechanism or dial system for communication with the control room. These are fixed components of the carrel. (Via such systems, connected with the school's public address system, the teacher could also receive information in the classroom.)

The growth pattern in some schools might evolve as a combination, with both the check-out of portable equipment as well as a central electronic system for transmitting information. If the school foresees such a pattern of growth, it should plan for the use of both types of carrels.

In either case, the carrels can be movable, an important consideration in the flexible arrangement and use of total library space. Their dividers would be of several types, some supporting a bookshelf, some containing cabinets or lockers where the student might store his materials between work periods without having to go through the tedious task of assembling them each time.

Because the cost of providing each student with his own study carrel is likely to be well beyond the means of many schools, some carrel dividers could be designed to contain two storage cabinets to permit double use of the space. Additional cabinets for triple use of each space could be hung on the uprights of adjacent book stacks.

INDEPENDENT STUDY PROGRAMS: CASE STUDIES

Ideal conditions for independent study require facilities and equipment, instructional materials, and administrative arrangements quite different from those found in most schools and colleges today. It remains to be seen how soon educational institutions will be equipped regularly with electronic, multi-media, or other modern study facilities for individual students. But a growing number of schools and colleges are developing plans, programs, and facilities that are designed for independent study. Some schools use carrels or "Q" spaces of the type just described; others simply give more attention to the concept of individual work stations and opportunities and materials adequate to make independent study profitable. Apparently, no single pattern or formula for independent study programs and facilities meets all requirements. The following examples of independent study programs represent variations on a theme. Although their differences are evident, each has reference to matters of persistent and common concern.

Flexible-schedule program: Wayland, Massachusetts

Seeking to improve the quality and efficiency of the total instructional program and with a distinct regard for the needs of individual students, the high school has developed a pattern of instruction employing a variable group-size format in combination with a flexible master schedule. For each course, an initial decision is made as to the amount of time to be given large-, medium-sized-, and small-group instruction, and laboratory work.[27] A typical student's schedule calls for about two-thirds of the school week to be spent in classroom work and the remainder in independent study. Facilities for various types of independent work that involve different types of activities, include the following:

> *Language center,* including a thirty-six-pupil language laboratory
> *Mathematics and science center,* including laboratory areas and applied science workshop
> *Art center,* including central areas for library, reference, and audio-visual services
> *Social science and business center,* including workshop facilities for machine operations
> *Physical education center*

All facilities are used in various ways for independent study, but the heart of the Wayland program is an ingenious organization of instruction and a system of scheduling that promotes optimum flexibility in designing individual study programs for students: [28]

> The master schedule is a function of individual needs. It is constructed to include the many combinations of courses and the basic arrangements within which the large, medium, labs, and small groups sections meet. The decision of placing an instructional group into the master schedule depends upon the following set of conditions: Are the appropriate students available? Can the teaching team supply an

[27] William M. Griffin, "The Wayland, Massachusetts, High School Program for Individual Differences," *Bulletin of the National Association of Secondary-school Principals,* vol. 47, pp. 118–127, March, 1963.
[28] *Ibid.,* pp. 122–123.

appropriate member or members? Is there a suitable room available? Does this placement maintain a desirable sequence of groups of different size and purpose?

The flow chart with its set of priorities which describes the process of constructing the master schedule calls for electronic sorting since many possibilities need to be examined. The results are rewarding inasmuch as the school is becoming more ungraded. Counselors feel fewer restrictions in arranging individual programs and a very high percentage of students pursue studies of significance to them.

In planning how classes meet over a period of five days, the schedule maker thinks in a total matrix. This matrix consists of 35 modules inasmuch as our school day is usually divided into seven modules of 50 minutes each, one-half hour for lunch, and an optional half hour for cultural arts programs.

A pupil does not necessarily meet a particular course every day or at the same hour each day. Steps however are taken to insure that instruction continues as planned. The days of the week are coded, A B C D E, and instruction throughout the year follows within this planned order of days. In this way, school vacations and emergency "no school days" do not cancel out important segments of the total program.

Thinking in terms of three levels of scheduling responsibility clarifies how the instructional program works throughout the year. The *first level* includes the arrangements for the large, medium, lab, and small-group classes, designating pupil membership, teacher assignment, time of day, and room. The principal, guidance counselors, center coordinators, and data processing personnel have key roles of responsibility in this process.

Many refinements come from this administrative team effort as the staff develops a working understanding of the flexible features within the total schedule. This basic master schedule may appear somewhat rigid, but the *second level* of responsibility for scheduling, under the authority of the team leaders and coordinator in each Center, opens many options similar to a football play. To call these plays in the best interest of the learners calls for perceptions of high order with readily available diagnostic information. This second level, for example, permits revamping the roles of team members in ways thought more effective with students, deciding appropriate membership for an instructional group, and making arrangements for use of other facilities within or outside of the immediate center. These are but a few of the many kinds of arrangements within the learning situations at the instructional center level which lie beyond the scope of the central schedule maker.

The *third level* of schedule making concerns the arrangements between individuals that cannot be "scheduled" at all. The learning experiences under the independent study program depend upon pupil-teacher planning quite independent from the master schedule. Through this dimension, for example, facilities and equipment anywhere in the school become open to students on an individual basis, members of teaching teams become available for tutorial work of a remedial or advanced nature, and the student takes charge of his own learning through projects which have little regard for subject matter boundaries.

Individual-study center: Blackwell, Oklahoma

The senior high school, constructed in 1962 to accommodate 600 students, makes provision for independent study a dominant feature of its design. Its central structure is an individual-study center that houses a "home base" for each student. This base is a station at a four-man desk, with drawers serving as lockers. The individual-study center also contains the school library, as well as a circular enclosure for teacher consultations and faculty dining. The liberal space provided for independent study is made possible because the center replaces the conventional study hall and also serves as a cafeteria. The students get their food from a nearby serving kitchen and take it to their home-base desks, which they use as dining tables. Since the students' desks are not divided by partitions, the center can also serve as an assembly hall, if desired.

The organization of the instructional program provides for a combination of instructional activities that involve groups of varying sizes which meet in smaller classroom buildings adjacent to the center. However, students actually spend the major portion of their time working in the central independent study facility.

Plan for a continuous-progress school: Bassett, California

The plan for the Bassett high school reflects two major goals: (1) that children be educated to the level of their capacities, and (2) that the school aid in developing in each student a sense of individual responsibility. The initial planning of the instructional program for this school was conducted by a committee that consisted of the board of trustees, the superintendent, representatives of the California State Department of Education, architects, and representatives of the School Planning Laboratory of Stanford University. Planning expenses were borne partly by the Bassett Unified School District and partly by the Educational Facilities Laboratories.[29]

Bassett High School has been built around an instructional-materials center, which is the core of the complex of buildings. Immediately adjacent to this center is a cluster of study units, each containing studio offices and a sizable group of study carrels. Each carrel serves as a home base for a student; it is a work area and includes the usual provisions for reading, writing, and related study activities. In addition, each carrel includes provisions for a television receiver and facilities for scheduling or dialing video-tape lectures or demonstrations. Plans

[29] The Educational Facilities Laboratories, Inc., supported by the Ford Foundation, is located at 477 Madison Avenue, New York, N.Y.

have been made to develop an electronic communication system to enable students to communicate with teachers or aides, and vice versa.

The organization of the instructional program is modeled on a continuous-progress plan to permit each student to operate on the basis of his unique objectives for the semester or year. Thus each student's program stipulates not only the courses or learning sequences he is to complete, but the length of time in which these activities should be accomplished. Once the student's general plans have been determined: [30]

> He will then be provided with a personal program—a prepared sequence of activities—to help him reach these objectives. Incorporated into the program will be directions for use of autoinstructional materials, programed textbooks, study kits, books, audiovisual aids, and a variety of technological teaching devices.

Computer-controlled teaching system: University of Illinois [31]

A teaching system known as PLATO has been developed by the Coordinated Science Laboratory at the University of Illinois in an effort to find a means of automated teaching to serve large numbers of students with concurrent, individualized instruction. PLATO uses a single high-speed general-purpose digital computer capable of controlling simultaneous programmed instruction for as many as 1,000 students, thus permitting each student to proceed with one of a variety of programs at his own speed.

Each student taught under this system occupies a station supplied with an electronic keyset to communicate with the computer. He also has a small TV set with which to view materials selected or composed by the computer. The student communicates with the computer by operating keys on the keyset, whose functions are previously designated by the teacher (or lesson designer). Key functions are of two types: (1) character-writing keys, including numerals and letters used in answering questions; and (2) logic keys to provide to the computer instructions such as "continue," "reverse," "help," "lab," "aha," "judge," and "erase." The computer accepts each student's requests in sequence, but because of its high speed each is served without delay.

Information selected by the computer and displayed on the student's own TV screen comes from two sources: (1) a central slide selector having a capacity of 122 slides, and (2) the student's electronic blackboard, on which the central computer writes characters and draws diagrams. Although the slide selector itself is shared by all students being instructed, the individual student has access to any particular slide at will. Slide projector and electronic blackboard images are superimposed on the student's TV screen.

[30] Edward Eisman, "What's Brewing in Bassett?" *Audiovisual Instruction,* vol. 8, p. 136, March, 1963.
[31] This description of PLATO was furnished by Mrs. Elisabeth R. Lyman, Coordinated Science Laboratory of the University of Illinois, Urbana, Ill.

The PLATO response unit is part of a computer-controlled system in experimental use at the Coordinated Science Laboratory of the University of
Illinois. It employs a single general-purpose digital computer programmed for
the simultaneous tutoring of large numbers of students. Keysets in front of
these students permit a variety of reactions to problems presented on viewing
screens. (*University of Illinois*)

Although any pattern of programed or nonprogramed teaching
logic may be written for PLATO, two types of logic have been explored to date—"tutorial" and "inquiry."

"Tutorial" programed lessons for PLATO are divided into a main
sequence, plus a number of help sequences. The main sequence includes questions the student is required to answer. Help-sequence material, for students needing help in answering main-sequence questions,
typically presents further information based on computer diagnosis of
the kind of help needed, and asks leading questions to aid students
in finding correct answers to main-sequence problems. The student
uses "continue" and "reverse" buttons to move forward or backward
in the material. When the computer asks a question, the student must
answer correctly before being allowed to proceed. In practice, the
student inserts his answer to a question and pushes the "judge" button;
the computer answers "OK" or "No." If correct, the student proceeds;
if incorrect, he erases his answer and tries again or asks to see the
help sequence by pushing the "help" button. In the help sequence, as
well, the student must answer correctly before going on; if he cannot

answer a help question correctly, he can ask for "help-help." When all help is exhausted, the student is so informed and given a choice of returning to the question and trying again or of having the computer insert the correct answer for him. The "aha" button is for the student who, having asked for help, discovers he no longer needs it; it takes him back to the main-sequence question. A periodic evaluation check of student responses during the lesson is made by the computer. Superior students satisfying predetermined criteria automatically skip some main sequences, thus proceeding faster through the lesson material.

The "inquiry" lesson material, in contrast to the tutorial logic, allows a student to decide how he wishes to approach a general problem and answers the student's requests for information he needs to solve it. Here, the student exercises almost complete control over his progress. The principal control key in the inquiry logic, usually labeled "lab," transfers the student from any one point in the program to a position which opens up the complete choice of information he can request. One interesting inquiry feature is a simulated laboratory situation for the student in which he can communicate specifications for experiments to the computer by designated keys and receive the experimental results on his display as a computer-drawn picture, diagram, or printed result.

Versatility in the presentation of lesson material to the student is possible since tutorial and inquiry logic may be mixed either with questions being asked of the student or with those constructed by the student for the computer to answer. Such a program permits the lesson designer to create a special teaching logic to suit each subject being taught.

As students proceed through the lesson material, the computer keeps detailed records. These data are available as: (1) raw data which can later be reingested into the computer for analysis, and (2) sorted data suitable for printing out in a format which permits easy visual inspection and provides timed information pertaining to pages on which students have studied, answers submitted and judged by the computer, correctness of answers, requests for help-help, answers or other information supplied by the computer, and experiments performed. "Finger trouble" (hitting wrong keys, etc.) is also recorded.

The availability of a detailed accurate record of each student's progress is an outstanding PLATO feature. Feedback of such data aids the programmer in developing improved lessons.

Self-instructional laboratory facility: Purdue University

At Purdue University, a freshman course in botany has been organized to permit independent work on laboratory assignments, making use of a special facility in which booths fitted for individual students contain all materials and equipment necessary to carry out given study tasks. This experimental program divides the course into four types of study sessions: (1) a general assembly for one hour per week, (2) independent home study, (3) a small-group assembly of approximately thirty students for one hour per week, (4) supervised (independent) study with audio tapes and laboratory materials for approximately four hours per week.

The weekly general assembly offers large-group instructional presentations for all students taking the course. These include general directions and announcements, introductory and orientation lectures, guest presentations, films, and the handling of various course details. In the small assembly sessions, groups of thirty students meet with an experienced discussion leader to deal with such matters as homework questions, quizzes, and discussion of problems related to any aspect of the course.

The independent study facility, which is also the laboratory, is open daily from 7:30 A.M. to 10:30 P.M. and is monitored by a teaching assistant. Students report to the laboratory at their own convenience, and each is allowed to work as long as he wishes. The laboratory is divided into booths, each containing a tape-playback unit. Each student is checked in by the laboratory monitor, provided with the tape for the week, and assigned to a booth. The tape directs the student's activity in a manner somewhat analogous to a teaching machine. The booth is equipped with such items as living plants, preserved specimens, microscope and slides, pictures, diagrams, charts, and materials for experimentation that are placed at specific locations about the booth and identified by numbers or letters. The tape presents information and directs the student's study as he takes notes, makes observations, and completes various exercises. A typical tape might be programmed as follows: [32]

> The tape begins with a general discussion of twigs. The student is asked to obtain a twig from location A in the booth and to notice specific structures (these structures would be identified by pointers attached to the twig and labeled 1, 2, 3, etc.). The nature and function of these structures are discussed while the student observes the specimen. He is then requested to obtain a twig diagram from another location in the booth and to label the structures noted previously. Then he is asked to turn off the tape and to read certain paragraphs in his text; a tape discussion follows which emphasizes important points in this reading. Other twigs which exhibit variations from the first twig (without specific labels) are called to the student's attention. The study of twigs ends with the completion of certain laboratory manual exercises.

Comment on case studies

Consideration of the descriptions of independent study programs carried on at Wayland High School, Blackwell Senior High School, and Bassett

[32] James W. Brown and James W. Thornton, Jr. (eds.), *New Media in Higher Education,* Association for Higher Education and Department of Audio-Visual Instruction, NEA, 1963, p. 128.

High School, as well as the special programmed units in use at the University of Illinois (PLATO) and Purdue University, points up a variety of related problems. In the Wayland High School situation, for example, emphasis is placed upon design of a flexible *scheduling* system for instructional activities so that students may work out programs suited to their individual needs and interests. The facilities provided do not seem to afford unusual or highly specialized arrangements for independent study beyond those found in many modern high schools. Although the design was not a matter of primary concern, the facilities that developed appear to have been well-suited or readily adapted to the instructional plan that ensued.

In the cases of Blackwell Senior High School and the Bassett Unified School District, on the other hand, somewhat greater emphasis was placed on facilities design with a view to implementing specific instructional goals—no doubt this was partly because these new high schools were not yet built when organizational plans were developed. It should be noted, however, that both the Blackwell and Bassett schools illustrate markedly different concepts in design and construction. In the one case, large and highly flexible open space was used in which to house desks that were not separated by partitions; in the other, carrels provided some measure of visual and acoustic privacy, plus added technological features for the convenient use of a variety of media by individual students.

The PLATO plan of the University of Illinois suggests an arrangement in which sophisticated instrumentation becomes the dominant consideration. The resulting instructional program could be achieved only through use of a computer. The over-all problems of instructional organization and scheduling still remain, but in so far as the specific functions subsumed under PLATO are concerned, such problems are relatively minor and mechanical.

Finally, the Purdue self-instructional laboratory plan is an example of a highly structured, carefully developed program of self-instruction that might be adapted quite easily (with the preparation of proper materials and the scheduling of study stations and related equipment) to various types of instruction at any level—elementary school through college.

SUMMARY

This chapter has dealt with the growing emphasis on independent study and with some of the methods, facilities, and programs designed to enhance individual learning. Programmed learning is one method of structuring and facilitating independent study. From an administrative standpoint, problems connected with it mainly concern the total assessment of this new development and its role in education, the selection of programmed materials and devices to fit various instructional situations, and scheduling.

Similar problems are encountered with language laboratories, except that the techniques for them have already gained wider acceptance, and their instrumentation is by now reasonably well standardized, at least with respect to audio components.

The fact that the language laboratory is frequently used as a group instructional facility should not be allowed to obscure its value as a system for self-instruction. Autoinstructional features are especially evident in the level 3 laboratory, which has the capability of permitting the student to record his own voice and to monitor his speaking and compare it with a recorded model.

As we regard the organization and administration of independent study in general, two types of administrative concern stand out. One cluster of problems has to do with the organization and scheduling of independent study in a framework that takes account of the total instructional program, group instructional activities, and various appropriate uses of available space. The other has to do with the design and detailed planning of facilities—the floor space, construction, equipment, and materials that will create an optimum environment for independent study. In general, both sets of problems concern the educational media program directly, although the specific ways in which they are solved will vary.

A distinction should be drawn between independent study centers that serve an entire instructional program and those having more limited purposes—a typical language laboratory, or a facility for a single course, such as the college botany laboratory that was described earlier. It now seems clear that central facilities should be planned cooperatively by those having comprehensive responsibilities for instructional planning and the administration of media and instructional materials; such facilities should be serviced in the context of the total media and materials program. In planning and developing independent study facilities to serve more specific programs, the initiative frequently may be taken by the responsible departmental faculty member or teacher, with encouragement, support, and cooperative assistance from the central administration and media staff.

FOR FURTHER INFORMATION

Bushnell, Donald D.: *The Role of the Computer in Future Instructional Systems,* Monograph 2, Technological Development Project, NEA, 1963. (Published as a special supplement of *AV Communication Review*)

Center for Programed Instruction: *Programs '63: A Guide to Programed Instructional Materials Available to Educators by September 1963.* U.S. Office of Education Publication OE 34015, 1963.

Center for Programed Instruction: *The Use of Programed Instruction in U.S. Schools,* U.S. Office of Education Publication OE 34022, 1963.

Clemens, Thomas D. (ed.): *Research Grants and Contracts Involving Teaching Machines and Other Self-instructional Media,* U.S. Office of Education, 1963.

Coulson, John E. (ed.): *Programmed Learning and Computer-based Instruction,* Wiley, New York, 1962.

"Criteria for Assessing Programed Instructional Materials: 1962 Interim Report of the Joint Committee on Programed Instruction and Teaching Machines" (American Educational Research Association; American Psychological Association; Department of Audio-Visual Instruction, NEA), *Audiovisual Instruction,* vol. 8, pp. 84–89, February, 1963. (Prepared with the cooperation and support of the Educational Media Branch, U.S. Office of Education under NDEA Title VII)

Ellsworth, Ralph E., and Hobart D. Wagener: *The School Library: Facilities for Independent Study in the Secondary School,* Educational Facilities Laboratories, Inc., New York, 1963.

Finn, James D., Donald G. Perrin, and Lee Campion: *Studies in the Growth of Instructional Technology. I: Audiovisual Instrumentation for Instruction in the Public Schools, 1930–1960: A Basis for Take-off,* Occasional Paper 6, Technological Development Project, NEA, 1962.

Finn, James D., and Donald G. Perrin: *Teaching Machines and Programed Learning, 1962: A Survey of the Industry,* U.S. Office of Education Publication OE 34019, 1962.

Four Case Studies of Programed Instruction, Educational Facilities Laboratories, Inc., New York, 1964.

Grubb, Ralph E., and Lenore D. Selfridge: *The Computer Tutoring of Statistics: A Preliminary Report,* International Business Machines Corp., Yorktown Heights, N.Y., 1963.

Hayes, Alfred S.: "Procedures for Language Laboratory Planning," *Bulletin of the National Association of Secondary-school Principals,* pp. 123–125, March, 1962. (The same article in different format is listed as *Step-by-step Procedures for Language Laboratory Planning: Some Suggestions for Schools and Colleges.*)

Hayes, Alfred S.: *Language Laboratory Facilities: Technical Guide for the Selection, Purchase, Use, and Maintenance,* U.S. Government Printing Office, 1963.

Hocking, Elton: "Language Laboratories," *The Nation's Schools,* vol. 67, pp. 83–86, February, 1961. (Reprints available from Dr. Elton Hocking, Department of Modern Languages, Purdue University, Lafayette, Ind.)

Hocking, Elton: *Language Laboratory and Language Learning,* Monograph 2, Department of Audio-Visual Instruction, NEA, 1964.

Hutchinson, Joseph C.: *Modern Foreign Languages in High School: The Language Laboratory,* U.S. Office of Education Bulletin 23, 1961.

Improving Instruction through Audio-Visual Media: Techniques in Teaching Mathematics, Science, and Modern Foreign Languages, California State Department of Education, Sacramento, Calif., 1963.

Lumsdaine, A. A.: "The Developing of Teaching Machines and Programmed Self-instruction," *New Teaching Aids for the American Classroom,* U.S. Government Printing Office, 1962.

Nostrand, Howard Lee, and others: *Research on Language Teaching: An Annotated Bibliography for 1945–61,* University of Washington Press, Seattle, Wash., 1962.

Ofiesh, Gabriel, and Wesley C. Meierhenry (eds.): *Trends in Programmed Instruction,* Papers from the first annual convention of the National Society for Programmed Instruction, Department of Audio-Visual Instruction, NEA, and National Society for Programmed Instruction, 1964.

Oxhandler, Eugene K.: "Bringing the 'Dons' up to Date," *Audiovisual Instruction,* vol. 8, pp. 566–569, October, 1963.

Planning Schools for New Media: A Guide for Boards of Education, School Administrators, and Architects, Division of Education, Portland State College, Portland, Ore., 1961. (Produced pursuant to a contract with the U.S. Office of Education)

Regenstreif, Harry: "Why Stop at Language Labs?" *Audiovisual Instruction,* vol. 7, pp. 282–283, May, 1962.

"The Teacher and the Machine," *The Journal of Educational Research,* vol. 55, pp. 405–531, June–July, 1962.

White, Laurence B.: "Analysis of Problems of Maintenance and Operation of Language Laboratories in California High Schools," *California Schools,* vol. 32, pp. 437–455, November, 1961.

chapter 12

Media services
in the single school

The several varying patterns for supplying single-school educational media services in this country reflect differences in philosophy, economic support, and the restraining effects of tradition. Generally, most may be subsumed in four categories, and in a continuum of responsibility, as follows:

❯ *Complete decentralization,* with no central instructional-materials collection; no specialized staff. The school principal or clerk provides what assistance he can for the program. Chief responsibility for obtaining materials for room libraries rests with individual teachers.

❯ *Centralization of library materials and services only,* with a central book library in the school that is supervised by a professionally trained librarian or teacher-librarian. Nonbook (audio-visual) materials are handled by individual teachers.

❯ *Centralization of separate library and audio-visual services,* often with separate professionally trained librarian or teacher-librarian responsible for book collections. A second interested or professionally trained teacher (who may or may not have had special training for the work) handles the school's audio-visual materials collection and services.

❯ *Centralization of instructional-materials-center services,* with fully integrated book and nonbook facilities and resources. Stress is upon applications of instructional technology and systematic, insightful uses of materials as basic, rather than supplementary, elements of the instructional process.

THE INSTRUCTIONAL–MATERIALS CENTER: EMERGING CONCEPT

Despite the apparent lack of uniformity in administrative organization for educational media services in the past, numerous signs now point to a speed-up in the development of the single-school instructional-materials center. This new service is characterized by providing in one organization the services that students and teachers formerly associated with separate library, audio-visual, textbook depository, duplicating, photo lab, language lab, listening lab, programmed learning lab, and similar facilities.

Perhaps it was to be expected that new media—the films, film-strips, recordings, programmed materials, radio, television, and others—would be accepted somewhat reluctantly at first as responsibilities of the book-oriented school library. Usually its librarian had been trained to handle print items; he had not been trained nor had he ever expected to be required to grapple with unfamiliar "new media" problems—operating (and training others to operate) electronic-playback, projection, or recording equipment; scheduling out-of-library projection services; handling projection club activities; organizing listening laboratory schedules; and the like. Nevertheless, early moves toward integrated instructional-materials services came in widely separated school systems: Portland, Oregon, 1941; the state of Virginia, 1941; Rochester, New York, 1941; the state of Washington, 1947.

The Virginia State Department of Education used the 1945 Legislature's special one-year appropriation of $2 per enrolled student (more than $1 million) to expand collections for bureaus of teaching materials in divisional and single-school centers throughout the state, thus establishing a continuing interest in all instructional materials—printed, audio-visual, realia, as well as books.[1]

In 1947, the Washington State Department of Public Instruction appointed the State Instructional Materials Planning Committee.[2] Using the contributions of more than forty individuals from various branches of education and various disciplines, the committee developed *A Temporary Guide for the Instructional Materials Program*,[3] which was revised in 1960, offering valuable and highly needed assistance to school personnel interested in establishing expanded instructional-materials programs throughout that state. In its foreword, this then somewhat novel viewpoint was expressed: [4]

> The school library is probably as old as our schools. Its function has been recognized as an essential part of our public school program. In the modern educational program a well-equipped school library is more important than ever. The emphasis now placed on meeting the needs of individual boys and girls, on developing their varying interests and capabilities, makes a wealth of instructional materials imperative. The importance of knowing and understanding the whole world community, of which we are now more than ever a part, necessitates the fullest utilization of all avenues of modern communication. Books, magazines, newspapers, other printed materials, radio broadcasts, recordings, community resources are utilized to provide children and youth a knowledge of the world about them and an understanding of their own relation to it. The school must provide these facilities. ˙

[1] James W. Brown, *The Virginia Plan for Audio-Visual Education,* The University of Chicago Press, Chicago, 1947. 31 pp.

[2] Under the general chairmanship of Dr. John E. Hansen, consultant on instructional materials.

[3] Office of the State Superintendent of Public Instruction, Olympia, Wash., 1950. 52 pp.

[4] *Ibid.,* p. 5.

Most of the educators in the State of Washington are convinced that the educational needs of pupils and teachers can best be met through an integrated instructional materials service. [Italics added.] When materials and information about resources are organized in one center their use will be facilitated, and a program better geared to the needs of all pupils will be made possible. Economy in personnel and materials can also be effected through this arrangement.

As early as 1949, the American Association of School Librarians sponsored publication of Margaret Rufsvold's *Audio-Visual School Library Service.*[5] In this useful book appeared details (most still valid) to guide the traditionally book-oriented librarian in setting up and administering "new media" materials and services.

In 1956, during the Miami Beach conference of the ALA, the following statement of the American Association of School Librarians was adopted as official policy, reflecting the continuing interest of this group in the expanding character of "library" services:

The American Association of School Librarians believes that the school library, in addition to doing its vital work of individual reading guidance and development of the school curriculum, should serve the school as a center for instructional materials. Instructional materials include books—the literature of children, young people and adults—other printed materials, films, recordings, and newer media developed to aid learning.

Teaching methods advocated by leaders in the field of curriculum development and now used in elementary and secondary education call for extensive and frequently combined use of traditional along with many new and different kinds of materials. Since these methods depend for their success upon a cross-media approach to learning, a convenient way of approaching instructional materials on a subject or problem basis must be immediately at hand in each school. Historically, libraries of all types have been established to provide convenient centers for books and reading and for locating ideas and information important to the communities they serve. The interest a modern school now has in finding and using good motion pictures, sound recordings, filmstrips and other newer materials simply challenges and gives increased dimension to established library roles.

The school librarian has always encouraged development of appreciation for and ability to make good and continuing use of printed materials and library services. Taking into account individual differences of children and young people, the school library stimulates and guides each child in the selection and use of materials for the building of taste on appropriate levels of maturity. Now in good library practice, the school library also helps both pupils and teachers to discover new materials of interest and to determine their values. It may provide these

[5] Margaret Rufsvold, *Audio-Visual School Library Service,* American Association of School Librarians, ALA, Chicago, 1949.

materials and the equipment needed for their use for both individual and classroom study and teaching.

The function of an instructional materials center is to locate, gather, provide and coordinate a school's materials for learning and the equipment required for use of these materials. Primary responsibility for administering such a center, producing new instructional materials, and supervising regular programs of in-service training for use of materials may be the province of librarians, or it may be shared. In any case, trained school librarians must be ready to cooperate with others and themselves serve as coordinators, consultants, and supervisors of instructional materials service on each level of school administration—in the individual school building, for the city or county unit, for the state.

School librarians are normally educated as teachers and meet state requirements for regular teaching certificates. They must also receive special training in analysis, educational evaluation, selection, organization, systematic distribution and use of instructional materials. The professional education of school librarians should contribute this basic knowledge as well as provide understanding of fundamental learning processes, teaching methods, and the psychology of children and adolescents. Also, school librarians must be familiar with the history and current trends in development of school curricula.

In summary, the well-trained professional school librarian should anticipate service as both a teacher and as an instructional materials specialist. Where adequate funds and staff are available, the school library can serve as an efficient and economical means of coordinating the instructional materials and equipment needed for a given school program. It should always stand ready to provide informed guidance concerning selection and use of both printed and newer media.

More recently, basic textbooks for use in college classes have also stressed the importance of the integrated administration of instructional-materials programs.[6,7,8] In one of them appeared a statement that is commonly, but by no means uniformly, accepted in all quarters: [9]

It is neither possible nor desirable to separate into neat categories the instructional materials and techniques we use. Neither is it possible to rank them arbitrarily in ways which attempt to demonstrate the relative superiority or inferiority of items in such a list. Educators no longer think this is necessary. We serve little purpose by trying to prove that sound films or recordings are "better" than books. . . . Instead, we prefer to examine the entire gamut of instructional resources—including the important segment known as "printed" text and reference materials—and to support curriculum plans which en-

[6] James W. Brown, Richard B. Lewis, and Fred F. Harcleroad, *A-V Instruction: Materials and Methods,* 2d ed., McGraw-Hill, New York, 1964. 592 pp.

[7] Murray Thomas and Sherwin Swartout, *Integrated Teaching Materials,* Longmans, New York, 1960. 545 pp.

[8] Louis Shores, *Instructional Materials: An Introduction for Teachers,* Ronald, New York, 1960. 408 pp.

[9] Brown, Lewis, and Harcleroad, *op. cit.,* p. vii.

courage the use of many different types. We understand the desirability of using these resources *together,* in ways which allow varied approaches to learning problems. And we see exceptional possibilities in capitalizing upon the fact that different instructional materials strengthen and reinforce each other.

But perhaps the most significant stimulus for establishing instructional-materials centers has been the changed approach to the organization and administration of school programs as espoused in the Trump plan and similar proposals described earlier. Most such changes have highlighted the need to coordinate and enrich offerings of instructional resources and services and to improve the physical environment for their use. The most significant trends in this regard have been:

> Increasing technicality of educational media and media devices (projectors, teaching machines, language labs, recorders, for example) which require professionally qualified personnel to supervise their selection and use.
> A move away from a single textbook and toward uses of many different kinds of instructional materials—visual, printed, audio, and real.
> A move toward more individualized or small-group learning activities (library research, listening to recordings, viewing filmstrips, engaging in small-group discussion) and the resulting requirement of space in which to conduct them and personnel for their supervision. The former concept of the library as a "study hall" has changed radically.
> The realization that—with only so much money to go around—it is necessary to avoid the needless expense of building separate and perhaps duplicating media and equipment collections and to seek an integrated approach instead, through a single set of specifications of educational requirements for materials and equipment.
> Recognition that good personnel policies suggest the wisdom of performing for teachers in some central service agency many tasks for which they were once individually responsible—duplicating worksheets or tests, preparing transparencies, arranging field trip details, ordering films, setting up projectors, and the like—leaving them the tasks that they alone can perform proficiently.

The 1963 statement "The Function of Media in the Public Schools" [10] succinctly and effectively summarized the position of the Department of Audio-Visual Instruction of the NEA with respect to the foregoing trends. It first identified two general functions of instructional media in the schools:

> To supplement the teacher through enhancing his effectiveness in the classroom.
> To enhance over-all productivity through instructional media and systems that do not depend upon the teacher for routine execution of many instructional processes or for clerical-mechanical chores.

[10] Barry Morris (ed.), "The Function of Media in the Public Schools," *Audio-visual Instruction,* vol. 8, pp. 9–14, January, 1963.

In serving these two important functions, according to this same statement, the instructional-materials or media generalist is expected to:

❯ Establish a favorable climate for application and development of technology in the instructional program by (1) leading the community and the educational staff to recognize the potential of instructional technology for improved learning and increased productivity, and (2) developing among teachers a concept of instructional technology as the coordination of the elements of environment, staff, methods, and media to educational ends

❯ Participate in the development and implementation of the curriculum by (1) influencing the selection of materials and methods in relation to curricular goals, (2) helping to plan for the allocation of space, time, and financial resources, (3) facilitating the detailed application of instructional technology in specific learning areas and situations, (4) promoting and assessing experimentation and innovation, and (5) continually evaluating and upgrading applications of instructional technology, leading to systems design where appropriate

❯ Provide services that will facilitate the effective use of instructional technology, by (1) designing and producing new materials, (2) making materials and machines readily available to teachers and students, and (3) procuring, maintaining, and operating the necessary equipment

❯ Provide technological support for research, public interpretation, and administration

The position paper continued: [11]

Within these activities fall the traditional services of the school audiovisual center and the school library. Also incorporated are newer concepts of storage and retrieval, of local production of specific teacher-designed materials, of electronic systems for communication and for processing of response data, and of sophisticated visual and audio installations for both individual learning and large-group presentation —installations such as instrumented study carrels, audio laboratories, teaching auditoriums, and programed learning centers.

INSTRUCTIONAL-MATERIALS CENTER

Further analysis of activities in which students and teachers engage in the single school while using the comprehensive services of instructional-materials centers aids in defining their logical functions. Ellsworth and Wagener itemize *student* activities in the center: [12]

❯ Finding answers to questions arising from the teaching process or from ordinary curiosity

❯ Seeking information alone or as members of committees

❯ Carrying out study hall assignments—that is, spending a specific amount of time studying in the library

[11] *Ibid.,* pp. 12–13.
[12] Ralph E. Ellsworth and Hobart D. Wagener, *The School Library: Facilities for Independent Study in the Secondary School,* Educational Facilities Laboratories, Inc., New York, 1963, p. 25.

❯ Finding material for objects, such as written reports, book reviews, debates, or research papers
❯ Learning to use the keys to the library—its card catalogs, bibliographies, reference books, or periodical indexes
❯ Viewing motion pictures, filmstrips, or other audio-visual materials; studying with teaching machines; auditioning tape or disk recordings; listening and recording voice for language study
❯ Locating quotations, excerpts, or data for speeches or projects
❯ Reading just for the fun of reading—one book or a hundred
❯ Browsing through current magazines and newspapers, or looking at the new-book section
❯ Talking with other students

In addition, *teacher* uses of the instructional-materials center are described by the same authors: [13]

❯ Conferring with the center staff on relevant materials to use for classwork —those appropriate for general presentations in the classroom, those most suitable for students working in small groups, and those appropriate for use on an individualized basis
❯ Previewing films and filmstrips; conferring on the purchase or rental of audio-visual materials or on their local production
❯ Consulting on matters pertaining to materials purchases, on the handling of special materials (pamphlets, sample magazines, government documents, and the like), on classification and cataloging problems, and on problems and difficulties of student users of the service

The instructional-materials center in operation

The center contributes in many ways to the improvement of instruction. Its regular day-to-day pattern of utilization by students and teachers is suggested by the following activity analysis: [14]

❯ The teacher and the materials generalist, working together, clarify objectives of the unit topic and study school and class records to discover pertinent facts concerning backgrounds, needs, interests, or special problems (including those of reading) of students in the class.
❯ Center personnel, working closely with the teacher and perhaps with a class committee, choose a variety of suitable and applicable materials from the center's collections—printed, audio, visual, and real.
❯ The materials generalist and the teacher together provide the students with a prefatory overview of the collected materials, giving special attention to those considered most helpful for special purposes of the study.
❯ Decentralized room libraries or subject laboratories may be set up at this time to provide more convenient student access to materials. In such cases, students may serve as room librarians to control distribution.

[13] *Ibid.,* pp. 26–27.
[14] Adapted, in part, from J. Lloyd Trump and Dorsey Baynham, *Focus on Learning;* also, *The School Instructional Materials Center and the Curriculum: The Library Audio-Visual Center,* Pennsylvania State Department of Education, Harrisburg, Pa., 1962, pp. 3–4; Ellsworth and Wagener, *op. cit.,* pp. 25–36.

> The materials generalist and the teacher continue to guide students in selecting and using materials throughout the course of unit study. As they discover a need for additional time to use the center's collections (as in independent study, for example), the schedule is arranged. The materials generalist stimulates interest in materials through appropriate displays and exhibits.

> Center production services are provided as needed to duplicate materials, to prepare slides or large transparencies, to duplicate or make original recordings, and the like.

> The materials generalist indicates the availability and appropriateness of other instructional resources not in the center (field trips, resource visitors, TV programs, loan films from district or other collections) and arranges their use, as desired.

> The materials generalist schedules and monitors student use of teaching machines, small-group conference rooms, listening booths, carrels, recording studio, projection or viewing rooms, and similar facilities, as needed.

> At the conclusion of the study, the teacher, class, and materials generalist evaluate the suitability and adequacy of center resources and services, indicating areas of strength and of needed improvement or additions.

Materials resources

Instructional materials to be found in any single-school instructional-materials center vary, of course, according to enrollment, sophistication of student body, teacher demands, characteristics of the curriculum, and adequacy of the economic base supporting the educational program. They also vary in accordance with the adequacy and policies of other instructional-materials centers at district, county, and state levels. An efficient and well-stocked county or district center, for example, may support the policy of maintaining smaller single-school collections, provided, of course, that they may be borrowed for sufficiently long periods of time to satisfy the requirements of other schools in the area. Groups of items that one might expect to find in the single-school center in varying amounts are:

Printed

Enrichment reading
Basic and supplementary textbooks
Reference and source books
Magazines and newspapers
Pamphlets and other vertical-file
    materials
Microcards (or microfilms)
Programmed materials
Professional library materials
    (guides, courses of study)

Audio

Tape recordings
Disk recordings

Graphic and Photographic

Maps and globes
Flat picture sets
35mm filmstrips
16mm and 8mm films
2- by 2-inch slide sets
Large transparency sets
Art prints

Other

Kits (multi-media units)
Specimen collections
Community resources file
Models and mockups
Exhibits and displays

In addition, the instructional-materials center must arrange to store and monitor the distribution of many expendable materials—blank tapes, raw film, duplicating supplies, tagboard, inks and paints, brushes, sensitized paper for various reproduction processes, dry-mounting tissue, rubber cement, and the like—all of which are needed by teachers, students, and educational media personnel in the school.

The materials of the single-school instructional-materials center are usually inventoried and recorded in the card file or other records of the center, although many of the items are kept in the places where they will be most frequently used. Thus, while a teaching team for subject x may have in its preparation area a complete set of filmstrips, large transparencies, still pictures, reference books, supplementary books (including additional textbooks), and other materials, this fact is recorded in the center, and the items are still available to others, if they are needed.

Equipment resources

As with the materials resources discussed above, the single-school instructional-materials center accessions, services, and maintains distribution and utilization control of various items of equipment.[15] Some items are distributed directly to classrooms on a "permanent custody" basis (i.e., for an extended period of time, up to an entire school year); others are loaned for briefer periods. All media equipment in the building is inventoried on center records whether or not it is physically maintained there. Equipment in the single-school center might include:

Projectors

8mm and 16mm film
2- by 2-inch slide
Combination 35mm filmstrip and 2- by 2-inch
Large transparency (overhead)
3¼ - by 4-inch
Opaque
Individual filmstrip and slide viewers
Microfilm or microcard readers
Microprojector

Audio-TV

Tape recorders
Disk playbacks
Public-address amplifiers
Radios

Television receivers
Video-tape recorders
Image-magnifier TV cameras

Photographic

Still cameras (35mm, 2¼ by 2¼, 4 by 5)
Motion picture cameras (16mm, 8mm)
Darkroom equipment (larger schools)
Photocopiers
Tripods

Graphic

Lettering devices and guides
Laminators

[15] Recommended quantitative equipment standards for individual schools are included in Chap. 7 along with a discussion of budgeting procedures and practices; they will not be duplicated here.

Picture trimmers
Paper cutters
Dry-mount presses
Typewriters
Duplicating machines (spirit, stencil-and-ink, offset)

Other

Portable screens
Temporary darkening equipment

Loan chalkboards, bulletin boards, felt boards, magnetic boards, pegboards
Easels, flip-chart stands
Student-response devices
Teaching machines
Tachistoscopic and other timed-exposure or reading-improvement devices
Wheeled carts
Projection stands

Here again, it is necessary that the center maintain and monitor the distribution of supplies of easily installed and frequently needed replacement parts and accessories for equipment, such as (1) projector belts, reels, exciter lamps, and projector bulbs; (2) tape-recorder take-up reels, splicing blocks; (3) camera filters and copying lenses; and (4) microphones and mixer units.

FACILITIES OF THE INSTRUCTIONAL-MATERIALS CENTER

The general arrangement and physical layout to serve the needs of a comprehensive single-school instructional-materials center have been identified by DeBernardis and others. They recommend that: [16]

❯ The storing, cataloging, inventorying, and distributing of books and of all other teaching materials should be combined in one center.
❯ To facilitate its efficient use by teachers and students, the center should be centrally located. A ground floor location is preferable.
❯ In buildings of more than one floor, elevators or ramps (sloping floors) should be provided to facilitate transportation of heavy materials and equipment.
❯ Floors and entryways through which carts must pass should be free of obstructions. Provide kick plates and jamb covers where equipment must pass through doors.
❯ Center facilities should be sufficiently large and flexible, capable of being rearranged or expanded to suit changing conditions and future requirements and to permit multiple uses of space.
❯ Noise-producing areas of the center should be isolated from classrooms or "quiet reading" areas.

The various types of specialized facilities required for the comprehensive single-school instructional-materials center include:

Control center
Reading rooms, study, and book storage areas
Textbook room
Professional library
Teacher preparation room

[16] Amo DeBernardis and others, *Planning Schools for New Media,* Portland State College, Portland, Ore., 1961, pp. 12–13.

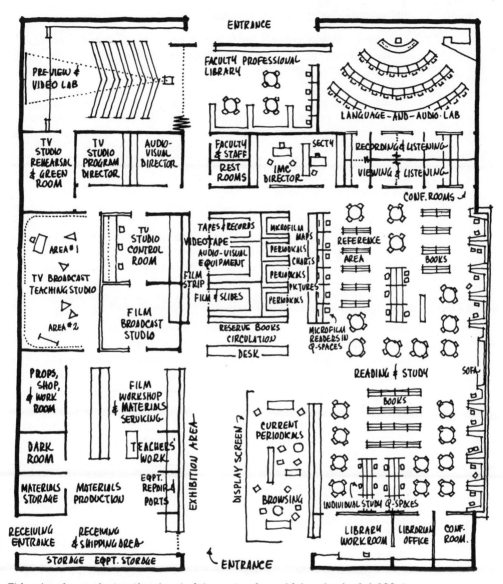

This plan for an instructional-materials center for a high school of 1,000 to 2,000 students includes space for the comprehensive educational media services demanded by today's educational programs. (*From Amo DeBernardis and others,* Planning Schools for New Media, 1961 *p.* 20.)

Technical processes room
Equipment storage and scheduling room
Nonbook materials storage
Materials preparation room
Classroom
Studio and TV-audio control room

Features and uses of each of these facilities are discussed next.

271

Instructional-materials control center

The center should contain space for the variety of "keys" essential to all the student-faculty use of facilities and resources that the center contains. Needed will be: [17]

❯ Instructional-materials center card catalogs, in which are interfiled (in properly color-coded form) carded data on all instructional resources in the center, with separate, smaller files, perhaps, for inventories of community resources (speakers, field-trip destinations, special equipment) and other items.
❯ Shelved reference collections of encyclopedias, almanacs, dictionaries, and other resource books.
❯ Reference consultation desk, near the card catalog, for easy access by students.
❯ Circulation or charging counter, at which are maintained records of all loans and visual control of in-and-out traffic. Staff for the circulation counter might also supervise activities in facilities mentioned below.

An essential function of the control center is to schedule, monitor, and regulate *student use* of teaching machines, listening banks, study carrels, small conference rooms, and the various items of audio-visual equipment (mostly portable) in the center itself or held in other locations. Students wishing to sign up to use a *teaching machine,* for example, check in with the control center, indicate the program desired, and reserve a machine in a bank of teaching machines for the required length of time. The attendant may then accompany the student to provide whatever service is required and to give necessary operating directions. With *individual viewing* of filmstrips or motion pictures, similar arrangements are made. *Study carrels* and *small conference rooms* are also handled at the control center. Some may be "open," others available only by reservation. If sound or TV materials are required in carrels or conference rooms, students leave directions at the control center.

Listening banks (which, in the future, may include video-tape viewers as well as audio from earphones) are also scheduled from the control center. Assigned listening for student groups may be scheduled in advance; individual listening may be available through several channels, into any one of which the listener may tune by use of a simple switching arrangement at his station. Some spaces may also provide opportunities for several students to operate equipment themselves in listening to prerecorded tapes or disks or to radio programs piped from the sound studio.

Reading room, study, and book-storage areas

The general reading room and study areas of the instructional-materials center appear to require less space in schools that emphasize individual-

[17] For a more detailed description of catalog facilities and their uses, see the earlier discussion of this topic in Chap. 4.

This tape and disk playback-listening facility permits students at San Jose State College to study a variety of recorded materials regularly assigned in their courses. (*San Jose State College*)

study approaches to learning than in schools stressing more traditional "study-hall" procedures. But whatever space is saved through this changed condition is likely to be used—and more—in providing individualized study carrels, small conference rooms, and other needed special facilities as mentioned above. Ellsworth and Wagener,[18] for example, recommend the following allocation of the 15,000 square feet of reading-room study space they believe to be needed in a 2,000-student secondary school (based on the seating of 30 per cent of this enrollment at 25 square feet of floor space per station):

Study space	Per cent of students
Carrels	60
Group-study rooms (serving also for use of audio-visual equipment)	15
Flat-top tables	8
Lounge	17
Total	100

[18] Op cit., p. 51.

The Pennsylvania State Department of Education [19] recommends, on the other hand, that no single reading room should accommodate more than 100 students and that enough separate reading rooms should be supplied to accommodate at one time 15 per cent of the school's enrollment, allowing 30 square feet of floor space per student. Included in this space should be all facilities necessary to shelve the center's book and nonbook material. The department estimates that, by these standard, from 15 to 50 per cent of the students in the school may also have space in which to conduct independent study activities.

Ellsworth and Wagener [20] estimate that, on the average, 1 square foot of floor space will be needed for each fifteen volumes in the book collection. They also recommend that books be stored in free-standing, bracket-book stacks (which come in 3-foot unit lengths, plus 2 inches for end panels of each range), and that shelves be no more than one-third full when newly constructed centers are first occupied. This limit will permit a future doubling of size without forcing shelves beyond the recommended "two-thirds full" (more than this amount is said to excessively wear the books). Rows of ranges should be spaced 4 feet and 6 inches apart, measuring from column centers, with five or six shelves per section. No more than 10 per cent of the shelves need be 10 inches wide; all others may be 8 inches, but special atlas cases are recommended. A 5-foot space should be left between the book-stack face and edges of adjacent tables.

Textbook room

A textbook room is usually needed in most schools; it is recommended that it be made part of the instructional-materials-center complex. In it are a limited number of copies of textbooks in use in the school, as well as limited quantities of other supplementary textbooks. Records of regular textbook distribution are maintained here. Textbook repairs may be done in the textbook room or in the technical processes room, which is discussed later. In some secondary schools, it is now customary to assign to the textbook clerk the responsibility for operating a school bookstore, from which paperbacks, school supplies, and certain other items are sold.

Professional library

Each school center should also maintain a collection of professional library materials that contain courses of study, selected professional textbooks and reference books, sample tests, professional magazines, pamphlets, and similar materials. In some cases, this collection might be placed in one corner of the teacher preparation room, which is discussed below.

[19] *The School Instructional Materials Center and the Curriculum: The Library Audio-Visual Center,* p. 15.
[20] *Op. cit.,* pp. 78–79.

Teacher preparation-conference room

In the teacher preparation-conference room, facilities and space should be provided to accomplish the many activities now required of teachers as they plan classwork and select instructional materials. Here teachers may come to consider items that the materials specialist has collected, as discussed previously, and to seek opinions of other teachers about resources best suited to their special requirements.

The teacher preparation-conference room finds other uses, too. It may be used as a committee-meeting room; or teachers may use its earphone-equipped tape or disk playbacks or motion-picture projectors, individual filmstrip viewers or projectors, illuminated slide sorters, or similar equipment for their own detailed studies of nonbook materials considered for use in their classes. The professional library should be easily accessible from here; it may be combined into one facility.

Technical processes room

The center itself requires a room in which the many technical processes of readying for circulation, cataloging, inspecting, mending, repairing, displaying, labeling, or packaging instructional materials may be carried out. There must also be space in which to check, clean, oil, or replace bulbs or belts on various items of audio-visual equipment.

As more and more centralized services are performed for school centers (including those of cataloging and preparing books and other materials for the shelves), space requirements for technical processes rooms diminish.

Equipment storage and scheduling room

Space should be provided to store and schedule the use of audio-visual and other types of instructional equipment. This same area might also be used as a "ready room" for student projectionists or center assistants who handle assignments in classrooms or auditoriums throughout the school plant.

This area should be accessible to hallways and/or elevators or dumbwaiters. Its furnishings should include:

❯ Adjustable shelving in racks sufficiently large to store all regularly scheduled equipment items sent out on short-term loans to teachers or students or taken by student assistants assigned to handle equipment operation in classrooms
❯ Some extra space for at least part of the equipment usually left in classrooms or team-teaching areas on long-term bases
❯ Separate space (perhaps blocked off from those just mentioned) for storing loan items such as microscopes, typewriters, stand lights, globes, bulky maps (such as large spring-roller types), large models (the human body, for example), and similar items that do not ordinarily circulate to students

275

but which would be delivered to classrooms or other teaching areas in the school on request.

The full inventory of audio-visual equipment in the building, as well as preventive maintenance schedules for oiling, cleaning, checking belts, etc., would also be kept here. Needed would be (1) a counter or desk space at which the chief projectionist (student) may work and maintain his records and operator assignments, (2) one large bulletin or magnetic board on which to post schedules for the day or week, (3) a second, smaller bulletin board on which to place notices for students and instructors, (4) an illuminated slide sorter, (5) a tape splicer, and (6) a number of wheeled projector carts, book carts, and/or demonstration tables.

Nonbook materials storage

The storage requirements for various different kinds of nonbook materials were discussed earlier in Chapter 4. For example, it was pointed out there that some easy-to-handle disk recordings may be stored in their jackets in the individual study or reading area and near the listening bank referred to earlier. When this is done, students and teachers alike may browse through the collection, read dust-jacket comments, and if they so desire, go directly to the playback machine to hear recordings. But perhaps a second collection of disk recordings may also be kept in another location and made available only to teachers or to specially authorized students.

Decisions concerning the most suitable storage control for other kinds of items must take into account some of the special difficulties (miscanning, scratching, snarling, and the like) that are likely to arise as they are handled by persons unfamiliar with details of their proper care. What usually results is a stack-type storage system that permits only minimum "browsing." With this arrangement, students and teachers check out items and schedule equipment necessary for previewing or auditioning them within the center.

Materials-preparation room

Such a room in the center is used primarily by teachers and the center staff; secondarily, by students having special requirements in connection with class assignments or individual research. This facility, mentioned earlier in Chapter 6, must provide space and equipment in which to produce simple charts, copy 2- by 2-inch slides, prepare materials for bulletin boards or other displays, edit film or tape footage, and develop and print (or enlarge) black-and-white pictures in larger schools. It should also contain one or more photocopiers (capable of making projectable large transparencies or instant paper copies), as well as spirit, stencil-and-ink, or offset duplicators. Space and equipment must be provided, of course, to facilitate the assembling and stapling of duplicated materials.

Instructional-materials classroom

An important part of the center is a special classroom, adjacent to the reading room, in which entire classes may be assembled quietly to receive special instruction in use of the center's materials and equipment or to hear or see other special presentations related to their studies. This room should be equipped with light-control devices, ventilation facilities, electrical outlets, chalkboard, and acoustical treatment of the usual classroom, as discussed in Chapter 3.

Studio and control room

The studio and control room of the center finds a variety of uses. It may:

❯ House the school's central sound system and central TV and reception facilities and be the focal point of distribution to classrooms throughout the school plant
❯ House facilities for originating live TV or audio materials for use in various parts of the school, for *live* transmission elsewhere, or for making tape and video-tape recordings from the air, from closed lines (as from the downtown center), or from the studio itself
❯ Provide space in which to photograph simple motion pictures or to pose various kinds of still pictures

INSTRUCTIONAL–MATERIALS CENTER ORGANIZATION AND STAFFING

The administrative organization of the single-school instructional-materials center may first be examined with respect to its relationships to other administrative offices of the school and the system of which that school is a part.

The NEA Department of Audio-Visual Instruction recommends the appointment to the central district or county staff of an assistant superintendent for educational media at a level commensurate with the importance of his work in the administrative hierarchy. Working with this individual are others whose special interests are in systems design, television, library resources, programmed instruction, audio-visual equipment, and materials production.

The single-school instructional-materials center should preferably be organized as one administrative unit, under the supervision of a person trained in instructional materials; in turn, he is directly responsible to the school principal and indirectly to the district or county educational media director. In some schools, other staffing arrangements have developed through custom. This may perhaps include the establishment of a separate "book" library under a librarian and an "audio-visual service" under a part-time teacher-director; in this case, suitable arrangements should be made to either combine these services, or to continue the separate services but facilitate their future coordination through combined information (catalog) services, inventories, policies, student staff assignments, faculty advisory committees, and the like.

With fully combined services, the pattern of staff organization and responsibilities usually results in assignments of the following types:

> An instructional-materials generalist in charge—one who is broadly trained in all aspects of educational media, who is familiar with the entire range of educational media and media services, who can perform proficiently as both a "librarian" and an "audio-visual specialist."

> In larger schools, one or more additional professionally trained media specialists to assume "library" or "audio-visual" responsibilities.

> One or more instructional-materials clerks to handle nonprofessional tasks within the center, such as typing, duplicating, filing, and maintaining records; shelving, mending, repairing materials; supervising student aides; assisting center personnel as needed; maintaining card catalogs and the shelf list; [21] handling additional clerical duties, such as booking films, searching for bibliographical information, maintaining special files of pictures and realia, handling charging desk routines, reserving books and other materials, sending notices, assisting students with audio-visual equipment in the center.[22]

> One or more nonprofessional technicians (depending upon size and support) to handle the making of photographs, large transparencies, and slides, audio and video-tape requirements, television or sound studio operation, "first-echelon" equipment adjustment and maintenance, graphic productions, and the like. In large centers, these individuals would most likely report to the "library" or "audio-visual" professional specialist, according to assignments involved.

> Student aides in various numbers, in accordance with need, to handle essential details (operating projectors, arranging materials on shelves, checking materials in and out, typing, duplicating tapes, servicing teaching machines, and the like). In making such assignments, care should be taken to avoid merely exploiting the students rather than helping them to derive valuable learnings from the experiences.[23]

[21] As recommended by the Pennsylvania State Department of Public Instruction in *The School Instructional Materials Center and the Curriculum: The Library Audio-Visual Center,* p. 12.

[22] In some schools it is also the practice to assign shipping-receiving functions to such a clerk. In carrying out these responsibilities, all shipments for the school —in or out—arrive at his room and shipping dock. He orders and receives films, for example, or picks them up and returns them to the district center; textbooks are his responsibility—to procure from the central warehouse, to distribute, and to account for.

[23] For a succinct and valuable discussion of ways of organizing and managing student aide clubs, see Fred Winston and others, *Guiding Students in the School AV Club,* Department of Audio-Visual Instruction, NEA, 1962. 72 pp.

SUMMARY

The "instructional-materials center" concept has recently experienced considerable growth in American education. This has been due, in part, to increased attention to multiple uses of all kinds of educational media occasioned by recent curricular and administrative changes. Phillips develops the following case: [24]

> The rationale for an instructional materials center is based upon the obvious fact that . . . [no] one medium of communication is adequate to the task of providing information and concepts which are unambiguous to students. . . . Only the use of a wide variety of materials—the multi-media approach—can insure that the weakness of any given type of material will be compensated for by the strengths of one or more of the other materials. . . . [The] problem is how best to make this wide range of materials convenient to teachers and students. . . . The simplest answer is to make all the media available through a single facility: an instructional materials center. It is the simplest answer because it makes possible the most efficient use of the students' and teachers' time. Only one place need be visited, only one catalog consulted. All necessary help is available from one source. . . .
>
> All types of audiovisual materials, not only the printed materials classically associated with libraries, are circulated from and used within the center. The use and selection of these materials are coordinated with the use and selection of radio and televised programs, both broadcast and closed-circuit. A formal and informal inservice program is constantly in operation to improve usage of materials. Consultation service is at hand for students, teachers, and administrators concerning the best resources available to help solve particular learning and teaching problems. A wide variety of materials is locally produced to supplement commercially produced materials. . . . An instructional materials center is more than a library plus an audiovisual center. Its collection of printed materials includes publications not ordinarily found in the libraries: curriculum guides, courses of study, specimen standardized tests, catalogs of all types of commercial instructional materials and equipment, and sample textbooks from many publishers.

FOR FURTHER INFORMATION

American Association of School Librarians: *Standards for School Library Programs,* ALA, Chicago, 1960, 152 pp.

Audio-Visual and Other Instructional Materials, Kansas State Department of Public Instruction, Topeka, Kan., 1961. 28 pp.

Audio-Visual Education: A Manual for Administrators, North Carolina State Department of Education, Raleigh, N.C., 1962. 37 pp.

[24] Murray G. Phillips, "Instructional Materials Center: The Rationale," *Audiovisual Instruction,* vol. 5, p. 326, December, 1960.

"The Audio-Visual Instructional Materials Center," *Planning Schools for Use of Audio-Visual Materials,* no. 3, Department of Audio-Visual Instruction, NEA, 1954. 80 pp.

"Complete with Reading Rooms," *Audiovisual Instruction,* vol. 5, p. 333, December, 1960.

Daniel, Wanda, and James J. McPherson (eds.): *Teachers' Audio-Visual Instructional Materials Handbook,* Wayne State University, Detroit, Mich., 1958. 32 pp.

DeBernardis, Amo, and others: *Planning Schools for New Media,* Portland State College, Portland, Ore., 1961. 72 pp.

Ellsworth, Ralph E., and Hobart D. Wagener: *The School Library: Facilities for Independent Study in the Secondary School,* Educational Facilities Laboratories, Inc., New York, 1963. 139 pp.

Ford, Harry J.: "The Instructional Resources Center," *Audiovisual Instruction,* vol. 7, pp. 524–526, October, 1962.

Glenn, Magdalene: "Organizing a Materials Center," *National Elementary Principal,* vol. 40, pp. 28–30, January, 1961.

Goldberg, Albert L., and Richard A. Darling: "Is the Instructional Materials Center the Answer?" *Audiovisual Instruction,* vol. 6, pp. 194–195, May, 1961.

Greer, Phyllis: "A Materials Center That Really Works," *Audiovisual Instruction,* vol. 5, p. 332, December, 1960.

Handbook for the Student Assistant in the School Library, Arkansas Library Commission, Arkansas State Department of Education, Little Rock, Ark., 1959. 28 pp.

Harcleroad, Fred F. (ed.): "The Education of the AV Communication Specialist," *A-V Communication Review,* vol. 8, September–October, 1960. 96 pp.

Helfrich, John E.: "A Laboratory for Total Communication," *Visucom,* Tecnifax Corp., vol. 2, 1963, pp. 2–8.

Hyer, Anna L.: "Setting Quantitative Standards," *Audiovisual Instruction,* vol. 6, pp. 506–510, December, 1961.

Instructional Materials, Illinois Curriculum Program, Verne Stockman (chairman), Administration and Supervision Series, Bulletin A-3, Springfield, Ill. 1961. 146 pp.

Instructional Materials Services for Washington's Schools, State Superintendent of Public Instruction, Olympia, Wash., 1960. 56 pp.

Larsen, John A., and Jewel Bindrup: "The Library Curriculum Center: Hub of the School Program," *Audiovisual Instruction,* vol. 7, pp. 526–527, October, 1962.

McMahan, Marie: "Building Coordinator: Professional Partner?" *Audiovisual Instruction,* vol. 7, pp. 662–665, October, 1962.

Mahar, Mary Helen: *The School Library as a Materials Center,* U.S. Office of Education, 1963. 84 pp.

Mitchell, Malcolm G.: "What's Going On in the School Library?" *Phi Delta Kappan,* vol. 45, pp. 44–47, October, 1963. ·

Nicholson, Margaret E.: "The I.M.C.," *School Libraries,* pp. 39–43, March, 1964.

Phillips, Murray G.: "Instructional Materials Center: The Rationale," *Audiovisual Instruction,* vol. 5, pp. 326–332, December, 1960.

Planning Materials Centers, Florida State Department of Education Bulletin 22E, Tallahassee, Fla., 1958. 49 pp.

Planning the Instructional Materials Center for Elementary and Secondary Schools, Michigan State Department of Public Instruction, Lansing, Mich., 1958. 13 pp.

Rufsvold, Margaret: *Audio-Visual School Library Service,* ALA, Chicago, 1949. 116 pp.

Staffing the Instructional Materials Center in Elementary and Secondary Schools, Michigan State Department of Public Instruction, Lansing, Mich., 1960.

Taylor, Kenneth I.: "Instructional Materials Center," *The Nation's Schools,* vol. 66, pp. 46–50, December, 1960.

Taylor, Kenneth I.: "West Leyden's Center for Instructional Materials," *Library Journal,* vol. 86, pp. 16–48, Apr. 15, 1961.

"The Instructional Materials Center," *Overview,* vol. 3, pp. 25–28, July, 1962.

The School Instructional Materials Center and the Curriculum: The Library Audio-Visual Center, Pennsylvania State Department of Public Instruction, Harrisburg, Pa., 1962. 36 pp.

Trump, J. Lloyd: "Images of the Future for School Libraries," *ALA Bulletin,* pp. 129–131, February, 1961.

Wartenberg, Milton: "A Comprehensive Service Center for Randolph High School," *Audiovisual Instruction,* vol. 7, pp. 542–543, October, 1962.

Winston, Fred, and others: *Guiding Students in the School AV Club,* Department of Audio-Visual Instruction, NEA, 1962. 73 pp.

Wittich, Walter A.: "A–V Tools Talk; Schools Listen—and Look," *The Nation's Schools,* vol. 71, pp. 61–80, May, 1963.

Wittich, Walter A., and W. Henry Durr: "The Audio-Visual Tools of Learning: How to Make Them Work," *The Nation's Schools,* pp. 35–54, July, 1962.

chapter 13

Media services
in counties and districts

The early development of audio-visual education as a separate activity in school systems of the United States has been traced from the school museums and bureaus of visual education that were organized in some large cities in the first three decades of this century. The St. Louis educational museum was established in 1904, and Saettler notes that it was the first organization for visual education in a city school system.[1] By 1923, sixteen city school systems had established bureaus or departments of visual education, as reported in a survey by F. Dean McClusky.[2] These progenitors of the modern educational media programs consisted mainly of slides, museum exhibits, pictures, charts, and models; they changed gradually as motion pictures grew in importance during the 1920s and 1930s.

At first, many schools and school systems found ways of using visual materials without a central organization, but the nondepartmentalized use of newer media became less and less practical as the modern technology of instruction developed—as the continued and accelerating growth of audio-visual and instructional-materials programs since the early 1930s, and especially since World War II has shown.

In 1953–1954, the NEA conducted a national survey of audio-visual education in urban school districts. This survey revealed that departments of audio-visual education had been established in most large metropolitan school districts: in districts having a population of 100,000 or more, 86 per cent had such departments. Formal centralization of audio-visual services occurred much less frequently in smaller districts. In cities ranging from 30,000 to 100,000, the frequency was 48 per cent; this dropped to 25 per cent in cities of 10,000 to 30,000.[3]

A comparison of the 1954 data with a 1946 survey showed that the number of audio-visual departments, bureaus, or divisions had increased sharply in the intervening period, especially in medium-sized

[1] Paul Saettler, "The Origin and Development of Audio-Visual Communication in Education in the United States," unpublished doctoral dissertation, University of Southern California, Los Angeles, Calif., 1953, p. 364ff.
[2] F. Dean McClusky, "The Administration of Visual Education: A National Survey," unpublished report to the NEA, 1923.
[3] NEA, Research Division, *Audio-Visual Education in Urban School Districts, 1953–1954,* Research Bulletin 33, October, 1955, p. 95.

and small districts. There are many indications that this trend has continued and possibly accelerated in recent years. At present, most urban school districts have their own centralized services or benefit from a cooperative program serving a number of small districts. Likewise, a very large number of small rural districts (and consolidated districts) are now served by centralized educational media programs of the sort described in the next section.

COOPERATIVE COUNTY PROGRAMS

The 1954 NEA study revealed that a large proportion of small cities did not have centrally organized audio-visual services. Despite a trend toward consolidation and larger districts, most school systems in the United States are still relatively small, and an adequate, well-rounded education media program requires a larger pupil base than most small cities or small districts have. In many localities, small districts have overcome this limitation by developing cooperative programs through which media services can be provided to a number of participating school systems. Such programs are usually operated through the office of a county superintendent of schools, although other administrative units may be used. The cooperative program may be administered in any one of a variety of ways, as shown in the following definition: [4]

> A cooperative audio-visual program is one which extends services to two or more school districts in one or more counties. The audio-visual center may be organized under legal authority of the state legislature, state education agency, county board of education, and/or by mutual consent of the participating local school districts. The policy-making body of the program may be a county board of education and/or a board of school superintendents or representatives of the schools participating in the financial support and services of the cooperative audio-visual center.
>
> The cooperative program may be financed by state funds, county funds, local funds, or any combination of these financial sources. In some cases higher education institutions contribute financial support, physical facilities, and administrative support to encourage the establishment and operation of the programs. The audio-visual services provided are generally limited to the schools participating in the program. The center does not necessarily serve all the public schools in the county or service area.

In California, for instance, a highly successful cooperative plan is supported in part by state funds and administered by the county offices, which provide contracted services to participating districts. This plan was initiated in 1947 on a wholly state-supported basis. In the mid-1950s, it was gradually modified so that districts would participate on

[4] Henry R. McCarty and Horace C. Hartsell, *The Cooperative Approach to Audio-Visual Programs,* Department of Audio-Visual Instruction and Department of Rural Education, NEA, 1959, pp. 20–21.

a matching-funds basis. Although the present law does not require the state to allocate matching funds or to designate any portion of the school-service allocation specifically for audio-visual services, county cooperative programs continue to operate on the basis of joint support from state and districts, very much as in the past.

In 1959, a special committee jointly sponsored by the Department of Audio-Visual Instruction and the Department of Rural Education of the NEA published a report of a survey of 104 cooperative audio-visual programs throughout the country.[5] Commenting on their geographical distribution, the report identified the West Coast, the Middle West, and some Southern states as the areas showing greatest growth in this respect. The relative lack of cooperative programs in the Plains, Mountain, and Southwestern states was attributed to distance between communities, sparsity of population, and the large number of very small districts. Relatively few cooperative programs were found in the Eastern and New England states, although favorable conditions prevailed in those areas. The general rate of growth of the cooperative pattern had slowed down somewhat since 1950, but the authors concluded that "increasing interest in the need to develop effective intermediate units as a means of making specialized services available for all schools points up the probability that the greatest growth is yet to be made." [6]

Although cooperative educational media programs are sometimes set up on a regional basis or occasionally to serve only part of a county, most operate through the office of the county superintendent of schools. Programs of this sort are found in such widely scattered locations as Alameda County, California; Snohomish County, Washington; Pratt County, Kansas; Cook County, Illinois; Vanderburgh County, Indiana; Dallas County, Texas; and, of course, many others.

County educational media programs are also found in a number of states that employ a county-unit-district form of organization for school services. In Florida, Nevada, West Virginia, Maryland, Louisiana, and other states, the county (or parish) is the only available administrative unit—aside from some large independent city systems or the state itself. Media programs administered on a county-unit-district basis are not cooperative in the strict sense, but they are similar to the county cooperatives in other ways and have about the same advantages in terms of economy and efficiency. Such programs are found in Dade County, Florida; Fulton County, Georgia; Kanawha County, West Virginia; and in many other locations.

FUNCTIONS OF A CENTRALIZED EDUCATIONAL MEDIA PROGRAM

The preceding discussion suggests a variety of organizational patterns. Most early programs were known as bureaus or departments of visual

[5] *Ibid.*

[6] *Ibid.*, p. 13.

instruction or, later, audio-visual instruction. In the 1950s and early 1960s the audio-visual center was still the predominant pattern, but this was modified in many cases by two important developments.

Some counties and districts preferred an integrated system of services that encompassed printed as well as audio-visual materials—the complete, integrated instructional-materials center. As educational television developed in the 1950s and continued to grow vigorously in the 1960s, a variety of administrative bases and patterns came about. Sometimes television became a part of the county or district audio-visual or instructional-materials program, sometimes not (see Chapter 10). Frequently the county or district was served by an educational television station operated by a university or as a community public-service enterprise. In such cases, the county or school district might support a consultant or coordinator to assist schools and teachers in the cooperative planning and utilization of televised instruction.

Still another factor that contributed to the growing complexity and diversity of the centralized educational media program was the expansion of educational technology—programmed instruction and teaching machines, language laboratories, electronic classrooms, computer-based instructional systems, etc. While the county or district center was not always directly involved in the planning, purchase, and use of such materials, school personnel needed consultation, research services, and informed leadership to keep up with the bewildering array of technological developments, and properly staffed centralized programs were in a strategic position to make a vital and continuing contribution to education in the 1960s.

No list of specified functions would apply to all centralized programs. The following composite list outlines the range of operations of the modern county or district program, whether it be called "audio-visual," "instructional materials," "educational communication," "instructional resources," "instructional services," "curriculum materials," or "library and audio-visual services":

❯ Participating in the planning of instructional programs with respect to printed and audio-visual materials, instructional devices, media, and systems
❯ Coordinating the selection and organization of collections of instructional materials for students and professional library resources for teachers
❯ Circulating instructional materials
❯ Coordinating the selection, processing, and distribution of textbooks
❯ Planning and producing instructional television and radio broadcasts and closed-circuit television programs in cooperation with appropriate curriculum or other committees
❯ Coordinating the use of instructional television and radio services
❯ Planning, designing, and preparing instructional materials, such as graphics, photographs, slides, filmstrips, motion pictures, recordings, and programmed materials, in cooperation with teachers
❯ Circulating appropriate printed, broadcast, and other information to

schools and the lay public to acquaint them with the services, facilities, and materials of the educational media program

❯ Consulting with teachers and school administrators to identify instructional problems or opportunities related to the use of media and materials and to assist in solving problems or exploiting opportunities

❯ Planning and coordinating a variety of in-service training activities to assist teachers in the effective use of instructional media and materials

❯ Participating in the planning and design of school buildings and facilities to ensure the most effective and efficient use of technological resources in teaching

❯ Promoting and coordinating appropriate experimentation and research to ascertain the values of various instructional materials, techniques, and media and to develop better ways of using them

GUIDELINES FOR THE ADMINISTRATION OF CENTRALIZED EDUCATIONAL MEDIA PROGRAMS

The administration of materials and equipment was discussed earlier (see Chapters 4 and 5), and such key matters as criteria, selection, specifications and bids, accessioning and cataloging, shelving and storage, circulation, and maintenance need not be repeated here. However, some guidelines, cautions, and suggestions apply particularly to the administration of centralized instructional-media programs and warrant discussion. These guidelines are freely adapted, in part, from an evaluation instrument developed by the Bureau of Audiovisual and School Library Education of the California State Department of Education and the Audiovisual Education Association of California.[7]

Size of administrative unit

Most individual schools do not enroll enough students to support a complete and independent media program, but a county or district frequently constitutes a suitable administrative base. State funds are available to districts through cooperative programs that are administered at the county level in some states.

General requisites

An educational media program is successful to the extent that it facilitates effective use of appropriate media and good instructional materials in the classroom. To do so, the central program must (1) maintain a collection of good instructional materials that are not readily, conveniently, or economically available in the individual schools, (2) provide appropriate media facilities and services not otherwise available,

[7] *AVEAC Cooperative Evaluation Instrument for County and District Audiovisual Programs,* Bureau of Audiovisual and School Library Education, California State Department of Education, Sacramento, Calif., 1965.

(3) keep teachers, principals, and supervisors adequately informed about media services and materials and procedures for using them, (4) develop and maintain a booking and circulation system that makes services and materials readily and conveniently accessible to teachers, (5) provide or coordinate in-service education to ensure skillful and discriminating use of resources, and (6) provide technical assistance and advice to administrators and teachers to aid them in conducting the essential and highly personal business of teaching.

Staff

Educational media services involve professional, clerical, and technical personnel (staff functions for professional personnel required to implement county and district programs were briefly discussed in Chapter 2). Much of the success of the program depends upon clerical and technical personnel who must carry out numerous and detailed functions such as ordinary bookkeeping; processing of purchase orders and rentals; accessioning and cataloging; booking orders for the circulation of materials and equipment; shipping, delivering, and receiving materials and equipment; maintaining and repairing materials and equipment; and sundry other duties, such as operating and maintaining television systems, language laboratories, computers, or other devices, depending on the scope of media services and operations. The importance of having sufficient well-trained personnel for such functions cannot be overemphasized, particularly for expanding programs, which must obtain financial support, recruit and train personnel in advance or on the job.

However, the most critical shortage is frequently found at the professional level. A county or district program is usually headed by a full-time professionally trained person, but all too often, he does not have sufficient professional staff to carry out supervision, in-service training, or evaluation and experimentation in more than the most cursory way. Thus earlier discussion (see Chapter 8), which deals with improving utilization practices, assumes that the head must usually function primarily as an instigator and coordinator of in-service training and experimental efforts to develop better uses of instructional media.

Organization and administration

In central offices that provide various instructional services to county or district schools, most staff members act as supervisors or consultants. This applies also to the educational media director. However, he differs from his colleagues, who supervise in such areas as instruction, languages, social studies, or fine arts in that he must also administer a large and complicated enterprise that involves special facilities, services, technical operations, a staff, a large budget—with the associated problems of planning and management. In short, he is called upon to play two roles: supervisor and administrator, and the organization of the center must take both of these often conflicting roles into account. The professional staff should devote its time to professional duties; however, the director should have full administrative authority over other members of his staff, including technical and clerical personnel. Lines of authority should be clearly defined. The director should have the authority to carry out his assigned responsibilities, but he should delegate sufficient authority to staff members to facilitate operations, avoid becoming a bottleneck, and free his own time for professional functions. The administrative structure (both internal and external) should have sufficient flexibility to encourage initiative.

Appropriate ties of cooperation should be established also between the center and related community, county, state, and Federal agencies and services.

Media and materials

Criteria and selection procedures for instructional materials and equipment have been discussed earlier in some detail (see Chapters 4 and 5), and there is no need to add to that discussion here, except to emphasize the importance of properly dividing instructional resources between those which should be centralized and those which should be contained in the single school. In Chapter 12, the instructional-materials center was described as a facility that brings a complete spectrum of instructional materials to individual schools. It was noted that relatively expensive materials, such as motion pictures, would not ordinarily belong to the school collection. In addition, television and radio services usually require facilities, staff, and a degree of coordination that can best be provided at the county or large-district level. Sometimes television and other mass-media services are administered at the state, regional, or national level and several examples of national network educational television have been given (see Chapter 10). In addition, the development and coordination of instructional-materials centers or libraries for individual schools and selection, storage, distribution, and textbook-maintenance services may also be administered at the district or county level. Finally, the collections of county and district centers may include relatively expensive and/or infrequently used items—mounted specimens of animals, models of human organs, plants, mockups of molecules, human skeletons, scientific instruments, such as barometers or vacuum pumps, etc.

The four factors most pertinent in determining which materials, media, and services should be centrally administered at the county or district level are (1) expense, (2) relative frequency of use, (3) size and geographical distribution of the audience (as in the case of the mass media), and (4) the need for central coordination of materials and services at the single-school level.

Those responsible for selecting materials should be guided by established and recorded policies. Evaluative criteria for selecting all materials should be developed and used.

The collection and resources should be sufficiently balanced and complete to meet various instructional needs and implement various curricular objectives. Records should show that teachers are using the materials frequently and effectively and with precision and discrimination and that the use of materials is well distributed throughout the collection and throughout the schools served.

Equipment

Needs of county and district centers are governed by considerations similar to those just cited for materials, media, and services. Criteria and selection procedures have been discussed earlier (see Chapter 5). Additional factors to be considered are the center's needs for equipment to carry on certain internal operations, including preparation of some instructional materials, and the trend toward greater use of electronic computers and related equipment. Principal categories of required equipment may include the following:

❯ *Equipment for storage, inspection, cleaning, and repair,* for films, books and other printed materials, projectors, tape recorders, and other equipment. This ordinarily includes an automatic film-inspection and cleaning unit; it frequently includes a shop containing mechanical, power-driven, and electronic tools for the maintenance and repair of projectors, tape recorders, sound playback units, and various other classroom instruction devices that cannot be maintained economically by individual schools.

❯ *Preview and listening equipment,* including projectors, tape recorders, and disk playback unit. This is used mainly by center staff and visiting teachers.

❯ *Equipment for circulation to schools,* for occasional loan. Audio-visual equipment commonly used in the classroom is usually owned by the individual school or stationed there on permanent loan from the district or county. However, in some cases there may be a need for supplementary or occasional use of equipment available from a central source. Some centers keep limited amounts of circulating equipment to meet such demands.

❯ *Production equipment,* for graphic, photographic, and authority instructional materials. A detailed discussion of equipment needs for county and district educational media centers offering such production services is contained in Chapter 5.

❯ *Transmitting equipment,* for radio and television. This would also include a distribution system where schools are served by closed-circuit television. A detailed discussion of the various types of systems used for transmitting television signals is included in Chapter 10. Of course, many school systems do not provide broadcasting services. Systems using broadcasting may or may not include it as one of the functions of the central educational media program. Finally, it should be noted that television and/or radio programming does not necessarily mean that the school system owns the equipment. Some counties and districts provide broadcasting services to the schools through commercial facilities.

❯ *The electronic computer,* rapidly gaining recognition and acceptance in education. It is used to store and process pupil data; facilitate clerical operations, such as the preparation of catalogs and listing of instructional materials; book instructional materials and services; and implement certain kinds of instructional and experimental functions, including the simulation of instructional programs and techniques. Further anticipated uses include the development of information-retrieval systems that can be operated on a regional basis to serve local school systems through data-link transmission lines and satellite computers.[10] While the direct application of the computer to instruction is still largely experimental, and the information-retrieval system for educational institutions is still in the future (because of cost), it seems evident that the computer has an impressive potential in education and not unlikely that computer equipment will be employed to help implement modern instructional techniques at the district or county level. Some centralized educational media centers are already making use of such equipment for cataloging and booking functions. To explore and expand the use of the computer may be one of the most important challenges now facing educational media administrators who are engaged in the direction of centralized instructional facilities.

There should be established, written policies and criteria to provide guidance in the selection, testing, and demonstration of new equipment, as well as materials. Such policies and criteria should be designed to make sure that the proper kinds and quantities of equipment will be on hand to meet genuine needs, and that the equipment collection will be justified by its regular and frequent use. The media center staff should exercise appropriate leadership in evaluating, testing, and demonstrating new equipment and uses of equipment.

Facilities

A county or district center is essentially a service facility. Sufficient space, furniture, fixtures, and equipment must be allocated for display and circulation of materials; administrative and clerical functions, including processing, cataloging, filing, and booking; storage of equipment and materials; technical and production functions, such as broadcasting or closed-circuit television, maintenance and repair, recording, preparation of graphic and photographic materials; preview and listening, professional library, and conference room. In addition to these more or less conventional requirements, it would appear (as discussed in the previous section) that a truly modern design for a centralized instruc-

[8] See Chap. 4.
[9] See Chap. 16.
[10] Donald D. Bushnell, "The Role of the Computer in Future Instructional Systems," Monograph 2, Technical Development Project, NEA, *AV Communication Review,* vol. 11, March–April, 1963. (Entire issue)

tional facility should include provisions to make use of the electronic computer and related equipment for card punching, card sorting, and, in due course, information storage and retrieval.

The center should be a pleasant place, and working conditions should be such as to attract and retain desirable personnel and promote efficient work. Location and layout of space should facilitate workflow and efficiency. Adequate facilities must also exist in the schools being served (see detailed discussion in Chapter 3).

Communication, information, and field relations

The effectiveness of professional staff members depends largely upon contact and communication with teachers and administrators in the school and other professional central office staff—especially those working in supervision, curriculum, and library services.

❯ *County.* To amplify and sustain the efforts of the county staff, it is often helpful to establish a liaison group or groups at the district level. In this way, the district offices can join forces with the county to facilitate policy development and improve communication with individual schools and teachers.

❯ *District.* Where central services are organized on a district basis it may be desirable to form a small liaison group that includes administrators from the individual schools.

The director should be available to provide professional assistance to the superintendent's staff and the schools served. He should conduct or arrange in-service educational activities as required and should develop a strong program at the individual school level. Teachers should be involved in the implementation of the media program; their involvement might be measured by imaginative recommendations and productive changes in policies and procedures.

Supervisory and consultative services should be coordinated with similar activities conducted by other county or district supervisors and curriculum workers, and the effectiveness of such services should be measured in terms of improved instructional practices and teacher attitudes.

An effective cataloging system and other information procedures should be developed for all clients and constituents of the program.

Research, experimentation, and evaluation

A vital instructional program requires constant evaluation and experimentation to find better ways of doing what is already being done and to deal with new teaching needs or problems. Aside from studies that must be made in the laboratory and "pure" research, such means of developing the program are probably most helpful when used by teachers and those working closely with them. The county or district center should be a source of stimulation and guidance for teachers who wish to evaluate and improve their use of instructional media and materials, and typical research functions that can be discharged at the district or county level are described later (see Chapter 16). Whether or not the educational media staff actually includes members who are qualified and have the time to engage fully in research activities, the director of the media program may assume responsibility for instigating, planning, and coordinating research efforts that relate to the better organization and use of instructional resources. The close relationship of research and the planning of instructional systems is examined in Chapter 16.

CASE STUDIES

The evolution of the modern audio-visual center from its primitive counterparts—the educational museums and bureaus of visual education of the turn of the century—is a remarkable story of technological change and progressive organization of instructional services. But the coming of age of the newer media in education has led to something much more complicated than just a "grown-up" collection of visual and auditory learning aids. The increasing recognition of the power of the new media and the importance of a variety of instructional materials has given impetus to a multi-media approach. This multi-media approach has been reflected not only in the growing diversity of the audio-visual center's functions and of concepts about the instructional-materials center but also in organizational plans.

Just how comprehensive should the educational media program become? Should it rest content with the conventional audio-visual materials and devices? Should it reach beyond them to teaching machines, electronic classrooms, television and radio? Should audio-visual and printed materials join forces with the newer electronic devices and media, moving toward a total mustering of all instructional resources in one integrated plan of organization?

There is evidence that the scope of audio-visual services tends to expand with the technology and to embrace the newer technological developments, with occasional exceptions. The integration of printed and audio-visual materials, on the other hand, is somewhat different. Here practice is not consistent, and there are many conspicuously successful programs in both integrated and nonintegrated patterns. Over a period of years, arguments have been advanced in behalf of the integrated center by many strong supporters, including Louis Shores and Murray G. Phillips.[11] Others have argued that the integration of printed and audio-visual materials is unnecessary or undesirable if there is suitable cooperation and coordination for administrative planning and su-

[11] Murray G. Phillips, "Instructional Materials Centers: The Rationale," *Audiovisual Instruction,* vol. 5, pp. 326–327, December, 1960.

pervision.[12] Both points of view are represented in the three county and district case studies that follow.

Los Angeles County, California

In this county, 856 schools in 92 districts are served by the Division of Audio-Visual Education, which administers one of the largest and most fully developed county film, radio, and television programs in the United States. As in other California counties, this cooperative program is supported by district and state funds. Major functions include the circulation of motion pictures, art reproductions, and other audio-visual materials; the administration of instructional television and radio programs; and consultative and in-service training services related to the planning and use of educational media and materials.

The director of the Division of Audio-Visual Education, who reports to the chief deputy superintendent of schools, is assisted by a staff of 46 regular employees (5 consulting, 24 clerical, 11 technical, 3 shipping, 3 distributing), plus occasional professional and clerical workers.

The size of this large operation is suggested by a recent annual budget of $651,000; a motion-picture collection consisting of almost 32,000 prints; and a circulation of approximately 128,000 films per year. In addition, the division operates a regional instructional television program that serves 86 school districts in 8 counties on a (recent) budget of approximately $227,000, as well as an instructional radio program that is conducted in cooperation with the Los Angeles city schools.

Policy for the television project is determined jointly by the Regional Educational Television Advisory Committee, the executive committee of the office of the county superintendent of schools, and the Los Angeles County Board of Education. Planning for program presentations is initiated by curriculum committees from the participating districts, which set the content areas, levels, and the in-service training programs necessary to implement the telecasts. These recommendations are submitted to the regional committee for approval, and thence to the Los Angeles County superintendent of schools and the county board of education. After the board gives its approval, implementation becomes the responsibility of the Division of Audio-Visual Services. Actual programming entails the purchase of airtime in the amount of about three hours per day from a commercial station. Professional TV consultants serving on the division staff take part in planning and editing scripts.

Other professional services afforded by the Division of Audio-Visual Education include the following: [13]

[12] Albert Goldberg and Richard A. Darling, "Is the Instructional Materials Center the Answer?" *Audiovisual Instruction,* vol. 6, p. 194, May, 1961.
[13] This description is based upon information supplied by Robert C. Gerletti, Director, Division of Audio-Visual Education, Los Angeles County Schools.

> Editing radio and film scripts
> Consulting with producers of audio-visual materials and equipment
> Consulting with districts regarding all aspects of the audio-visual program, such as in-service programs, physical facilities, and organization
> Serving as a coordinating agency to disseminate best practices found in the county schools
> Serving on state-wide professional committees to develop common standards and procedures
> Cooperating with business and industry committees relative to services in this area
> Consulting with teacher-training institutions regarding the preservice and in-service training of teachers

Newark, New Jersey

The purposes of the Newark Department of Libraries and Audiovisual Education are listed in a recent annual report as follows: [14]

> To coordinate materials of instruction for the schools of Newark through the development, organization and promotion of all media:
> 1. The printed word, including library and text materials
> 2. Audiovisual materials
>   a. The production and broadcasting of educational radio programs
>   b. Projected and recorded materials, including films, filmstrips, slides, tape and disc recordings
> To assist in the development and supervision of libraries as centers of instructional materials in the individual schools
> To compile, for the Textbook Council, the data needed for the selection and listing of textbooks, including the maintenance of an information service and the preparation of inventory reports on textbooks
> To cooperate with the Newark Public Library and the Newark Museum in their work with schools

The foregoing statement is notable for its inclusive orientation to the wide span of educational media and materials and also for the explicit reference to the cooperating community agencies, the public library and the museum. All expressed purposes are reflected in the actual program of the Department of Libraries and Audiovisual Education, whose organization is shown on the next page.

The library division houses a professional library for teachers and a school library office, which maintains examination collections of new books and periodicals approved for use in the schools. The audio-visual division maintains a collection of films, filmstrips, and other audio-visual materials and equipment for use in the schools, produces photographic and other materials, and provides related services, which are spelled out below. The textbook division provides a reference collection of listed textbooks and a collection of textbooks, maps, and educational

[14] *Annual Report, 1963–64,* Department of Libraries and Audiovisual Education, Newark Public Schools, Newark, N.J. (Mimeographed)

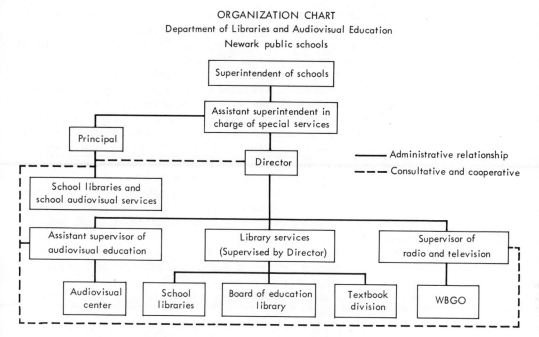

ORGANIZATION CHART
Department of Libraries and Audiovisual Education
Newark public schools

supplies submitted for evaluation. Specific services are indicated below. The radio and television division is responsible for planning and coordinating the use of these media, although until recently actual production of instructional programs has been limited to radio. Specific functions to be carried out by the four divisions are given in the following list: [15]

❯ To provide for the evaluation and selection of printed and audio-visual materials.

❯ To make available curriculum materials that will supplement and enrich the resources of individual schools.

❯ To provide materials and research services for professional growth in service.

❯ To provide advisory services for school personnel in the areas of book selection, use of audio-visual instructional materials, selection and use of audio-visual equipment, organization of school libraries as information centers.

❯ To encourage and assist in the production of instructional materials in areas where they are not available commercially and/or where a permanent record of school activities is required.

❯ To prepare *Price List of Textbooks, Maps and Educational Supplies* based on materials approved by the Textbook Council.

❯ To compile an inventory of all books in the Newark public schools from reports of individual schools.

❯ To approve all book and periodical orders for school libraries.

[15] This description is based upon information supplied by Edward T. Schofield, director, Department of Libraries and Audiovisual Education, Newark Public Schools, Newark, N.J.

> To provide lists of teaching materials to accompany courses of study.
> To issue a list of outstanding professional books annually.
> To develop radio and television programs of significance for the Newark schools, which involves analysis of community needs; consultation with school and other resource personnel; research, preparation, writing of script, casting, selection of music, and sound effects; production and taping; broadcasting and evaluation of pilot programs; construction of manuals for use by teachers; development of programs covering a wide range of experiences.
> To use radio programs from outside sources and to contribute to the national supply of school programs such as is provided by WBGO membership in the NAEB. The school advisory committee assists in auditioning and evaluating programs; manuals are adapted by staff of WBGO.
> To provide for pupil participation in radio programs, the division initiates contests, discussions, and quizzes, with pupil representatives from various schools; trains talented children in drama techniques through radio programs.
> To provide in-service training for teachers, including introduction and interpretation of new courses of study; demonstration of teaching techniques.
> To serve as a means of rapid communication from the superintendent of schools to individual schools.

Montgomery County, Maryland

A complete instructional-materials program is administered by the Office of Instructional Materials for the 141 schools of Montgomery County, Maryland. The specific functions of this county service agency are discharged by a staff of forty-five members grouped in five sections, as shown by its organizational plan. It is headed by a director, who reports to the assistant superintendent for instructional and personnel services.

The *instructional-materials center* operates a telephone booking service for efficient distribution of instructional materials, supplies graphic arts service for the design, layout, and production of materials for instruction, and provides professional and technical staff services to schools for more effective utilization of materials and equipment. The *curriculum laboratory* houses professional textbooks, courses of study, copies of approved textbooks used in the county schools, newly published textbooks, professional periodicals, programmed materials, and other printed materials for use by teachers in instructional planning. The *review and evaluation section* coordinates the review, evaluation, and selection of all instructional materials and equipment for the school system, annually publishes an elementary and secondary textbook list, and periodically releases approved lists of print and nonprint instructional materials for use by schools in the system. The *processing center* processes instructional materials for all school libraries in the county and for the curriculum laboratory. This is done for economy and also to eliminate the repetitive work done in each school in order to release additional time for librarians to assist individual students and teachers.

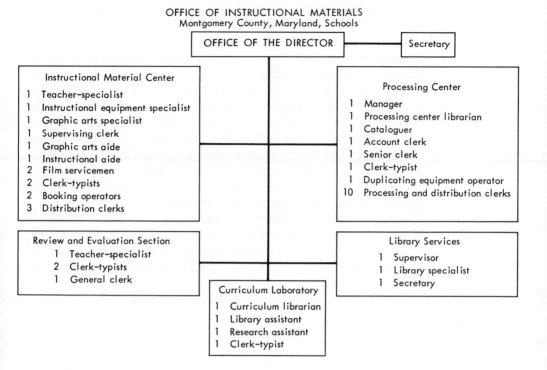

OFFICE OF INSTRUCTIONAL MATERIALS
Montgomery County, Maryland, Schools

OFFICE OF THE DIRECTOR — Secretary

Instructional Material Center
1 Teacher-specialist
1 Instructional equipment specialist
1 Graphic arts specialist
1 Supervising clerk
1 Graphic arts aide
1 Instructional aide
2 Film servicemen
2 Clerk-typists
2 Booking operators
3 Distribution clerks

Processing Center
1 Manager
1 Processing center librarian
1 Cataloguer
1 Account clerk
1 Senior clerk
1 Clerk-typist
1 Duplicating equipment operator
10 Processing and distribution clerks

Review and Evaluation Section
1 Teacher-specialist
2 Clerk-typists
1 General clerk

Library Services
1 Supervisor
1 Library specialist
1 Secretary

Curriculum Laboratory
1 Curriculum librarian
1 Library assistant
1 Research assistant
1 Clerk-typist

Library services selects and orders new materials in cooperation with other professional members of the school staff, provides instructional-materials consultation service to all school personnel, maintains school instructional-materials collections, maintains a comprehensive card catalog of all instructional materials both print and nonprint, organizes the work of the library aides, helps conduct workshops in the use of instructional materials, and carries out numerous other functions.

A *central textbook depository,* although not administratively assigned to the office, handles all elementary and secondary school orders for all new textbooks, all excess textbooks, and all discarded elementary and secondary textbooks. The textbooks are processed and sent out to the schools. All used textbooks can be returned to the depository for credit, thus extending the textbook budget for individual schools.[16]

SUMMARY

This chapter has reviewed the development of comprehensive educational media programs as formally constituted activities of county and large-district school systems throughout the United States. The rise of such programs in the 1940s, 1950s, and 1960s enabled increasing numbers of smaller school districts and county school units to enjoy the numerous advantages of centralized media services.

[16] Information provided by James W. Jacobs, director of Office of Instructional Materials, Montgomery County Public Schools. Montgomery, Md.

Characteristic county and district programs discussed in this chapter emphasized services peculiarly adapted to this administrative level. It was pointed out, for example, that the services of such centers usually involve the more expensive or complex media—circulation of motion pictures or of less frequently used and expensive scientific equipment, television programming and broadcasting, the writing and publishing of texts or booklet materials, electronic computers, large-scale graphics production, and the like. It was also stressed that such centers must seek to contribute importantly to the achievement of educational goals through adequate communication and cooperation with other instructional services, administrators, and teachers; through their own in-service and consultative activities; and through vigorous and sustained programs of research and experimental evaluation.

Case studies describing the organization of central educational media services in Los Angeles County (California), Newark (New Jersey), and Montgomery County (Maryland) schools suggested essential similarities and differences in purposes and administrative organization of such agencies.

FOR FURTHER INFORMATION

Erickson, Carlton W. H.: *Administering Audio-Visual Services,* Macmillan, New York, 1959.

Goldberg, Albert L., and Richard A. Darling: "Is the Instructional Materials Center the Answer?" *Audiovisual Instruction,* vol. 6, p. 194, May, 1961.

McCarty, Henry R., and Horace C. Hartsell: *The Cooperative Approach to Audio-Visual Programs,* Department of Audio-Visual Instruction and Department of Rural Education, NEA, 1959.

Morris, Barry (ed.): "The Function of Media in the Public Schools," *Audiovisual Instruction,* vol. 18, p. 9, January, 1963.

NEA, Department of Audio-Visual Instruction: *Planning Schools for Use of Audio-Visual Materials,* no. 3, The Audio-Visual Instructional Materials Center, January, 1954.

NEA: *Audio-Visual Education in Urban School Districts, 1953–54,* Research Bulletin 33, October, 1955.

Office of the Superintendent of Public Instruction: *Instructional Materials,*

Bulletin A-3, Administration and Supervision Series, Illinois Curriculum Program, Springfield, Ill., 1963.

Phillips, Murray G.: "Instructional Materials Centers: The Rationale," *Audiovisual Instruction,* vol. 5, p. 326, December, 1960.

Schuller, Charles F. (ed.): *The School Administrator and His Audio-Visual Program,* Department of Audio-Visual Instruction, NEA, 1954.

chapter 14

Media services
in universities and colleges

The number of students enrolled in public and private universities, colleges, and schools of technology in 1900 barely exceeded 115,000. This enrollment had increased by 1963 to 4.4 million; today it continues to mount at an accelerating rate as the war babies enter college. Increasing enrollments in higher education are due, partly, to sheer population growth; in addition, more young people now enter institutions of higher education and stay longer. In Kansas, for example, college and university enrollments actually increased about 50 per cent in the ten-year period from 1950 to 1960, although the number of college-age youth actually decreased. On the basis of birth records alone, the prospects are that the number of young people of college age will rise sharply in the years immediately ahead. This, combined with the growing tendency to continue education beyond high school, recently prompted the prediction that by 1980 college enrollments would rise 250 to 300 per cent.[1]

No doubt, some of this growth is due to economic factors. In the United States and other prosperous societies, for example, more and more families can afford to send their sons and daughters to college, and they do so to ensure their children's future as well as that of the family unit. However, the deeper and considerably more significant factor is simply that constantly advancing science and technology create a persistent demand for more highly educated people. Automation and other technological developments reduce the demand for blue-collar and farm workers. As machines take over mechanical and repetitive tasks, modern society calls for more highly trained professional workers, managers, planners, research specialists, and skilled technicians to perform increasingly complex tasks. A high level of training is required of the individual, and he needs, as well, a broad cultural orientation in order that he may view his own specialized work as a meaningful and constructive part of the total social enterprise.

The plight of higher education today is apparent and well known:

[1] Alvin C. Eurich, "A Twenty-first Century Look at Higher Education," *Current Issues in Higher Education: 1963,* Association for Higher Education, NEA, 1963, p. 39.

More students require more and better education—but who will teach them? This problem is discussed in a recent report: [2]

> The problem of teaching staff is the reverse of the problem of students. Not enough graduate students are preparing rapidly enough to replace the annual loss in numbers of professors from death, retirement, and movement to better paid positions and to staff the colleges that must be created to care for the imminent doubling of enrollments. Nationwide, about 40 per cent of college professors now hold earned doctorates. It has been estimated that by 1975 this proportion will drop to 20 per cent. Steps such as reducing the time span between the bachelor's degree and the doctorate and making college teaching competitively more attractive by increasing salaries and technical assistance can help in a small way to maintain student-faculty ratios. These efforts, however, seem unlikely to provide enough new recruits to college teaching to maintain even present standards of class size and present practices of student-professor interaction.

Shortages, of course, are not confined simply to the human factor. Eurich estimated in 1963 that if colleges continued to operate along conventional lines, it would be necessary to build more new facilities than had been built in all our previous history during the next fifteen years. Surveying the explosive population growth now in progress, he concluded that "we obviously cannot accommodate such numbers within the conventional framework of our educational system. We are virtually forced to consider how we can use available resources more effectively and efficiently." [3]

In view of the explosive growth in enrollments, the corresponding shortages of qualified instructors and facilities, and the changing character of higher education, several critical questions that have particular application to the subject of this book are raised: [4]

❯ Can the valid, traditional purposes of higher education, as well as its new and emerging purposes, continue to be attained economically and effectively by its traditional media of communication?

❯ Can newer media of communication contribute, without loss of quality and perhaps with some hope of betterment, to improving large-group instruction?

❯ Can desired flexibility and quality of instruction result from combinations of large-group presentations with discussion groups of moderate size, tutoring, independent study, programmed learning, or other procedures?

❯ Can new media contribute to effective self-instruction, and thus free the professor for more face-to-face contact with students?

❯ Considering the increasing complexity of interrelationships and abstraction of conceptualization in the several disciplines, will certain forms of

---

[2] James W. Brown and James W. Thornton, Jr. (eds.), *New Media in Higher Education,* Association for Higher Education and Department of Audio-Visual Instruction, NEA, 1963, p. 4.
[3] Eurich, *op. cit.,* p. 29.
[4] Adapted from Brown and Thornton, *op. cit.,* pp. 1–5.

nonverbal presentation prove more effective than oral or printed words in transmitting some kinds of ideas?

> Is it possible that experimentation with new media may lead to improved effectiveness of the professor as well as to an extension of his influence?

> What changing conditions emphasize the need to speed the processes of evolution in higher education, and how do these changes relate to uses of new media?

COLLEGE TEACHING AND THE CHALLENGE OF TECHNOLOGY

Modern communications technology affords abundant opportunities to meet some of these problems, and new dimensions of teaching in higher education are being explored. Substantial changes have already occurred. Some experimental applications of the new educational media have been tried, for example; many are in progress; more are still to come. But large numbers of college teachers and administrators continue to resist impending developments in educational technology and to be doubtful of their results.

Someone has observed that college teachers are inclined to hold progressive views regarding almost everything but the practice of their own profession: teaching. Such a statement is probably unfair. Yet there is strong evidence that many highly educated professors do fail to demonstrate effective communication skills in their own classrooms. The two greatest faults of college teaching appear to be: (1) an undue reliance upon the lecture method, and (2) failure to use an adequate and varied repertoire of communication techniques. Many college teachers appear to be unconcerned or unaware of such faults. Opportunities to launch instructional innovations involving uses of new media or a wider range of learning resources are often viewed with apathy or suspicion and sometimes with downright hostility.

Why do some professors resist so firmly the advances of technology in college and university teaching? Edgar Dale has described the feelings of the professor who rejects new media as a threat to his academic privacy and autonomy. In a world that makes "more and more intrusions upon his time, his choices, his feeling of self-esteem, the classroom is one place where his dreams and ideals can hold full sway, where he can have some choice of what he is going to do." [5] Here he can take pride in his own unique effort to achieve excellence in teaching. His discipline is internal. However, Dale continues: [6]

> Now come the new media which will impose an external discipline. When the machine says "start," the professor starts and he stops when it says so. Further, the presentation may be better than he can do.
> If he is making the presentation for a large group he must plan

[5] Edgar Dale, as quoted in *ibid.*, p. 14.
[6] *Ibid.*

his lectures with others, follow what group consensus dictates. The applause, if any, is no longer individual. It is dispersed, nebulous. And when he must expose his teaching to the view of others, he may feel that he is not quite up to it. The professor's classroom is no longer his castle.

Further, where do planning and systematizing end? What will prevent his being engulfed in an enforced cooperation, a kind of intellectual collectivism?

Of course, this fear of technology is not confined to the college classroom alone. Modern man has learned to rely upon machines for his livelihood and his protection, and yet there is a dread of the consequences of the continuing advance of technology because of its apparent power to alter conditions of human life and growth—for evil, as well as for good. In an age when machines intrude upon the life and privacy of individuals in so many threatening ways, many have a strong urge to run away, to return in nostalgic memory to a time when life was simpler, or somehow to halt the terrible and relentless advance of technology. Unfortunately, though, there is no place to hide, not even within the ivy-covered walls of the temple of learning.

CHANGING PATTERNS OF MEDIA SERVICES IN HIGHER EDUCATION

Media services afforded today's college students are rich and varied, as compared with those of thirty years or perhaps even fifteen years ago. But to view the present scene in perspective, it is helpful to look still farther. A century ago, the traditional library was indeed a meager resource: [7]

Until the last quarter of the nineteenth century the pattern of college library service was relatively simple. The library was recognized in the abstract as an important symbol in the establishment of colleges but was honored more frequently in words than in performance. Research on the history of the American college library indicates that the inadequacy of most college libraries was felt so keenly by students that the literary societies, which began to appear after the middle of the nineteenth century, undertook to establish student libraries as one of their major purposes. The office of the librarian was one of the first to be differentiated after that of the presidency, but the duties of the librarian, usually a member of the teaching faculty upon whom was laid the added responsibility of caring for the library, were largely custodial. He carried the key to the room where the books were kept and saw to it that the room was tightly locked except during the few periods of the week when students were permitted to use the books. Not until the twentieth century, and for many colleges not until the

[7] Guy R. Lyle, *The Administration of the College Library,* H. W. Wilson, New York, 1961, p. 1.

twenties and the thirties of this century, was there any pronounced change in the traditional role of the library as a storehouse of books and of the librarian as guardian of these books.

The dramatic changes that produced the great college and university libraries of today required the better part of a hundred years— even longer, if one looks back to the beginnings of higher education in the United States. Technological developments of the twentieth century, and especially of the last thirty years, have initiated a new cycle in communication and instruction. Although this development now proceeds with accelerating speed, it is a very young revolution and far from maturation.

Organized visual education first appeared in the colleges and universities in conjunction with extension divisions that were formed in the early 1900s. Among functions of The University of the State of New York (established in 1891) for example, was the distribution of still pictures and lantern slides. The Bureau of Visual Instruction was established by the extension department of the University of Texas in 1910. By 1914, similar departments or bureaus were operating as extension activities in 5 other universities in the country. This number had increased to 23 by 1940, and to 36 by 1948.[8]

Expansion of media services to include on-campus activities was a somewhat later and overlapping development that dated from the establishment of audio-visual centers in the 1930s and 1940s.[9] Such newer media programs prospered as more suitable motion pictures and other audio-visual materials became available and as there was some gradual—though sometimes reluctant—recognition and acceptance of audio-visual techniques by college teachers everywhere. As on-campus media services expanded, they were sometimes allied to extension programs, sometimes not.

In the 1950s and 1960s, the growth of educational television, language laboratories, and other electronic teaching devices, as well as the advent of programmed instruction, stimulated and hastened the development of additional media services. Frequently, these are included in expanding audio-visual organizations or in inclusive educational media programs that are known by some other name. Patterns of administrative organization for such programs reflect a variety of functions. The extent of this variety is suggested by the following list of names given to educational media programs in colleges and universities around the country:

Audio-Visual Center (or Audiovisual Center)
Library (including other than printed materials)

[8] Paul Saettler, "The Origin and Development of Audio-Visual Communication in Education in the United States," unpublished doctoral dissertation, University of Southern California, Los Angeles, 1953, p. 351.

[9] The term "visual education" gave way to "audio-visual" in the 1940s. For instance, the Bureau of Visual Education at Indiana University was changed to Bureau of Audio-Visual Aids in 1941 and to Audio-Visual Center in 1946.

Instructional Materials Center
Instructional Resources Center
Division of Instructional Services
Division of Learning Resources

Units that are frequently organized as discrete media services are:

Educational television stations
Instructional television centers
Film-production units
Language laboratories

The various functions discharged by these educational media agencies include:

❯ Circulation of motion pictures and other audio-visual materials and equipment for on-campus instructional purposes
❯ Circulation of printed materials, involving the use of modern information storage and retrieval systems
❯ Off-campus circulation of educational materials through extension services and/or by means of cooperative "service-area" programs
❯ Production of instructional materials such as motion pictures, graphics, and photographic materials
❯ Services and facilities for large-group instruction, including open- and closed-circuit television, and special classrooms designed for large groups or for groups of varying sizes and equipped for use of various media or for multi-media presentation
❯ Television and radio broadcasting for regional and community education (in the broad sense), and for off-campus instruction of enrolled students
❯ Provision of language laboratories and other electronic teaching or learning facilities for independent study and automated instruction
❯ Programmed instruction, including the use of teaching machines
❯ Technical services such as the design, installation, maintenance, and operation of instructional equipment of all kinds, including television and radio transmitters, electronic components for language laboratories, classroom communication and student-response systems, projectors, magnetic recorders
❯ Provision of facilities and coaching for faculty members who wish to prepare their own inexpensive instructional materials, such as overhead transparencies, slides, and charts
❯ In-service education and dissemination of information regarding instructional media developments, techniques, and research findings
❯ Assistance in the planning and design of new buildings and instructional facilities to accommodate optimum use of various educational media
❯ Experimental trial and development of instructional devices, techniques, and materials
❯ Systematic analysis and evaluation of instructional functions, costs, and results for the purpose of improving teaching effectiveness and reducing unnecessary expense
❯ Design of instructional systems, a process involving the comprehensive analysis of human and nonhuman factors and their interrelations in teach-

Dr. Edwin L. Peterson, University of Pittsburgh, uses the overhead transparency projector to provide "luminous" English instruction in a course in composition. (*University of Pittsburgh*)

ing, a concept to be examined at some length in the final chapter of this book ❯ Professional education of specialists and "generalists" who are qualified to assume positions of leadership in planning and directing educational media programs and research in this area.[10]

The list just given is rather comprehensive. Ordinarily, not all these services are offered as part of any single educational media program. In most cases in higher education, the conventional library and

[10] While this is a function frequently associated with educational media programs operating in conjunction with some appropriate department of instruction, it is not an administrative service function and will not be considered further in this chapter.

the audio-visual program are administered as two discrete entities. Television and radio services may be combined with other audio-visual services or not. Language laboratories are sometimes administered as part of a centralized media program; frequently they are not. This is also true of programmed instruction. Experimental trial, analysis, and development of new or stronger instructional techniques and materials are often decentralized, sporadic, or frequently nonexistent. The idea of a centralized, systematic program of instructional research and/or instructional-systems design is new and still largely untried in most institutions.

The following case studies suggest in more detail the nature and implications of these varying patterns of administrative organization.

CASE STUDIES: THE MODERN AUDIO-VISUAL CENTER

It was noted earlier that educational media programs in institutions of higher education are known by various names and that they differ in the scope of their instructional services as well. In the following sections, case studies illustrate certain of these differences—from the contemporary audio-visual center through several variants of the combined instructional resources organization, including those handling both print and nonprint materials. The final group of case studies deals briefly with a research emphasis, which may be a promising pattern in the development of instructional services and resources in institutions of higher learning.

Indiana University

A classic example of the educational media program built along nonprint lines is the Audio-Visual Center at Indiana University. As in the case of some other large universities, the present organization evolved from an earlier extension activity that was concerned primarily with off-campus rentals of motion pictures and other visual materials. The Bureau of Visual Education, formed in 1914, became the Bureau of Audio-Visual Aids in 1941, and finally was named the Audio-Visual Center. Since 1946, this program has been administered jointly by the Division of Adult Education and Public Services and the School of Education.

The director of the Audio-Visual Center reports jointly to the administrative heads of the Division of Adult Education and the School of Education. Under his direction, the ten line departments discharge the functions of an integrated program that includes the following services:

❯ *Off-campus rental circulation* (throughout the United States) of a comprehensive film library

LINE–STAFF ORGANIZATION CHART
AUDIO–VISUAL CENTER, INDIANA UNIVERSITY

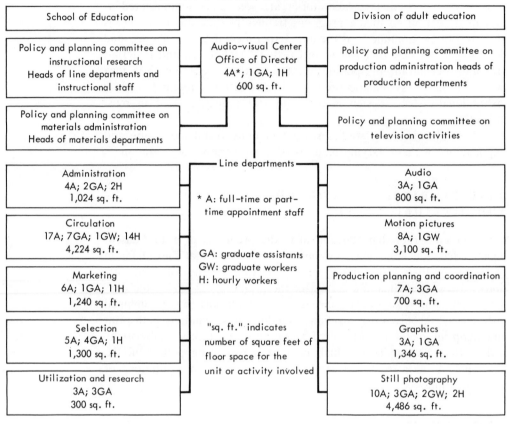

> *On-campus audio-visual services* to all university departments, including distribution of university-owned films and other audio-visual materials and equipment
> *Consultation and minor production services and facilities* for faculty members
> *Services to improve utilization and evaluation* of audio-visual materials by members of faculty and off-campus groups
> *Production activities,* including 16mm films, photographic and graphic materials, as well as tape and disk recordings; motion pictures made for national distribution and marketed by the Audio-Visual Center
> *Closed-circuit television* for on-campus classroom instruction
> *Professional education and research* that leads to the doctoral degree in audio-visual education

Similar audio-visual programs are found in some other colleges and universities, with some variations. Frequently, the director of the media program reports to the chief administrative officer in charge of instruction or academic affairs. Such an administrative arrangement is shown in the following account of the program at San Jose State College, where the head of audio-visual services reports to the dean of the college.

San Jose State College

Educational media services other than those related to printed materials are operated under the Division of Audio-Visual Services. The functions of this division may be described under four major categories: (1) utilization, (2) materials preparation or production, (3) technical, and (4) instructional television.

Utilization Services

❯ *Materials collection.* The center maintains a permanent collection of films, filmstrips, and tape recordings for instructional use. These are available for use by any instructor and may be borrowed or used with or without operator service.

❯ *Equipment.* The center maintains several models of each of the major types of audio-visual equipment for classroom instruction. This equipment may be borrowed for any instructional use on campus, by the instructor and with or without operator service.

❯ *Operator service.* The center provides student operators for audio-visual equipment for classroom instruction. Operators deliver equipment and materials to classrooms, operate equipment during the class period, and return equipment and materials to the center.

❯ *Rental services.* Motion pictures not included in the center collection may be obtained by rental or loan if desired for instructional uses. In such

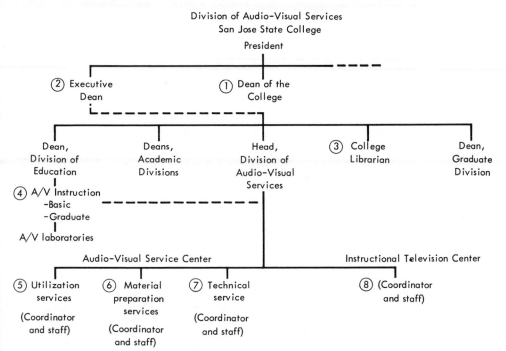

cases, the center pays rental charges and handles all details of correspondence and shipping.

❯ *Information and preview services.* The center maintains major resource and reference materials and provides preview facilities to assist instructors in locating, screening, and evaluating films and other prospective additions to the audio-visual library.

❯ *Purchase of materials.* Materials are purchased for the permanent college collection upon specific recommendations of faculty members, when the indicated frequency of use provides economic justification of purchase as opposed to rental.

Materials Preparation Services

❯ *Consultation.* Staff members aid faculty members in analyzing instructional problems and planning with them for the development and local production of appropriate materials.

❯ *Production.* Photographs, slides, large transparencies, charts, mounted materials, reproductions, tape recordings, motion-picture footage, and other materials are prepared for instructional use. Production costs are borne by the center; materials produced are in the custody of the department using them. This service emphasizes production of materials that are unavailable from commercial sources but needed for specific instructional purposes.

Technical Services

❯ *Maintenance and servicing for on-campus audio-visual equipment on the campus.* In addition to such services, the center assists faculty and staff in planning for and obtaining necessary physical facilities for effective use of audio-visual materials both in existing buildings and buildings in planning stages. Coordination of purchase and use of equipment is also a responsibility of the center.

Instructional Television Services

❯ *Televised observation.* Five nearby public schools—three elementary, one junior high, and one senior high school—are linked with the college by coaxial cable. College classroom activities can also be televised and broadcast to the public school on this same cable. Two-way audio-video communications are part of the system.

❯ *Direct teaching by television.* Lessons, demonstrations, and special presentations are originated from the studio for transmission to all wired points on campus, to the local public schools, or to a local television station.

❯ *Resource television.* A single television camera is scheduled for use as a class teaching tool. The use of resource television is especially effective as a "magnifier," for showing manipulative skills, for demonstrating microscope techniques or slides, and for meeting other instructional needs.

❯ *Broadcast television.* Weekly television lessons are originated in the studio for broadcast over a local TV station as in-service training for teachers and administrators in the college service area.

❯ *Programs from commercial and educational stations.* The college closed-circuit television system receives programs from several local television stations. The center receives and distributes advance schedules and other in-formation.

❯ *Staff services.* The center staff assists instructors and departmental groups in presenting televised instruction or in receiving and using televised programs. Study guides, lesson plans, seating charts, and other materials used with telelessons are duplicated for instructors. A full-time graphic artist assists instructors in preparing program televisuals. Monthly schedules, bulletins, orientation guides, and similar materials are also prepared and distributed to the faculty. A resource library (nearly 3,000 items) relating to instructional television is maintained at the center, as well as a photo file containing slides and pictures for instructional purposes.

❯ *Technical facilities.* Television receivers are available in nearly half of the more than 120 campus classrooms. The center operates three remotely controlled television cameras from a mobile trailer unit, as well as a three-camera studio containing a video-tape recorder and complete facilities for televised instruction.

❯ *Faculty orientation.* All faculty members are invited to visit the center to become acquainted with the facilities, to practice with cameras, to test television teaching techniques, and to gain familiarity with the utilization of television in college teaching.

CASE STUDIES: PROGRAMS COMBINING PRINT AND NONPRINT MATERIALS

Most colleges and universities continue to follow the traditional practice of separating audio-visual services from the library that contains printed materials. Many educators have questioned this separation on theoretical grounds: Why should not the various media, materials, and services connected with their use be combined administratively for the greater convenience of instructors and students—also, perhaps, to ensure their appropriate use as reciprocal or complementary elements of the instructional process? As technological factors assume new importance in implementing communication processes generally, it would seem logical that coordination might be a means of reducing operating costs while improving the quality of the service. In view of such considerations, some institutions of higher education have set up integrated media or learning resources centers that combine print and nonprint materials, as illustrated by the following examples.

Stephens College

The Stephens College Learning Center was established in 1963 to bring together the many modern technological aids to learning with the more traditional library materials, making them readily available in combined facilities for faculty and student use. The purposes of this center are (1) to provide a wealth of modern educational materials resources and aids for study of the arts and sciences, (2) to create a favorable learning environment, (3) to develop student capacity for self-education, (4) to enable instructors to utilize their time and ability with greater effectiveness, and (5) to provide instructional space and facilities designed for versatility and maximum utilization.

The center includes five separate facilities that are planned and equipped to form a central system of communication, providing unity in the use of all educational media. One building houses a general library of books and other printed materials, various departmental collections, and a loan collection of original pictures and reproductions, films, slides, filmstrips, records, and tapes. Another contains television and radio studios, a film-production department, and instructional facilities for the science department. Still others contain the humanities and English departments, the Fine Arts Center, learning laboratories, and other office and classroom areas for the religious, philosophy, and language departments.

Instructional and learning spaces have been designed for flexibility to accommodate individuals and groups in spaces of varying sizes and shapes. The center and other campus facilities also provide for large-group presentations for as many as 2,900 students. The library contains complete listening and viewing facilities, reading areas, and autoinstructional laboratories for language, drama, and music training. The electronic heart of the center is the television, radio, and audio-visual center, which is equipped for transmitting closed-circuit television and radio programs, broadcasting tapes and films, and originating live programs for use in classrooms in the center or across the campus. The center itself is a major instructional facility, operating through a divisional and departmental structure under a dean of instruction and a director of educational development.[11]

Central Washington State College [12]

A library building constructed in 1961 at Central Washington State College, Ellensburg, contains the following facilities: (1) a closed-circuit television unit servicing various academic buildings and connecting them with nearby public school buildings; (2) extensive audiovisual materials and services, (3) a curriculum laboratory, (4) an instructional-materials production laboratory, (5) student "do-it-yourself" production facilities, (6) audition and preview rooms, (7) a tape learning (language) laboratory, (8) a music collection and listening area, (9) an art collection and display area, (10) programed learning materials and equipment, (11) museum collection and display cases, (12) a map collection, (13) a library science teaching laboratory, (14) a room for special displays and demonstrations, (15) seminar-conference rooms, (16) a classroom, and (17) the conventional library for the college. Also in the Campus demonstration school is an elementary school library collection. All services thus afforded are administered by a single officer having the title of Director of Libraries;

---

[11] Adapted from Brown and Thornton, *op. cit.,* pp. 142–144.

[12] This description of the Central Washington State College program was provided by J. Wesley Crum, dean of instruction of that institution.

CENTRAL WASHINGTON STATE COLLEGE

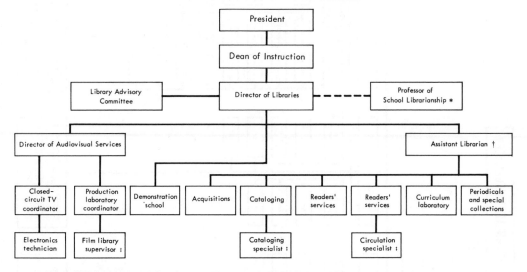

* Library Science and audiovisual classes are taught in the Department of Education

† The Assistant Librarian position has not been filled. The Director of Libraries performs this function at present.

‡ Subprofessional Civil Service personnel.

he is assisted by a staff of ten professional, four sub-professional civil service, nine clerical, and numerous part-time student employees.

This total facility, known as the Victor J. Bouillon Library, was designed so that students and faculty would have ready access, in one place, to the books, periodicals, films, phonodiscs, art prints and slides, tapes, and other materials and services required for modern study, teaching, and research. All materials and services are available for individual or group use throughout the hours the library is open. The total facility is operated in such a way that students and faculty members are encouraged to use freely a wide variety of learning materials in any individual study or research project. Although not yet fully implemented, plans call for listing all materials in the main card catalog file so that individuals may readily locate all kinds of materials relevant to a given topic.

The library operates on an open stack basis, with reader tables, open and closed carrels, typing rooms, microfilm reading areas, and small conference rooms interspersed or adjacent to the stacks. Users are permitted and encouraged to bring together various types of materials to facilitate their topical studies.

Florida Atlantic University

A third interesting plan involving integration of print and nonprint media forms is represented by that of the Division of Learning Resources at Florida Atlantic University, established at Boca Raton in

313

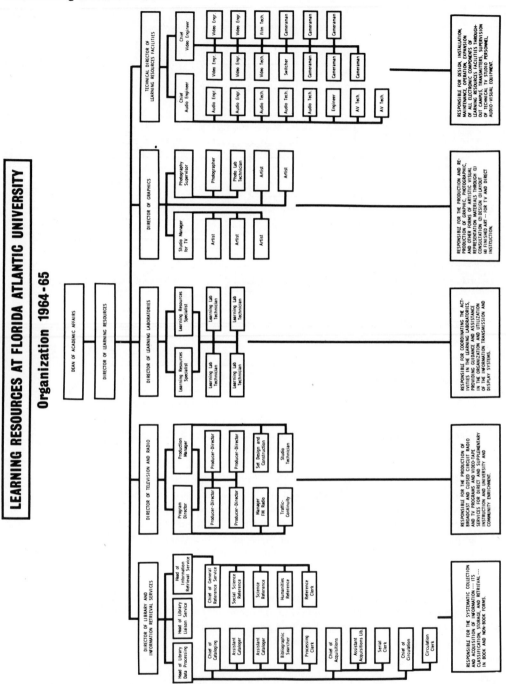

LEARNING RESOURCES AT FLORIDA ATLANTIC UNIVERSITY

Organization 1964-65

1962. This organization is administered by a director of learning resources, who reports directly to the dean of academic affairs. Under his direction are five departments: (1) library, (2) television and radio, (3) learning laboratories, (4) graphics, and (5) technical facilities. This institution's somewhat novel program has been described

314

as "concerned essentially with nonhuman tools and [embracing] virtually all media, technology, and services that contribute to the communication of ideas in the university life of the learner and instructor."

Two functions are involved: [13]

To put at the disposal of the teaching faculty all media, technology, services and systems which will enhance the effective communication of ideas in the pre-programed phase of learning

To put at the disposal of the student all media, technology, services and systems which will enhance the effective communication of ideas in a self-programed phase of learning.

The three major units of this facility will be the Library and Information Storage and Retrieval Center, the Television and Radio Production Center, and the Learning Laboratories Center. The library will stress a utilization approach to the storage and circulation of learning materials and use data-processing equipment as part of its modern system of information storage and retrieval.

[13] Len Singer, "Florida Atlantic University: Where Tomorrow Begins," *Audiovisual Instruction,* vol. 8, pp. 236–242, April, 1963.

These four buildings, comprising the facilities of the Learning Resources Center of Florida Atlantic University, are (1) Learning Laboratory Center, containing facilities for large-group instruction, small-group discussion, and independent study, (2) Television and Radio Production and Distribution Center, containing television studios, dressing rooms, conference rooms, offices, and a viewing gallery, (3) Library and Information Retrieval Center, and (4) Science Building, containing laboratories for physics, chemistry, biology, and mathematics. (*Florida Atlantic University*)

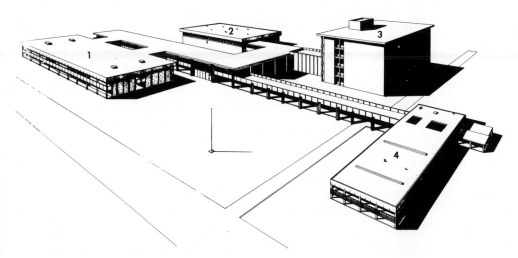

CASE STUDIES: THE RESEARCH APPROACH

Probably one of the most notable recent developments in higher education is a growing emphasis upon research that relates to innovations in instructional practices. Many colleges and universities are investigating their teaching methods, seeking to find better and more efficient ways to accomplish their objectives. Prompted in part by the challenge of the new media and the changing technology of instruction, recent experimentation has been further stimulated by appropriations resulting from the National Defense Education Act (NDEA) and support from private foundations such as the Ford Foundation, which continues to take a strong interest in educational television, programmed instruction, and other new approaches to instruction. While many such efforts based on these external sources of financial support are sporadic and temporary, some show promise of having lasting effects. In a few institutions, permanent administrative arrangements are being established to continue instructional research. The following example is indicative of this gradual, but perhaps growing, trend.

The Pennsylvania State University [14]

The Division of Instructional Services of the Pennsylvania State University contributes to that institution's instructional program in the following areas: (1) instructional research and course development, (2) examination services, (3) instructional television, (4) instructional graphics, (5) motion-picture production, and (6) still-photography services. Established in 1958 and formerly known as the Division of Academic Research and Services, the present organization grew out of a complex of research activities that originated with the widely known Instructional Film Research Program sponsored from 1947 to 1958 by the Office of Naval Research through the Special Devices Center. In the intervening period, this earlier research emphasis upon film as a training medium was transformed into an institutional research effort integrally related to the on-going instructional program of the university. At the outset, it was focused, upon the experimental development of closed-circuit television.

According to C. R. Carpenter, who was director the division until November, 1963, the program was based upon the assumptions that:

❯ Research conducted in the realistic context of academic learning, although difficult to accomplish, can be done, and when results of importance are found, the probability of their application and use is increased over the results of research conducted in a different context.

❯ Contextual research, which requires the cooperation and involvement of

[14] Information concerning this program was supplied by C. R. Carpenter, formerly head of the division, and by L. P. Greenhill, its present director.

faculty members and administrators, emphasizes the needs and possibilities for improving instruction and the conditions required to produce better learning.

❯ The facilities and personnel needed for the creation, production, and use of instructional resources and services for research are those also required for the improvement of regular on-going academic programs.

The division is supported financially by institutional funds that cover the costs of all services to instructional programs, including limited amounts for research. Some research projects are supported by Federal grants and some by funds received from foundations and industrial sources.

Organized on an all-university basis, the division works cooperatively with academic departments and directly with faculty members in areas of instructional services and research. It also assists faculty members in designing experiments, in preparing proposals for grants, and in conducting and evaluating research projects that are designed to improve teaching and learning. The director reports to the vice-president for resident instruction. L. P. Greenhill, present director of the division, recently summarized current research activities as follows:

❯ *Course development.* It has been found impractical to make substantial changes and improvements in courses or blocks of instruction while they are being taught daily in classrooms. The concept has been developed and is now being put into effect whereby courses are moved into a "laboratory" situation to be worked on by a team of individuals of varying competencies. This procedure involves the restatement of course objectives in detail in terms of behavior desired of students as a result of studying in the course. Next comes the development of examinations to be used to determine the extent to which students achieve these objectives. The course content is then selected and organized, and appropriate and varied methods of presenting it and of obtaining student interaction are chosen. The course is tested out with groups of students and, on the basis of an analysis of their test performances, revised and made ready for regular use in the classroom. Several such course development projects are now in various stages of activation.

❯ *Faculty development.* Another program now being initiated is aimed at developing certain instructional skills on the part of faculty members and selected graduate students. This program will include discussion and examination of various instructional methods and media and new developments in laboratory instruction, the construction and analysis of tests, grading procedures, the advising and counseling of students, and the recording on videotape and critiquing of faculty members' and graduate assistants' classroom presentations.

❯ *Examination development.* Much emphasis is also being placed on the improvement of examinations for the advanced placement of students and for the evaluation of their performances in courses. To the extent possible, and desirable, examinations are being developed that will test a variety of learning outcomes and which can also be scored on new high-speed test-scoring machines. With the aid of computer programs, print-outs of examination results and analyses of test items can be made available to faculty members within 24 hours.

❯ *Development of instructional facilities.* A major activity is the planning and construction of a building containing four teaching auditoria each seating 395 students. Special provision has been made for a wide variety of display systems including several kinds of projectors for each auditorium. These are located in a central projection core of the building from which images are shown on rear-projection screens in the classrooms. The equipment can be remotely controlled by the instructor. Instrumentation for obtaining and recording student responses to problems and test questions is also being planned. Continuing work on the design of appropriate facilities for learning is anticipated.

In all of the above activities an effort is made to base new developments upon research findings and to test these developments empirically in the context of regular classroom instruction.

Rensselaer Polytechnic Institute [15]

For more than eight years, Rensselaer has developed applications of new educational media as part of its institutional research program. Broadly defined, institutional research is the study of problems connected with the academic programs of a college or university. Application of new media, with a research emphasis, becomes involved in the study of many of these problems, as well as in the implementation of solutions. For example, studies of faculty effectiveness in handling student load may include the utilization of television, locally produced films and other media, and the design of experimental facilities. Likewise, curricular and course development and revision, taking cognizance of research findings concerning the resources of new media, may give consideration to similar applications. The many experimental possibilities inherent in the institutional research approach requires the involvement of many faculty members, preferably through their own organizational units, while coordination and service are provided, as needed, by the Office of Institutional Research.

During its first five years, Rensselaer's institutional research program was known as "Project Reward," whose dual objective was to assist faculty in improving their instructional methods, and, at the same time, to keep the unit costs of instruction reasonably constant. This overall objective of greater instructional productivity still prevails, supplemented by increased effort—by faculty, administration, and institutional research staff—to improve the total educational experience of each student. The steps in the implementation of this program, by activity, have been (1) continuous statistical analysis of instructional programs for administrative purposes, (2) production of multimedia materials for faculty, including instructional films, (3) provision of technical assistance, as needed, for educational research projects and teaching, and (4) interinstitutional research participation, especially by institutional research staff.

In 1961, "Project Reward" was redesignated as the Office of Insti-

[15] This description was prepared by Philip H. Tyrrell, director, Office of Institutional Research, Rensselaer Polytechnic Institute.

tutional Research. It is academically oriented, and reports to the Vice President and Provost. This educational and organizational orientation, as well as the research emphasis of its program, is compatible with the larger orientation of Rensselaer, namely, that instruction and research are complementary.

The impact of institutional research as an "idea" to which many faculty and staff actively subscribe is not always susceptible to precise measurement, because both the units and methodology of measuring interacting activities are less than adequate. In matters of educational innovation, the judgment of informed men must often substitute for such time-consuming, sophisticated measurement methodologies as now exist. In programs like the one being described, it appears that both experimentally designed research projects and informal studies are necessary to substantial accomplishment. The former, of course, should be evaluated by appropriate analytical techniques; the latter appear to contribute to institutional progress in proportion to the wisdom of those who carry the burden of making operational decisions. Both approaches toward finding ways to attain selected institutional objectives may be justly called "applied research," and it is interesting to note that what may be experimental one year often becomes standard operating procedure the next.

Although precise measurement of total impact is impossible, helpful indicators do exist. Some of the indicators used each year at Rensselaer are teaching materials production data; television utilization data; faculty effectiveness in handling the student load, as measured in terms of student credit hours or student contact hours per instructor contact hour; unit costs of instruction, per student credit hour, student contact hour, and instructor contact hour; number and type of projects initiated; and number of projects in progress, with some indication of potential value. The last two categories may be experimentally designed educational research projects or more informal studies. Thus, the programmatic approach to institutional research may well have built into it a variety of checks and balances. To date, the previously mentioned indicators show trends that indicate steady progress in the attainment of program objectives.

In addition to the long-term objectives stated earlier, the future of Rensselaer's program is also based upon short-term objectives which are no doubt shared by other institutions. They are (1) greater involvement of faculty in educational research projects, including applications of new media to instruction, (2) increased participation in cooperative projects with other institutions, (3) development of more precise units and methodologies of measurement for programmatic approaches to the solution of instructional problems, and (4) the maintenance and nurture of innovative thinking on the part of both faculty and institutional research staff.

A LOOK TO THE FUTURE

In his 1961 annual report to his board of trustees, John A. Hannah, president of Michigan State University, included the following significant paragraph: [16]

[16] John A. Hannah, *Annual Report to the Trustees,* Michigan State University.

It is proposed to put to use discoveries already made concerning the learning process itself, and to stimulate further research through the establishment of a Learning Resources Center to include and encourage the use of closed-circuit television, film, teaching machines, programed studies, and other aids.

This explicit reference to such matters of instructional technology was unusual in the annual report of the president of a major university, even in 1961. Subsequent events make it seem less unusual now. So swift and so compelling is the march of events that it is becoming respectable and even commonplace to discuss the new media and modern technology as proper and important means to the achievement of the objectives of higher education. What, then, is the future shape of educational media programs in higher education? Alvin C. Eurich, speaking at the 1963 National Conference on Higher Education, suggested that some of the most profound changes would be in the use of learning resources. The following lines, which bear on educational media, are spoken as though it were now 2000 A.D.: [17]

> The most prominent difference between today's colleges and those fifty years ago, however, is not in the curriculum, but in the use of learning resources. We have introduced devices and techniques which were not even thought of prior to the mid-twentieth century. Curriculum has always been the subject of educational debate and reform. But the learning resources which our students now take for granted were developed for the first time in the 1950's and 60's. These enabled us to fulfill the psychologists' dreams of making the best teaching available to all students, and of truly adapting instruction to individual rates of learning.

Eurich goes on to discuss the specific results of wide-scale uses of television and programmed instruction. He emphasizes that "nowadays" (2000 A.D.) a professor rarely lectures to a group of thirty or forty students as he once did (half a century ago). Rather, he meets with students individually or in small groups after they have mastered a given block of knowledge through the use of diverse learning resources. He continues: [18]

> Our professors now do only what no text or other learning resource can ever accomplish: they develop the mind of the individual students through intimate give and take based on sound knowledge and understanding. Under this system the three-year colleges, far from becoming obsolete, have rediscovered their primary function in education. Instead of pretending to the microcosms of all human knowledge, the individual colleges now lean heavily on the use of learning resources to provide the base of their instructional programs. But this firm foundation enables them to build real understanding and creativity

[17] Eurich, *op. cit.*, pp. 39–46.
[18] *Ibid*, p. 44.

in their students through their achievements in the higher reaches of teaching. Never before have they had such an opportunity.

In his "journey into the future," Eurich also describes some of the revolutionary effects of miniaturization and electronic information-retrieval systems in library services and various other sweeping changes, including provisions for complete individualization of a student's rate of progress throughout the period of his college education. He concludes that "these reforms are merely the beginning. Changes will come more rapidly and more sweepingly—of necessity—in the early decades of the twenty-first century; changes so great, so fantastic, that the imagination can barely keep pace." [19]

His final note is provocative too: "Each of us can make his own projections—they will differ widely, of course—but the point is, we must make them. The old ideas will no longer do." [20]

SUMMARY

The increasing use of new media in higher education has occurred partly as a response to mounting pressures of expanded enrollments, a demand for a more highly educated population, and a growing scarcity of trained personnel to fill teaching positions in our colleges and universities. Many look to these new media to play increasingly important roles in alleviating such problems; but some college instructors continue to regard them with doubt, perhaps because they fear in this advance of technology a harmful impact upon the processes of instruction and their own roles as teachers.

The growth of modern services and facilities in higher education to administer programs of educational media, old and new, has produced a variety of organizational and administrative patterns—some showing the centralization and unification of all media resources into one administrative unit; most following the traditional separation of print from nonprint or audio-visual services; others using still different arrangements, sometimes in behalf of a single medium (as with television) or linking a particular instructional facility to a departmental activity (as with language laboratories). Case studies used here illustrated these various types of centralized administrative organization for educational media services, as well as the research-oriented approach such as that employed at Pennsylvania State University.

FOR MORE INFORMATION

Audio-Visual Centers in Colleges and Universities, Department of Audio-Visual Instruction, NEA, 1955.

[19] *Ibid.,* p. 46.
[20] *Ibid.,* p. 46.

Brown, James W., and James W. Thornton, Jr. (eds.): *New Media in Higher Education,* Association for Higher Education and the Department of Audio-Visual Instruction, NEA, 1963.

Brown, James W., and James W. Thornton, Jr.: *College Teaching: Perspectives and Guidelines,* McGraw-Hill, New York, 1963.

Erickson, Clifford G., and Hyman M. Chausow: *Chicago's TV College: Final Report of a Three Year Experiment,* Chicago City Junior College, Chicago, August, 1960. 98 pp.

Fulton, W. R., and O. J. Rupiper: *Selected Vicarious Experiences versus Direct Observational Experiences of Pre-service Teachers in the Foundation Areas of Professional Preparation at the University of Oklahoma,* College of Education in cooperation with the Research Institute, University of Oklahoma, Norman, Okla., 1961. 105 pp. (Prepared under U.S. Office of Education Title VII Project no. 192)

Lepore, Albert R., and others: *Project Number Two: An Experimental Study of College Instruction Using Broadcast Television,* San Francisco State College, San Francisco, Calif., Fall, 1958. 77 pp.

Lyle, Guy R.: *The Administration of the College Library,* H. W. Wilson, New York, 1961.

Meaney, John W.: *Televised College Courses,* Fund for the Advancement of Education, New York, 1962. 88 pp.

Morton, F. Rand: "The Language Laboratory as a Teaching Machine," *International Journal of American Linguistics,* vol. 26, pp. 113–116, part II, 1960.

Smith, Kerry G. (ed.): *Current Issues in Higher Education,* Association for Higher Education, NEA, 1963.

Smith, M. Daniel: *New Instruction Media: Self-instruction, Guided Instruction, and the Role of the Teacher,* Earlham College, Richmond, Ind., 1962. 70 pp.

chapter 15

Media services in state departments of education

The basic over-all responsibility for managing public education in most of the United States resides with state boards of education. While specific duties and responsibilities of these boards vary greatly from state to state, all give attention to developing educational policy and to generally overseeing its administration through appointed or elected state superintendents of public instruction and their professional staffs.

The typical state department of education staff is subdivided to provide several specialized offices and personnel to care for such matters as the development and supervision of curriculum and instruction, departmental administration, the administration of various specialized state-supported schools (such as those for the deaf and blind or for vocational rehabilitation), school plant planning, school district reorganization, educational research, the selection and distribution of state-adopted textbooks, and in some cases, the administration of state instructional-materials and library services, and others.

Growing demands for the equalization of educational opportunities have led to increased participation by state departments of education in providing state-wide educational media and media services of many different kinds. In Virginia, for example, a $1.25 million legislative appropriation immediately after World War II was used on a matching-funds basis to bring the advantages of audio-visual materials and equipment to all public schools in the state, many of which were then without either libraries or electricity.[1]

Connelly's study [2] of state laws relating to audio-visual media revealed that as of 1962, 12 states made no legal provision for the media (although they are used in the schools); 9 refer only to simple basic types (maps, teaching aids, charts, other instructional material, instructional apparatus); 4 refer to audio-visual materials, but make no reference to specific types; 2 provide for the simple basic types as well as audio-visual; 7 provide legislation *only* for educational television and

---

[1] James W. Brown, *The Viriginia Plan for Audio-Visual Education,* The University of Chicago Press, Chicago, 1947.

[2] John W. Connelly, Jr., *Report of State Laws on Audio-Visual Media of Instruction in Public Schools and on Establishment of Educational Television Stations,* U.S. Office of Education, 1962.

for no other forms of audio-visual media; and the remaining 16 have made broader legal provisions for them.

EDUCATIONAL MEDIA ACTIVITIES

The principal educational media activities of the fifty state departments of education in the United States may be classified generally as falling within one or more of eleven broad and somewhat overlapping categories, as follows:

Fact finding. Determining the current and predicted future status of educational media and media programs within schools and colleges of the state; reporting findings; making recommendations based on results.

Example. The Colorado State Department of Education, with the assistance of Dr. Robert DeKieffer (University of Colorado) conducts every third year a survey [3] of existing school audio-visual programs, with special reference to personnel, facilities, and utilization. Factors investigated include (1) the number of school systems having system-wide directors of audio-visual education, (2) the titles of these directors, (3) the mean percentage of time devoted to their duties, (4) the number of individual schools with audio-visual directors and the mean percentage of time devoted to the audio-visual program, (5) the incidence of various titles applied to audio-visual directors, (6) the mean percentage of time frequency of student assistants for the audio-visual program, (7) numbers and percentages of classrooms with outlets, darkening facilities, and bulletin boards, (8) purposes and kinds of use of audio-visual materials and equipment—by teachers, by grade levels, by subject areas, (9) incidence of in-service education programs for stimulating improved uses of audio-visual materials, and (10) location and size of school-owned collections of audio-visual materials and equipment.

Experimenting. Obtaining grant support for conducting research studies pertaining to uses of educational media; supervising the design and administration of such studies; interpreting and applying their results.

Example. The Washington State Department of Education's Technical Research Advisory Committee sponsored a study to determine the amount and nature of teacher help necessary for optimum achievement through uses of programmed learning devices. The four teaching conditions of the study were (1) the teacher merely monitored the programmed learning session, (2) the teacher gave no help but completed the program himself, (3) the teacher answered individual student's questions, and (4)

[3] *The Biennial Audio-Visual Report for Colorado Schools,* John H. Swenson, acting commissioner of education. Denver, Colo., Colorado State Department of Education, 1960. 15 pp.

the teacher supplemented the program by reviewing basic concepts. The research staff concluded that "programmed learning directed towards achievement of mathematical concepts is as effective as other forms of instruction conducted with the same time span, and, administratively, programed learning can be used to save substantial amounts of teacher time. Programed learning supplemented by systematic teacher instruction can result in a significantly superior level of achievement." [4]

Setting and enforcing standards. Obtaining cooperative assistance of appropriate groups of personnel in determining teacher certification and institutional accreditation standards as they pertain to educational media; materials and equipment selection, criteria and procedures; recommending minimum equipment and materials quotas; developing building, classroom, auditorium, or instructional-materials-center criteria based on currently valid engineering and construction principles; evaluating various aspects of existing programs—citing existing strengths and weaknesses and recommending needed improvements.

Example. The Office of the Illinois State Superintendent of Public Instruction appointed a special curriculum subcommittee [5] to develop and publish a comprehensive manual on instrucional-materials characteristics, procedures, and standards. This publication stressed particularly the point of view that "instructional materials should be regarded simply as a combination of audio-visual materials and printed matter to form a unified collection of teaching resources," and stated six principles to guide their proper utilization in teaching. Included in this publication were recommended minimum standards for school collections of books, newspapers, magazines, filmstrips, recordings, pamphlets, slides, professional materials, globes, and maps. Also included were descriptive standards for shelving, tables and chairs, audio-visual and other types of equipment, recommended minimum school expenditures for instructional materials and services, and standards for school classroom, auditorium, and instructional-materials-center facilities.

Planning. Working with curriculum personnel in the state department itself and in the state's schools and colleges; determining desirable ways in which curriculum practices can and should be improved through proper applications of the potential of educational media; predicting future requirements for educational media and media personnel; analyzing and producing specifications for physical facilities for the proper utilization of educational media.

[4] Larry Wriggle and Herbert Hite, *The Amount and Nature of Teacher Help Necessary for Optimum Achievement through Use of Programed Learning Devices,* Office of the State Superintendent of Public Instruction, Olympia, Wash., 1962. 32 pp.
[5] Verne Stockman (chairman), Illinois Curriculum Program, State Department of Public Instruction, *Instructional Materials,* Illinois Administration and Supervision Series, Bulletin A-3, Springfield, Ill., 1961. 146 pp.

Example. The Division of Educational Communications of the New York State Education Department recently produced (with NDEA Title III support) the booklet *Developing an Electronic Language Classroom* [6] "to provide administrators, business managers, language teachers, and audio-visual directors with information, standards, and equipment specifications to facilitate the planning or implementation of audio-lingual programs designed to strengthen modern foreign language instruction." Standards and specifications for equipment appearance, installation, operation, and performance were included, as well as suggested bid forms and ordering procedures.

Budgeting. Determining total budgetary needs to support proposed or established goals for educational media programs; presenting the case supporting the need to appropriate such funds; allocating and supervising (through appropriate departmental accounting offices) their proper expenditure.

Example. Two reports of the Division of Instructional Materials of the Hawaii State Department of Education illustrate the budgeting function with respect to educational media programs. In *An Hawaii Public School Audio-Visual Program"* [7] a budgetary analysis is made to answer four questions: (1) What is now available? (2) What is wanted (goals)? (3) What is needed in addition to what is now available to reach intended goals? (4) What will these additional resources and services cost? By careful and methodical progression, the analysis proceeds first to point up the present value of audio-visual equipment in a "typical" Hawaiian school, of servicing and maintaining that equipment each year, of replacing it each ten years, and of bringing equipment offerings up to minimum levels within five years. The report then gives attention to similar aspects of educational media, suggesting the dollar value of present numbers now on hand in the typical school, to budgeting for its replacement each five years, to expanding the collection into new areas and to bring present offerings up to minimum standards. Finally, there is attention to the costs of increasing in this same hypothetical school the number of rooms in which facilities for light control (darkening) are satisfactory.

In its second leaflet, *Primary Long Range Audio-Visual Objectives Having Budget Implications,* [8] the Hawaii Department of Education, Division of Instructional Materials, analyzes the budgetary costs of increasing to satisfactory size and depth the number of 16mm sound films in its central and regional collections, of adding filmstrips to individual school collections, of buying the proper numbers of projectors, recorders, screens, and the like, and of darkening a sufficient number of classrooms. To solve these three top-priority objectives alone would have required, in 1963,

[6] Thomas D. Paolucci, *Developing an Electronic Language Classroom,* New York State Education Department, Albany, N.Y., n.d. 38 pp.

[7] Division of Instructional Materials, *An Hawaii Public School Audio-Visual Program,* Hawaii State Department of Education, Honolulu, Hawaii, 1963. 7 pp.

[8] Division of Instructional Materials, *Primary and Long Range Audio-Visual Objectives Having Budget Implications,* Hawaii State Department of Education, Honolulu, Hawaii, 1963. 5 pp.

$1,260,000 for films and filmstrips, $250,000 for equipment, and $600,000 for classroom light control—$2,110,000 in all.

Developing liaison relationships. Working closely with various state organizations and institutions also concerned with improved uses of educational media (state audio-visual and library professional associations), educational materials and equipment dealers and dealer associations, county, district, and college educational media program directors and supervisors, college and university instructors of teacher-education courses (especially those teaching audio-visual, librarianship, television, and educational communications classes).

Example. The Bureau of Audio-Visual and Library Education of the California State Department of Education works closely with the Audio-Visual Education Association of California (an NEA Department of Audio-Visual Instruction affiliate), the California School Library Association, the National Audio-Visual Association (independent dealers), state colleges and universities (through their directors of audio-visual services and the instructors of special classes in audio-visual and library education), and various educational and commercial television and radio groups in the state whose interests lie in educational applications of these media. The NDEA-financed publication *Improving Instruction through Audio-Visual Media*[9] recently characterized this cooperative approach to develop bases for agreement on new media utilization principles and policies among groups representing the state department of education, public schools, and private and public colleges and universities.

Selecting. Organizing programs to facilitate the actual selection and purchase of educational media, equipment, services (as in the case of contracted repair or maintenance services for educational media equipment), and supplies.

Example. NDEA, Title III, caused considerable attention to be given to developing approved specifications to guide in selecting materials, equipment, and services to strengthen instruction in science, mathematics, and modern foreign languages in each state. The Oregon State Department of Education's publication, typical of those which were to aid in this, was *A Guide for Oregon Projects under Title III, NDEA*.[10] Included were specifications and recommendations (developed by the department's staff members—especially those related to educational media—and representative public school administrators, teachers, and supervisors), as follows: general provisions of the Title III program; general procedures for applying for, expending, and accounting for funds; criteria by which to judge equipment and materials; and suggested minimum lists of equipment and materials

[9] William H. Allen, and Harry J. Skelly, *Improving Instruction through Audio-Visual Media: Techniques in Teaching Science, Mathematics and Modern Foreign Languages,* California State Department of Education, Sacramento, Calif., 1963. 69 pp.
[10] *A Guide for Oregon Projects under Title III, NDEA.* Oregon State Department of Education, Salem, Ore., 1960, Instructional Services Section. 31 pp.

for elementary and secondary science, mathematics, and modern foreign languages. For the foreign-language program, level 1 (listening only), level 2 (listening and responding), level 3 (listening, responding, and recording), electronic installation standards were prescribed. Criteria were given for projection and sound equipment in general, for opaque and overhead transparency projectors, for filmstrip and slide projectors, for 16mm motion-picture projectors, for record players and tape recorders, as well as for various types of printed instructional materials. Finally, minor remodeling standards were included to guide improvements in providing electrical, gas, or water facilities, room darkening, ventilation, or acoustical changes.

Procuring.   Actually placing orders for educational media, equipment, or services in accordance with state specifications and requirements; verifying their receipt in good condition; authorizing payments.

Example.   The Georgia State Department of Education's textbook distribution program provides an example of centralized purchasing based on specified standards. Each year, a specified amount of money is appropriated by the state budget commission and reallocated to local districts on the basis of the total number of pupils enrolled. The Division of Instructional Materials and Services of the Georgia State Department of Education is responsible for coordinating textbook selection through officially appointed committees, negotiating bids, receiving and placing orders for items on the official list, and for monitoring the actual payment of charges as invoiced.[11]

Distributing.   Distributing (on temporary- or permanent-custody bases) textbooks, supplementary enrichment books, films, filmstrips, tape and disk recordings, artifacts, official publications, and similar items; loaning equipment to department personnel.

Example.   Distribution activities of state department of education educational media offices vary greatly. Some maintain centralized depositories for direct distribution to schools; most do not. The Division of Audio-Visual Education of the Ohio State Department of Education maintains one of the country's most complete film and slide distribution services, listing in its catalogs [12] several thousand available film titles. Films, ordered and delivered by mail, may be used without charge, except for a $10 annual insurance fee. Special funds to be used to add to film library collections are derived from fees charged for censorship approvals of theatrical films shown in Ohio.

Producing.   Producing educational media as instruments in aiding the achievement of goals of various state department or other gov-

---

[11] Hal Clements, "How Textbooks Are Adopted in Georgia," *Georgia Education Journal,* vol. 54, February, 1961.

[12] *Manual No. 16: Educational Films and Slides,* Division of Audio-Visual Education, Clyde K. Miller, Ohio State Department of Education, Columbus, Ohio, 1960. 213 pp. (Supplements)

ernment agency programs; selling, loaning, or broadcasting those media to schools within the state.

Example. The Film Production Section of the Division of Publications and Teaching Materials, Virginia State Department of Education, has since 1946 conducted a program for planning, producing, selling, and loaning instructional materials (particularly 16mm sound films and 35mm filmstrips) to the state's public schools and school divisions. Film productions emphasize topics somewhat unique to Virginia, which may not have been covered adequately through existing or contemplated offerings of commercial and educational film companies. Two recent productions include *Marine Invertebrates of the Chesapeake Bay* (8 minutes, 16mm sound, color), made in cooperation with the Virginia Institute of Marine Science; and *The Refuse Problem* (13 minutes, 16mm sound, color), filmed in conjunction with the Virginia Department of Health. A revolving fund, supplemented by direct legislative appropriations, underwrites the cost of productions.

Stimulating and informing. Providing information concerning educational media and media programs through various channels (for example, catalogs listing and describing loan films, approved textbooks and audio-visual media, television or radio programs, and the like); developing background materials as bases for news releases, leaflets, or brochures to inform school personnel and the general public; holding conferences, clinics, and special training sessions for purposes of studying and encouraging wider and better utilization of educational media, equipment, and services.

Example. *The Audiovisual Handbook for Teachers,* produced by the Audiovisual Office of the New Jersey Department of Education [13] in cooperation with representatives of the state's school and colleges, provides an example of a brochure intended to inform teachers about qualities, advantages, and requirements of use of various educational media. Succinct utilization suggestions are given for chalkboards; felt boards; bulletin boards; flat pictures; posters; cartoons and comics; charts or graphs and diagrams; maps and globes; exhibits and displays; dioramas, mockups, models, and specimens; flash cards; demonstrations; field trips; slides or transparencies; filmstrips; motion pictures; television; radio programs; and tape and disk recordings. A look to the future is also provided for programmed materials and machines; 8mm films; sound filmstrips; closed-circuit television; Polaroid color pictures; automated tape-slide programs; remedial reading devices; and language laboratories. The booklet includes suggested sources of information and assistance as well as recommended standards for choosing, using, evaluating, and administering these educational media. Several thousand copies of the illustrated brochure were distributed.

[13] *The Audiovisual Handbook for Teachers,* 2d ed., Audio-Visual Office, New Jersey State Department of Education, Trenton, N.J., 1963. 46 pp.

CASE EXAMPLES

California

The California State Department of Education provides an example of the administration of a decentralized state-level educational media program. Basic to a description of the program is a concept of size and numbers. Third largest of all the states (158,693 square miles), California contained in 1963 nearly 16 million people, of whom approximately 85 per cent resided in what may be classed as "urban" areas. The state now contains eighty-six cities whose separate populations exceed 25,000. Within the state during the same year were approximately 2.5 million elementary students, 1.2 million secondary students, and 125,000 teachers. The state's per pupil expenditure of approximately $500 for 1960–1961 ranked it fourth in the nation.

California school organization continues to develop under an administrative pattern that retains much authority in the state's *Education Code* and its *California Administrative Code, Title V. Education,* but at the same time, there is considerable delegation of authority to county and district boards of education for the development of local educational policies. A total of 53 of the state's 58 counties now maintain their own educational media programs involving audio-visual materials and services; 5 contract for these services with other county units. A total of 128 cities and districts within the state maintain regular audio-visual service centers employing professional educational media personnel.

The Bureau of Audio-Visual and School Library Education, which now functions as an administrative unit within the Supplementary Education Services Section of the Division of Instruction (see organization chart), was first organized in 1944 with the appointment of Dr. Francis W. Noel as chief. The bureau itself parallels administratively several other bureaus of the Division of Instruction (elementary education, secondary education, adult education, health and physical education, and others).

Principal responsibilities of the bureau staff, as outlined recently by Dr. Harry Skelly, present chief, include:

> Seeking to improve teacher competency in the selection, use, and evaluation of instructional materials through a variety of means
> Developing immediate and long-range plans with regard to state-level financial requirements to implement objectives of the total instructional materials program of public schools and colleges within the state
> Consulting with intermediate county school units and other city, junior college, college, university, and nonschool groups within the state with regard to plans for improving and extending the utilization of educational media
> Stimulating research and experimentation and disseminating information with regard to such media
> Cooperating with various other state and local groups that also seek to

STATE OF CALIFORNIA DEPARTMENT OF EDUCATION

State Board of Education

Superintendent of Public Instruction and Director of Department of Education

Deputy Supt. of Public Instruction
Chief of Departmental Administration

Assoc. Supt. of Public Instruction
Chief, Div. of Higher Education

Assoc. Supt. of Public Instruction
Chief, Div. of Public School Administration

Assoc. Supt. of Public Instruction
Chief, Div. of Instruction

Deputy Supt. of Public Instruction
Chief, Division of Special Schools and Services

State Librarian

Consultant, Curriculum Div.

Chief, Bureau of Elementary Education

Chief, Bureau of Secondary Education

Chief, Supplemental Education Section

Chief, Bureau of Audio-Visual and School Library Education

Consultants
Audio-Visual Education

Consultant
School Library Education

Photographer

Graphic artist

Chief, Bureau of Pupil Personnel Services

Consultants

Chief, Bureau of Health Ed., Physical Ed., and Recreation

Consultant
School Health Ed.

Consultant
Physical Education

Consultant
School Recreation

Chief, Bureau of National Defense Education Act Administration

---

Chief, Vocational Educational Section

Chief, Bureau of Agricultural Education

Chief, Bureau of Business Education

Chief, Bureau of Homemaking Education

Chief, Bureau of Industrial Education

improve the utilization of educational media, including radio and television interests, commercial producers, distributors, and manufacturers of educational media and equipment, and others

During the 1964–1965 school year, the bureau's budget included approximately $107,000 for salaries, $18,000 for in-state and out-of-state travel, $4,000 for printing and publications, $12,000 for educational materials and related expenses—as parts of a total separate bureau budget of $142,000. During 1963–1964, total expenditures for audio-visual or new media materials, equipment, and services in the state were estimated at approximately $11 million. Of this total, approximately $2 million were provided by the State Department of Education to county units from the County Service Fund; this was matched by another $2 million by the recipients. During this same period, the 128 cities and districts (Los Angeles, San Francisco, San Diego, Alameda, and Sacramento, for example) also spent another $4 million of their own funds. In addition, an estimated $1.5 million NDEA, Title III, funds, matched with a similar amount from school units all over the state, was used in purchasing approved audio-visual materials and equipment, in constructing approved language and science laboratories, and in other similar ways—to bring the total expenditures from this source to $3 million.

Participating largely on a request basis, the bureau's five professional staff members work directly with representatives of county school units and with as many as 200 other educational media service centers in school systems and colleges and universities throughout the state during any one year. During a typical year, these staff members participate in nearly 200 meetings in which educational media and their utilization are discussed or demonstrated.

Within the bureau is a small but carefully selected collection of audio-visual equipment that is intended largely for the use of departmental staff members in performing their regular office or field duties. The bureau also maintains a collection of audio-visual materials (more than 700 films, 250 filmstrips, many slide units, for example) for similar purposes. Its graphics unit (photographic and art) provides some locally made visual materials for departmental use, but no large-scale production plans are under way.

The bureau's interest in educational television extends well into the past. As early as 1952, following a preliminary planning meeting called by the state superintendent, the Governor's Conference on Educational Television was called for nearly 2,000 participants, who represented various geographical, occupational, and institutional interests of the state. An outgrowth of this conference was the appointment of the Governor's Citizens Advisory Committee on Educational Television, which later recommended and was instrumental in obtaining legislative approval for the use of state funds for educational television. In 1961, the California State Department of Education successfully sponsored another bill to authorize counties and school districts to operate their own educational television stations.

The California Legislature recently approved a pilot program in San Bernardino County to explore the effects of uses of state matching funds to encourage participation by local school districts in educational television activities. The staff of the Bureau of Audio-Visual and Library Education is directly involved in developing and evaluating plans for administering this program. It is hoped that its results will provide needed guidance for the future development of more comprehensive financing programs at the state level.

Additional educational media responsibilities are carried out through other offices of the State Department of Education. The Bureau of Textbooks and Publications, for example, supervises the work of selecting, seeking bids for, and distributing officially adopted textbooks within the state. The California State Library, under the supervision of the state librarian, also functions under the state superintendent of public instruction. Services of its main library in Sacramento are supplemented through branches in other parts of the state. The Department of Education also maintains a curriculum library, under the chief of the Division of Instruction. This unit serves as a source of various kinds of curriculum reports, courses of study, and similar materials applicable to the work of the department's professional staff. In addition, a special administrative staff for the NDEA cooperates with personnel of the department and school units throughout the state in administering the selection and purchase of materials, equipment, and services for approved projects under the provisions of this program.

Hawaii

Newest of the fifty states, Hawaii is an interesting case of centralization in the organization and administration of educational media programs. This state maintains a single school system; it is administered by a state superintendent of public instruction and his staff, with the aid of seven district superintendents on the islands of Kauai, Oahu, Maui, and Hawaii. School finances come largely from state appropriations, although the counties provide the school buildings. Enrolled in the public schools of Hawaii are more than 90,000 elementary students and 60,000 secondary students, who are taught by some 5,000 teachers.

Educational media responsibilities in the Hawaii State Department of Education are assigned to its Division of Instructional Materials. Its first director, William Henry Durr, assumed his position in 1961. Development of the state's educational media program was stimulated by results of a 1960 [14] survey that had been requested by the State Department of Education and the University of Hawaii and completed under terms of a special NDEA grant. A later five-year plan that was based

[14] *Audio-Visual Education in Hawaii: Its Status and Needs,* U.S. Office of Education, 1960. 60 pp.

HAWAII STATE DEPARTMENT OF EDUCATION

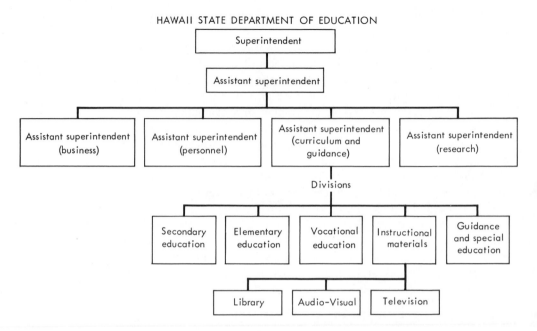

on this survey had to do largely with goals to be sought for educational media, equipment, services, and facilities.

The Division of Instructional Materials is administratively responsible to the assistant superintendent for curriculum, instruction, and guidance. In 1961, its staff included six professional, six technical, and three secretarial-clerical assignments. Professional-level positions included the director, a program assistant, and an audio-visual graphic artist, each of whom works on a state-wide basis. Central processing of library materials is performed cooperatively with the public libraries (which are also administered by the Department of Education).

The primary responsibilities of the director of the Division of Instructional Materials and his staff are to:

❯ Develop state-wide policies and practices for instructional-materials services (including educational television) and supervise their implementation at the district levels

❯ Effect liaison in educational media matters with other educational and public officials

❯ Encourage and aid, through district staff personnel, the in-service education of teachers with respect to the utilization of educational media and equipment

❯ Supervise the operation of certain educational media distribution and production services as a function of the central office

❯ Direct research and the preparation and distribution of various publications related to educational media

❯ Assist staff members of the State Department of Education in obtaining and using appropriate educational media in the conduct of their official responsibilities

A recent budget (1961) for the Division of Instructional Materials included approximately $57,000 for salaries, $2,000 for travel, $5,000 for publications, $110,000 for materials to be circulated to schools from the various state and regional centers, $75,000 for materials to be purchased by and left in individual schools, $7,500 for other expenses— for a total outlay of approximately $250,000. In the 1964 budget, a total of $285,000 was appropriated for the purchase of materials for circulation to schools from state and district collections, as well as materials and equipment to be left permanently in the collections of individual schools.

In Hawaii, in the period from 1962 to 1964, a total of $100,000 was spent in purchasing 16mm films for the main audio-visual distribution center in the State Department of Education and for films to be distributed from three district centers. Films for the regional centers were allocated according to a formula based on numbers of schools to be served.

A library of 6,000 prints of educational motion pictures is maintained in the Division of Instructional Materials office and in regional offices. Their circulation (free or rental) is restricted to Hawaii public schools, including technical and community evening schools, classes conducted under the direction of State Department of Education personnel in hospitals or other locations, and the University of Hawaii (including its elementary and high school). Films are normally loaned on a one-week basis.

The Governor of Hawaii has appointed an educational television advisory committee, which is undertaking the problem of drafting and seeking passage of enabling legislation that will permit installation and operation of educational television stations with matching Federal funds. Some experimental use of television, particularly that regarding foreign-language instruction, has been made.

New York's educational media program

New York's State Department of Education educational media program, like the departmental organization itself, is large and complex. Its Division of Educational Communications, headed by Lee A. Campion, is directly responsible to an associate commissioner of education for cultural education and special services. It serves schools in which were enrolled (in 1964) approximately four million elementary and secondary pupils. Fourteen professional persons, including the division head, plus nineteen specialist, technical, and clerical personnel, comprised the 1964 staff. The principal elements of the division's present organization include: (1) the director's office, (2) dissemination and evaluation section—involving Project CUE (Culture, Understanding, Enrichment), staff members involved with the Project Manpower Development and Training Act, and Project AIM (Appraising Instructional Materials), (3) the Bureau of Mass Communications—involving an educational broadcasting section and a technical support section (educational media-materials distribution), and (4) the Bureau of Classroom Communications—involving a communications media-materials section (teaching machines and programmed instruction, electronic classroom and school building design, educational films, curriculum liaison) and the Graphic Communications Center (involving graphic designers and illustrators).

Director, Division of Educational Communications. Over-all responsibilities of the director of the Division of Educational Communications are to:

❯ Plan, organize, and direct the work of the division
❯ Plan and coordinate the effective programs for the development of educational communications activities
❯ Assist in the development of broad plans for educational communications based on need and financial and engineering practicality
❯ Serve as consultant on technical communciations problems to staff members of the Department of Education, schools, colleges, and other participating groups
❯ Initiate plans for research in educational communications and recommend procedures for carrying out research projects
❯ Promote understanding and use of facilities for educational communications
❯ Conduct negotiations with officials of other levels of government concerned with development, financing, and regulation of educational television and radio
❯ Recommend policies and legislation necessary to achieve objectives in educational communications

DIVISION OF EDUCATIONAL COMMUNICATIONS,
NEW YORK STATE DEPARTMENT OF EDUCATION

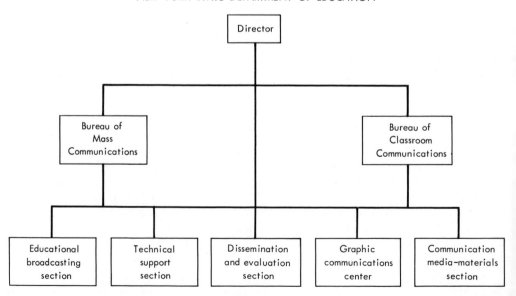

In carrying out these responsibilities, special assignments are given to various subsections of the division.

Bureau of Mass Communications. The bureau is chiefly responsible for the New York State educational television plan. An important activity of this bureau is its ETV council program. An ETV council is described as an organization serving an entire community, including schools, with enriching and educational and cultural television programs. The council puts a television station on the air, offering the best available in programs to a wide geographic area. In the first phase (now completed) of a projected four-phase construction program, approximately 88 per cent of the state's population will be within receiving range of an open-circuit ETV signal. The State Department of Education now contracts with six of the present nine ETV councils in New York State for the production of television programs. Approximately $340,000 was budgeted for this service in 1964.

A second emphasis of the bureau is its school-aid program. In 1964, fifteen school districts will be aided by a $600,000 appropriation to develop their own ETV facilities and to produce educational and cultural television programs. A school system qualifying for aid (on a matching basis) is helped financially for a five-year period, at the conclusion of which time it is expected to operate alone. At least half the appropriated money is to be used for television equipment and facilities. Educational and technical personnel to assist with these developments are also provided through the State Department of Education.

Bureau of Classroom Communications. The bureau fosters leadership by encouraging the acceptance and use of various types of educational media in classrooms throughout the state. Its communications media-materials section concentrates upon new developments in programmed instruction, language laboratories and electronic classrooms, the improvement of film utilization, curriculum consultation, and graphics communication. Typical activities include (1) selecting, utilizing, and evaluating programs and programmed methods, (2) consulting with school districts on NDEA Title III and Title VII projects, (3) aiding school personnel in writing educational and technical specifications for electronic and language-laboratory facilities, (4) stimulating improved use of such facilities, (5) assisting in the development of specifications for improved physical facilities, (6) experimenting with the feasibility of using television to distribute classroom films, (7) stimulating film purchases through use of matching funds, (8) supervising the application of state contract procedures to school district purchases of educational media and equipment, (9) cooperating with curriculum committees in the State Department of Education and in districts throughout the state—including evaluative studies of current practices with respect to educational media and services, and (10) preparing graphic materials primarily for the use of department and division personnel. The bureau's "Cinelib" maintains an up-to-date film center that deals with films in the field of educational communications. These are loaned free of charge for use in teacher-education programs.

Under a Project CUE program, Federal and state funds are being used to underwrite the preparation of 13 humanities kits for thirteen experimental schools. Qualifying schools receive from this program curriculum guides and packages of instructional materials—including filmstrips, films, slides, recordings, and various types of realia—comprising what is described as "an integrated system of instructional materials and techniques." Teachers using the curriculum guide and materials in the selected schools evaluate the materials and report their findings to Project CUE staff members. Pre- and post- testing techniques are used to measure their instructional effectiveness; curriculum guides and descriptions of the packaged materials will be available at the conclusion of the study for use by schools throughout the country.

The bureau's Project AIM seeks to provide a continuous, organized approach to the evaluation of the plethora of new educational media now appearing on the market. It is anticipated that in the final stages of this project, media evaluation reports will be issued regularly for the guidance of school personnel involved in purchasing and using the media.

SUMMARY

Most state departments of education have recently extended their activities into the new media field, partially as a response to established trends toward the equalization of educational opportunity. Principal activities at this level have been defined here as (1) fact finding, (2) experimenting, (3) setting and enforcing standards, (4) planning, (5) budgeting, (6) developing liaison relationships, (7) selecting, (8) procuring, (9) distributing, (10) producing, and (11) stimulating and informing.

In carrying out these several functions, state departments of education have tended to organize separate divisions, bureaus, or offices and to staff them with professional, technical, and clerical personnel having qualifications similar to those found in such offices at other administrative levels. The interrelationships of state, county, district, regional, and college and university offices involved with aspects of new media are usually a primary concern of this state staff.

FOR FURTHER INFORMATION

Allen, William H., and Harry J. Skelly: *Improving Instruction through Audio-Visual Media: Techniques in Teaching Science, Mathematics and Modern Foreign Languages,* California State Department of Education, Sacramento, Calif., 1963. 70 pp.

Audio-Visual Coordinator's Handbook, Hawaii State Department of Education, Honolulu, Hawaii, 1962.

Audio-Visual Education in Hawaii: Its Status and Needs, U.S. Office of Education, 1960. 60 pp.

Audio-Visual and Other Instructional Materials, Kansas State Department of Public Instruction, Topeka, Kan., 1961. 28 pp.

Beach, Fred R.: *The Functions of State Departments of Education,* U.S. Government Printing Office, 1960.

Bell, Walter S.: "How Georgia Utilizes Her AV Surveys," *Audiovisual Instruction,* vol. 3, pp. 209–210, October, 1958.

Connelly, John W., Jr.: *Report of State Laws on Audio-Visual Media of Instruction in Public Schools and on Establishment of Educational Television Stations,* U.S. Office of Education, 1962.

"Florida Testimony to Title III," *Audiovisual Instruction,* vol. 3, pp. 4–5, January, 1960.

Instructional Materials, Illinois Curriculum Program, Verne Stockman (chairman), Superintendent of Public Instruction, Administration and Supervision Series, Bulletin A-3, Springfield, Ill., September, 1961. 146 pp.

Noel, Francis W.: "State Programs of Audio-Visual Education," *Audio-Visual Materials of Instruction,* Forty-eighth Yearbook of the National Society for the Study of Education, The University of Chicago Press, Chicago, 1949, pp. 162–179.

Noel, Francis W., Paul V. Robinson, and Elizabeth S. Noel: *Practices of State Departments of Education in New Media: Audio-Visual Education during 1960–61.* School of Education, University of Southern California, Los Angeles, Calif., 1963.

Ruark, Henry C., Jr.: "ACCSAVO Looks Ahead," *Audiovisual Instruction,* vol. 8, pp. 444–445, June, 1963.

Ruark, Henry C., Jr. (ed.): *Douglas County Instructional Materials Center Survey,* Division of Instruction, Oregon State Department of Education, October, 1963. 84 pp.

State Department of Education Leadership in the Development and Use of New Educational Media: Preliminary Draft. Study Commission of the Council of Chief State School Officers, Hartford, Conn., 1963. 23 pp. (Offset)

chapter 16

Research and the systems approach in education

A highly developed instructional program in a static society might be able to persist for a long time with very little change. But the expanding educational system of a rapidly changing society presents quite a different problem—especially when there is dissatisfaction with results. In this case, the question is not whether change is required, but rather how to control it—how to develop, test, and implement desired innovation.

No one should seek change merely for the sake of change; but to neglect needed alterations or to permit changes already in progress to proceed without careful scrutiny and evaluation is irresponsible. If changes are required or in progress, it is necessary to consider alternatives, to establish systematic and controlled procedures for evaluating them. To the extent that such procedures are formalized and made scientific, they may be regarded as research.

In the past, educational research has been considered a more or less autonomous enterprise primarily to aid in the development of a science of education. Research still serves this important function, to be sure. But in the latter half of the twentieth century, it has become difficult to administer an educational institution or system effectively without various applied research services that contribute systematically to planning and development. While smaller programs may continue to rely upon research of others or occasional research projects sponsored by outside agencies, larger educational systems (including institutions of higher education) require their own research units to deal with their problems of growth and change in a technological society.

RESEARCH, PLANNING, AND DEVELOPMENT

Most state departments of education, many large school systems, and some institutions of higher education now include research departments concerned with the conduct of instructional programs. But their limited resources are frequently spent in statistical data gathering or in functions closely related to fiscal, reporting, or public relations rather than the instructional program—which should be an object of study in its own right.

Indeed, although we live in a period of rapid social transition and although we recognize that we need to modernize and improve education through better use of human and technical resources, the actual rate of improvement is slow. Brickell reported a threefold increase in the innovation rate in New York State schools after the launching of Sputnik, for example, but the schools included in his sample still showed an average of only one innovation per year. And most of the school systems he observed remained stable during the period of his study.[1]

Regarding the forces that tend to stabilize educational programs or to prevent their changing, the following adapted comments from Miles [2] are suggestive:

❯ Maximum energy goes into current operations and maintenance; the development and implementation of new programs appears to require the addition of money and staff over and beyond that required for regular operations.

❯ The hierarchically arranged subsystems in the over-all organization tend, over time, to become progressively segregated and independent.

❯ Durable feedback loops tend to develop between individuals and subsystems and operate to restrict communication in self-confirming, stabilizing ways. Thus, the longer the tenure of individuals—either administrators or those lower in the structure—the more stable the patterns of interaction that develop, and the more difficult change becomes.

❯ Another set of forces for conservatism arises from the connection of the target system with other relevant systems. For example, the target system's autonomy to make changes may be limited by other systems. In addition, comparison processes occur; innovations in other systems, when noted at all, are often defined as "no better—and perchance a trifle worse than what . . . [we are] already doing."

It would be a mistake, of course, to assume that forces of stabilization such as those just described represent an iron grip that prevents planned change from becoming a significant feature of American education. On the contrary, a number of strong and forward-moving forces are gradually effecting and accelerating changes, as has been already noted.

Proposed innovations in instructional systems are frequently the subject of experimental investigation. Thus, educational institutions that have no research staffs and facilities are handicapped because they are not likely to be able to conduct such investigations. In recent years, however, substantial Federal appropriations through the NDEA have helped to surmount this problem considerably. In the field of educational media, for example, hundreds of studies and experimental demon-

[1] Henry M. Brickell, "State Organization for Educational Change: A Case Study and a Proposal for Educational Change," in Matthew B. Miles (ed.), *Innovation in Education,* Bureau of Publications, Teachers College, Columbia University, New York, 1964, chap. 20.

[2] Matthew B. Miles (ed.), *Innovation in Education,* Bureau of Publications, Teachers College, Columbia University, New York, 1964.

stration projects that have led to significant and lasting changes in school and college teaching and, hopefully, in general concepts of instructional practice have been underwritten by such funds. The Ford Foundation has also contributed financial support to such efforts. But while both Federal and foundation support of seminal research in education are vital, it appears that any long-term growth of the instructional system must have support at the *local* level.

Miles's observation that implementing new programs requires money and staff above and beyond what is required for regular operation is especially relevant to research. Research programs or experimental demonstrations supported by outside agencies may serve to establish prototypes; frequently they will instigate local innovations. But if such programs are to be fully successful, continued study, modification, further development, and support of such programs must, in time, become a matter of local concern and responsibility. For unless nurturing and sustaining functions are discharged at this level, outside "seeding" and promulgation of innovations may serve little purpose. Functions and responsibilities that become (or should become) matters of interest to local departments or offices of instructional research are:

❯ Serving as centers of research information where administrators, instructors, or persons conducting individual experimental studies can examine research journals and reports or obtain needed bibliographical information
❯ Planning and conducting local surveys, studies, or experimental investigations of instructional practices, the uses of instructional resources, or similar matters related to the achievement of instructional objectives
❯ Exploring and exploiting outside sources of support to finance special research projects that require funds or other resources exceeding local capabilities
❯ Working with outside agencies that may require local cooperation in conducting experimental studies of instructional problems
❯ Cooperating with local administrative staff members and instructional departments, committees, teachers, or professors in planning and analyzing instructional functions, making experimental studies of procedures, interpreting and evaluating research information from other sources, and studying and improving the instructional system as a whole

If we are asked whether such research activities are "pure," "applied," or "developmental," the answer must surely be that they are all three to some degree, but mostly the latter two. In the strict sense, pure research is not designed to evaluate or develop specific programs, but to generate new knowledge or extend the range of scientific inquiry. Perhaps some would argue that any research that seeks some practical outcome is bound to be something less than pure. Certainly, most educational research is applied, since it is usually conducted in classrooms or other regular instructional situations. The difficulties of generalizing from the results of such studies—because of the variables involved— are well known, but sometimes overstated.

Developmental research may be described as research carried on with deliberate regard to developing some specific program or demonstrating the feasibility of some instructional system or technique. The term seems to imply that the aims are closely linked to implementing innovations in an on-going program of instruction. This relationship between the practical and the experimental is not without disadvantages and controversy. Research is never quite so pure, action never quite so positive, when one is joined with the other. Nevertheless, it is difficult to see how any truly significant instructional research can be carried on without at least some orientation toward programmatic development in the schools themselves, and vice versa.

In sum, it would appear that vigorous educational research must operate at both pure and applied levels. And it would seem desirable for some large school systems and universities to maintain instructional-research departments that divide their interests between both pure and practical or applied research.

Let us return now to Miles's analysis of forces that resist dynamic solutions to educational problems and consider his comment that hierarchically arranged subsystems tend to become segregated and independent. By combining this observation with the idea that research should be a constant factor in planning and developing the instructional program, we may hypothesize that research orientation should encompass the instructional system as a whole. A research activity thus directed becomes a program of *operations research* or *systems analysis*—a subject to be discussed next.

THE PROSPECT OF A SYSTEMS APPROACH

What can be gained from a systems approach to educational planning? One viewpoint is that it provides a useful conceptual framework for designing and implementing various kinds of educational change.[3] Such a framework makes it possible (1) to identify specific functions that are required to achieve various instructional goals, and (2) to divide such functions appropriately between *men* and *machines*. Systems analysis and design procedures also make possible the identification of strengths and weaknesses in resources, prediction of future needs, and the orderly development of an instructional program in which the proper combinations of human and technical resources become available as required at the proper times and places.

The particular relationships of educational media to the process of systems analysis are explained in this way: [4]

[3] *Fundamental Processes in Education: Report of a Study under Advisory Board on Education, National Academy of Sciences (Woods Hole, Massachusetts, September, 1959)*, Washington, D.C., 1959.
[4] *Ibid.*, pp. 5–6.

A system framework makes possible the use of advances in technology. At the present time, the use of such devices as films and television, not to mention various types of laboratory apparatus, suffers from the viewpoint that these are "aids" which are to be introduced at the whim of the teacher, perhaps to occupy a spare hour or two of class time. From the systems standpoint, a machine is to be used when it will best accomplish a specific educational purpose, and not otherwise. The systematic integration of the various available machines and of machine technology into the educational system is an enterprise that has scarcely begun, although steps have been taken in that direction.

Processes of systems analysis in education

The general processes involved in developing a systems design for education have been outlined by Carpenter as follows: [5]

❯ Define achievement or performance goals.
❯ Translate these goals into subsystems of general and specific functions.
❯ Specify the means of executing these functions and define the components of the systems including human capabilities, machines, materials, and interactions within the system.
❯ Distinguish between functions that can best be performed by persons with known competencies and functions that can best be performed by instrumentation and materials with known characteristics.
❯ Plan schedules and sequences of events so that all components of the designed system, when tested and retested, maximize performance of the system as a whole in accomplishing projected goals or objectives.

Egbert has proposed a similar list of steps for planning systems for schools: [6]

1. As a first step to guide the development of systems for schools, operational goals must be stated. Furthermore, priorities must be attached to these goals to enable the system designers to plan effectively.

2. The second step is to produce a descriptive model of the system. The system thus stated must be so designed as to permit achieving the stated goals. Thus, the initial description must be "ideal" oriented and must be divorced from restrictions imposed by reality. To ensure internal consistency and to permit close analysis of the plan, logical flow diagrams must be constructed.

3. Step three involves computer simulation of the model. This simulation should include representation of students, school personnel, cur-

[5] Adapted from C. R. Carpenter, "Approaches to Promising Areas of Research in the Field of Instructional Television," in Wilbur Schramm (ed.), *New Teaching Aids for the American Classroom,* The Institute for Communication Research, Stanford University Press, Stanford, Calif., 1960, pp. 75–76.
[6] R. L. Egbert, "System Design for Schools," in Don D. Bushnell (ed.), *The Automation of School Information Systems,* Department of Audio-Visual Instruction, NEA, 1964, pp. 128–131.

STEPS IN DESIGNING NEW SYSTEMS FOR SCHOOLS

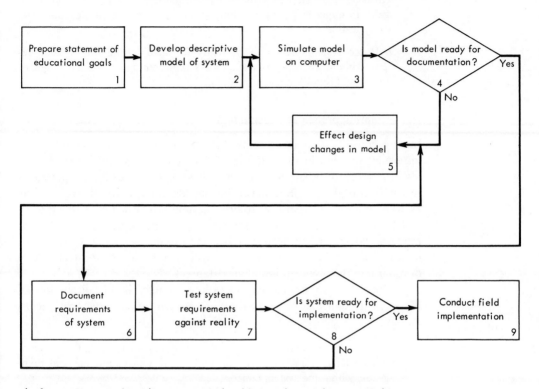

riculum, space, and equipment, and should examine various operating rules. Computer simulation will enable manipulation of the model and will give additional information about its characteristics and requirements.

4. Based on experience in simulating the model, a decision must be made whether the model is ready for initial documentation. The making of this decision is indicated as step four.

5. If the model requires changes before documentation is accomplished, the designer moves to step five, which calls for making necessary modifications in the model. He then proceeds through another simulation phase.

6. If the simulation study demonstrates that the model is theoretically sound, a document should be prepared detailing personnel and material requirements of the system as represented in this model.

7. With the requirements of an ideal system specified, the next step is to test these requirements against reality—both as to availability of personnel and material and feasibility of applying the program. (By feasibility, we refer to such problems as cost and relationships with school patrons.)

8. The reality test described as step seven provides the basis for another decision—whether the system is ready for implementation.

If the system is not ready for implementation, the designer must return again to step five, make modifications in the model, and move again through steps three, simulation; five, documenting; and six, reality testing.

9. If the system proves to be ready for field testing, the system designer should attempt tests in schools representing as wide a range of designs and requirements as possible.

The systems approach and technology

In any consideration of systems analysis or operations research, it is important to keep in mind the close relationships of technology to the modern tools of planning. Ackoff [7] has pointed out that operations research moved into prominence during the early years of World War II, when it became imperative to bring seriously retarded military strategy and tactics rapidly abreast of the advanced technological capabilities of modern warfare. (The need first became evident when the German air invasion of Britain suddenly made it necessary to absorb the technology of radar into the organization of air defense.)

Hoban brings similar considerations to light in his discussion of the systems concept in education, as related to an advancing technology: [8]

With the introduction of any new educational medium and its accompanying technology, many problems become understandable and manageable within the system concept. . . .

It can be postulated that the more complicated the system technology becomes and the more often machines take over functions performed by man, the greater the probability of human resistance to the introduction of the technology becomes. Man does not surrender his historical prerogatives to machines without a battle, nor does he easily reconceive his historical role in the accustomed order of things. . . .

Applied to education, this means that the development of a new technology of communication forces change in the general and specific means by which educational objectives can be attained—change that is frequently resisted as disturbing and discomforting to the *status quo*.

If we are to cope adequately in educational media research and in the implementation of research findings, use of the system concept is intellectually and practically inescapable.

[7] Russell L. Ackoff, "The Development and Nature of Operations Research and Its Relevance to Educational Media Research," paper prepared for the Conference on New Dimensions for Research in Educational Media Implied by the "Systems" Approach to Instruction, conducted by the Center for Instructional Communications, Syracuse University, April 2–4, 1964, pp. 4–5. (Mimeographed)
[8] Charles F. Hoban, Jr., "The Usable Residue of Educational Film Research," in Wilbur Schramm (ed.), *New Teaching Aids for the American Classroom,* The Institute for Communication Research, Stanford University Press, Stanford, Calif., 1960, p. 110.

Systems analysis in education

Large-scale acceptance of operations research or systems analysis in education is still for the future. It is popular to believe that any large and complex undertaking should be administered with proper regard for the total organization and its elements. Viewing a problem in its entirety has already been identified as the "systems approach," and as Mood observes it, it is favored by almost everyone "in the same sense that almost everyone is in favor of God, country and motherhood."[9] It is only when the systems approach moves toward the rigorous norms that are implied by operations research and the more precise methods of systems analysis that questions and doubts arise. Two major questions that may be anticipated are these: Is systems analysis (involving quantitative methods of operations research) appropriate to education? Is a rigorous form of systems analysis really feasible in education?

The question of appropriateness comes quickly to mind when one examines the common assumption that teaching is an art. If we combine this perfectly valid notion with the opinion that technology and highly contrived instructional procedures can only get in the way of the good teacher—as some do—it is not difficult to draw the somewhat analogous conclusion that systems analysis is suspect and dubious and possibly actually threatening to highly regarded educational values. Of course, scientific "neutrality" and "cold" quantitative precision of operations research do not necessarily lead to denial of the importance of personal contact or other cherished values. Unfortunately, however, such erroneous reasoning continues to beguile many whose humanistic defenses are quickly triggered by the idea of "trying to reduce teaching to a set of mathematical formulas."

In approaching this same problem from a philosophical standpoint, Burns raises two penetrating and related questions: [10]

❯ Are there some man-machine systems which, for whatever reasons, simply do not lend themselves to operations research or systems analysis?

❯ Can this methodology be useful for moral systems or systems based on an ethic, such as education, law, or religion; can you clean up these systems, as, say, you might clean up a nuclear delivery system or an automotive production system?

[9] Alexander M. Mood, "Some Problems Inherent in the Development of a Systems Approach to Instruction," paper prepared for the Conference on New Dimensions for Research in Educational Media Implied by the "Systems" Approach to Instruction, conducted by the Center for Instructional Communications, Syracuse University, April 2–4, 1964, p. 1. (Mimeographed)

[10] Robert W. Burns, "An Exiological Dimension of Systems Analysis in Education," paper prepared for the Conference on New Dimensions for Research in Educational Media Implied by the "Systems" Approach to Instruction, conducted by the Center for Instructional Communications, Syracuse University, April 2–4, 1964, p. 11. (Mimeographed)

Burns's questions are not intended to repudiate the notion of a systems approach in education, but they do point up the difficulties of the "means technologist" in education—the one who must address himself to the specification of ends. Some implications of this person's tasks are considered in the following paragraphs. While the questions Burns proposes are perhaps not insuperable, it will be some time before they can be answered with complete assurance.

The second question, which asks whether rigorous systems analysis is really feasible in education, relates to the earlier question of its appropriateness. If a quantitative approach to analyzing and solving instructional problems seems either distasteful or dangerous, it may also be regarded as somewhat questionable from a purely technical standpoint. Systems analysis, which involves typical operations-research methods, is mathematical; thus, it involves the quantification of variables. Of course, various factors in instructional process must be related to some goal—the criterion that the analyst is trying to optimize—and it must also be expressed quantitatively. It is difficult to define the human behavior that constitutes an instructional goal in this way; although educational research workers—especially those interested in developing programmed materials—have given some attention to the problem in recent years.[11]

Supporting the idea that the experimental development of instructional systems requires exact specification of the criterion, Gilpin [12] proposes a "dichotomous" concept of testing. The criterion is specified with precision as an absolute goal. After instruction, students are classified in accordance with whether they reached the goal or did not. Students are not rated in terms of relative or "discriminating" scores that represent performance at some presumed percentile level of achievement. The student either attains the criterion behavior or he does not. However, it is still possible to scale his performance in terms of time-to-criterion—i.e., the time he requires to master what the program teaches. Time-to-criterion thus becomes a measure of the effectiveness of the program (system) for the average student and, incidentally, a measure of student aptitude as well. Essentially, Gilpin's argument is that experimental comparisons of alternative systems (or different versions of the same system) are ineffectual unless the criterion is precisely specified. While he recognizes the difficulties in making such "absolute" specifications, he insists that they are important: [13]

Wouldn't the detailed specification of objectives for any really sizable instructional task be prohibitive in cost? Those who have done such work know that the costs *are* high. The lesson we might take from this

[11] See R. F. Mager, *Preparing Objectives for Programmed Instruction,* Fearon Publishers, Inc., San Francisco, Calif., 1961; Benjamin Bloom and others, *A Taxonomy of Educational Objectives: The Cognitive Domain* and *Taxonomy of Educational Objectives: Affective Domain,* McKay, New York, 1956 and 1964.

[12] John Gilpin, "Design and Evaluation of Instructional Systems," *AV Communication Review,* vol. 10, pp. 77–78, March–April, 1962.

[13] *Ibid.,* p. 82.

fact is that the technology of such specification is inadequately developed, and that we should be putting more effort there, rather than multiplying further our media and methods research. Indeed, *the main burden of this paper* is this point: *the focus of research at this stage of development of instructional science should be in criterion-specification and measurement, not in methods of presentation.* We cannot produce a technology of instruction while we are still proceeding intuitively to specify goals, nor can we attach much confidence to the results of our experiments in methods or presentation while evaluative methods are so sketchy. When you start out to do something, it is advisable to have a way to express precisely what you wish to do, and a way to tell when you've successfully done it. These are exactly the things we do not now have.

Two observations regarding Gilpin's point of view should be noted. One is that the substitution of time-to-criterion for conventional testing seems to require a setting in which each student is allowed to progress at his own rate—a setting, presumably, in which programmed instruction plays a central role. The other is that Gilpin's insistence on the need for "absolute" specification of the criterion must be carefully examined to measure the full dimensions of the problem he poses. Obviously, we cannot produce a technology of instruction while specifying its goals intuitively. But is it possible to specify educational goals with absolute precision? In some fields, it may not be too difficult; in others, there are serious obstacles, to say the least. What does one do about lack of philosophical clarity or consensus concerning education's broader aims, for example? If we add the view that educational goals are generated partly by the process of education itself, the over-all problem of stating measurable goals becomes formidable indeed.

Were it not for the fact that operations-research methods have already proved workable in other equally large and complicated systems that also involve human values, the case might appear hopeless. It is often much simpler to establish a system performance criterion when the output is readily specified in quantitative terms; but it should not be assumed that perfect quantitative specification of all factors is always the absolute requirement. Operations research has developed a kind of built-in flexibility and a tolerance of appropriate degrees of looseness in situations where analysis appears desirable, although a completely "tight" model may be impossible. Operations research has been constructed to facilitate the ordering of complex human tasks (typically those involving man-machine systems), even though such systems are not reduced to quantitative specifications. In such cases, a limited and judicious use of mathematical method may be more desirable than completely qualitative analysis, if the latter is ever possible. Qualitative judgments are involved in all quantitative analyses and vice versa; the choice is not "either-or." One must be careful not to "force" the use of quantitative method to the point that judgments that ought to be acknowledged as purely qualitative show up as invalid statistical coefficients.

Systems analysis as "housekeeping"

One further comment regarding the method of systems analysis may be helpful. Practically speaking, educational administrators cannot always be looking to the system as a whole. Systems run by their parts, and unless the parts continue to function properly, the total enterprise will fail anyhow. Hence, administrators constantly find themselves straightening out the operations of parts or subsystems, while still working on the total systems analysis. Churchman [14] has emphasized this aspect of operations research, which he calls "housekeeping"; he characterizes systems design as a continuous dialectical process in which the good designer listens carefully to the debate between the "system-as-a-whole" and the "housekeeping" principles. He suggests that the good administrator is a systems designer; he is also trying to patch up the leaks and fix the broken parts, while keeping the system going and seeking to improve its design. He also reminds us that "very few of the large systems we humans inhabit are understood by anybody. And yet people act in them every day." We do this by "housekeeping," even while we dream of a better house to keep.

In education, housekeeping is a continuously necessary and important administrative task. But there is a difference between Churchman's concept of housekeeping as an aspect of the design process and the kind that does not go beyond the immediate straightening up of a mess. Housekeeping as an approach is not intended merely to fix up the parts (which, of course, has merit); it also seeks "to find those problems of the parts, the study of which enables us best to think most adequately about the whole." [15] In other words, the good administrator can make repair and upkeep an occasion for experimental action and evaluation—if he has courage and imagination and is sensitive at all times to the costs and benefits of any single part to the system as a whole.

Some experimental overtures

In view of the success of operations research or systems analysis in military and industrial applications, the fact that it has stirred so much interest in education is hardly surprising.

The current use of the systems concept in education is promising, but not extensive. There has been more talk about systems than actual systems approaches, more systems planning for new programs than analysis (and modification) of already operating systems, more development of systems (actually subsystems) of instructional procedures and

[14] C. West Churchman, "A Design for Systems Research on Instruction," paper prepared for the Conference on New Dimensions for Research in Educational Media Implied by the "Systems" Approach to Instruction, conducted by the Center for Instructional Communications, Syracuse University, April 2–4, 1964, pp. 16ff. (Mimeographed)

[15] *Ibid.*, p. 17.

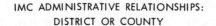

IMC ADMINISTRATIVE RELATIONSHIPS:
DISTRICT OR COUNTY

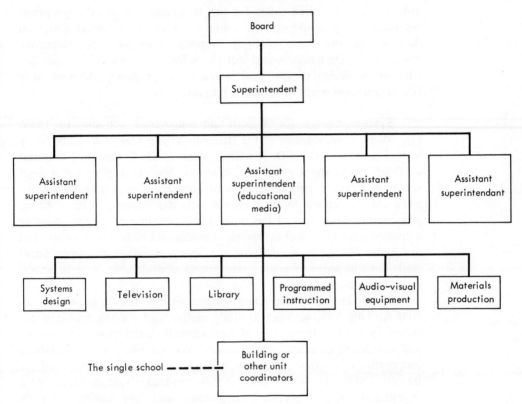

The Department of Audiovisual Instruction, National Education Association, emphasizes the relationships of the administrator of educational media services to other administrators in a centralized public school organization. Note the inclusion of "systems design" in the allotment of functions under this unit. (*From Barry Morris, ed., "The Function of Media in the Public Schools,"* Audiovisual Instruction, *vol.* 8, *p.* 13, *January, 1963.*)

materials for limited and specific purposes than for total instructional programs.

Systems design for instructional planning and coordination. Some educational institutions have provided (or planned to provide) staff and facilities to assist instructors in developing curricula to implement courses of instruction based on the systems concept. The integrated learning resources program at Florida Atlantic University is one such example.[16] The long-range plan for this program involves a team of systems designers, each of whom would be content-oriented and a representative of one of the institution's instructional divisions.

[16] See the earlier description of this program included in Chap. 14.

These designers would also serve as communications media specialists; in this capacity, they would work with instructors to achieve coordinated instructional plans that called for the systematic use of all appropriate resources. They would operate within the learning resources program; they would also have teaching responsibilities in their respective disciplines.[17] Designers would not be individually concerned with the analysis or design of the *total* instructional program, although their efforts as a team might be turned in that direction.

System design for a continuous-progress school. In 1959, Dr. Edwin Read, director of the Brigham Young University Laboratory School, and Dr. Asahel D. Woodruff, dean of the College of Education of Brigham Young University, began to develop a plan for a high school program to permit students to progress at varying rates toward goals closely related to their capabilities and interests. The resulting plan involves a system of individualized scheduling of student learning activities and wide use of instructional media and materials. Programmed materials, which are needed for the heavy emphasis on independent study, are included. Students also spend considerable time in small-group instruction.

In 1963, the System Development Corporation[18] negotiated an NDEA, Title VII, contract to study methods of solving problems involved in implementing uses of instructional media "through analysis and simulation of school organization." As one phase of this study, a cooperative effort was initiated with Brigham Young University and the Bassett, California, School District[19] to produce a system design for a "continuous-progress" school. Beginning with the concept already under study at the Brigham Young University Laboratory School, further steps were taken to work out a system design suited to the goals of both collaborating schools. A report issued in 1964 describes the plan.[20] Its principal features are described as the "Materials Center" and the "Information Processing Center." In the materials center are housed the bookstore; such equipment as motion-picture projectors and tape recorders; related films and tapes; the library; and a construction area where students, faculty, and staff can build and have built various devices and materials needed for effective course work.

The information processing center is described as much more significant in the continuous-progress school than it is in a traditional school. In the continuous-progress school, the information processing center mediates the day-to-day scheduling of students, faculty, staff,

[17] Len Singer, "Florida Atlantic University: Where Tomorrow Begins," *Audiovisual Instruction,* vol. 8, pp. 236–242, April, 1963.

[18] Santa Monica, Calif.

[19] The high school program of this district, emphasizing administrative arrangements and facilities for independent study is described in Chap. 11.

[20] Robert L. Egbert and John F. Cogswell (David G. Ryans, principal investigator), *System Design for a Continuous Progress School: Part 1,* System Development Corp., Santa Monica, Calif., 1964, p. 9.

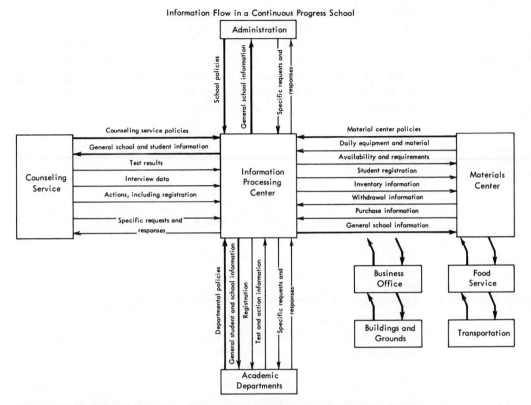

Information Flow in a Continuous Progress School

This chart emphasizes the importance of the Information Processing Center in scheduling instructional activities, space, instructional materials, and equipment in a continuous-progress school. (*System Development Corporation*)

space and equipment, in addition to the traditional functions of attendance, grades, and pupil records. These activities require the acceptance, processing, and reporting of quantities of information—such as that provided by the school administration, the materials center, the counseling service, and the students. To handle these data, modern methods and equipment are required; in a fully implemented and effectively functioning continuous-progress school, a stored-program computer will probably be essential.[21]

Another function that plays a more important role in the continuous-progress school program than it does in the traditional school is the counseling service. Its increased importance derives from the fact that the students' programs are quite flexible, and student progress is largely self-determined; thus more frequent consideration and reevaluation of student programs is required.

Elaboration of this system design includes a series of highly detailed charts and flow diagrams that illustrate various organizational patterns, processes, and relationships. One of these flow diagrams represents the

[21] *Ibid.*

student's progress, step by step, through preregistration and registration. Another represents his progress through a typical course of instruction in a continuous-progress school. Together with verbal description, these charts and flow diagrams constitute a descriptive model of a working system. The development of such models and their manipulation and testing by computer simulation before actual tryout is characteristic of the method of systems analysis and design.

SUMMARY

A changing society requires educational research not only to develop and expand the science of teaching but also to provide a basis for scientific control and responsible direction of technological innovation. Federal appropriations and efforts of some private foundations have given special impetus to instructional research in recent years, but the success of the experimental approach in the long-term development of instructional programs requires firm local support to ensure continuity and fruition of research efforts. Research activities in this field now show a strong developmental emphasis, but there appears to be no reason why both pure and applied types of experimentation should not be conducted, as needed, with mutual benefits.

A research orientation directed toward the total instructional program moves toward systems analysis. The size, complexity, and rapidity of change in modern education seem to require a systems approach to planning that begins with a comprehensive analysis of objectives and functions and then seeks to match performance goals with optimum configurations of human and technical resources. Systems analysis and design have been applied with satisfactory results in both military and industrial operations, where technology has moved sharply ahead of methods and procedures and where the magnitude and flux of the enterprises concerned have combined with a tardy and imperfect assimilation of technology to produce confusion, inefficiency, or a lack of coordination of human efforts and machine functions.

A growing number of educational planners and educational media administrators now look to operations research to facilitate effective planning and to expedite the orderly assimilation of the new technology of instruction. Some regard this prospect with grave doubts, questioning whether systems are appropriate or workable as methods of solving educational problems. They also wonder whether it is ever possible to specify instructional goals with the necessary precision or whether just attempting to do this imposes an undesirable fixed terminus to this important process.

To temper the more pronounced points of view with regard to this question, two additional observations are made. First, systems analysis is a method that is only as good as the judgment and adequacy of the related research and mathematical tools employed by those who conduct the analyses, and it is still not clear how well various types of instruction or phases of the instructional process lend themselves to the method.

Secondly, systems research is adaptable within limits and can be used profitably without going all the way to the completely tight mathematical model. It can be tempered by recognizing that there are limits to the precision with which some goals can be specified and that quantification of all variables with impeccable mathematical rigor may never be possible, nor is it necessary in order to gain some of the benefits of systems analysis. This is not to deny that a combination of systems research and machine technology could—on wrong assumptions and for wrong reasons—proceed to put education in a kind of conceptual strait jacket that would contradict the essentially creative and open-ended role it should play in a democratic society. But while the risk is apparent, it should not be the cause of turning back to a nostalgic past that can no longer shelter education from the disturbing present. The problem is to minimize this risk without summarily dismissing the potential of the powerful tools of modern science and technology to aid in planning improved instructional systems.

FOR FURTHER INFORMATION

Ackoff, R. L., and Ruett: *A Manager's Guide to Operations Research,* Wiley, New York, 1963.

Bern, Henry A.: "Toward Educational Engineering," in Henry A. Bern (ed.), *New Directions in Audio-Visual Communications,* Bulletin of the School of Education, Indiana University, vol. 36, November, 1960.

Bushnell, Don D. (ed.): *The Automation of School Information Systems,* Department of Audio-Visual Instruction, NEA, 1964.

Bushnell, Donald D.: *The Role of the Computer in Future Instructional Systems,* Monograph 2, Technological Development Project, NEA, *AV Communication Review,* vol. 8, March–April, 1963. (Special supplement)

Cogswell, John F., Robert L. Egbert, Donald G. Marsh, and Frank A. Yett (principal investigator, David G. Ryans): *New Solutions to Implementing Instructional Media through Analysis and Simulation of School Organization,* System Development Corp., Santa Monica, Calif., 1964. (Report prepared under grant from U.S. Office of Education, NDEA Title VII)

Egbert, Robert L., and John F. Cogswell (David G. Ryans, principal investigator): *System Design for a Continuous Progress School,* System Development Corp., Santa Monica, Calif., 1964. (Report prepared under a grant from the U.S. Office of Education, NDEA Title VII)

Miles, Matthew B.: *Innovation in Education,* Bureau of Publications, Teachers College, Columbia University, New York, 1964.

Panel on Educational Research and Development, The President's Science Advisory Committee, *Innovation and Experiment in Education,* 1964.

Index